Worthy of the Cause for Which They Fight

The Civil War in the West

Series Editors: T. Michael Parrish
and Daniel E. Sutherland

Worthy of the Cause for Which They Fight

THE CIVIL WAR DIARY OF BRIGADIER GENERAL
DANIEL HARRIS REYNOLDS, 1861–1865

Edited by
Robert Patrick Bender

THE UNIVERSITY OF ARKANSAS PRESS
FAYETTEVILLE • 2011

Copyright © 2011 by The University of Arkansas Press

ISBN-10: 1-55728-971-9
ISBN-13: 978-1-55728-971-1

15 14 13 12 11   5 4 3 2 1

Text design by Ellen Beeler

⊗ The paper used in this publication meets the minimum requirements of the
American National Standard for Permanence of Paper for Printed Library Materials
Z39.48-1984.

Library of Congress Cataloging-in-Publication Data

Reynolds, Daniel Harris, 1832–1902.
    Worthy of the cause for which they fight : the Civil War diary of Brigadier General
    Daniel Harris Reynolds, 1861–1865 / edited by Robert Patrick Bender.
        p. cm. — (The Civil War in the West)
    Includes bibliographical references and index.
    ISBN-13: 978-1-55728-971-1 (pbk. : alk. paper)
    ISBN-10: 1-55728-971-9
    1. Reynolds, Daniel Harris, 1832–1902—Diaries. 2. Confederate States of
    America. Army. Arkansas Mounted Rifles, 1st. 3. United States—History—Civil
    War, 1861–1865—Personal narratives, Confederate. 4. Arkansas—History—Civil
    War, 1861-1865—Personal narratives. 5. United States—History—Civil War,
    1861–1865—Regimental histories. 6. Generals—Confederate States of America—
    Diaries. I. Bender, Robert Patrick. II. Title.
    E553.61st .R49 2011
    355.0092—dc23

                                                                    2011027202

To Sarah Beth,
who arrived like a spring day after a long hard winter

CONTENTS

SERIES EDITORS' PREFACE

The Civil War in the West series has a single goal: to promote historical writing about the war in the western states and territories. It focuses most particularly on the Trans-Mississippi Theater, which consisted of Missouri, Arkansas, Texas, most of Louisiana (west of the Mississippi River), Indian Territory (modern-day Oklahoma), and Arizona Territory (two-fifths of modern-day Arizona and New Mexico), but also encompasses adjacent states, such as Kansas, Tennessee, and Mississippi, that directly influenced the trans-Mississippi war. It is a wide swath, to be sure, but one too often ignored by historians and, consequently, too little understood and appreciated.

Topically, the series embraces all aspects of the wartime story. Military history in its many guises, from the strategies of generals to the daily lives of common soldiers, forms an important part of that story, but so, too, do the numerous and complex political, economic, social, and diplomatic dimensions of the war. The series also provides a variety of perspectives on these topics. Most importantly, it offers the best in modern scholarship, with thoughtful, challenging monographs. Secondly, it presents new editions of important books that have gone out of print. And thirdly, it premieres expertly edited correspondence, diaries, reminiscences, and other writings by participants in the war.

It is a formidable challenge, but by focusing on some of the least familiar dimensions of the conflict, the Civil War in the West series significantly broadens our understanding of the nation's most pivotal and dramatic story.

Daniel H. Reynolds was born in Ohio but settled in Chicot County, Arkansas, in the late 1850s. When the Civil War erupted, he cast his lot with his Confederate neighbors. More than that, he raised a company of mounted rangers that was eventually mustered into service with the First Arkansas Mounted Rifles. Reynolds was a captain at the time, but by 1864 he was a brigadier general and commanded the "Arkansas Brigade" of the Army of Tennessee.

In as much as few general officers kept a diary through the entire war, Reynolds's journal is something of a rarity. It is rare, too, in that it traces one man's evolution from company commander to brigade commander. Students of the war will learn much about the internal workings of the Confederate army, from its lowest to its highest military levels, including problems of supply, breakdowns in discipline, and bickering within the officer corps. Reynolds's personal accounts of the battles and campaigns in which he participated, from Wilson's Creek, Missouri, to Bentonville, North Carolina, add revealing layers to his official reports of those actions.

Editor Robert Patrick Bender has provided something more than a diary, too. In identifying the people, places, and events described, he offers readers an astonishing amount of detail about the general's world. Indeed, given the slender body of correspondence left by Reynolds, Bender has crafted the closest thing to a biography that we are likely to have. As editor, he has also done a splendid job, through his chapter introductions, of placing the several stages of Reynolds's career in the context of larger wartime military and political events. Consequently, even though Reynolds, his regiment, and, eventually, his brigade traveled far beyond the usual geographical limits of this series, their story, as preserved, recorded, and expanded by Bender, makes a valuable contribution to our understanding of the war in the West.

T. Michael Parrish
Daniel E. Sutherland
Series Editors

EDITOR'S PREFACE

The Special Collections Department of University Libraries at the University of Arkansas holds the typewritten transcription of Daniel Harris Reynolds's Civil War diary. That typescript provides the content used in this publication. The original handwritten diary probably remains in the possession of a Reynolds descendant, but its current location is unknown.

Although many published firsthand accounts of the Civil War are available to researchers and history enthusiasts, the diary of Daniel Harris Reynolds stands out as a historical resource. Given the strategic significance of the Western Theater to the outcome of the conflict, and the comparative rarity of full-length wartime accounts by Confederates, the need for additional voices to tell the complex and intriguing story of the star-crossed Army of Tennessee remains strong.

Reynolds began his diary in May 1861, shortly after the secession of Arkansas and the mobilization of Confederate troops, and maintained it until shortly after his return to Chicot County in June 1865. During the intervening years, Reynolds and his command witnessed the full scope of war as it developed in the Western Theater and the often-overlooked Trans-Mississippi Department. Thus, Reynolds presents the reader with a panoramic view of two major regions of the conflict through vivid descriptions of battlefields and camp life. Some of these descriptions, such as Pea Ridge, the Kentucky invasion, Chicamauga, Atlanta, and Nashville, do not appear in the published reports found in the *Official Records,* or appear in somewhat altered form.

In addition, Reynolds bears witness to some of the personal squabbles and political machinations that undermined the western Rebel army's command hierarchy through much of the war. The fresh and emotional nature of these encounters adds to our understanding of their depth and influence across the higher ranks of the Confederate army.

Reynolds's diary also offers an inside look at the daily nature of command at the company, regimental, and brigade levels. Although a strict commander, Reynolds devoted himself to the daily needs of his men and repeatedly advocated their rights in relation to issues such as conscription and the desire to return to Arkansas to defend their families and homes.

Finally, the diary of Daniel Harris Reynolds illuminates the story of the role played by Arkansas volunteers throughout the war. In no other arena of the conflict did Arkansas soldiers play a more significant role than the Western Theater. And yet, despite the valor they displayed on numerous battlefields, many Arkansawyers believed their contributions and sacrifices went unappreciated by their Confederate peers. Publication of a diary written by one of the state's most prominent wartime participants adds new depth to our understanding of the multifaceted contributions made by Arkansawyers to the overall Confederate war effort, both inside and outside their native state.

While editing the typescript of this diary, the following considerations have influenced the process. The diary is presented with as few changes as possible, in order to preserve the original content and style. Reynolds's style is clear and direct, but also often characterized by truncated or run-on sentences. For the sake of clarity, some of these characteristics have been addressed. Abbreviations have been standardized to their full spelling and misspelled names are corrected. Modern punctuation has replaced the use of dashes, as well as the excessive use of "and" as a conjunction. Brackets are used only to clarify meaning in the event of a missing word. Italics are used to identify newspapers or theatrical productions mentioned by name and to replace underlined words. All quotation marks are original to the text.

Reynolds placed several documents within his diary that relate to his service. Some of these items have been included in the publication, when they add to the general narrative of the diary. These documents are particularly useful on the rare occasions when Reynolds missed a significant event while absent from the regiment, such as the battle of Murfreesboro (for which he included the report by Col. Robert W. Harper). Certain documents in the Reynolds collection, such as newspaper clippings about the terms of surrender or a list of Confederate currency held by Reynolds at the end of the war, have not been included because they are either readily available in other sources or do not add substantively to the narrative.

Finally, considerable effort has been expended to identify as many as possible of the individuals named in the diary. Despite these efforts, a few individuals eluded positive identification. This is most often the result of incomplete original references, such as individuals mentioned exclusively by initials or without a surname.

Robert Patrick Bender

ACKNOWLEDGMENTS

During the completion of this manuscript, numerous people provided valuable assistance and encouragement. The Special Collections Department of Mullins Library at the University of Arkansas preserved the original transcription of D. H. Reynolds's diary and graciously agreed to its publication. As friends and former colleagues, they have always expressed supportive interest in my career; in particular, Andrea Cantrell rendered very helpful assistance.

My friends and colleagues at Eastern New Mexico University–Roswell provided considerable encouragement and support for my research interests. Jenny Ward, of the ENMU-Roswell Learning Resource Center, provided particularly valuable assistance in the acquisition of numerous interlibrary loan materials.

Richard and Connie Cox, who own Reynolds's Lake Village home, immediately expressed genuine interest in the project. They graciously shared photographs and stories about Reynolds and his family, their community, and home. Their assistance helped make the final manuscript more complete. Through their ongoing restoration of the Reynolds home and their sincere enthusiasm for this project, they reflect positively upon the general's legacy of generosity and devotion to the Lake Village community.

My family and friends, as always, consistently encouraged my work. My wife, Sarah Beth, and her family have also expressed much-appreciated interest in this project and my career.

Worthy of the Cause for Which They Fight

INTRODUCTION

Returning to the Arkansas delta in the summer of 1865, Daniel Harris Reynolds reflected on the surrender of the Confederate field armies and measured the cost of four hard years of service against the failure of the southern cause. "The war is over," he noted with melancholy, "and we failed." The fresh sting of defeat, however, could not diminish his devotion to the South or suppress the deep sense of pride associated with the men of his command; nothing in his life, he emphatically declared, gave him greater satisfaction than leading "Reynolds's Arkansas Brigade" in the Army of Tennessee during the South's struggle for independence.[1]

Reynolds first settled among the Mississippi River plantations of southeast Arkansas exactly seven years prior to this pointed pronouncement. Born in the village of Centerburg, Ohio, on December 14, 1832, Reynolds descended from southern pioneer families of colonial Virginia and Maryland who followed the pattern of westward migration that typified the first generation of independent Americans. By the early years of the nineteenth century, his paternal and maternal grandparents obtained property in the upper region of the Ohio River basin, where they broke land for crops and raised their families. Reynolds grew into early adulthood on the family farm, but tragedies common to frontier life forced an early bloom of the self-confidence and independent spirit that later characterized his military service, as both parents died prior to his eighteenth birthday.[2]

In spite of these personal losses, Reynolds moved within the year to the town of Delaware and enrolled at Ohio Wesleyan University. During his collegiate years, he befriended fellow future Confederate general Otho French Strahl and joined the Masonic Order. With a solid educational foundation formed by the mid-1850s, he soon envisioned a legal career as the most likely route to long-term success and the southern frontier as the most likely location from which to pursue those ambitions. After a short stay in Iowa, therefore, he joined his old friend Strahl in Somerville, Tennessee, where both men pursued private legal studies.[3]

Drawn further south by the lure of opportunity, in 1858 Reynolds settled in Lake Village and established a thriving law practice. During the antebellum years, he resided at the Parker House hotel and remained a bachelor while he established his financial and social status. Like many ambitious young southern men of the era, Reynolds modeled his goal of upward mobility on the example set by the delta's old planter class—acquisition of status through the purchase of land. During his early years in Lake Village, therefore, Reynolds invested significantly in real estate; by 1860, he owned property valued at approximately $8,500 as well as a personal estate of $500. Although Reynolds owned no slaves, his stance during the secession crisis revealed genuine acceptance of the institution as a cornerstone for the region's economic and social structure.[4]

In the last years of peace before the nation divided, Reynolds emerged as a community leader with a deep-rooted attachment to his adopted state, its people, and their ideals. As a self-described States' Rights Democrat, Reynolds viewed the presidential election of Abraham Lincoln as an act of "hostility" by the northern states and openly supported secession as the only means by which southern states could defend and maintain their "political rights and institutions." In January 1861, therefore, he placed his name before the public as a candidate to serve in the state secession convention scheduled to convene in March. For the next two weeks, he repeatedly addressed "the citizens of Chicot County" on the dire issues of the day. As with his fellow candidates, Reynolds hoped to steer "the wealthy cotton-growing county of Chicot" toward independence for the "self-preservation" of the South. Although not selected to serve at the convention, Reynolds remained a staunch supporter of secession and a man of growing reputation as a leader in the county.[5]

As the state's political leaders debated whether to cast their lot with the Confederacy, Reynolds increasingly focused his energies on martial options and initiated recruitment of a "gallant little company" of mounted volunteers to defend southern rights and institutions. In the wake of secession, these "true sons of the South" mustered into Confederate service as "the Chicot Rangers"—Company A of the First Arkansas Mounted Rifles. Before the end of their first summer under arms, the regiment drew its first measure of Yankee blood and began an odyssey that witnessed innumerable struggles with heat, cold, privation, disease, dust, mud, and bureaucracy—in addition to the Federal army.[6]

Over the next four years, Reynolds chronicled these experiences in a meticulous and detailed account. Characterized by frank and articulate assessments, Reynolds's diary offers valuable insights into the nature of command from the company to brigade levels and the evolution of the Army of Tennessee—the primary Confederate force in the Western Theater.

As with his civilian endeavors, Reynolds succeeded in his military career through a combination of talent and drive. Rising steadily in rank, he commanded the regiment by late 1863 and the brigade by the next spring. As his rank increased, however, Reynolds's observations and commentary lost none of their honesty or verve. A naturally intelligent and decisive leader, Reynolds showed little patience for inefficiency or incompetence—especially among superior officers. His anger and displeasure simmered in early campaigns, but soon found vent. Whether disputing strategic decisions or holding firm against slights to regimental or individual honor, Reynolds unapologetically voiced the concerns of his Trans-Mississippi command. Such candor put him at odds with at least two division commanders and, on one occasion, resulted in his arrest.

Such strained personal relationships proved a persistent problem throughout the Army of Tennessee. Indeed, the often-fractious leaders of the western Rebel army fought themselves nearly as furiously as they did the Yankees. For Reynolds and the First Arkansas Rifles these conflicts often seem rooted in the belief that Confederate high command held the defensive needs of Trans-Mississippi states in low regard and viewed Trans-Mississippi soldiers with contempt. Such perceptions of inequity only deepened when the regiment transferred east of the Mississippi River in 1862, with orders to serve dismounted, and thereafter found themselves begrudgingly assigned as infantry, in a theater of operations far removed from their homes and families.[7]

Despite these combative relationships and periodic frustrations, Reynolds proved an exceptional leader. Citations in wartime correspondence and postwar memoirs attest to his personal courage and leadership abilities and reveal a high measure of respect among superiors and subordinates alike. He showed genuine concern for the welfare of his men and fought the necessary bureaucratic battles to advance their needs and interests. Reynolds also expressed genuine pride in the courage and ability of his troops. Throughout the war, Reynolds accepted difficult assignments as opportunities for his hard-fighting Arkansawyers to excel. Even under difficult circumstances, the brigade consistently met his high expectations and "punished the enemy severely." During the Atlanta campaign, for example, they defended the Macon and Western Railroad at Lovejoy Station against a raid by the flamboyant Union cavalryman Judson Kilpatrick, thereby briefly prolonging the South's lifeline to that vital supply hub.[8]

The passion displayed in his periodic displeasure with command decisions reveals the depth of Reynolds's symbolic investment in the Confederate cause. Through most of the war, he remained optimistic about the potential for victory, even as resources and manpower began to wane. Only after a series of heartbreaking defeats through the summer and autumn of 1864 did his enthusiasm begin to wane. Nonetheless, Reynolds remained in the field with his beloved Army of Tennessee until he finally fell with a serious wound at Bentonville—just prior to capitulation.

The emotional impact of surrender is evident in the final months of Reynolds's diary, as he weighed the reality of defeat against considerable uncertainties for how the conditions of peace would alter southern society. The end of slavery caused particular concern. Despite the numerous unanswered social and racial questions that persisted at the close of hostilities, Reynolds remained resolute and unapologetic, immensely proud of his service and sacrifice.

The close of hostilities also brought manifold challenges and opportunities, which Reynolds faced with the same intelligent resolve that characterized his military service. As noted during his journey home, the first issue to command attention concerned his legal status. As a former Confederate general officer, exempt from the amnesty issued by President Andrew Johnson on May 29, 1865, Reynolds carefully weighed his options in regards to a special application for presidential pardon during the first summer of peace. He took counsel on the matter from Edward Cary Walthall, who initially refused to comply and expressed legal concern that the process implied guilt for a crime. After numerous prominent Confederates submitted applications, however, it soon became apparent to both men that no organized resistance to the process would materialize. Thus, on the express advice of Walthall and a general concern that lack of a pardon might inhibit his pursuit of future ambitions or responsibilities, Reynolds submitted an application on August 21, 1865, which closely resembled that of his former division commander. In a carefully worded statement he recounted the ideas and events that shaped his support for secession and the Confederate war effort, but also acknowledged defeat and pledged faithful compliance with the terms of his oath. When the application drew no response after five months, Reynolds submitted a second letter on January 15, 1866, and followed up in October with concerns about his eligibility to accept a seat in the Arkansas State Senate. With endorsements that included Unionist governor Isaac Murphy, he received a full presidential pardon on November 13, 1866.[9]

With the war behind him, Reynolds quickly regained his professional and personal status. He reestablished his law practice and soon gained a reputation as "the most forceful member" of the Chicot County circuit court. Always a leader in the communities of the southeast delta, he represented Chicot, Ashley, and Drew Counties in the state senate from 1866 to 1867—prior to the disfranchisement of former high-ranking Confederates during the radical congressional phase of Reconstruction. Despite early encouragement from Walthall to pursue a seat in the U.S. Congress and later efforts by the state's Democratic Party to draft him as a gubernatorial candidate, Reynolds never again sought public office—even as restrictions against former Confederates eased. For the remainder of his years, he focused his energies on his legal career and personal life.[10]

Shortly after his return to Lake Village, he met and courted Martha Jane "Mattie" Wallace. Born in Holmes County, Mississippi, on May 3, 1845, to Jeremiah and Eleanor Wallace, Mattie lost her father by the age of three. The widow Wallace eventually moved her family to Arkansas in 1859 and remained in Lake Village throughout the war years. Reynolds and Mattie married on November 24, 1868, and produced five children. Born between 1869 and 1883, the Reynolds children included Kate, Robert, Eleanor, Ruth, and Daniel Jr. As his family and law practice expanded, Reynolds acquired considerable acreage among the county's former elite plantations. His holdings grew to include the former Johnson family plantation known as "Tecumseh," purchased in 1869 in partnership with William B. Streett. At the height of his postwar prestige, Reynolds owned approximately sixty thousand productive acres in Chicot County and established "Lakeside"—a stylish home overlooking Lake Chicot. For many years, the Reynolds home served as an elite venue of entertainment for the county and state's political and social leaders, as well as a warm and loving family environment. Reflective of this prominence, in November 1890, Kate married Joseph Morrison Hill—future chief justice of the Arkansas Supreme Court and son of former Confederate lieutenant general (and University of Arkansas president) Daniel Harvey Hill—on the grounds of Lakeside.[11]

Reynolds's loyalty oath and postwar prosperity, however, did not diminish his devotion to the historical legacy of the Confederacy. As with many southern veterans, Reynolds took an active interest in the literature and history of the "Lost Cause," a highly romanticized view of the conflict that attempted to sanitize the fundamental sectional disagreements over the institution of slavery. Thirty years after the war, Reynolds publicly expressed the hope that Confederate veterans would speak and write about their philosophical motivations for secession as much as the drama of their combat experiences, so that "a fair and impartial" history of the conflict might emerge and, thereby, create "a more correct idea" about the war among the younger generation of southerners. The growth and endurance of Lost Cause mythology across the South attests to the fact that this wish came to fruition in his lifetime.[12]

In his final years, Reynolds's finances began to decline as his landholdings gradually diminished through acts of philanthropy and misfortune. In 1884, he donated the land on which Lakeside United Methodist Church established a still-thriving congregation. Likewise, he bestowed generous acreage to his children as wedding gifts. A few months prior to Kate's marriage Reynolds mortgaged seventeen thousand acres with Lloyd's of London, with the expectation that Hill would join the family practice and help pay the note. Despite this financial commitment, Kate and Joseph instead moved to Fort Smith, which left Reynolds to absorb an unexpected financial burden late in his career. Near the end of the decade, Reynolds made a wedding gift to Robert and Julia Reynolds of a two-thousand-acre plantation at Macon Lake. In his last decade, Reynolds sold further acreage to help pay medical expenses as his health began to fail. Despite these setbacks, Reynolds remained a figure of prominence and respect throughout Arkansas for the rest of his life.[13]

After a long bout with apoplexy, a condition of internal bleeding that left him an invalid in his last years, Daniel Harris Reynolds died in his home at the age of sixty-nine on March 14, 1902, surrounded by loved ones. As his family laid him to rest the following day in Lake Village Cemetery, his contemporaries eulogized him as a devoted family man, an accomplished soldier and attorney, a staunch supporter of the Democratic Party, and a devoted citizen of Lake Village. As an expression of respect for his many achievements, the Chicot County circuit court adjourned on the day of his funeral. The citizens of Lake Village also named Reynolds Street, which intersects Lakeshore Drive near the family home at Lakeside, in his honor. Likewise, Masonic Lodge 563 and the United Confederate Veterans camp of Lake Village named their facilities in his honor.[14]

Although several prominent Arkansas Confederates remained alive at the time of his death, few could claim a more distinguished war record than Daniel Harris Reynolds, and few exercised a longer lasting influence upon their community.

1861

Took Up the Line of March

As the fire-eaters of the Lower South rushed toward disunion during the seces-sion winter of 1860–1861, residents of Arkansas pursued the more prudent course of the Upper South. Inspired by the conservative approach of Virginia— "the mother of states and statesmen"—voters of Arkansas issued a restrained call for a state convention in March to select delegates and debate their connec-tion to the national Union. Despite strong support for secession among the cotton-growing counties of the southeast delta, Unionists continued to express faith in the South's ability to protect its rights and gain redress for grievances without resorting to the "mad fanaticism" of secession. As the first convention came to a close, the Unionists emerged with a majority and Arkansas remained in the nation. After their initial rejection of secession, Arkansawyers awaited more definitive events to decide the debate and determine their stance.[1]

In the aftermath of the attack on Fort Sumter and President Abraham Lincoln's call for state volunteers to suppress rebellion, opinions changed quickly and loyalties shifted across the Upper South. In Arkansas, as the temperate days of spring gave way to hotter passions of early summer, the debate over secession bloomed anew and support for disunion took deeper root in the state. In spite of lingering debate about the legitimacy of secession, many Arkansawyers per-ceived Lincoln's call as a usurpation of executive authority that justified seces-sion. At an emergency convention in Little Rock, characterized by distinctly pro-secession loyalties, an ordinance of secession gained easy passage and Arkansas became the ninth state to join the fledgling Confederacy.[2]

Throughout the cotton-producing lowlands of southeast Arkansas, citizens greeted the news of secession like a day of jubilation. Recruiters took to the streets and beat the drum to enroll eager volunteers, who poured forth in a wave of southern patriotism. As an early advocate of southern independence and military preparations, Reynolds played an enthusiastic role in these early recruitment efforts. Fully enrolled since mid-January, he and the Chicot Rangers quickly stepped forward as one of the state's first companies to answer the call to arms.[3]

After public and private celebrations to honor the new troops, Reynolds and the Chicot Rangers took up "the line of march" on May 25 and arrived in Little Rock five days later. After additional celebrations in the capital they proceeded to Fort Smith for muster. Despite some initial reluctance to enlist beyond twelve months, by mid-June the company took the oath of service and elected officers. When company commanders drew lots for position, the luck of the draw placed Reynolds and the Chicot Rangers in Company A—a position of honor on the regiment's right flank.[4]

For most of the summer their activities consisted of extensive practice in the foundations of military discipline: drilling, marching, establishing camp, and preparing for the eventuality of combat. During their transition from civilians to soldiers they endured a variety of difficulties including accidents, desertions, and even one murder. In addition, they suffered through the physical strain of early marches, infrequent and inadequate supply, and the demands of military bureaucracy.[5]

On August 10 the regiment took to the field of battle at Wilson's Creek, Missouri, in the first major contest of the Trans-Mississippi Department. The fight, which held potential strategic significance for the South's designs on Missouri, marked an inauspicious beginning for Reynolds as a battlefield leader. Thrown from his horse early in the engagement and knocked briefly unconscious, he narrowly avoided capture, and injuries kept him out of most of the day's fighting. The company and regiment, however, performed well. The men and officers, Reynolds proudly reported, "conducted themselves as men worthy of the cause for which they fight."[6]

Bloodied by this first campaign, Reynolds and the Chicot Rangers spent the remainder of the year performing additional mundane tasks, marching throughout Missouri and Arkansas, drilling, and preparing winter camps. Although their victory at Wilson's Creek eventually proved of limited strategic value, they closed the year with high hopes for the prospects that lay before them, that their fragile crop might yet yield a fruit worthy of harvest.

MAY 25, 1861, SATURDAY

Reveille was sounded at the Court House in Lake Village at 7 a.m. by A. C. Wells and orders given to march at 10½ a.m. and part of the company sent in advance to get horses shod. At 10½, the company formed and listened to a speech by W. H. Sutton and after bidding adieu to friends took up the line of march for Little Rock. Took dinner at Bellvue with Mr. J. M. Craig and elected him an honorary member of the company. At 3½ p.m., left Bellvue for Mr. Ben P. Gaines's to share his hospitality (by invitation). Reached Mr. Gaines at sunset all well, where we were kindly received and everything was prepared to make our stay comfortable.[7]

MAY 26, SUNDAY

Left Mr. Gaines's at 7 a.m. and were joined by the remainder of the company at Gaines' Landing. Took lunch at Mrs. Bowie's and fed our horses at Mr. Trippe's and reached Mr. Cheer's [Chairs's] place in Desha County. The overseer refused to assist our teams that were stalled, or to furnish forage for our horses though it was after dark and bad road to next place, where we could get corn. After his refusal we took corn and fodder for our horses and teams and meat etc. . . . for the men and sent back Negroes and mules to assist our teams out of the mud. We paid the overseer liberally for what belonged to him and arranged with Mr. James W. Bowie to settle for corn, etc. . . . Mr. Prewitt's overseer brought more corn to us.[8]

MAY 27

Morning elected the officers of the company except Captain, 2nd Lieutenant, and Orderly Sergeant. The officers of the company are D. H. Reynolds, Captain, Richard J. Shaddock, 1st Lieutenant, Abner Gaines, 2nd Lieutenant, William B. Streett, 3rd Lieutenant, B. F. Cason, Orderly Sergeant, Eli T. Wills, 2nd, Chas. C. Ferguson, 3rd, and Frank Estill, 4th Sergeant, etc. . . . Left Camp Holmes at 8 a.m. and reached the "hills" at 12 m. Lt. Shaddock and 15 men went on in advance to Pine Bluff to have some horses shod. The company reached Mr. Emett's at 8 a.m. and were furnished with corn and provisions. All well except one man who had a slight spasm.[9]

MAY 28

The company left early and reached Mr. McGehee's 10 miles from Pine Bluff. I left the company and went into Pine Bluff, where I found the advance part of the company with horses all shod. Here I heard the rumor that the state had been invaded in Randolph County by Gen. Harney with 8,000 men and received a request to move on rapidly for Little Rock. All well and in fine spirits.[10]

MAY 29

The rear of the company came up early and had horses shod, traded for a new wagon and left for Little Rock at 2 p.m. Reached Mr. Hudson's place 12 miles from Pine Bluff and stopped for the night, good accommodations. Placed out guards for the 1st time.[11]

MAY 30

Left Hudson's at 6 a.m.; missed the road and did not reach Little Rock until 9 p.m. Men and horses very tired and hungry. No preparations made for us and after much trouble we got accommodations for our horses and the men eat at the Anthony House and slept at the "Theatre Hall."[12]

May 31

Moved up to St. John's College grounds after breakfast and not finding good provisions for us we again eat at the Anthony House and then we commenced our camp life in reality, though entirely without tents. We slept on the floor in one of the college rooms. No sickness and but little dissatisfaction. The captains of the regiment drew for position in the regiment and I fortunately drew No. 1, which gives the letter "A" and position on right of the regiment.[13]

June 1, Saturday

The day was spent providing camp equipage for the company.

June 2

Parade of companies present at 9 a.m. when I received orders to march with my company and Capt. Galloway's "Pulaski Rangers" for Fort Smith. Drilled in the evening. Gen. Bradley, Gen. Gaines, and other prominent men present to see the drill. Had the measures taken for uniforms for the company by J. C. Ray of Little Rock, who done so free of charge. Jacob McConnell left for Memphis with $1,000 to buy uniforms for company.[14]

June 3

Obtained camp equipage and got horses shod etc. . . . Drilled in morning and evening. In evening received written orders to proceed with my own company and Capt. Galloway's company to Fort Smith, on tomorrow (morning) at 7 a.m.

June 4

Daniel Hines and B. F. Allen were permitted to withdraw from the company. The company left camp at 7 a.m. followed by Capt. Galloway's company. The companies crossed the Arkansas River and marched 18 miles and camped near Cadron Bayou and were furnished with corn by B. F. Danley.[15]

June 5

Left camp at 6 a.m. and marched 20 miles and camped at Dr. Menefee's. Good water and camp, one man sick. One wagon broke down, took wheel off of another and sent back and brought it up. Andrew Aeker mended wheel.[16]

June 6

Dr. Menefee loaned us a wagon to go to Lewisburg, where we took the wheel off of one of Mr. Hanger's wagons and replaced our broken one. The broken wagon belonged to Mr. Hanger. Marched about 20 miles and camped at Mr. Kurtz's on Point Remove Bayou. Plenty of corn and good camps. Rained very hard about 10 p.m. and part of Capt. Galloway's went to the house, most of the men slept in the house, but I with 5 or 6 others slept in the corn cribs.[17]

JUNE 7
Left camp at 9 a.m. and went 20 miles and camped at Mr. Pott's on Galley Creek near "Carrion Crow Mountain." Mr. P. a very clever man, but very stingy. All well and in good spirits.[18]

JUNE 8
Left camp early and marched 18 miles and camped at Mr. Cozort's at Russellville, the men sent forward to buy corn for us took one road and we took another. Procured corn at 60 cents a bushel and got provisions and got Mr. Cozort's negroes to cook our suppers, it being very late when our wagon's arrived.[19]

JUNE 9, SUNDAY
Passed through Clarksville and marched 20 miles and camped on Little Horseshoe Creek and Capt. Galloway's company on Big Horseshoe ½ mile apart. The best camp ground since we left home.

JUNE 10
Marched 31 miles and camped on west bank of Mulberry Creek, a hard day's march.

JUNE 11
Marched 20 miles and camped ½ mile east of Van Buren on Dr. McGehee's place, and by the way one of the stingiest and most eccentric man I have ever seen. Went to Van Buren, saw Mr. Scott, who has an interest in the Drennen Estate in Chicot. He treated me very cleverly etc. . . . .[20]

JUNE 12
Companies crossed the river at Van Buren and camped at the "Half Way House." Reported to Lt. Col. Matlock, was introduced to Gen. Ben McCulloch. Men in good health, horses in tolerable condition considering the march.[21]

JUNE 13
Went out on Massard Prairie with Capt. Galloway to look for a camp ground. I selected a camp near Mr. Tatum's. Received notice that Capt. James McIntosh, Adjutant General, wished to muster my company in on tomorrow.[22]

June 14

At 10 a.m. Capt. McIntosh and two other men arrived in camp and mustered in the company and appraised the horses. In the evening the company moved out to the new camp ground near Mr. Tatum's where we find plenty of good water and grass. Camp 4 miles from Fort Smith.

June 15, Saturday

Henry W. Stedman, James B. Lyerly, Eli T. Wills, and Boelfield W. Mathis left for home for the purpose of recruiting for the company and getting some money etc. . . .[23]

June 16

Attended dress parade at 6 p.m. Moved camp ½ mile, more convenient to water and a cooler place.

June 17

Drilled twice today. Full rations for the men, only 2/3 rations for horses. Men all seem anxious to keep horses in good condition.

June 18, 19, 20, 21, 22

Nothing worthy of note, except that Capt. McConnell returned from Memphis with hats etc. . . . Dug a well near camp and called it the "Chicot Well." Drill once or twice a day. Men all well.

June 23, Sunday

Dress parade of the whole regiment at 8 a.m., had part of the rules and articles of war read to us. Rained quite hard while on our way from parade to camp.

June 24

Men much displeased because they are required to take "flint lock muskets," and many say they will only consent to take them to drill with. Drill on horseback in morning and on foot in evening.

June 25 and 26

Getting horses shod preparatory to a march to Missouri.

June 27

Procured saddles and bridles for part of the company. Received orders to cross the Arkansas River and camp at Camp Winchell 3 miles north of Van Buren.

JUNE 28

Left camp at 9 a.m. and passed through Fort Smith and Van Buren to Camp Winchell, where we arrived about dark. While in Van Buren, Mr. Charles G. Scott presented me with a fine Maynard rifle. Mr. Madison was appointed pioneer for Gen. McCulloch and his connection with my company ceases. McConnell elected 2nd Lieutenant.[24]

JUNE 29

I went back to Fort Smith to settle up some business and returned to camp. Daniel Robinson of the company was killed today on his way from Van Buren to camp by a fall from his horse. Martin Worthington and Columbus Simpson left camp today without permission. I fear they have deserted.[25]

JUNE 30

Had the body of Robinson decently buried by a corporal and 8 men and his grave marked. The regiment commenced leaving camp 5½ a.m. and at 6½ all were off. I had been appointed officer of the day and my company was to leave first and march to front in rear. Marched 20 miles and camped in military order, being the first time the whole regiment were ever together.

JULY 1, MONDAY

Reveille at 3½ a.m. and marched at 5 a.m. Lt. Wair of Des Arc company officer of the day. Crossed Boston Mountain, marched about 13 miles, and camped ¼ miles North of Evansville.[26]

JULY 2

Marched 23 miles and camped ½ miles north of Cincinnati. Find much better country than I had anticipated and as good water as I ever drank and plenty of it. We marched on the "Line Road" and were a part of the time in Arkansas and part of the time in Cherokee nation. Men all well.[27]

JULY 3

Marched 13 [miles] and camped at 8 a.m. on a "camp meeting ground." Had dress parade at 6 p.m. After drill and parade we received a dispatch from Gen. McCulloch to march to Camp Walker at once, with 8 days' rations and leave all baggage, sick, bad horses, etc. behind; the news was received with a shout by the men. All were so anxious to go forward that details had to be made to stay behind, in one hour we were on the march and at 2 a.m. on 4th we camped ½ miles west of Camp Walker.

July 4

Left Camp Walker at 11 a.m. for Neosho, Missouri, with our own regiment, Col. Carroll's regiment [of] State Troops, and Capt. Woodruff's Battery. Passed through Gen. Price's camp on "Cowskin Prairie" and camped at Scott's Mills on Cowskin on Elk River. Marched 18 miles during day. Men and horses in pretty good condition and men in fine spirits at prospect of getting a fight with the U.S. troops at the town of Neosho.[28]

July 5, Friday

Left camp at 5 a.m. for Neosho. At 11 a.m. halted and fed our horses one sheaf of oats and rested two hours, when I was ordered to examine all my horses and to leave behind all that are not in a condition to make a force march. At 1 a.m. we left for Neosho, 5 companies on one road and 3 on another. My company with Col. Churchill's. When we got within 5 miles of town we moved forward rapidly and when ½ mile from town halted and fixed bayonets and prepared for a charge. We entered the town and surrounded the public square when almost 100 U.S. troops were stationed and who had just surrendered to the other detachments under Capt. McIntosh, Adjutant General, and were in the act of laying down their arms. The prisoners were put in the courthouse and the "Stars" and "Stripes" taken down from the Court House and the "Stars and Bars" put up in their place. We camped ½ mile from town for the night. Capt. Carroll's company of Arkansas State Troops was sent out north of town and took 8 wagons loaded with rations and 30 prisoners and brought them. Men all behaved very well when we expected to meet the enemy.[29]

July 6, Saturday

One of the main objects of our entering Missouri being to unite Gov. Jackson and Gen. Price's forces (the enemy being between them) and hearing that Jackson had repulsed them and was pressing them in a running fight, we left at an early hour to assist him. When 8 miles from town we heard the enemy were only two miles distant marking toward us. We prepared to meet them and kept on advancing and shortly after learned that the report was false. We camped near Jackson's forces for the night and 4 miles from Carthage. The enemy had been repulsed by Jackson and were retreating rapidly for Springfield and were at least 20 miles ahead of us and we declined further pursuit. In the fight Jackson had 8 killed and a few wounded, the enemy lost 40 killed and several wounded. Gov. Jackson regretted very much that we were not there for had we been there we could have taken them all prisoners beyond a doubt. The people seem very grateful for our visit to assist them. They have been badly treated by the U.S. troops, who are nearly all Dutch.[30]

July 7

Our main object, the uniting of Price and Jackson, being accomplished at 5 a.m., we left camp for Neosho, where we arrived about 2 p.m. Our horses a little worsted from the force march and men tired and hungry. The road was very dusty. Camped ½ mile from town, were joined by wagons and men left behind. Men in good spirits but disappointed that they did not have an opportunity of fighting the U.S. troops.

July 8

Left Neosho at 5½ a.m. for the south. Camped 20 miles from town on a creek. Considerable difficulty in getting oats for our horses. Complaints against the Missouri State Troops for taking what belonged to us.

July 9

Left camp at 6 a.m. and marched 11 miles and camped for the night at a fine large spring 4 miles south of Scott's Mills on Elk River. B. W. Mathis returned and Frank Whitten joined the company.[31]

July 10

Came down into Arkansas and camped one mile east of Camp Walker; named the camp "Camp Jackson" in honor of Gov. Jackson of Missouri.

July 11

Sent 5 horses to be traded off to Missourians for better ones if possible, learning that they were going to change from cavalry to infantry. Failed to make any trade. James B. Lyerly and James Shaddock came to camp and informed me that 40 men recruits were on their way to us.[32]

July 12

Recruits all came in, in one time, and at 5 p.m. were mustered into service of Confederate States and muster rolls dated of same date as those mustered in at Fort Smith. Men all in good health.

July 13

Left Camp Jackson for Bentonville, Arkansas, and marched 17 miles and camped at Alex McKissick's. Lt. Gaines Captain of Guard today. My company first on the march. 3rd Louisiana regiment also left Camp Jackson and moved in direction of Bentonville.[33]

July 14

Passed through Bentonville and camped on a prairie 2½ miles southeast of town at 10½ a.m. and, being officer of the day, I placed guards around our camp, which in honor of William L. Yancey was named "Camp Yancey." Troops in good health except a few cases of measles, none in my company. Five companies each left 15 horses in Bentonville to be shod.[34]

July 15

Nothing worthy of note.

July 16

Mr. John C. Bush of Drew County came to the company under an escort of a guard, but guard was soon dismissed as I vouched for him being all right.[35]

July 17

Drilling is the order of the day.

July 18 and 19

At Camp Yancey and drilling.

July 20

Rained hard last night, and men being but poorly supplied with tents, some of them were quite ill from their drenching but none seriously so.

July 21, Sunday

Inspection at 9 a.m.

July 22

General Court Martial for the trial of Lt. Alexander of the Napoleon Company for the murder of Private William Finnerty of same company. Convened at 9 a.m. and adjourned at 3 p.m. I am Judge Advocate of the court and Major Harper, President.[36]

July 23

Court met at 8 a.m. and adjourned at 3 p.m. Evidence closed and leave granted to parties to prepare final defense. Company drill in morning and battalion drill in evening.

July 24

Court met at 9 a.m. and the case of Lt. D. A. Alexander was decided at 12 m. and court adjourned. Orders to leave for Missouri on tomorrow morning. Private T. N. Lambe of my company received a discharge from the service on account of disability.[37]

July 25

Left camp at 6 a.m. and 12 m. camped 8 miles from Missouri state line. My little wagon broke down and I sent back after it and had it repaired. Our camp 3 miles south of Elkhorn Tavern. Eli T. Wills accidentally cut a horse of the Pulaski Company with his saber, which created quite an excitement and came near terminating in a serious difficulty. T. N. Lambe left for home this morning with boy Monroe. Monroe not being able to attend to work.[38]

July 26

Left camp early and entered Missouri and camped ½ miles east of Reatsville and 3 miles from state line. Good water, camp ground, and good forage. Named camp "Camp Sevier."[39]

July 27

Took 20 men and Captains Basham and Daniels, Lieutenants Gaines, Griffin, and Hardesty and went in pursuit of wagons that were taking goods from Keetsville. Two miles south of Cassville we separated and I with part of the force went over to the Granby road and there got 8 Missourians to prosecute the search and returned. The other party heard of wagons but they were so far gone they did not pursue them.[40]

July 28

Early in morning heard the rumor that was a fight progressing some 20 or 25 [miles] northwest of this camp. Men all anxious to go. During day 25 men, 22 of them from Company D, had a skirmish with the enemy on Flat Creek and killed [or] wounded several and had 4 horses wounded. Deserter Worthington brought back.[41]

July 29

All quiet in camp.

July 30

Still at Camp Sevier. Two men sick, bilious fever. No orders to move yet. Missourians glad to see us among them. Horses improving. Troops assembling at this place.

July 31

Troops still coming up and moving forward to Cassville, 8 miles north of this place. General orders to march upon Springfield were read in camp today. We are 1st regiment in 3rd division in the march. Leave tomorrow morning at 5½ o'clock. Left W. Mabry at McCult's, near camp, to remain until he recovers. Remainder of men well.[42]

AUGUST 1

Left camp at 5 a.m. and passed through Cassville and camped on creek 2½ miles north of town. Forage very scarce and Quartermaster negligent; was compelled to take my company at 3 p.m. and go in search of forage. Got wheat and a few bundles of oats. Men all well and anxious to push forward.[43]

AUGUST 2

Left camp early. Were detained during day by the slow march of the infantry in our advance. Camped for the night at "old" John I. Smith's place. The old fellow is a strong Union man, has a son in the Union Army at Springfield, a captain commanding a company. We bought grain etc. . . . for our horses from him as if he were a southern man, and yet the Union men shoot or hang all Secessionists in arms and rob and plunder their farm and houses.[44]

AUGUST 3

Left camp at daylight for McCulloch's camp, leaving our train to come on after us. When we arrived at his camp we were ordered to go five miles in advance and apparently bring on an engagement with the enemy. When we arrived at the place appointed we got two bundles of oats and fed our horses. Soon, it was announced that the enemy were advancing. We prepared to receive them and sent a message to Gen. McCulloch. He came up and ordered us to fall back to his camp to the ground selected by him for a fight, feeling certain that they would try to follow us. We fell back to the place and formed with balance of the army, but the enemy did not come. We were well prepared to receive them. In evening, camped one mile west of main or center camp.[45]

AUGUST 4

During the day it was reported that the enemy were in a short distance of our camp and we were called into line at once. It was some Missourians who had narrowly escaped being captured by going into the enemy's camp by mistake. In the evening we moved and camped 1½ miles east of center camp. Received orders to cook one days' rations and be prepared to advance on the enemy's camp 7 miles distant at 12 midnight. All were prompt and soon all things were ready and some laid down to sleep and others remained up waiting for the time to come. At 12 o'clock (p.m.) we were called out and were soon on the march; went up to center camp and took our place in line.[46]

AUGUST 5

Commenced moving about 3 a.m. Daylight found us still on the road and momentarily expecting to hear the roar of artillery, but we found the enemy had left their camps on the previous day for Springfield. We moved on and camped at Moody's Spring. The enemy had only left the ground some 4 or 6 hours before, their campfires had not entirely died out. We started in advance of 3 divisions and when we stopped to camp we were in advance of the whole army. Had good camp and plenty of forage. Our wagons still behind and I got Mrs. Dixon, who lives near, to cook some for the company. I fed my horse some oats and I laid down near him on some oats and while asleep he pawed me in the face making quite a painful wound.[47]

AUGUST 6

Left camp early. Most of infantry had passed forward before daylight. Moved up one-half mile and went into camp. Men thought they were going to Springfield. Wound in face, which was undressed and on side of my nose, is painful and feverish. Had I been closer I would have been killed. It has been a lesson to me not to lay too close to my horse in future.

AUGUST 7

In camp on Wilson's Creek. Men all well and anxious to go forward to Springfield, 10 miles distant. Suffered very severely from my wound in face. It commenced swelling early in evening and swelled very much. Bathed in cold water, but obtained no relief, then tried warm water and got easier and continued application. Lt. Shaddock's prescription and he made the application and remained with me during the night.

AUGUST 8

Still in old camp, anxious to go on to meet U.S. forces. Our regiment was ordered out to cut off a train of the enemy going to town, but it got too near before the regiment could get to it and had to abandon and return to camp. Wound so very painful that I could not go with my company, and very much swollen. Still applying warm water for relief.

AUGUST 9

Wound improving slightly, still very much swollen. Late in afternoon received orders to have two days' rations cooked and be ready to march at 9 p.m. At 9 all were ready, but myself, and I had made arrangements to go on toward daylight and join my company before Springfield. After company was found ready to march, orders came to retire and await further orders.

AUGUST 10

About 6 a.m. just after some of my men had eaten and while others were eating breakfast we were fired upon by the U.S. troops who had completely surrounded and surprised us. I had just given orders to my men to saddle up. Some had saddled; these I ordered to the northwest of camp to form out of range of the shots and I hurried up to get my horse saddled and sending the men forward as fast as possible; and as I was not expecting or prepared for so early a move (being almost confined to my bed by wound) I was about the last to get ready to leave; and when I mounted my horse and before I was securely in the saddle he was struck by a ball and away he bounded, jumping a fence and throwing me and injuring me, very severely.[48]

Camp on Wilson's Creek, Missouri

August 11, 1861
Col. Thomas J. Churchill,

Sir: I have the honor to report to you that on yesterday when our camp was attacked, part of my company had their horses saddled. These I ordered to form up in the field to the northwest of us and ordered the remainder to saddle up and join them. I, though considerably disabled from a wound inflicted on my face by my horse on the night of the 5th instant, saddled my horse to go with my company. As I mounted my horse he was slightly cut in the hind leg by a ball from the enemy and dashed forward, struggling to throw me off; when about 150 yards from my tent he threw me, injuring me severely.

I was taken up insensible by Lt. Gaines and some of my men and carried to my tent. Finding we were between the fire of two batteries, Lt. Gaines then carried me to the skirt of timber that ran through our camps. Here I remained some time. When I came to my sense I ordered Lt. Gaines and the men that had remained with him to leave me and join the company, being unable to go myself. I remained in the timber some time, the enemy passing near me; shortly afterward they commenced falling back and plundering the wagons, camps, etc. . . . , then to prevent being taken prisoner, I with three of my sick men that had joined me left the timber and went over to the hill on the east of our encampment where we remained until after the retreat of the enemy from the field, we narrowly escaped being taken several times.

By my fall the command devolved upon 1st Lt. R. I. Shaddock, and he with Lt. McConnell formed the company in the field northwest of our camp and led them on to attack the enemy near where the Missourians were encamped; and so far as I can learn they, both officers and men of my company, conducted themselves as men worthy of the cause for which they fight.

I have to report that two of my men are missing, to wit: Davis S. Stephenson and Josiah Knighton, and 14 wounded to wit: Eli T. Wills, A. J. Beakes, Jasper Dugan, William F. Estille, S. S. Stuart, L. Harmon, B. W. Mathis, Robert Mathias, Richard Thurman, Frank Cable, James A. Yuill, Nelson M. Lynch, Peter J. Smith, and Frank Smith; five being severely and 9 only slightly wounded. I lost from my company 2 horses killed and several wounded and missing number not yet known, our camp equipage except a few taken by the enemy was all saved.[49]

I have the honor to be, sir etc. . . . ,

D. H. Reynolds,

Capt. Chicot Rangers

AUGUST 11

Remained in camp on battlefield during part of the day and then moved to camp 5 miles northwest on same creek, visited the wounded men of my company and found them all doing very well considering their locality. Much crowded and place becoming offensive, on account of dead men and horses being so near. A. J. Beakes had his leg taken off. I came to camp late in the evening.[50]

AUGUST 12

Had wounded removed to Springfield and they were placed in the "Christian Church," all of our regiment placed same house and it small. Nothing worthy of note in camp, only that many feel anxious to write and many anxious to go back towards Arkansas on account of treatment of Missourians to us. As many of our guns, horses, saddles, blankets, etc. . . . were taken by them from our wounded and those waiting on the wounded. A. J. Beakes died late this evening.[51]

AUGUST 13

I went to Springfield and found the wounded getting along tolerably considering their comforts and attention. I procured a house and had them moved to it and separated from other companies in a cool quiet place, where I think they will do better. Wills' wound not dressed yet nor examined until today, nor any others. All in good spirits. Men not satisfied with camp; want to change and follow the enemy.[52]

AUGUST 14

Went to Springfield, found wounded doing well and in fine spirits. Great trouble in getting them food in town, in fact we are all rather short rationed somehow. Visited U.S. wounded. They are all well cared for by the ladies of Springfield, to my surprise. I expected to find many good secessionists, but have been rather disappointed. Missourians have the town, and we cannot trade at stores for them. This is not right and many of us are not pleased at this course.[53]

AUGUST 15

Men much displeased with the Missourians, but hope all will be right soon. Wound in my face is still very sore though I have been riding about. I have suffered very much from it and it is still quite troublesome and am suffering some from my fall from my horse at opening of battle.

AUGUST 16

Heard from sick, all doing quite well. Great difficulty in getting suitable food for them. Several men sick. Don't get as much provisions as desirable, nor of proper kind. Received orders to march to Pond Springs on tomorrow for new camp.

AUGUST 17

Left camp for Pond Springs at 7½ a.m., where we camped, 9 miles west of Springfield. Road dry and dusty and men not in good spirits on account of treatment of the Missouri troops in stealing our guns, horses, flour, etc. . . . and refusing to give them up. Camped in a low bad place on a stream running near the spring. Heard from wounded men, all doing well and in good spirits.

AUGUST 18

Still at Pond Springs. Some of my men went to church and others did not as the minister is a man of doubtful character. I did not go. Josiah Knighton returned; he left the "Dutch" 58 miles from Springfield by escaping. Stephenson with them and did not want to leave.

AUGUST 19

Rations scarce and some of my men suffering for want of blankets, but there is no chance of getting any in Springfield as the Missouri troops have taken all the "Dutch" left and some of my men have not tents. Col. A. C. Wellborn of Chicot County came up to see us and be with us during the fight before Springfield and then go on with us to St. Louis, but got here too late.[54]

AUGUST 20

First dress parade since the battle of "Oak Hills," the name given to the late battle on Wilson's Creek by Gen. McCulloch; not 200 men present. No orders for leaving. Col. Hindman passed through our camp, going after our state troops to get them turned over to the Confederate service and to join Hardee. Col. Wellborn still with us. Heard from wounded men and all doing very well. Rations still very scarce and of roasting ears principally.[55]

August 21

Rained hard during night and men much exposed on account of scarcity of tents and blankets. Received orders to march to Mt. Vernon tomorrow at 5½ a.m. Lent my ambulance to the country to get some provisions and got $8 worth of potatoes, meal, and chickens.

August 22

Raining early and order to march countermanded. Col. Wellborn made me a present of his sword for the war or forever if he should not then call for it. He left for home today and took letters for members of the company. Continued to rain during early part of the day. About 12 m. I started to Springfield to see my wounded men, found them all doing very well and in good spirits. Learned that some of them were to be taken to Bentonville, Arkansas. I left $27½ including 17½ by Mr. Emanuel with those slightly wounded and $10 with those that wait on Eli T. Wills. Reached camp at 9 p.m.[56]

August 23

Left camp at 5½ a.m. and reached Mt. Vernon and camped 4 miles east of the place on the farm of a Mr. Woods, a strong Union man *and* some say a Black Republican. William F. Estille and Davis H. White received discharge from the service on account of disability and left for home. We have a fine camp ground, good water and road convenient, named "Camp Harper" in honor of James Harper, Adjutant of regiment who was killed in battle of Oak Hills.[57]

August 24

Gen. R. M. Gaines of Chicot reached camp today and we were all glad to see him as he has from the first taken a deep interest in our welfare and assisted us by means and by his presence. He brought news from home and none but those who have been absent for a long time can tell how to appreciate news from home.

August 25

No drill or dress parade today. Provisions scarce. Men in tolerable health except L. Harmon, who is quite unwell and has been removed to a house nearby for better protection and assistance.

AUGUST 26

Camp alarmed early in evening by rumor of an attack by Union men.

AUGUST 27

Shoeing horse. B. W. Mathis kicked O. L. Mathis in the eye, hurting him very much, and left camp before being arrested. Still at same camp.[58]

AUGUST 28

Orders to leave for Neosho on tomorrow morning at sunrise. B. W. Mathis and J. B. Lyerly placed under guard for disorderly conduct. Coulter sick and Sappington improving slowly; will try to take them with us. Will take Harmon with us.[59]

AUGUST 29

Left camp early, my company in advance and myself officer of the day. Passed through Mt. Vernon and reached Sarcoxie, 18 miles from Mt. Vernon. Most of the country poor and thinly settled. Several men have taken the measles. Almost no provisions at all.[60]

AUGUST 30

Left Sarcoxie and come to within 4 miles of Neosho. Left Mr. Harmon at Sarcoxie and Mr. Robinson with him is sick with typhoid fever. Forage and provisions scarce.

AUGUST 31

Made arrangements to have 16 horses shod on Monday. Men of my company all well except W. Mabry, who is sick with measles. Lt. McConnell returned from trip to Cassville where he had gone to bring a load of provisions. He was in command of the escort, [companies] B [and] I.

SEPTEMBER 1, SUNDAY

Moved to within two miles of Neosho. Gen. Gaines, Lt. Gaines, Isaac Newton, and C. C. Ferguson returned from Springfield and battleground, their men some of the wounded, and saw remainder in Springfield all doing very well except Yuill, his chance not being good to recover. Saw Mr. Harmon at Sarcoxie. He is improving.[61]

SEPTEMBER 2

At Camp McIntosh. Sent 16 horses to be shod. Talk of a ball in Neosho. Forage and rations scarce.

SEPTEMBER 3

Still at Camp McIntosh. Ball at night at Neosho, not present but Lieutenants Shaddock and Gaines and 8 men went. Ball very pleasant affair.

SEPTEMBER 4

Left camp for Scott's Mills on Elk or Cowskin River 12 miles from state line. Marched 24½ miles and camped for night, and for the first time in several days we have plenty of forage and plenty to eat except bacon.[62]

SEPTEMBER 5

Moved 5 miles and camped south of Scott's Mills; men all in good health. Named camp "Camp Gaines" in honor of Gen. R. M. Gaines.

SEPTEMBER 6

I started to Sarcoxie to see L. Harmon, who is very sick. Reached Neosho at 4 p.m. Got dinner and went 10 miles further and stayed with Crouch during night.[63]

SEPTEMBER 7

Started early. Took breakfast 7 miles from Sarcoxie, where I am satisfied the breakfast was gotten quicker than any I ever saw. Reached Sarcoxie and found Mr. Harmon very bad indeed, not able to converse with any one on any subject, remained during day.

SEPTEMBER 8

Left early for camp at Scott's Mills, reached Neosho at 12 m. and the house of Mr. Hopkins, 6 miles from Mills at dark and remained all night.[64]

SEPTEMBER 9

Reached Camp Gaines early. No change in my absence.

SEPTEMBER 10

Still at Camp Gaines, Gen. Gaines left for Camp Walker where he will remain a day or two and then proceed to Chicot County. Men all in good health, except a few cases of measles. Heard from wounded at Bentonville, all doing very well.

SEPTEMBER 11

Moved to Camp Wells 5 miles south of Camp Gaines. Rained very hard at night. Provisions very scarce and unfairly divided and men much dissatisfied at not being supplied. Officers think of trying to have these things remedied.

SEPTEMBER 12

Officers held a meeting and drew up a request to Col. Churchill to have stricter discipline and some changes made in the management of regiment and presented same to Col. Churchill. He did not receive it in the proper spirit, but spoke harshly and ordered us back to our tents. We held another meeting and freely expressed our views and agreed to meet on tomorrow.

SEPTEMBER 13

Held meeting and Col. Churchill was invited and made an apology for treatment, which satisfied many and some it did not satisfy. After meeting Captains Gibbs, Daniels, Jones, and Lieutenants Thompson and Campbell and myself started to Camp Walker. Stayed all night near Camp Walker.[65]

SEPTEMBER 14

Lieutenant Campbell and myself went to Bentonville and saw the wounded and agreed to send them home on furlough and returned to Camp Walker and stopped all night at Mr. Gray's.[66]

SEPTEMBER 15

Started into camp and when near Camp Mills learned that the camp was changed to a place 5 miles north of Scott Mills. Reached camp about 12 m. Saw the sick at hospital on the roadside, all doing well. The camp named Johnston.

SEPTEMBER 16

At Camp Johnston 21 miles south [of] Neosho, a good camp and plenty to eat for man and horse.

SEPTEMBER 17

At Camp Johnston. Sick doing very well, some new cases of measles. John Brawner and Robinson returned and informed me of the death of L. Harmon, who died at Sarcoxie, Missouri, on last Saturday 14th, he was a true man and excellent soldier.[67]

SEPTEMBER 18

Officer of the day, up late at night making "Grand Rounds," find all guards doing their duty.

SEPTEMBER 19

Col. Churchill received orders at 3 a.m. to report with 5 companies at Camp Jackson. My company and 4 others were off at daylight and reached Camp Jackson at 11 a.m. We were ordered to camp and await further orders; if necessary we were to go to Fayetteville and take possession of some arms held by Col. Hindman.

SEPTEMBER 20

Sent some men back to Camp Johnson, they being unwell. A. Griffith died at hospital, M. V. Worthington restored to duty by order of Gen. McCulloch. Lieutenant Abner Gaines tendered his resignation.[68]

SEPTEMBER 21

Returned to Camp Johnston. Learned that in our absence the camp had been alarmed by rumor of Jayhawkers.[69]

SEPTEMBER 22

Col. Churchill with a small detachment of men went to Lost Creek to select a new camp and I being senior captain was left in charge of regiment. Gave orders to leave for new camp on tomorrow, at 5 a.m. Lt. Gaines left for home having resigned on the 20th. Lt. Shaddock went a short distance with him. B. W. Mathis and P. E. Bush sent home on detail to get some clothing.[70]

SEPTEMBER 23

Left Camp Johnston at 5 a.m. in charge of regiment and went over to Sparling's Store 12 miles west of Neosho, named Camp "Lee" in honor of R. E. Lee of Virginia. Camped men in center and horses on each side. Camp 7 miles southeast of corner of Kansas, report of Jayhawkers not far distant.

SEPTEMBER 24

The forenoon spent in fixing up camp, arranging tents, etc. . . . John MacLean elected 2nd Lt. in place of Lt. Gaines resigned. At 2 p.m., I with H. C. Stamps and 10 men left camp for Cherokee Nation with dispatches from Gen. McCulloch and Col. Churchill to Col. Stand Watie, a Cherokee. We marched 22 miles and reached the house of one Mr. Cockerel on the "Texas and Missouri Road" and 13 miles north of mouth of Horse Creek. Named camp "Camp Talbot" after one of the company.[71]

SEPTEMBER 25

Raining in the morning and we remained in camp until 8 a.m. Took breakfast with Mr. Cockerel, bill for supper and breakfast for 12 of us and our horses only $3. Left for Col. Watie's camp. Kept on main road 10 miles until we crossed Horse Creek; here we met with a Cherokee named "Neo Woodard" who told me that his grandfather was a chief and assisted "White man Jackson to fight Creek Nation long time ago." He acted as guide for us and we left main road and went over to Col. Watie's plantation where we found Captains Buzzard and Parks and their companies and left dispatches with them. They gave us a dinner. Col. Watie has a very good plantation here and several slaves. Continued to rain and after waiting until near night, left and crossed Grand River and came to Mr. Carey's house on the river. He keeps a ferry here. We put up for the night. Mr. Carey is a white man and about 70 years old, but has a young Cherokee wife about 16 years old. He has lived with the Cherokees since 1837 and now has his second Cherokee wife. He is a strong southern man.[72]

SEPTEMBER 26

Left Carey's early in the morning, a clear cool day. Young Mr. Carey showed us a nearer way to our camps. We came to Gilstrap's Ferry and crossed and got oats from a Seneca Indian to feed our horses, but could get no dinner. The country through which we passed in the Cherokee Nation was quite good and some good arms; through the Seneca Nation land not so good and farms poor. The Cherokees that we saw are anxious to fight for the South. Col. Stand Watie was absent at the Grand Council at Tahlequah, several nations of Indians represented. Reached camp at 5 p.m.[73]

SEPTEMBER 27

Nothing worthy of note. Men in good health and fine spirits, except a few cases of measles and they are doing very well.

Still at Camp Lee. Capt. J. D. Latimer, Assistant Quartermaster of our regiment, joined us from Chicot. He brought letters and news from home. The boys all glad to see him and hear from home. Capt. Latimer comes up to commence the duties of his office.[74]

SEPTEMBER 28, SUNDAY

Church at 11 a.m. and after church spent the day in repose. D. M. Mathis, William H. Robb, T. J. Wilson, William D. Phillips, and James M. Carpenter and a Mr. Woods came up to join my company, and D. H. White and Mr. Hurley arrived with letters and papers etc. . . . from home. Several of the boys got articles of clothing from home and nearly all got assurance that clothes would be sent shortly by Mr. J. W. Bowie. Sent 7 men on a scout with Maj. Harper.[75]

SEPTEMBER 30

Officer of the day. Men with measles doing very well.

OCTOBER 1

All recruits were mustered into the service except Mr. Woods. Lieutenant Shaddock and 10 men went out on a scout. Mr. J. Shaddock sick with measles.

All the sick sent to a house near by to be used as a hospital. All the sick doing well.

OCTOBER 2, 3, 4, 5, 6, 7, 8

Nothing worthy of note in camp. Drilled once or twice each day. Sick men doing very well.

OCTOBER 9, WEDNESDAY

Moved from Camp Lee, to a camp 2 miles east. Myself and Orderly Sergeant went to Neosho.

OCTOBER 10

Procured house in Neosho for sick and returned to camp.

OCTOBER 11

Left Camp Stein for Carthage via Neosho. Camped at Neosho and had a ball at night, a quiet and pleasant affair, many present.

OCTOBER 12

Left for Carthage early, camped 5 miles west of Carthage, a hard day's march. Men all doing finely. A few sick, but none dangerously so.

OCTOBER 13, SUNDAY

Moved camp ½ miles west, named Camp Pickens in honor of Gov. Pickens of South Carolina. I went to camp of Col. McIntosh to see about pay rolls.[76]

OCTOBER 14 AND 15

At Camp Pickens and engaged in making out pay rolls.

OCTOBER 16

Completed pay rolls and the company was paid each man $20 in Confederate money. Sent I. Newton and D. Hines to Springfield with money that belonged to men there, Eli T. Wills, Henry W. Stedman, E. G. Molero, Frank Whitten, and J. A. Yuill.[77]

OCTOBER 17 AND 18

All quiet in camp. Sent some sick men to a house near camp.

OCTOBER 19

All quiet in camp. 7 sick men that had been sent to house in country lost their horses. Served in General Court Martial as Judge Advocate, 3 cases of men sleeping on post. Punishment in one case public reprimand and forfeiture of one month's pay, and 2 cases public reprimand and forfeiture of 2 month's pay.

OCTOBER 20

Officer of the day. Rumors that the Federals are only a few miles off. Kept out strong pickets and scouts during day but no enemy seen by them. Camp lively and men ready for the fray. About 4 p.m., Company F on a scout came dashing into camp and reported the enemy advancing on them and Company C was called out; but it was soon ascertained that Company F had mistaken Company G for Federals. The fact, when explained, created considerable merriment in camp at the expense of Company F. At night received orders to fall back on Neosho. We left camp at 9 p.m. I marched all night with rear guard, a very cold night. Camped at 4 a.m. on 21st, 8 miles north of Neosho. Everything brought up but the picket guard and they ordered to follow.

OCTOBER 21

Received orders early to fall back to Bentonville, Arkansas. Passed through Neosho and took the Pineville Road and camped for the night within 10 miles of Pineville. Horse threw me today but did not hurt me seriously. Gen. Price at Neosho with 12 or 13 thousand men well armed. Gen. McCulloch very much annoyed because Gen. Price failed to carry out an arrangement made with him sometime previous by which Gen. Price was to fall back slowly from Lexington, Missouri, and fight Fremont at every favorable place, and when he reached Springfield he was to take Fayetteville Road and Gen. McCulloch was to join him near Springfield with all his infantry and artillery while his cavalry under Col. McIntosh was to enter Kansas and destroy all its depots of supplies etc. . . . All of Gen. McCulloch's forces were disposed in accordance with said plan, but when Gen. Price fell back upon Neosho the plan was entirely disconnected and northern Arkansas left exposed to invasion from Springfield and the base of our supplies be thus endangered. We are now being pushed rapidly forward to Bentonville to prevent so great a calamity if possible. I sent my sick men from Neosho to Camp Walker.[78]

OCTOBER 22

Left camp early and marched 20 miles and camped 10 miles east of Pineville. Camped in a thicket. All well in company. The regiment is said to march faster than any regiment in the brigade. Boys say they caught some "Foxes."

OCTOBER 23

Left camp early and camped at Camp Stephens 5 miles north of Bentonville. Camped as we marched in line. Stephens a good camp and near good water, a pleasant place.

OCTOBER 24

Nothing worthy of note.

OCTOBER 25

James W. Bowie and Mr. Woods with 9 recruits, Mack P. J. Smith and George Young came up from Chicot County with clothing for the company, part of it divided out, a good supply and much needed by the men. Several played too freely with the "bottle" and were put under guard for fighting.[79]

OCTOBER 26

Balance of clothing divided out and all surplus baggage ordered to be put up in boxes and sacks and to be deposited in Bentonville for safe keeping and to save transportation. Sent orders and deposited it with Mr. Dinsmore, a merchant.[80]

OCTOBER 27

Received orders to march northward with 10 days' rations, leaving all extra baggage, sick men, etc. . . . behind.

OCTOBER 28

Left Camp Stephens at 6½ a.m. and reached our old Camp Sevier at 12 m., each company occupying its old ground. All in fine spirits and expecting to march in search of the enemy soon.

OCTOBER 29 AND 30

Nothing worthy of note.

OCTOBER 31

Took 10 men of my company and went on a scout down on Roaring River and down the river to its junction with White River in search of bands of Union men. Heard of a band on Hickman Prairie before leaving camp, but on examination a rough road and wild scenery. Had an adventure with "Greasy Bill Smith," a noted character in them parts. Returned to camp at 8 p.m., having marched about 40 miles.[81]

November 1, 2, 3, 4, 5

At Camp Sevier, a Court Martial progressing. Gen. Price is at Cassville with 12 or 15 thousand men and Gen. McCulloch south of us with all his men except 4 regiments, including ours. Three regiments north of us.

November 6

Left Camp Sevier and marched back into Arkansas and camped at Miser's camp ground 8 miles north of Bentonville and called place "Camp Harris" in honor of a Missouri General and sent to Camp Stephens for balance of clothing and sick men.[82]

November 7, 8, 9, 10

At Camp Harris and nothing worthy of note.

November 11

Took 10 men from each company of the regiment and went up 7 miles north of us to Col. Greer's camp to assist in blockading the roads leading south from Keetsville, Missouri.[83]

November 12

Blockaded the road in 3 places by falling trees across it and then returned to Camp Harris, all quiet and orderly. The company in good health.

November 13

At Camp Harris and Judge Advocate of a General Court Martial.

November 14

At Camp Harris discharging the duties of Judge Advocate. Orders to have 5 days' rations cooked and on hand at all times.

November 15

Prospects of a fight, the principal topic of conversation.

November 16

Received orders to take 40 men from each company with 5 days' rations cooked and 5 uncooked rations and march on Springfield, Missouri.

November 17

Took up the line of march for Springfield, Missouri, at 6 a.m. and camped 3½ miles south of Cassville, Missouri.

NOVEMBER 18

Left camp 2 hours before daylight. Marched 29 miles and camped at John I. Smith's place at 12 m.

NOVEMBER 19

Left camp before daylight and camped ½ mile south of Oak Hills battleground at 2 p.m. Heavy shower of rain just as we reached camp. I with others went over the battleground. I found a Bowie Knife and others got different relics. In evening I, with Messrs. Bowie and Woods, went to Springfield to see Eli T. Wills and Steadman. Wills had been left badly wounded, we found recovering and able to be moved.

NOVEMBER 20

The regiment camped 4 miles south of town, the enemy had fled and his rear Division was at Rolla. Price is moving after the enemy and is at Sarcoxie with his main force, a part being in advance. McCulloch has 2,200 men here, being cavalry entirely.

NOVEMBER 21

Awaiting the result of a scouting party sent to the vicinity of Rolla. Eli T. Wills started home.

NOVEMBER 22

Men growing fat on Crenshaw's fine pork and our horses faring finely on his corn and hay.[84]

NOVEMBER 23

Main part of our forces left for Arkansas. Our regiment left to bring up the rear. Orders to march on tomorrow.

NOVEMBER 24

Left camp at 4 a.m., the weather pinching cold. The secession portion of the citizens anxious for us to winter with them. Camped at John I. Smith's place having marched 31 miles.

NOVEMBER 25

Left camp early and marched 32 miles and camped at Camp Sevier at 1½ p.m. Fair marching.

November 26
Left camp early 7, camped 6 miles south of Bentonville, making in 3 days a march of 96 miles without the loss of a single man, horse, mule, or wagon. Men all in fine spirits.

November 27
At camp 6 miles south of Bentonville.

November 28
Orders to move south and to build winter quarters.

November 29
Went to Bentonville and got wagon to haul clothing for my company. Regiment camped 3 miles south of Fayetteville near the residence of Judge Walker. Saw T. N. Lambe at house near Fayetteville, he is very low.[85]

November 30
Regiment moved at 4 a.m. and marched 23 miles and camped on Mr. Buck's place. I went to Fayetteville and settled some business and did not overtake the regiment; stayed at Mr. Mill's 6 miles from camp.[86]

December 1, Sunday
Learned the charm of how to cure a horse of the bots, but I have not faith. Overtook regiment at foot of Boston Mountain on north side. Regiment only marched 9 miles.[87]

December 2
Regiment crossed Boston Mountain and camped at foot of Boston and Mulberry Mountain. Here we were compelled to leave a part of the company clothing under charge of a guard.

December 3
Crossed Mulberry Mountain and camped on Little Mulberry Creek 15 miles west of Clarksville. Smallpox in Clarksville. Orders to camp at Spadra Bluff 4 miles south of Clarksville.[88]

December 4
Officer of the day. Regiment camped at Spadra Bluff and very poor camp and the stables the government is putting for us are miserable things. Men and officers dissatisfied. Efforts to keep the men in camp to prevent them from taking smallpox.

December 5

Maj. Harper, Dr. Lawrence, and myself started in ambulance to Van Buren, stayed all night with Mr. Bryant 25 miles east of Van Buren.[89]

December 6

Reached Van Buren at 11 a.m. and stopped at the Planter's House. Took supper with my friend Mr. Scott and spent a very pleasant evening at his house. Captain Stuart presented me with a fine hat. Captain Carroll vaccinated me.[90]

December 7

Left Van Buren and reached Dr. Williams 20 miles east of Van Buren, a good place.[91]

December 8

Travelled 38 miles and put up for the night at Mr. Garrett's, 7 miles from camp.[92]

December 9

Reached camp early and found all things moving on quietly. Captain McConnell and myself are making arrangements to go home on a leave of absence. Orders to move camp on tomorrow morning.

December 10

Moved camp to the river bank, the ground better than last.

December 11

Nothing of interest. Our camp named Camp Bragg. Captain McConnell and myself obtained leaves of absence for 30 days from 14th instant.

December 12 and 13

Cutting timber to build winter quarters. Lieutenant Shaddock superintending hospital and other buildings. MacLean got instructions from Col. McIntosh about pay rolls.

December 14

Capt. McConnell, H. C. Stamps, and myself left for Chicot. Memorandum made by Lt. MacLean.

December 15

Ground to be cleared off to build houses.

December 16

Lieutenant Shaddock left with Capt. Latimer for Van Buren, intending to proceed from there to his home in Dallas County. P. G. Smith appointed corporal in T. J. Bateman's stead and Moses Graham in place of Joe Knighton.[93]

December 17

Nothing of interest at Camp Bragg.

December 25

Christmas and contrary to all my expectations remarkably quiet and all the boys distressingly sober, distressingly because it looks so much like the calm before the storm, although there was plenty of eggnog and the raw afloat.

December 31

Nothing of interest being the last day of the year, some of the boys think detailing themselves as a special escort and guard to his interesting and Honorable Highness Eighteen Hundred and Sixty-One and if practicable will return with the youthful and hopeful Eighteen Hundred and Sixty-Two.

Note.

Captain McConnell and myself arrived at home on the 21st [of] December and remained until 8th of January 1862, and during this time, and until the 19th of February 1862, I kept no diary. But during the time the men built themselves comfortable quarters and a good stables for their horses and enjoyed themselves by running horses and other sports. Many of them received furloughs and sent home. Drilled some. The health of the men has been very good. Remained in Camp Bragg until February 19th, 1862.

1862

THE MEN RAISED SUCH A SHOUT

Still buoyant from their victory at Wilson's Creek the previous summer, Reynolds and his company began the second year of war with a confident spirit. The new season, however, soon brought disappointment and discontent for Reynolds and his command, as well as for Confederate forces throughout the Trans-Mississippi Department and Western Theater.

The strategic picture took an early grim turn as the Rebels failed to hold their western defensive line at Forts Henry and Donelson and also lost control of southern Missouri and northwestern Arkansas. Influenced by these losses, Confederate authorities deemed it best to transfer the bulk of their Trans-Mississippi troops to the Western Theater. As part of this movement, Reynolds and the First Arkansas Mounted Rifles crossed the Mississippi River soon after the Pea Ridge campaign. Despite frequent requests for transfer back to Arkansas, so they might defend their homes and families, the regiment served in the armies of the Western Theater the remainder of the conflict.[1]

In addition to displeasure over the apparent abandonment of their home state, moving east of the big river also brought controversy related to the nature of their service. In mid-April, the regiment received orders to serve dismounted —essentially recasting the mounted rifles as traditional infantry. The men and officers complied—reluctantly—based on the impression that the change would be "best for the service" and temporary in duration. As the permanence of their new assignment became clear, however, it proved a growing source of resentment and protest among the Trans-Mississippi troops and reinforced the prevalent perception of their second-class status.[2]

The spring season also brought reorganization and the election of new regimental officers. This process placed additional responsibilities on Reynolds's shoulders as well as a new insignia of rank on his collar. Initially elevated to major, Reynolds quickly advanced to second in command of the regiment with a promotion to lieutenant colonel on the first day of May.[3]

The seeds of discord planted during service in the Trans-Mississippi Department germinated in the Western Theater, particularly in the aftermath of the unsuccessful Kentucky campaign. Gradual but growing displeasure

39

among Confederate commanders created factions that negatively affected the army's performance in the field as much as the Union's numerical strength. Always critical of ineffective performance or poor leadership, Reynolds added his voice to the chorus of dissatisfaction that rose in the wake of the Confederate withdrawal from the bluegrass state.[4]

In spite of this strategic setback, and late-season shortages in basic necessities, morale improved with the approach of autumn and, like a tenacious crop that survived unexpected damage from an early-season frost, the gray troops recovered their fighting spirit and prepared to finish the season in good order. Perhaps to bolster his own morale, Reynolds obtained an extended furlough in late November and used the opportunity to visit Lake Village until after the start of the new year. Although absent from the final battle of the year—Stones River—Reynolds stayed abreast of the war news as best as the distance allowed. As severe fighting outside Murfreesboro brought the year to a bloody climax, Reynolds and the rest of the western Confederate army expressed reasonable hopes for the coming year and a reversal of recent strategic losses in Tennessee.[5]

FEBRUARY 19, 1862

Left Camp Bragg for Fayetteville on a forced march to join Gen. McCulloch; about 50 men in my company and some 450 in the regiment marched 18 miles and halted and cooked 3 days' rations and took up line of march again at 9 p.m., leaving behind all baggage and supplies etc. . . . , crossed Mulberry Mountain and camped at foot of Boston Mountain on south side at 3 a.m. on 20th.

FEBRUARY 20

Crossed Mulberry Creek at 6 a.m. and fed our horses, and at 7½ a.m. again took up our line of march and crossed Boston Mountain; and at 12 m. fed our horses at Saillyville; and after feeding went on to Mr. Buck's and fed again; and here orders were received from Gen. McCulloch not to go to Fayetteville, but to take a left-hand road and join at Hogeye 12 miles south of Fayetteville. At 10 p.m., we left camp again in obedience to said order and moved on to a point 7 miles southeast of Fayetteville where we halted and fed at 5 a.m. on the 21st.

FEBRUARY 21

Moved again at 6½ a.m., and after winding our way over the spurs on north base of Boston Mountain, we arrived at Hogeye at 12 m., having marched a distance of 11 miles and cooked 3 days' rations in the short space of 50 hours, having crossed two mountains and the spurs of one again and the road being wet and in many places very muddy. On our arrival, we found Gen. McCulloch still here but that nearly all the artillery and some of the infantry had taken a position 8 miles south of this place. During the day, all the mounted force and some of the infantry passed us. The 3rd Louisiana, McRae's, and McNair's Regiments camped near us, bringing up the rear of our forces. The night was dark and raining.[6]

FEBRUARY 22

The 3rd Louisiana, McRae's, and McNair's regiments passed on up to the position designed to be occupied by our forces, 8 miles south of Hogeye, leaving our regiment as the advance; the other mounted regiments being between us and the main army. The men though faring roughly and without tents are cheerful and eager for the coming fight and confident of victory when it does come off, be it soon or late. Our pickets report the enemy at Cross Hollows, Sugar Creek, and Elm Springs, all being above Mudtown, which is 12 miles north of Fayetteville.[7]

FEBRUARY 23

Remained at camp at Hogeye during the day. At four p.m., our pickets came in and reported a large force of the enemy 4 miles south of Fayetteville and were thought to be advancing upon us. Being cavalry, we formed our line of battle, the regiment formed finely and were cool and ready to receive a charge from the enemy. We were to be supported by some companies of the Texas Cavalry and 2nd Arkansas Mounted Riflemen. We waited patiently for sometime but no enemy came and we camped in line of battle for the night. Night very cold but the men are cheerful. Tore down a picket fence and slept on the pickets. The enemy did not trouble us during the night.[8]

FEBRUARY 24

We left camp at 6½ a.m. and moved south 4 miles and camped on west side of Telegraph Road, leaving 3 regiments between us and the enemy, one of the infantry and 2 of cavalry. These three regiments went up to Fayetteville to draw the enemy out or take possession of the place again; when they appeared in sight of town the enemy drew up in time to fight but would not come out, and our forces returned without firing a gun.

FEBRUARY 25

Moved 4 miles further south and dismounted and sent our horses south of the mountain, even to Camp Bragg if corn cannot be had to feed them nearer. Detailed 8 men to go with the company horses and take care of them while we remain on foot. The boys did not like much to part with their horses but are willing to do anything to forward our cause; no sacrifice is too great for them when in the path of duty or on the road to success. I retained my horse as I had to act as major for the time being as the lieutenant colonel has left us to go to Pocahontas and leaves us short of a field officer. Our strength in the company, including the officers, amounts to about sixty men and our regiment to about 540, giving us a very respectable force considering the great number absent on furlough. Lieutenant F. Whitten has $40 to buy forage for horses on the road, if it can be had.

February 26

Nothing worthy of note. Morning drill and dress parade in the evening. 3rd Louisiana and McRae's Regiment on drill at same time and in same field. Some horses got away and got with the Texas regiments. G. M. Henry got in from Chicot County and brought some letters.[9]

February 27

Remained at camp, all quiet, no move by us or the enemy.

February 28

At same camp, nothing worthy of note.

March 1

At same camp and all quiet. Took some Federal prisoners and sent them to Fort Smith for safe keeping.

March 2

All quiet.

March 3

We received orders to cook six days' rations and be ready to march at short notice. At night received orders to march 7 a.m. tomorrow. The cavalry under Gen. McIntosh in advance and the infantry under Colonel Hebert. Goode's Battery goes with 3rd Louisiana regiment, Hart's Battery with our regiment, and Provence's Battery with McRae's Regiment. The batteries move in rear of the regiments to which they are attached. Wrote to Judge Hayes about taxes etc. . . . and sent money to pay state and county taxes and directed arrangements to be made in regard to my War and Levee Tax.[10]

March 4

We left camp at 7 a.m. in rear of 3rd Louisiana and followed by McRae's Regiment; was very cold and cloudy early in the morning and about 8 a.m. it commenced snowing and moved about 2 hours and quite fast most of the time and melted nearly as fast as it fell, making the road very moist, and as the day advanced it became milder. We camped 3½ miles south of Fayetteville at 3 p.m. for the night.

MARCH 5

Left camp at 6½ a.m., a very cold morning, and passed through Fayetteville. The town was almost deserted and many of the houses had been burned and much of the property fenced etc. . . . had burned and otherwise destroyed. Saw nothing of the enemy. Camped for the night at Elm Springs. A very cold night and some snow fell. We had a very hard march owing to our inexperience as infantry, many of the men being lame with blistered feet.[11]

MARCH 6

Left camp at 7 a.m. and marched through Bentonville at 12 m., where we found a large part of our cavalry in the town. They had been driven in by the enemy on their retreat from Bentonville to join Gen. Curtis at Elkhorn Tavern on the Telegraph Road. The cavalry then moved on and we followed some of our infantry in advance of our regiment. We camped near Camp Stephens 5 miles north of Bentonville at 6 p.m. and cooked our supper at 8 p.m. We again took up the line of march and having no preparations made to cross Sugar Creek, a small stream some 40 feet wide, it took us several hours to cross and march 3 miles where we at 3 a.m. on the 7th halted to rest and remained until daylight. It was very cold and men suffering terribly with sore feet.[12]

MARCH 7

At daylight we again moved slowly forward and when within 2½ miles of the Telegraph Road, where we were met by Gen. McCulloch and staff and ordered to countermarch and go back 2½ miles where a line of battle was soon formed and our regiment was held as a reserve and ordered to keep about ¼ mile behind the line of battle. At 5 minutes before 12 m. the enemy fired on our cavalry forming on the right of our line of battle; they did no harm; the enemy's battery was soon charged by our cavalry and Gen. Pike's Indians and taken after a very small loss on our part and some 30 or 40 on side of the enemy. Our line then moved on to the left of the point where the battery was taken and filed into the woods and our regiment with the two pieces of artillery assigned to it as a reserve; when we got within 400 yards of our line the enemy opened fire on us with a battery; we were in an open field; their battery was to the right of our infantry and to the left of our line of cavalry. In a few minutes, our cavalry charged and took 3 pieces of it. We advanced to the edge of the timber in which the enemy were stationed, the enemy firing a few shots at us from a battery in rear of the one just captured. We soon formed in line of battle at the place resigned for us to occupy as the reserve and laid down, the enemy continuing to fire upon us with their battery but doing no harm. Soon our line of infantry opened on the enemy and the firing of musketry became general and very heavy and continued with scarcely an intermission for nearly 3 hours, during which time the enemy continued to fire upon us and other regiments near us. At 10 minutes past 4 p.m., we were ordered to moved to the right to prevent being flanked by the enemy; and at 30 past 4 p.m., we were ordered to fall back to the support of Capt. Goode's Battery on the north side of the field where we first entered; and when we had fallen back near his battery, he moved and commenced a retreat toward Gen. Price's forces on the Telegraph Road; and to that point we were also ordered to go. Capt. Goode, by order of Col. Churchill after he (the colonel) had asked Gen. Pike to assume the command and he had declined to do so, placed one piece of artillery in rear of the regiment. We moved over to the Telegraph Road and turned south to join Gen. Price, and after going some half mile again countermarched and went toward Cassville, Missouri, some 1½ miles, and then again countermarched and went up to within one mile of Elkhorn Tavern and into Gen. Price's camp, where we arrived at 8 p.m. and camped for the night. Tired and worn down and without food, the men were soon asleep. Our forces held the field where McIntosh and McCulloch had fallen (and where we had been as reserve) until after night and then withdrew and joined the remainder of the army under Gen. Van Dorn at and near Elkhorn Tavern. Gen. Price's troops had driven the enemy back some two miles down the Telegraph Road and all troops in good spirits though worn down very much. Our trains were some 8 miles from the battlefield to the west and near to Bentonville and were attacked by the enemy's cavalry and were repulsed. Gen. McCulloch fell shortly after the fight opened and, in his fall, the Confederacy lost one of her noblest men. Gen. McIntosh fell some 20 minutes later, thus leaving our division without a leader. Col. Hebert had been taken prisoner shortly after McIntosh's death. Everything had went well with us though our loss had been very heavy and especially so in officers.[13]

March 8

About 3 a.m. we were aroused and moved up to Elkhorn Tavern; it was very cold and we could build but little fires; about 4 a.m. we divided our cartridges, each man of the regiment giving up 5 cartridges to men of other regiments who had been engaged on yesterday. Nothing for breakfast and nothing for supper last night or in fact since the evening before. At 5 a.m., we were placed in line of battle some 600 yards southwest of Elkhorn Tavern on the right of our line, the 1st Missouri Brigade on a hill in our rear. Col. Rector's Regiment on our left and Whitfield's Battalion on Rector's left and Burbridge's Missouri Regiment left of Whitfield's and other troops still to the left and rear. Some batteries in our front and to our left and to the left of the Elkhorn Tavern. Our orders were to hold our place and defend the hill immediately in our rear at all hazards; men confident of victory. About 6½ a.m., some of the batteries on each side opened and continued to fire slowly. About 7½ a.m., the enemy formed line of battle and advanced towards us, but our batteries soon dispersed them in great confusion and their batteries ceased for some minutes and took new positions when the cannonading recommenced with some pieces on each side, and it fairly made the earth tremble, though but little damage was done on either side except in a moral point of view. This tremendous cannonading continued until 10½ a.m., when nearly all of our [troops] withdrew owing to a want of ammunition. About 9½ a.m., they formed a new line of battle and about 11 a.m. advanced steadily on us, this time seemingly regardless of a few guns of ours, which were still firing. We were ordered to take position on the hill just in rear of our present position. We obeyed and found that Rector's regiment had also moved up on the hill. We were then ordered to the east side of the hill where we formed on the right of Whitfield's men, they having retained their position; here we awaited the enemy's approach. Soon the firing commenced on our left and, soon after, those on the hill we had just left, now to our right, opened fire. Orders were given to our regiment not to fire until the enemy were distinctly seen and not to waste their ammunition. Soon the whole line to our left commenced firing very heavily and was soon answered by the enemy and, in a minute, our left gave way and retreated toward Elkhorn Tavern. Then orders were given to the regiment to fall back, when my company and three others next to it fired a volley into the enemy, who could just be seen through the timber in our front, and then fell back according to our orders. The regiment reformed on the hill again. The side of the hill being very rough and but few places where it could be easily ascended, the regiment got in some confusion. Just as we were again formed, the enemy were advancing toward Elkhorn Tavern in the open field and nearly opposite to us, shouting as they went, when part of a company nearest them fired upon them and we were fired upon in return. Just at this time, Col. Churchill was notified that our whole army was on the retreat and that orders had been sent to him sometime previous (but they did not arrive). Orders were immediately given to retreat and we passed down the hill to the north and into a ravine and across the Telegraph Road some 400 yards north of Elkhorn Tavern, now in possession of the enemy. After crossing the road we took a southeasterly direction, over the hills without a road; after marching about 3 miles we got into a road and continued on to Van Winkle's Mill 11 miles northeast of Fayetteville. We were the rear of the infantry portion of our

army, and many of our men, being worn down by previous hardships, were
not able to keep up and fell by the wayside exhausted, and many of them I fear
have been taken prisoners. All our troops and some went west and many were
taken by the enemy's cavalry. It was only intended that we should make a
feint, and the main part of our army commenced retreating at an early hour
in the morning. Only 15 of my company, including Lt. McConnell and myself,
when we reached camp at 5 p.m. At night we got some pork, chickens, and
some parched corn and sent out and had a loaf of corn bread baked and got
8 or 10 lbs. of bacon and fared tolerably well under the circumstances.[14]

March 9

Left camp at 6½ a.m. and marched 20 miles and camped 16½ miles east of
Fayetteville, having marched 10 miles out of our way and by so doing had to
cross the White River five times; this was owing to a want of guides. During
the day it rained very hard and from the number of troops in the road it
became very muddy and we were much hindered by the Missouri wagons and
ambulances mixing up with us and compelling us to get out of the way. All
suffered very much with sore feet, particularly the dismounted cavalry, and we
went crippling on over the rough and stony road, and many declaring that
they could not hold out much longer; and to add to our sufferings, we were
fearful that our trains had been captured by the enemy, and if so our chances
for speedy relief are not very good, and still we trudged on in disorder and but
few men of any of our companies present and even that few were not in order.
Where camped at night we were compelled to take rails, as we had no axes to
procure other fuel. I sent out and got 17 lbs. of bacon, this with parched corn
and a little fresh beef furnished us with supper and breakfast on 10th. We have
some 20 men now in camp. Russ Ward on Mr. Cy Hank's horse acted as our
commissary and getting bacon for us. Mr. Hanks has been with the company
since the morning of the 7th, while under fire acted very gallantly.[15]

March 10

Left camp early and marched some 15 miles and camped southeast of
Fayetteville on Little Frog Bayou Road and were countermarched ½ mile to
our camp ground; more of our men overtook us during the evening. Drew
some meal and bacon, cooked bread on rocks and boards, and broiled meat
on sticks by holding in the fire. Night pretty cold and much coughing in the
regiment during the night, being too cold to sleep more than 10 or 15 minutes
at a time, being as we are without blankets for covering or protection from
cold ground.

MARCH 11

Moved camp 2½ miles further south. Heard that our trains are safe. Let some of my men go on to overtake the train. Drew more meal and bacon and killed some fresh pork and fared tolerably well; the little rest has made the men more cheerful and things look brighter than for a few days past.

MARCH 12

Took up line of march and, after going 4 miles south, countermarched 2 miles and crossed over to the Big Frog Bayou Road and then down that for some five miles and camped on bank of the bayou, and here as elsewhere we used fence rails. Our supply of provisions is very scant. Lt. MacLean and Isaac Newton joined us here, they having been on furlough at home.

MARCH 13

We crossed over the mountain to the Little Frog Bayou Road again, much dissatisfaction at having to countermarch and cross mountains so much for so little gain in distance. Made a hard day's march and camped 30 miles from Van Buren. Just before night it commenced raining and rained very hard, and after night it again rained very hard, so much so that it was with difficulty that we could keep a fire with plenty of dry and seasoned rails. We would stand up during the hardest of the rain and then lay down on wet rails and stones. We slept but little during the night and were all anxious to see daylight come. We had cornbread and fat bacon for our suppers and for breakfast next morning; having no cooking utensils, we carried water in our canteens and poured it in the meal sacks and thus made the dough, which we afterward baked on flat stones and boards.

MARCH 14

Marched down the Frog Bayou Road to the north bank of Cedar Creek and there took the Cedar Creek to avoid the deep water in Frog Bayou, which the men had been compelled to make several times and must still continue to do so or change the road; and, again to avoid the wading of Cedar Creek, we took a by-road or path over another spur of the mountains; and when we had gained the west side of the spur, and some 14 miles from Van Buren, we were informed that our train was three miles north of Van Buren and that we could get nothing more to eat until we reached our trains as our hitherto scanty supplies had entirely failed; and we were also informed that we could proceed on to our train or camp for the night; or, in other words, each man was allowed to look out for himself and report at the camp of the wagon train as early as possible. Owing to sore feet and exhaustion, I had fallen behind (for the 1st time) nearly all the regiment, but I made up my mind, though nearly night, when I reached the foot of the mountain on the west side, to try and if possible to reach the train. None of my company except Lt. McConnell and one or two others were ahead of me, so on I went with a "tobacco stick" for a cane. I soon met up with Capt. Lawrence of Col. Hill's Arkansas regiment, who said he would accompany me. I soon came to the creek again, and Capt. Gipson of the 2nd Arkansas Mounted Riflemen carried me over on his horse. A few hundred yards further on, I came to the creek again, and having suffered all day from wet feet from having waded Frog Bayou early in the morning, I determined to wait for some one to carry me over on a horse; seen a horseman came up; the horseman said that his horse was exhausted from assisting others and that he feared was not strong enough to carry us both but that he would try, so I got on behind him (and Capt. Lawrence on behind another horseman) and when about the middle of the stream the horse failed and down he went with both of us in the water some two feet deep, and my boots filled with water. I cut holes in my boots and determined to wade for the remainder of the trip and did wade 4 times during the evening, by which time it had become nearly dark; and the fords being dangerous to pass, I, with Capt. Lawrence, concluded to hunt a house on the roadside. At the second house, we found an invitation to share a smoke house with some fellow soldiers. The lady of the house cooked us supper and we slept before the fire on some straw in a really smoky house.[16]

March 15

We got something to eat and fell in with Col. Embry's Regiment, which was hunting a nearer mountain road to Van Buren and which we found by only crossing the creek once. Col. Embry let me ride his horse across the creek. I reached camp 3 miles northwest of Van Buren about 12 m., where I found that nearly all my men had preceded me; after getting something to eat I slept until night, then wrote a short letter to Judge Hayes.[17]

March 16

The regiment moved to a camp eight miles southeast of Van Buren. I got permission from Gen. Van Dorn and went to Fort Smith to buy a horse; went out and spent the night with Captain Woodruff about a mile from town, there being no hotel in town. Lieutenants Erwin and Cooke with me. The horse I went for was sold a few days ago.[18]

March 17

Lieutenant West and Mr. Stillwell and Capt. Woodruff came to Fort Smith with us, where we remained until 1 p.m. and left for Van Buren (loaned Lt.

Erwin $17). We waited until nearly night opposite Van Buren before we could cross the river and reached camp 8 miles southeast at 9 p.m. On 15th received a letter from Lt. Shaddock and D. O. Bowles informing me that they, with five others of my company, were in hands of the enemy prisoners.[19]

MARCH 18

All quiet in camp.

MARCH 19

Some furloughed men returned and some horses brought in.

MARCH 20

Went to Van Buren to try and have Lt. Shaddock and others exchanged as speedily as possible. Gave list of names to Gen. Van Dorn and he promised to try and get them exchanged as soon as possible, that Gen. Curtis had already proposed an exchange and he would effect it as soon as possible. The horses for my company arrived in camps.[20]

MARCH 21

Regiment started for Camp Bragg and camped for night at "Camp Meeting Grounds" west of Big Mulberry Creek. No forage for horses or teams.

MARCH 22

I left at 3½ a.m. with part of 7 companies, many of them having passed on during the night, as many of them were stopping on the byroads to feed their horses. I told those who were with me to report at Camp Bragg at 12 m. on tomorrow, and that each man might look out for himself and horse as it was not possible to get forage for them and keep them together. I came on to Clarksville and with Capt. Gibbs accepted an invitation to spend the night at the house of Judge Rose.[21]

MARCH 23

Went to camp early and found that nearly all the regiment had reached camp. The trains got in during the evening. Meeting of the officers at night and Col. Matlock made a speech.

MARCH 24

At Camp. Court Martial today and I acting as Judge Advocate.

MARCH 25

Court Martial still in session.

MARCH 26

Court Martial adjourned *sine die*. Tried 5 cases.[22]

MARCH 27

Left camp with 4 other regiments, to wit: Stone's, Young's, and Sim's Texas regiments and Gate's Missouri Regiment under Brig. Gen. Churchill on a secret expedition to Springfield, Missouri. Marched 23 miles on the road from Clarksville to Jasper in Newton County.[23]

MARCH 28

Marched 18 miles, crossing Piney Mountain and camping on headwaters of Big Piney. Left camp with 67 men, non-commissioned officers and privates.

MARCH 29

Marched 22 miles and camped on Hudson's Fork of Buffalo Fork of White River, having crossed Boston Mountain at one of its worst crossings. Left E. T. Smith with Dr. Kilburn, reducing our number to 66 men and 3 commissioned officers. Driver upset wagon and lost some few articles. Wagon did not get in until 11½ p.m.[24]

MARCH 30

In camp today, for Colonels Stone's and Sim's regiments to overtake us and for Gate's and Young's regiment[s] to pass a mountain in advance, as it would be impossible for all to pass together on tomorrow.

MARCH 31

Left camp early and marched 18 miles and camped [at] Crooked Creek near Mt. Pleasant. Passed through Jasper (but boy said Jasper was not at home); drew a special requisition for 7 days' rations and got flour and meat. Left P. J. Smith at Jasper and John Anderson with him. They are to make their way to Jacksonport as soon as possible.[25]

APRIL 1

Marched 7 miles and waited 5 hours and obtained forage and moved on 5 miles further and camped near a spring 5 miles from Brown's Prairie. Received orders to cook 4 days' rations and march 35 miles and camp at or near Forsyth, Missouri. Rained during afternoon and night, bad time to cook or sleep as we have no tents.

APRIL 2

Marched 35 [miles] and camped on south bank of White River opposite to Forsyth. Got forage on Forsyth side of river. Received orders to march [toward] Des Arc on White River by forced marches. White River rose during [night] so that we could not cross at the ford. We were on the way to Springfield but, owing to the above mentioned orders, we did not cross the river.

April 3
Marched on the Yellville Road 30 miles and camped on Crooked Creek.

April 4
Marched to Yellville and camped on north side of town, pleasant little place; most of the citizens of the place and vicinity are good and true men, as is evidenced by the county sending eight companies to the field.

April 5
Marched 20 miles and camped on Tomahawk Creek; for the first time on this trip we have plenty of forage.

April 6
Marched 18 miles and camped in Wiley's Cove near Dr. Stevenson's house. Passed through Burrowville, a very small place, and crossed a bad but short mountain.[26]

April 7
Marched 8 miles and camped at Page Hatchett's at foot of Boston Mountain.[27]

April 8
Crossed Boston Mountain and camped at Clinton in Van Buren County. Marched 18 miles and the best crossing I have yet seen of the Boston Mountain. Many horses of my company and, in fact, of the regiment almost unfit for service for want of shoes.

April 9, Wednesday
Marched down the Little Rock Road some 8 or 9 miles and then took the Searcy Road. Marched in all 13 or 14 miles.

April 10
Marched miles and camped where the Des Arc Road leaves the Searcy Road 25 miles from Searcy. Got plenty of corn but little fodder. Our horses are much in need of good forage.

April 11
Commenced raining about 4½ a.m. and rained slowly for nearly two hours, in the meantime we had taken up the line of march. We marched 17

miles over Black Jack (Oak) Flats; the road became very muddy. The wagons only moved 7 miles and we had to go to sleep supperless, after drying our wet blankets; many of our blankets had been left behind in the wagons, and the men had scanty bedding. We received orders from Col. Stone to cook one day's rations and leave our train and reach Des Arc as soon as possible. Col. Matlock remaining behind, I was in command of the regiment. I sent to Col. Stone telling him our condition and asking him whether I should stay for the train or move on. He sent back word to me that if I could not move to let him know, and thinking it was one day to starve either to stay or advance and so I concluded to advance.[28]

April 12

Moved at 6½ a.m. and came through Stony Point and down the Little Rock Road to Atlanta, where we took the Des Arc Road again and camped 7 miles east of Atlanta on Pigeon Creek. I sent out the Commissary Clerk and one man from each company to hunt for provisions; they got some bacon, which with parched corn and some little bread that the men got cooked at houses near camp furnished us with supper and breakfast for tomorrow morning. We obtained plenty of forage for our horses.[29]

April 13

Moved to Mr. Schnebley's place 4 miles from Des Arc. No forage for our horses and but little provisions for the men. Met with the part of our trains that had been left behind at Camp Bragg. Orders to dismount and privilege granted to send horses home or turn over to government agents to be taken care of at government depots near Camden, Arkansas. While dismounted we are to retain all the enrollments of other cavalry.[30]

April 14

Orders to elect a colonel in the regiment and to fill other vacant offices; election to be held at 12 m. today. Election held and Major Harper elected colonel and Capt. D. H. Reynolds elected major by acclamation. By my promotion, the captaincy of my company became vacant and Lt. Jacob McConnell was duly elected captain of the Chicot Rangers and John Maclean, 2nd Lt., and George M. Henry, Jr., 2nd Lt. Capt. Latimer gave Capt. McConnell $200 to defray the expenses of carrying the company horses to Chicot County and men were detailed to carry them. Men dismounted with great reluctance, but as it was insisted by our commanding officers that it was best for the service for us to do so, it was done without murmuring.

APRIL 15

My connection with the Chicot Rangers as their captain having ceased, I entered on the discharge of my duties as major of the regiment.

At 9 a.m., I received orders from Colonel Harper to move the regiment to town at once and at 10 a.m. we moved; and at 1 p.m., camped in the suburbs of the town. Orders were given to cook five days' rations and be prepared to go on board the steamboat early tomorrow morning, destined for the city of Memphis.[31]

APRIL 16

At 4½ a.m., the reveille was sounded and at 6½ a.m. our wagons were on their way to the steamboat landing. We followed soon after. The forenoon was occupied in getting horses, mules, and wagons on board, and the regiment went aboard at 1½ p.m. The steamer (the *J. A. Cotton*) pushed out for Memphis; being a large boat and many short bends in the river, she moved slowly and at 8 p.m. she tied up for the night at Clarendon. It rained very hard during the evening and night and our men suffered very much as they could not all get shelter. Gen. Churchill and staff are on board.[32]

APRIL 17

Moved out at daylight and got into the Mississippi River at 2 p.m. and stopped toward 8 miles below Helena on Mississippi side at 11 p.m. Passed a great many boats, the *H.R.W. Hill* carrying Whitfield's Legion, *Victoria* carrying Sim's Regiment, and the *Means* carrying Young's Texas Regiment, etc. . . . The Mississippi River very high and in many places out of its banks. It is said to be higher than in 1858.[33]

APRIL 18

Reached Memphis at 5 p.m. The day very foggy and banks of river all under water and raining most of the day. Remained in the boat all night.

APRIL 19

Left the boat and camped near Fort Pickering. Ground very [broken] and wood scarce. I went out and spent night with Captain Robinson of the Chicot Guards.[34]

APRIL 20

In camp. Sent my horse to the livery stable (of May and Tuft), the buffalo gnats being so bad that it is not safe to let a horse remain exposed to them.

APRIL 21

All quiet in camp near Fort Pickering.

APRIL 22

All same camp. Sent some men to Overton Hospital.[35]

APRIL 23

All quiet at same camp.

APRIL 24

Moved camp over to the fairgrounds this evening.

APRIL 25

Cooked 5 days' rations and the regiment was inspected at 4 p.m. by Maj. Haskell of Gen. Van Dorn's staff and after inspection sent baggage to the railroad depot and regiment moved over and took the cars for Corinth at 7 p.m. and run all night, running off on every switch etc. . . . , being very much detained.[36]

APRIL 26

Daylight found us 62 miles east of Memphis and run on at intervals all day and night, and men and horses having but little to eat, being as we are separated from our baggage train.

APRIL 27

Arrived at a point 2½ miles west of Corinth at 7 a.m., and our baggage train passed on to Corinth and returned at 8 p.m. to this our present camp, called Camp McIntosh in honor of General James McIntosh, killed at Elkhorn.

APRIL 28

At same camp; some few men sick and sent to the hospital at Memphis or Holly Springs.

APRIL 29

At camp, all quiet.

APRIL 30

Assisted Col. Embry to inspect Col. Turnbull's Battalion and Col. Harper to inspect Col. Embry's Regiment and was present when our regiment was inspected and mustered by Col. Embry and Maj. Brown.[37]

May 1

Our regiment reorganized under the New Conscript Law, many of the officers were left out, and many indifferent and many good ones elected, and some few retained. Field officers of the regiment are R. W. Harper, colonel; D. H. Reynolds, lieutenant colonel; and L. M. Ramseur, major. (The officers of the Chicot Rangers are Jacob McConnell, captain; G. M. Henry, 1st Lt.; J. W. Turner and A. J. Maxey, 2nd Lt.).[38]

May 2

Still in camp. Report of artillery heard in camp. Pickets fighting. All quiet in camp.

May 3

Fixed up muster rolls for Col. Turnbull's Battalion and assisted in fixing up same for Col. Embry's Regiment, and I have them ready to send to Richmond.

May 4

All up at 3 a.m. and at 5 a.m. moved out to Corinth, where we awaited to be ordered in the fight, if it should come off; our division being held as a reserve. It commenced raining at 11 a.m. and at 1 p.m. we returned to camp.

May 5 and 6

In camp, all quiet.

May 7

Moved to a point 3 miles southeast of Corinth. A little skirmish in the evening some 2½ [miles] northeast of our camp, nothing decisive.

May 8

At three p.m. were placed in line of battle and at 4½ p.m. took up line of march, and moved to within ¾ miles of Farmington and lay in line of battle all night, expecting to begin the attack early in the morning. A little affair occurred to mar the otherwise confident and harmonious movements of our forces. At dusk a company sent out by the 5th Arkansas regiment and returning to the regiment were mistaken for Federals and fired upon by part of same regiment, killing 4, wounding eighteen men.[39]

May 10

Remained in camp.

May 11

Moved over to the Mobile and Ohio Railroad 3½ miles south of Corinth behind some earth works.[40]

May 12, 13, 14, 15

Remained at camp; all quiet; many of the men getting sick on account of bad water etc. . . .

May 17

Took our regiment and 2nd Arkansas Mounted Riflemen and went out on picket on the Danville and Farmington road north of Memphis and Charleston railroad as advance pickets, being about ¾ miles from Farmington. Relieved Col. Moore's Texas regiment and guarded 1½ miles of front, assisted by a detachment of cavalry; 140 infantry and 20 cavalry on duty at a time, remaining force being a reserve. All quiet during the day and night and weather pleasant.[41]

May 18

During early part of the day, all quiet. About 5 p.m. the enemy came in sight on our front, both on right and left, and ambulances and ammunition wagons were seen by our pickets, passing toward our right from and near Farmington. Kept a vigilant lookout for the enemy, but no advance upon our lines.

May 19

The enemy's pickets in sight but all quiet until about 8 a.m., when they commenced passing to our right near the field in our front (right), and our pickets commenced firing upon them at long range, which was kept up during the day at intervals. They charged our cavalry pickets on our right and drove them in but were repulsed by our infantry pickets. About 12½ at night some few of the enemy made a little advance upon our pickets when some of them left their posts, but were soon repulsed by Major Ramseur and other officers on duty at the time. We were momentarily expecting an attack during day and night as the enemy were evidently in force only 800 or 1,000 yards from us.

May 19

We expected an attack early in the morning but were again disappointed. The men were all anxious to give them a tilt. We being only pickets of course would have been compelled to fall back, but we would have left our mark before doing so, or at least so the men thought. At 11 a.m. we were relieved by

Col. Danley with 3rd Arkansas cavalry and part of Col. Stone's Texas Regiment under Capt. Jack Wharton; when we came into camp Col. Harper was sick in camp.[42]

MAY 20

Prepared 3 days' rations and were ordered to be ready to march to meet the enemy at 5 p.m., but owing to rain and a threatening storm we did not march, but were ordered to hold ourselves to do so at any moment.

MAY 21

Received orders to march to meet the enemy at 3 p.m., at which time we left camp only with 3 days' cooked and 2 days' uncooked rations and marched out to a point a little south of the Memphis and Charleston Railroad, some 6 or 8 miles east of Corinth, where we lay on our arms during the night.

MAY 22

Gen. Price's and Gen. McCown's divisions of the Army of the West (Gen. Hardee's division having passed us) crossed the railroad and moved up some 2½ miles and formed a line of battle; shortly afterward we received orders to return to camp, where we arrived at 4 p.m. The men much disappointed that they did not have an opportunity to meet the enemy. Heavy cannonading commenced on the left of our lines at 6 p.m.[43]

MAY 23

At camp all quiet. Some cannonading on the left of our line, nothing definite. Raining during the greater part of the day.

MAY 24

All quiet in camp. Picket fighting on front as usual.

MAY 25

All quiet. Many men sick.

MAY 26 AND 27

All quiet. No movement.

MAY 28

Cooked three days' rations and in evening sent sick to the railroad depot and packed up baggage and sent train off and remained in camp during the night.

MAY 29

Moved out near the Memphis and Charleston railroad where our whole Army of the West was drawn up for battle, our brigade being held as reserve. During the day but little firing, except some cannonading in which we had the advantage.

MAY 30

During the day several rifle shells fell just in front of our brigade, wounding 3 men and two horses not more than 40 or 50 yards from our line and passing parallel with it; firing soon ceased. Our army commenced the retreat before dark, and at 11 p.m. we moved. Marched all night; before daylight on 31 all our infantry and artillery had withdrawn and was in retreat.

MAY 31

Continued march until about 12 m. and camped 2 miles from Rienzi, having made a very short march for the time employed.

JUNE 1

Took up line of march at 3 a.m. and moved on to a point 6 miles north of Baldwin, where we camped for the night.

JUNE 2

Moved at 4 a.m. and camped at a point 3 miles south of Baldwin.

JUNE 3

Remained at camp.

JUNE 4

Discharged some men in the evening. Changed camp about 300 yards to better ground and near better water.

JUNE 5

At same camp. Sent all sick who were too unwell to walk off on cars at 10 a.m., and all who were able to walk but not able to march with regiment were sent ahead at 4 p.m. In evening packed our wagons; ready to move at 3 a.m. on tomorrow.

JUNE 6

Wagons left at 3 a.m. Regiment still occupying same ground.

JUNE 7

Left campground at 3 a.m. and marched 16 [miles]. The day very hot and the troops suffering from want of water. Rained in evening but cleared up before night.

JUNE 8

Left campground at 4½ a.m and moved on to a point 2½ miles east of Tupelo, Mississippi, where we camped and have been digging wells and making preparations to stay for sometime.

JUNE 9

At same camp. Cleared up parade ground and worked on company grounds. The health of the regiment improving.

JUNE 10

All quiet and things begin to look like a campground. Men discussing the Conscript Law, many against it and desiring to go to Arkansas to fight etc. . . . Some threats about deserting and going home etc. . . . , but I think there will be nothing serious. Col. Harper sick at Jackson, Mississippi, and Maj. Ramseur sick in the country.[44]

JUNE 11

All quiet. Regular drills.

JUNE 12 AND 13

Everything moving on smoothly except that 8 men deserted from Company E.

JUNE 14

Twelve men from Company F laid down their arms and declared that they would do nothing more until they got their horses etc. . . . ; they were arrested and 4 companies of cavalry sent after the 9 deserters. Charges made out against the mutineers and court martial required and promised soon.

JUNE 15

All quiet. No more attempts to desert or mutiny.

JUNE 16, 17, 18, 19, 20, 21

At same camp and everything quiet. Men improving in health and many sick coming into camp.

JUNE 22

Sunday and everything quiet.

JUNE 23, 24, 25, 26, 27

All getting on smoothly and but few sick.

JUNE 28

Received orders to prepare to go to Chattanooga, Tennessee, tomorrow at 3 a.m. A busy day in making the necessary preparations, cooking rations etc. . . . ; at night, packed up the wagons so as not to be detained in the morning.

JUNE 29

Left camp at 3 a.m. Reached at 6 a.m. and after waiting until 8 a.m. got our baggage and three companies and part of another on the cars and left for Mobile. Travelled very slow all day and until low twelve, when we halted and laid until morning. During the day, Col. Harper joined us in good health.

JUNE 30

Reached Mobile at 6½ a.m. and regiment camped at depot. Men went about town to enjoy themselves. Col. Harper, Capt. Black, and myself went to Quartermaster's office to see about transportation to Montgomery and were informed that the quartermaster would not be in until 7½ next morning. Went to eating house and got supper, paying $8.50 for the same.[45]

JULY 1

At 3 p.m. we crossed the bay to Blakely, the terminus of the railroad to Montgomery, where we remained until next morning, waiting for the train of cars. Rained quite hard during the night and many of the men were exposed, but all quite cheerful under the circumstances.

JULY 2

Left Mobile at 7 a.m. and reached Montgomery at 3 a.m. on the 3rd. No accidents.

JULY 3

Left Montgomery at 3 p.m. and reached West Point at 10 p.m. and left West Point at 12 p.m. and travelled 34 miles by daylight on the 4th.[46]

July 4

Reached Atlanta at 10 a.m. and remained until 7 p.m. During the day a fire company paraded the streets in honor of the day.[47]

July 5

By stopping at night, we made very slow progress and did not reach Chattanooga until 5 p.m., where we found that Cabell's Brigade and nearly all his baggage. Part of his brigade had camped at Missionary Springs. Col. Harper reported to Gen. Heth and was ordered to camp at same place. Slept at depot.[48]

July 6, Sunday

Regiment moved out to springs at daylight and left men to send out baggage. I went back to town to assist the quartermaster, got some commissary stores, and got 6 or 7 loads out to the regiment.

July 7

Dr. Carroll and myself went out to forage for our mess; got some beans and potatoes and the promise of some 4 quarts of sweet milk this evening. Balance of the things brought out to the regiment, and I found to my sorrow that I had lost a lot of clothing and our mess lost some $10 worth of meat and 12 lbs. ($8.50) of coffee.

July 8

Dr. Carroll and I went over the mountain to the east from our camp some 3 miles out; found nothing. Bathed in Chickamauga Creek below the mill and returned to camp. Found a place 1½ miles from camp where we could get some clothes washed.

July 9

Part of the regiment moved to a new camp 1 mile west of old camp. Being short of transportation, but part of the regiment could move.

July 10

More of the regiment arrived today. Had a heavy shower of rain. A good place to camp; but one spring, which makes water rather scarce.

July 11

Balance of regiment arrived at our new camp, called Camp May in honor of major of 4th Arkansas.[49]

July 12, 13, 14, 15, 16

All quiet. Some difficulty in getting provisions from country owing to the fact that other troops had been here before us and things are scarce. Chickens sell for 50 to 75 cents, butter 50 cents, potatoes $4 per bushel, milk 25 cents a quart, etc. . . .

July 17

Remained at Camp May; all quiet. Drilling some and men in fine health. Drew some clothing.

July 22

Dr. Carroll and myself went up on Lookout Mountain and remained all night.

July 23

Drew Enfield rifles for our regiment, being the 1st draw of good guns we have had since our entry into service.

July 24

Moved camp some 2 miles to the southeast and camped at a very fine spring, though campground is rough and uneven.

July 25 and 26

At same camp. Health of men improving.

July 27

At same camp. Col. Harper sick.

July 28

Received orders to cook three days' rations and be ready to leave for London, Tennessee, at 4 a.m. tomorrow.

July 29

Went into Chattanooga at 4 a.m. and at 8 a.m. train left for London, where we arrived at 5 p.m. and camped below the railroad bridge next to town. Col. Harper left us, sick.

July 30

At same place. A good camp, campground.

JULY 31
Drilled morning and evening.

AUGUST 1, 2, 3, 4
In camp. Nothing of interest transpiring, drilling twice a day.

AUGUST 5
Went to Knoxville to have a tooth pulled. Knoxville a pleasant place.

AUGUST 6
Remained in town all day and got my work done.

AUGUST 7
Left Knoxville at 9 ¼ a.m. for London. On arriving I found the tents all struck and everything in readiness to move. At 4 p.m., we moved and camped near Lenoir's railroad station, having marched 6 miles.

AUGUST 8
Left camp at 4 a.m. 12 miles, the day very hot and many men left on the roadside exhausted, but they came to the regiment during the night.

AUGUST 9
Left camp at 4½ a.m. and camped at 12 m., 2 miles from Knoxville on the Clinton Road. Men much exhausted and many stragglers.

AUGUST 10, SUNDAY
Anniversary of the battle of Oak Hills. Day spent in camp. Cooked 3 days' rations and at 6 p.m. reviewed by Gen. E. Kirby Smith.[50]

AUGUST 11
Left camp for Clinton at 4 a.m. and at 10 a.m. camped ½ mile north of Bull Run. Men stood the march very well and but few stragglers.

AUGUST 12
Left camp at 4 a.m. and crossed the Clinch River at Clinton and camped 2 miles north of town on the Jacksboro Road near a very good spring.

AUGUST 13
Remained in camp and cooked days' rations and inspected the ammunition of men. Will leave for Jacksboro at 4 a.m. tomorrow.

August 14

Left camp at 4 a.m. and marched 16 miles and camped on some rough ground ½ mile south of Jacksboro.

August 15

Left camp at 4 a.m. and passed through Jacksboro and camped ½ mile east of Big Creek Gap at 8 a.m.

August 16

Left our trains to go through Big Creek Gap and meet us in Kentucky. Left our camp at 4 a.m. and marched 13 miles on the Cumberland Gap Road and camped for the evening at Rogers Gap. At 11 p.m. left our camp and crossed Cumberland Mountains. At Rogers Gap, detailed 80 men to assist in taking up 2 ambulances to the top of mountain. We reached the top of mountain at 3 a.m. on 17th, very weary but pressing on.

August 17

Daylight found us at the foot of Cumberland Mountains. On the north side, we moved on to within 2 miles of the Kentucky line and halted to rest. At 3 p.m. left camp and crossed Pine Mountain and camped at its foot, 17 miles from Barbourville, where we arrived at 8 p.m. and camped in an open field.

August 18

Left camp at 4 a.m. and at 10½ a.m. passed through Barbourville and camped 3 miles from town in Cumberland Gap Road. We crossed the Cumberland River on a hill dam.

August 19

Left camp at 4 a.m. and moved up toward the "Gap," my regiment being in advance; when 10 miles from Barbourville we prepared to drive some Federals from a point where they had taken shelter the day previous and driven back our cavalry. But on advancing, we found they had fled. We camped here at Pogue's for the night, on the bank of Cumberland River 6 miles from "Cumberland Ford."[51]

August 20

Remained at same camp and sent out scouting parties who found mules, wagons, meat, harness, arms, etc. . . .

AUGUST 21, 22

At same camp. Our trains have not yet arrived. Have to live on roasting ears and fresh beef and have no cooking utensils, but all the men are in fine spirits knowing almost to a certainty that there is a better day coming.

AUGUST 23

Moved up and crossed at Cumberland Ford and camped 1½ miles from "Ford toward the gap." My regiment on picket for the night.

AUGUST 24

Went up to Cumberland Gap in command of Flag of Truce, accompanied by Captains Johnson and Blackburn of Churchill's staff and a lieutenant with 10 men for an escort. We met from the Federal camp Cols. Cochran and Lindsay and Lt. Col. Gallop and Capt. Burton and 2 Surgeons and Lt. Montgomery A.D.C. on Gen. Morgan's staff and some others whose names I do not now remember. We came to a house about a mile this side of their line and took dinner and had a very pleasant time while waiting for the reply of Gen. Morgan. We started back to our camp at 5 p.m. and arrived at 8½ p.m.; our camps had been moved back across the river at Cumberland Ford.[52]

AUGUST 25

Remained in camp during the early part of the day. At 3 p.m. we moved back to Flatlick, 20 miles from Barbourville, and camped for the night.

AUGUST 26

Left camp at 4 a.m. and moved through Barbourville and camped one mile west of town, where we cooked 3 days' rations and at 4 p.m. left for Richmond. Marched 10 miles and camped for the night.

AUGUST 27

Marched to within 2½ miles of London and camped for the night on Laurel Creek.

AUGUST 28

Passed through London and marched to Rock Castle River 17½ miles from London.

AUGUST 29

Left camp at 4 a.m., crossed Big Hill, and camped on Clear Creek, having marched 21 miles. Sent out pickets. Gen. Cleburne's division was ahead of us.

A part of Scott's Cavalry who were in advance were driven in by the enemy and we lost one Mountain Howitzer, or as our men term it: "one piece of our Rice Bird Artillery."[53]

AUGUST 30

Our army moved up and our advance engaged the enemy near Kingston at an early hour. Our brigade was in the rear as reserve. We were moved up at a quick pace and when near the enemy we moved forward nearly ½ mile at double quick in order to reach a position. Immediately after reaching our position and before we were ordered forward, our force on our right (we were on the left of the turnpike) began the attack and nearly at the same time on our left also when the enemy gave way. Here the loss on our part was very small while the enemy's loss in killed and wounded was considerable. We moved forward about a mile and stopped to rest in the woods. The enemy continued to shell us occasionally at long range. This first fight was about 10½ or 11 a.m. At 12 [noon] our forces again moved forward and, at a point about 2 miles distant, again engaged the enemy. Our brigade was again in the rear as reserve. We double-quicked for nearly a mile but reached the field too late, the enemy had again fled. The firing of the small arms at this place lasted some 15 or 20 minutes. Our loss was again small but heavier than at first. The enemy's was not so great in proportion as at first. Our brigade took the place of the one that had been engaged and followed on some mile or more, when we found the enemy had taken a new position near Richmond and that their artillery commanded the hills between them and us. We then flanked off to the left and under cover of other hills and rolling ground moved to a point only 800 or 1,000 yards from them, entirely unharmed by their artillery. Here we halted and rested for a time, and I was ordered to take my regiment and examine a cornfield on the right of our brigade, my regiment being on the right of the brigade. I moved my regiment and formed a line of battle at right angles with the line of the brigade and against the cornfield fence and threw out my skirmishers through the field and soon found the enemy were not in the field, but beyond at nearly in front of the brigade. I then moved the regiment by the left flank to join the brigade, but before we joined it, it moved forward. We then moved at a double quick. At this time, the enemy opened fire upon us. I then gave the command "by the right flank march," when I found that we were just in the right place and right in front of the enemy's line. I then gave the command "Charge" and the regiment did charge in fine style and were well supported on our left by the 4th Arkansas. From the time they opened fire upon us until the enemy fled from the field our men never ceased to advance. Those in front would fire and stop to load again and those behind having loaded would pass on and fire and so on during the entire fight, which lasted 10 or 15 minutes after they opened upon us. Before I formed the regiment on the cornfield one company (H) were thrown forward as skirmishers and also one man from each company to throw down the fence in front of the brigade. When the enemy discovered these they opened fire upon them from their whole line; when the men who were to work on the fence, being unarmed, returned for their guns, the enemy saw this and thought our whole line had fallen back, and they raised a shout and were ordered to charge us, but they did not come. The men who had been detailed to throw down the fence got their guns and returned and threw it down. When I gave the order to charge the men raised such a shout that it made many a frightened Yankee leave his line before we had fired the first volley. The loss of the brigade was some 20 killed and 60 wounded.[54]

The enemy fled toward the Kentucky River but were intercepted some 4 miles from Richmond by Scott's Cavalry, which had passed to our left and to the rear of the enemy after the first fight. Scott captured nearly all their fleeing force.[55]

In short, it was a fine day's work. Our loss was about 300 killed and wounded and prisoners between 5,500 and 6,000 (some 600 being killed and wounded, 12 pieces of artillery, a large amount of arms ammunition, commissary stores, etc.). Our brigade camped on the north side of town in one of the Federal camps. Many of their men came into camp during the evening and gave themselves up as prisoners.[56]

AUGUST 31, SUNDAY

Remained in camp during the day. Prisoners still coming in and being brought in.

SEPTEMBER 1

Left camp at 4 a.m. on the Tates Creek Turnpike. McCray's Texas Brigade in front and ours next. When our advance reached Kentucky River they found the enemy posted on the opposite side and from reports supposed to be from 1,200 to 1,500 strong, but it was afterwards found to be only the 94th Ohio regiment, some 1,000 strong. Our batteries were placed in position, and after three or four fires the enemy fled. We crossed and moved up to within 8 miles of Lexington and camped for the night. Here our wagons were unloaded and sent to Kentucky River to bring up Heth's Division.[57]

SEPTEMBER 2

At 4 a.m., I was informed that the Federals had left Lexington and that my regiment had been selected by Gen. Smith to go on in advance and take possession of the town.[58]

The regiment was soon formed and took up the line of march. All along the road, as on the previous day, we saw great demonstrations of joy at our approach. When we reached the town, the streets were thronged. I have seen many demonstrations and many receptions but never saw anything to equal this. Shouts of "Welcome to Kentucky," "Hurrah for the heroes of Richmond," "Hurrah for the Confederacy," etc. . . . and waving of Confederate flags and waving of handkerchiefs and strewing the streets with flowers and showering on us bouquets, etc. . . . I was appointed Military Governor of the town. The day was spent in finding and placing guards over United States property. In the afternoon, the citizens raised a large Confederate Flag on the Court House and speeches were made by Gen. Smith and Col. Brent. During the day, the 12th regiment came into town to assist in guarding the stores, etc. . . . During the day, the ladies and citizens of the town and vicinity feasted our men upon the best provisions that could be had. It was a brilliant day for us and one long to be remembered.[59]

SEPTEMBER 3

Moved out to camp near the Covington Railroad depot and during the day my regiment and the 12th Tennessee were relieved from duty and ordered to be ready to move at 4 a.m. tomorrow.

SEPTEMBER 4

At 8 a.m., we left for Georgetown and camped on Gov. Robinson's farm near town. My old friend Ron Payne came to see me.[60]

SEPTEMBER 5

Left camp at 6 a.m. and moved up to within 5 miles of Cynthiana and camped for the night. It was a hard day's march, very hot.

SEPTEMBER 6

Left camp at 5 a.m. and moved through Cynthiana and camped on Licking River, 2 miles north of town. The enemy had built a small fort near town but had abandoned it before we arrived.

SEPTEMBER 7

Moved up to a point on the Cynthiana and Williamson Road, 13 miles southeast of Williamstown.

SEPTEMBER 8

Passed on through to Williamstown and camped 2 miles north of town on the east side of the Turnpike and 35 miles from Covington.

SEPTEMBER 9

Passed through Crittenden and camped 3 miles north of town and 22 miles from Covington.

SEPTEMBER 10

Moved through Florence and to within five miles of Covington, Kentucky, and immediately under the guns of the enemy for the night. Left our trains 2 miles in our rear. Our pickets, one brigade, were nearly a mile in advance and nearly in sight of the enemy's lines.

SEPTEMBER 11

Remained in same camps during the day and until 11½ p.m., when we prepared to retreat and moved in the direction of Florence, where we arrived at daylight on the 12th. It commenced raining in the evening and continued to rain during the night, and was very disagreeable, and the troops suffered.

SEPTEMBER 12

We continued our march until 11 a.m. when we camped 23 miles from Covington. Brig. Gen. Harry Heth had command of our force and I must say that, in my opinion, he managed the whole affair of the advance and retreat in a very unmilitary manner: 1st, in going forward unprepared to a position under the enemy's guns; 2nd, in relieving our pickets and exposing our whole force to an advance of the enemy, without a single picket to warn us of the approach and without even warning those in the rear that the pickets had been removed, our train being for sometime entirely in rear of the army; 3rd, for allowing the troops and trains to mix up so as to entirely obstruct the advance or fire movements of the troops, while yet in range of the enemy's guns. It was fortunate for us that the enemy did not advance on us.[61]

SEPTEMBER 13

Remained in camps all night.

SEPTEMBER 14 AND 15

At same camp, all quiet.

SEPTEMBER 16

Moved at 4 a.m. and came on to within 2 miles of Williamstown, and camped at same place where we did on the night of the 8th instant.

SEPTEMBER 17

Left camp early and marched 22 miles and camped on Eagle Creek where we arrived at dark. My regiment being rear guard of the army.

SEPTEMBER 18, 19, 20

Remained at camp. Discharged several men from the regiment who were entitled to discharge by reason of being over conscript age and having served their time (one year) and ninety days.[62]

SEPTEMBER 21

Came to Georgetown and camped on the farm of Mr. Thomson ½ mile from town on turnpike from Georgetown to Frankfort.[63]

SEPTEMBER 22

In camp all day and on the Military Court or Commission.

SEPTEMBER 23

Same camp. In command of brigade during the day. Received orders to leave for Frankfort on tomorrow at 5 a.m.[64]

SEPTEMBER 24

Left camp at 5 a.m. and marched on the Frankfort Pike 8 miles when orders reached us to return to Georgetown. We retraced our steps to our old camp ground and at sundown received orders to march to Paris and at 2 a.m. on 25th camped in open field 1½ miles from Paris.

SEPTEMBER 25

Cooked one days' rations and at 12 m. left for Mt. Sterling. Moved out 9 miles from town and camped in a very fine grove for the night.

SEPTEMBER 26, FRIDAY

My regiment in advance of brigade. Marched to within 3 miles of Mt. Sterling and camped for the night. An easy day's march. Nights are quite cold but it is warm in middle of the day; was frost this morning. Men in fine health and spirits.

September 27

At same camp. I went to town with Col. McNair.

September 28, Sunday

At same camp at 10 p.m. Received orders to march at daylight on 29th in the direction of Owingsville.

September 29

Moved at 5 a.m, on the Pike toward Paris instead of Owingsville. Passed through Middleville and camped 4 miles east of Paris. Received orders to move at daylight on tomorrow.

September 30

Moved at daylight. Passed Paris at an early hour. Paris is one of the oldest towns in Kentucky and is a neat pleasant place. Camped for the night at Newtown, 5 miles from Georgetown. Night cold and disagreeable and but little wood and men were compelled to use some fence rails.

October 1

Moved at an early hour and passed through Georgetown, and camped on old campground.

October 2

At 12 m. left for Frankfort and at 7 p.m. camped 3 miles east of Frankfort in open field. Our brigade in advance and it was late before we got anything to eat. It rained during the night and was very disagreeable.

October 3

Remained at same camp, in open field.

October 4

Went to Frankfort to witness the Inauguration of Gov. Hawes (a grand farce); did not get into the capitol on account of the immense crowd. Inauguration took place at 12 m. At 2 p.m. received orders to be ready to march at a moment's notice. At 5 p.m., we left camp for Versailles and camped 2 miles west of Versailles at 12 m.[65]

October 5, Sunday

Moved at 5 a.m. and came to and crossed the Kentucky River 4 miles north of Salvisa and camped until 8 p.m., when we moved up to Salvisa and camped 1½ miles south of town on Harrodsburg Turnpike.

October 6

Remained at camp during the day. All quiet in camp. Heard the roar of artillery some distance to the west.

October 7

Moved back to Kentucky River and camped for night on southwest bank.

October 8

Crossed Kentucky River and moved up to within two miles of Versailles, and at 3 p.m. moved back toward Salvisa and when some 6 miles from Versailles took a right hand road and moved down to the Kentucky River and crossed after dark (at 9 p.m.), the men wading the river, and moved up to the Harrodsburg and Frankfort Turnpike at 11 p.m.

October 9

Aroused at 1½ a.m. and moved up and across the pike and took a left hand road and moved to a point 5 miles south of Lawrenceburg and 8 miles west of Salvisa. Our advance captured some 450 prisoners and some stores etc. . . . At 1 p.m., we started back toward Salvisa and camped on Salt River 2 miles from Salvisa. The men out of rations and very tired but they bore the fatigue without a murmur. Our artillery that was detached from us on yesterday to go with Gen. Heth by way of Frankfort (our road being too rough for artillery) joined us. Saw Morgan's cavalry today for first time. The column of the enemy that was advancing on us and which we expected to meet today has retreated and I fear has made a junction with the column marching against Bragg near Perryville. Gen. Withers, who had charge of the portion of our forces here that was designed to bring on the attack, was too slow and the bird had flown.[66]

October 10

Left camp at 2 a.m. for Harrodsburg without any rations except raw bacon. The men roasted some hard corn. Reached Harrodsburg at 2 p.m. and prepared to cook rations, when we were ordered out into line of battle some 2½ miles southwest of town, where we lay during the night. It rained all the evening and night. Left some men to cook rations near town and bring them to us. Rations reached us during the night.

October 11

Aroused at 6 a.m. and moved to Harrodsburg and took the road to Bryantsville or Camp "Dick Robinson." Crossed Dick's River and camped 2 miles from the ford.[67]

October 12, Sunday

Our wagons arrived about 10 a.m. and we cooked three days' rations and in evening received orders to have the sick sent to Gen. Smith's headquarters with 4 days' rations; and all ambulances also ordered to be turned over to haul the sick along with the army; and wagons ordered to haul along men who might give out on the way. Things look like we were on the eve of a retreat. Received orders to be ready to go to Gen. Stevenson's assistance at a moments notice. Stevenson was in our rear.[68]

October 13

Remained at camp until 6 p.m. when we moved to Camp Dick Robinson and thence to Lancaster and there took the road to Big Hill and travelled all night on the retreat, all quietly and orderly.

October 14

Daylight found us on the march and at 9 a.m. we halted to rest and eat breakfast. Gen. Heth bringing up the rear of the army. No enemy on our rear yet. At 6 p.m. halted for camp. Men tired but in good spirits.

October 15

At 2 a.m. we were ordered up and moved on and camped 1½ miles north of Big Hill. Most of our train yet on north side of Hill and much confusion among the trains owing to the cowardice of those having charge of trains and the false rumors started for amusement; indeed there was some talk of burning the trains. Many things were destroyed to lighten the wagons. So as to get them over Big Hill. Made a detail of men and sent with Maj. Ramseur to assist the train.

October 16

Left camp at 2½ a.m. and passed up Big Hill through a tram. Road much crowded. Crossed and re-crossed Rock Castle River and camped on its banks for the night. Cannonading heard on Crab Orchard Road during day. Sent out a picket on the road leading from this to the Crab Orchard Road.

October 17

Daylight for once found us in camp. Had a good night's rest. At 8 a.m. we left camp and moved down to within 3 miles of London and camped for the night, having marched 14 miles.

October 18

Was aroused at daylight and our brigade sent up the Crab Orchard Road 5 miles to join our rear guard and relieve another brigade. Remained on the road all day. The cavalry in our front was driven back some ¾ of a mile; about 4 p.m. we were ordered to fall back; we moved toward London.

October 19

Daylight found us near London. We moved on to where the road forks leading to Cumberland Gap, one through Barbourville and the other through _____ being to the east of the Barbourville Road. We halted at this fork of the road (which is between 45 and 50 miles from Cumberland Gap) and rested 5 hours and cooked beef, the only provisions we have. Have been out of bread for 24 hours. At 4½ p.m., we moved out on left hand road some 4 miles where we camped for the night. Here we got half rations of bread.[69]

October 20

We moved to within 18 miles of Cumberland Ford and camped for the night. No bread rations but plenty of beef. I roasted some corn and some acorns.

October 21

Moved down to Cumberland Ford and camped for the night. Col. Harper met us on the road. This is first time he has been with us since we left Chattanooga last July. Half rations of bread and plenty of beef. Relieved Capt. Little as Regimental Commissary for neglect of duty.[70]

October 22

Passed through "Cumberland Gap" and camped one mile from Gap on the Jacksboro Road on a fine spring branch.

October 23, 24

At same camp; all quiet; Col. Harper assumed command of the regiment.

October 25, 26

Snow fell 12 inches deep, men poorly provided against such weather. Some nearly barefooted and with only one blanket and hardly axes enough to get wood to keep up fires.[71]

October 27

At same camp; all quiet and all things moving on smoothly. No money yet to pay off the troops who now have ten monthly pay due them.

October 28

Regiment relieved in afternoon and received orders to draw four days' rations and be ready to march at 7 a.m. on tomorrow. Snow is melting slowly, still several inches deep.

October 29

Moved at 7 a.m., the road very muddy for some 8 miles caused by melting snow. Marched some 12 miles on the Jacksboro Road. Camped in the woods. A good campground and men in fine spirits.

October 30

Left camp at 6 a.m. and moved down to within 7 miles of Big Creek Gap and camped on the farm of a Mr. Kincaid. A great many stragglers owing to the rapid marching.[72]

October 31

Passed through Jacksboro and camped 5 miles south of the town.

November 1

Moved down and camped ½ mile north of Clinton. Many of the men suffering more or less on account of the rough food which they are compelled to live on at present.

November 2

Passed through Clinton and camped 12 miles from Lenoir's Station, after a hard day's march. Much time being taken up in crossing Clinch River, being but one ferry boat and that a flat.

November 3

Left camp at 6½ a.m. and moved down to within two miles of London. Made the trip in good time and most of the men up. All stood the march well.

November 4, 5, 6, 7, 8, 9, 10

At same camp, getting men paid off and drawing clothing and letting men and officers have short leaves to get clothing made up for selves and friends. Weather in the main pleasant. Major Latimer and Mr. Hanks leave for Chicot. I applied for 10 days' leave of absence to get clothing made and was refused.

November 11

I went to Knoxville. Regiment at same camp and being slowly fitted out. Men in good health.

November 12

Returned from Knoxville and received order from Col. Harper commanding brigade to go to Augusta, Georgia, with Dr. Carroll and assist in procuring
clothing for the brigade.

November 13

Left London at 11 a.m., cars much crowded with passengers and soldiers.
Passed though Cleveland and Dalton, and when near Kingston the engine ran
off the track and we had to wait for 2 hours for the arrival of the up train. We
changed with the passengers on the up train, which returned toward Atlanta.
By the delay we did not make the connection.[73]

November 14

Daylight found us at Marietta 20 miles north of Atlanta. Here we got
breakfast and a drink at the bar for the first time in many months, 50 cents a
drink. Got a pretty fair breakfast. Met my old friend Kendrick from Natchez.
Arrived at Atlanta at 9 a.m. and stopped at "Washington Hall." Bought but-
tons, thread shirting etc. . . . for brigade. At 7¼ p.m. left for Augusta and travelled all night.[74]

November 15

Daylight found us at Augusta. Stopped at Southern States Hotel. Engaged
a tailor 6 or 8 doors east of hotel to make clothing. Went around town shopping and found everything very high. Had an idea of going to Charleston
tonight but gave it out being very tired, having been travelling two nights.[75]

November 16

Spent the day in Augusta and at 7¼ p.m. left for Charleston, cars not much
crowded. A little incident with conductor on the train.

November 17

Arrived in Charleston at 4¼ a.m. and stopped at "Mills House," went
about town shopping etc. . . . , and went down to the bay but did not have time
to visit any of the forts. Could see Castle Pinckney and Fort Sumter and a new
fort to the right of Fort Sumter and nearer Charleston. Could see Fort
Moultrie and Fort Johnson in distance and far in the distance could see a vessel in the blockading fleet. A few vessels in the bay at work on some new war
vessels.[76]

NOVEMBER 18

Spent the day in Charleston getting articles for self and friends. All things quiet here and citizens feel quite secure and have very little apprehension of a visit from the Yankees soon. At 7½ p.m. left.

NOVEMBER 19

Arrived in Augusta at 4 a.m. and spent the day about town in getting articles of clothing etc. . . .[77]

NOVEMBER 20

Remained in Augusta until 4 p.m. when we took cars for Atlanta.[78]

NOVEMBER 21

Arrived at Atlanta at 3 a.m. and remained until 7¼ p.m. when we left for Loudon, Tennessee.

NOVEMBER 22

Arrived at Loudon at 9 a.m. and at 11 a.m. left for Chattanooga, our regiment having left Loudon for that place on the 20th. At 6 p.m. reached Chattanooga. Went on train with Gen. McCown and learned that regiment had gone on to Bridgeport, Alabama.[79]

NOVEMBER 23

Left Chattanooga on train with Texas brigade and reached Bridgeport at 2 p.m. Regiment in good spirits. Maj. Ramseur in command, the colonel has gone to Huntsville, Alabama. During my absence, I had been ordered to Arkansas to take charge of the recruiting for our brigade, and one officer from each company has gone forward for that purpose. I am prepared to be off for Arkansas tomorrow morning. I have two of "Job's Comforters."[80]

NOVEMBER 24

Ready to start at 8 a.m. but train did not get off until 6 p.m. Dr. Gammage of the brigade handed me an article to be published in the Little Rock *True Democrat* ("A History of the Kentucky Campaign under Gen. Kirby Smith") and desired me to read it and superintend the publishing of it. After reading it I sent it back to him endorsed "Owing to the numerous errors in your article I cannot consent to carry and be instrumental in putting it before the public as facts." Reached Chattanooga at 8½ p.m. and could get no place at a public house, and Dr. Sayle got us in at Mr. French's.[81]

November 25

Dr. Sayle woke me at 3 a.m. and I went to the depot and was soon off for Dalton. There I stopped and got transportation on my order and the train left me, but I got on the freight train and overtook the passenger train before it reached Atlanta and changed cars. Arrived at Atlanta at 4 p.m. and at 6 p.m. left for West Point, where I arrived at 11½ p.m. and at 12 p.m. left for Montgomery.[82]

November 26

Reached Montgomery at 6 p.m. Remained during the day. Obtained transportation to Vicksburg and am ready to leave tomorrow morning.

November 27

Left Montgomery at 7 a.m. and reached Mobile at 9¾ p.m. and stopped at the "Battle House." Got supper at restaurant, $10.75 for 5 of us.[83]

November 28

Left Mobile at 7 a.m. for Meridian, the cars were not crowded though densely crowded from Chattanooga to Mobile. Arrived at Meridian at 9 p.m. and shortly afterward left for Jackson and Vicksburg.[84]

November 29

Passed through Jackson at 6 a.m. and reached Vicksburg at 11¼ a.m. and found I could not get conveyance on the west of the river before the 1st of December. Stopped at the "Washington Hotel."[85]

November 30, Sunday

Spent the day in going to Church M.E.S. and heard the Rev. Mr. Marshall preach. Saw James McMurray and heard from the "Chicot Guards" and the "Chicot Rebels," etc. . . .[86]

December 1

Left Vicksburg at 7 a.m. and crossed the river and went out ten miles to the end of the railroad and left there at 2 p.m., arriving at Monroe at 7 p.m., and found bad chance of getting conveyance to Camden, so I went to bed, being very tired.[87]

December 2

Found boy belonging to Mr. Brewer of Jefferson County, Arkansas, that had come after his master with a carriage, but his did not come, so I got a seat in the carriage to Warren, Arkansas. For $20 passed through Bastrop, Louisiana, and lodged all night at the house of Mrs. Whetstone, 3 miles north of Bastrop.[88]

DECEMBER 3

Out early and passed through Hamburg and stopped with Mr. Woods, 5 miles northwest of Hamburg.[89]

DECEMBER 4

Left early and reached Warren and put up with Pennington. Here I obtained a hack to go to Pine Bluff or Little Rock.[90]

DECEMBER 5

Left Warren at 9½ a.m. and came 30 miles. The road very bad in places and a poor team, but we'll persevere.

DECEMBER 6

Arrived at Pine Bluff and stopped at "Drew White's." Could not get conveyance from here to Little Rock for 3 days, so I kept the hack. Came to Judge Campbell's, 27 miles from Pine Bluff.[91]

DECEMBER 7

Arrived in Little Rock at 1 p.m. and stopped at the Anthony House. Gov. Jackson of Missouri buried in town today. Funeral preached at Methodist Church.[92]

DECEMBER 8

At Anthony House. Rumors of a fight near Cane Hill in Washington County, Arkansas, between forces under Gen. Hindman and the Federals. Hindman reported victorious. No particulars.[93]

DECEMBER 9

Still in Little Rock. Further news from Hindman saying that he is victorious, capturing 5 pieces of artillery, 250 prisoners, and 30 wagons loaded with clothing, etc. . . . Our loss in killed 100, enemy's 300. Called to Dr. Carroll's mother to deliver ambrotype and got order published for all the men belonging to our brigade, not members of regiments in the Trans-Mississippi Department, to report at once to proper officers.[94]

December 10, 11

At Little Rock, news from Hindman's fight at Prairie Grove. Victory on our side.[95]

December 12

Left Little Rock at 4 a.m. for Pine Bluff in public hack. Reached Pine Bluff at 6½ p.m. and stopped with Drew White.

December 13

Left Pine Bluff at 6 a.m. for Monticello. Rained yesterday and last night and the roads quite heavy.

December 14

Passed through Monticello and to Mr. Belser's place on Bayou Bartholomew.[96]

December 15

Rained all the forenoon and at 3 p.m. left for Lake Village where I arrived at 8 p.m.

December 16, 17

At Lake Village. No news.

December 18

Went to Bellvue. Stopped on my way to see Mr. Chapman, Dr. Proctor, and Capt. Gaines. Things very little changed except that the plantations seem to be almost a waste. The slaves have nearly all been moved back, further in the country and elsewhere.[97]

December 19

Went with Captain McConnell to Col. Llewellyn's and returned again to Bellvue.[98]

December 20

Came to Lake Village and crossed the Lake and took dinner with Mrs. Davies and after dinner went to Mrs. Read's, where I spent the night.[99]

December 21, Sunday

Went to Church at Lake Village and heard a sermon from the Rev. O. Hackett. Remained at Lake Village.[100]

December 22

Went out on Bayou Macon to see MacLean. Spent the night at his house.[101]

December 23

At Lake Village.

December 24

Seventy-two boats passed Columbia carrying troops who said they were going to take Vicksburg. Went to Mr. Diamond's to a party at night. Had a very pleasant time. Saw some old friends from the Macon Hills.[102]

December 25

At Col. Llewellyn's for dinner. Spent the night there. It is needless to say we had a pleasant time. We could have no other.

December 26

Came to Bellvue today and remained over night.

December 27

Came to Lake Village.

December 28, 29, 30, 31

Among my friends about Lake Village and vicinity. We have rumors of a fight at Grenada, Mississippi, and also at Vicksburg and both favorable to us. No particulars.

After I left the regiment on the 24th November they remained a short time at Bridgeport, then moved to Manchester, and thence to Readyville, and thence to Murfreesboro, where they were engaged in that sanguinary battle on the 31st day of December 1862. I here affix the official report of Col. Harper, commanding the regiment at the time.[103]

Headquarters 1st Arkansas Rifles (dismounted)
January 10, 1863
Sir:

I have the honor to submit the following report of the part taken by the regiment under my command in the battle of Murfreesboro on the 31st December, 1862.

In obedience to the order received from the brigadier general commanding, the regiment moved up 150 yards from the rear where it had bivouacked for the night and took its position on the right of the brigade then in line. A few minutes before six o'clock a.m., we moved to the front and on a line parallel with the road leading by Cowan's house. About six o'clock, our pickets became engaged with those of the enemy and soon after the firing opened along the whole line of the regiment. On account of a field fence my two companies were formed in rear and at this point we were severely enfiladed by the enemy's sharp shooters, some 200 yards distant on our right. The order to charge was given and, with impetuosity, our men scaled the fence, driving the enemy before them until we reached his encampment, which gave ample evidence of his want of preparation for a fight. Camped as he was on a heavy cedar brake, it would seem that our progress must be impeded, but nothing could withstand the fury of the outset. The enemy's lines were broken, and the rout, so far as my observation reached, became general. Wheeling to the right in the direction of the pursued, we moved constantly at a double quick over the field and brake, the dead and dying of the enemy but too plainly marking the track of the flying abolitionists.[104]

It was at this point that young Clark Jenkins, a private of Company D, killed a general officer who was endeavoring to rally his scattered columns, supposed to be Maj. Gen. Sill as his body was found soon afterwards in a hospital near by. We had driven the enemy about one and a half miles when finding a line of Federal infantry endeavoring to gain our rear. We halted for the purpose of cutting through his ranks to our main army, but the opportune arrival of Liddell's Brigade on our right relieved us.[105]

After a few moments pause I was ordered to move forward, my right resting on the left of Liddell's Brigade. We continued to move straight forward when Liddell became warmly engaged with a heavy force who had concealed themselves behind a fence on his front. I was ordered to file right, move forward some 150 paces and by the left flank and then received the order to charge. Forward rushed our men with the wild yell of an infuriate soldiery and for a few seconds the result appeared doubtful. The enemy almost securely posted, stubbornly held their ground and it seemed as if once during the war, our lines would clash in closest combat, but again the intrepidity of our troops was successful and the enemy's whole line gave way, swept from right to left by our galling fire. We were then only 50 or 75 yards from his lines and as he retreated across an open field of some 600 or 700 yards, he was terribly cut to pieces. Forward was again the order and forward moved our unwavering lines and, in the face of heavy volleys that were poured upon us from the opposite fence and the raking fire of grape and canister from two sections of a battery posted in the field, we charged and took two pieces of their artillery. It was at this point that Capt. W. P. Campbell, acting major, was severely wounded in the leg, while gallantly discharging his duty and urging his wing to another charge, and was compelled to leave the field.

Here we halted for a new supply of ammunition, having exhausted all but 3 or 4 rounds out of 40 to the men, which is the very best evidence of the severity of the contest. It was now 9½ a.m. We had charged and driven the enemy with impetuosity for three hours and a quarter over not less than 4½ miles of ground, captured and killed many field officers and officers of the line and privates without number, taken several pieces of artillery, while vast amounts of camp equipage and small arms etc. . . . were left in our rear, which our patriotic soldiers passed by unheeded.[106]

A few moments served to replenish our ammunition and again we moved forward for 1½ miles when skirmishers were ordered to be thrown forward to a cedar brake. Formerly we had advanced nearly north, but now our right as a pivot, and we made a right half wheel and were moving nearly due northeast. The left of our division becoming engaged, the order was given to charge the batteries strongly posted on an eminence beyond; another thrill of excitement ran along the lines and another yell of stern defiance rang out as they moved rapidly to the new scene of slaughter. The enemy being strongly posted with his batteries in echelon heavily supported by three lines of infantry, our regiment, after a most brilliant effort, was compelled to fall back, being nearly decimated. Here fell most severely and I fear mortally wounded Maj. L. M. Ramseur, acting lieutenant colonel of the regiment. He was gallantly leading the charge and had succeeded in driving the enemy from one of his batteries. We had now been under heavy fire almost continually for hours and had driven the enemy, and our troops were reformed and "rested" under the crest of a hill for an hour or so when we were again moved by the right flank some half mile or more and took position in a cedar brake where we remained posted with no casualties save a few wounded by pickets until we were withdrawn.[107]

Our loss in addition to the field officers already wounded is severe, but I am happy to add that the wounds are for the most part slight and not likely to render them unfit for active duty hereafter. Our loss in killed, wounded, and missing is 96 as already furnished in my official report, which I ask may be taken as a part of this. Where all exerted themselves and gave such evidence of individual heroism, it is impossible for a commander to discriminate. I must, however, mention color bearer Cotton, who always moved with unfaltering step in the front line. Our surgeons are also entitled to notice for the promptitude with which our wounded were cared for, and I conclude by saying that whatever fate betides the 1st Arkansas Rifles in future, that their actions on this day has shed imperishable glory on them and their cause.[108]

I have the honor to be sir,

Your obedient servant,

R. W. Harper

Colonel, Commanding First Arkansas Rifles

Capt. R. Foote, Assistant Adjutant General, Third Brigade, McCown's Division[109]

Daniel Harris Reynolds after his promotion to brigadier general, c. 1864. Bobby Roberts and Carl Moneyhon, eds., *Portraits of Conflict: A Photographic History of Arkansas in the Civil War* (Fayetteville: University of Arkansas, 1987), 202.

Daniel Harris Reynolds soon after the Civil War, probably taken during his term in the Arkansas legislature, c. 1867. Richard and Connie Cox Collection.

Daniel Harris Reynolds as the elder statesman of Chicot County, c. 1892. Richard and Connie Cox Collection.

Thomas J. Churchill served as colonel of the First Arkansas Mounted Rifles until his promotion to brigadier general in March of 1862. He later transferred back to the Trans-Mississippi and earned promotion to major general. Arkansas History Commission, Little Rock.

Benjamin McCulloch commanded a brigade at Wilson's Creek and a division at Elkhorn Tavern. The First Arkansas Mounted Rifles served under his command until his death at Elkhorn Tavern. Alabama Department of Archives and History, Montgomery, Alabama.

Evander McNair served as colonel of the Fourth Arkansas Infantry until his promotion to brigadier general in November of 1862. Wounded at Chickamauga, he served the remainder of the war in the Trans-Mississippi. Francis Trevelyan Miller, *Photographic History* (New York: Review of Reviews Company, 1911–1912), 259.

William Henry Talbot Walker.
The First Arkansas Mounted
Rifles served less than one
month in Walker's division
before personality conflicts
necessitated a transfer in the
summer of 1863. Augusta
Museum of History,
Augusta, Georgia.

Samuel Gibbs French. He and
his staff clashed repeatedly with
D. H. Reynolds and the First
Arkansas Mounted Rifles.
They transferred out of his
division shortly after Reynolds's
promotion to brigadier general.
Alabama Department of
Archives and History,
Montgomery, Alabama.

Edward Cary Walthall. D. H. Reynolds and the Arkansas Brigade joined Walthall's division in the spring of 1864 and remained under his command for the duration of the Civil War. Alabama Department of Archives and History, Montgomery, Alabama.

Alexander Patrick Stewart commanded a corps in the Army of Tennessee after the death of Leonidas Polk during the Atlanta campaign. Alabama Department of Archives and History, Montgomery, Alabama.

Otho French Strahl befriended
D. H. Reynolds at Ohio Wesleyan
University in the 1850s. A native
of Tennessee, Strahl commanded
a brigade in the division of
John C. Brown when killed at
the battle of Franklin on
November 30, 1864. Tennessee
State Library and Archives,
Nashville, Tennessee.

Charles B. Mitchel served briefly in the United States Senate prior to the secession of Arkansas and served in the Confederate Senate from 1861 until 1864. U.S. Senate Historical Office, Washington, D.C.

◄ This flag, donated to the Museum of the Confederacy in 1896, belonged either to D. H. Reynolds's Arkansas Brigade headquarters or the Ninth Arkansas Infantry (which transferred into the brigade during the Atlanta campaign). The Museum of the Confederacy, Richmond, Virginia. Photography by Katherine Wetzel.

Augustus Hill Garland represented Arkansas in the Confederate House of Representatives from 1861 until 1864, when he succeeded Charles B. Mitchel in the Confederate Senate. The Butler Center for Arkansas Studies, Central Arkansas Library System, Little Rock.

"Lakeside," the D. H. Reynolds family home at Lake Village, overlooking Lake Chicot. Richard and Connie Cox Collection.

◄ Mattie Reynolds sits (*front right*) with her mother (Eleanor Avent), her eldest daughter, Kate (Reynolds) Hill, and two granddaughters. Richard and Connie Cox Collection.

Daniel Harris Reynolds stands (*at left*) on the porch of his law office, located on the plot adjacent to his "Lakeside" home. The building no longer exists. Richard and Connie Cox Collection.

THREE

1863

A SAD THOUGHT FOR THE BRAVEST OF US

During the third year of war, Confederate fortunes in the Western Theater took a turn from which they would ultimately never recover. The year began with a bitter reversal at Murfreesboro, where early hopes for success turned into defeat and a general retreat toward the rail center at Chattanooga. By mid-summer, the loss of Vicksburg severed the southern nation and complicated its already significant communication and logistical problems. Despite a hard-fought victory at Chickamauga in early autumn, 1863 proved a year of lost territory and lost opportunities.[1]

In addition to strategic setbacks, conflicts rooted in politics and personality continued to characterize the western Rebel army in the crucial middle season of the war. Fueled by competing ambitions and frustrations from recent failures in the field, poor relations and factionalism within high command acted like a persistent blight upon the ever-shrinking Army of Tennessee as it contended with a numerically superior foe. As battlefield losses mounted, the Confederacy could ill-afford the additional problems associated with the growth of such factions.[2]

Reynolds and the First Arkansas Rifles experienced their share of these conflicts. With Col. Robert W. Harper frequently absent due to ill health and regimental business, Reynolds often commanded the regiment during its third year of service and witnessed the nearly immediate breakdown of relations with their new division commander—Maj. Gen. William Henry Talbot Walker. Deriding the discipline and quality of Evander McNair's Brigade within a week of his arrival, Walker and his staff made it transparently clear that they did not appreciate the abilities or sacrifices of Trans-Mississippi soldiers. By late June, after less than a month under Walker's command, the brigade received a much-desired transfer. Three months later, their gallant performance in Dyer's Field during the battle of Chickamauga inspired belated apologetic comments from Walker. However, neither apologies nor changes in division assignment alleviated the underlying complaints of Reynolds and his regiment about the treatment of Trans-Mississippians. In short order, many of the same attitudes and issues that plagued the relationship with Walker resurfaced during the tenure of their next division commander—Maj. Gen. Samuel Gibbs French.[3]

Despite these tumultuous relationships, Reynolds retained the respect of his fellow officers. The death of Col. Harper at Chickamauga permanently elevated Reynolds to regimental command and revealed the high regard of his peers. Although he ranked as junior colonel, one month after his appointment a majority of the brigade's senior officers formally petitioned the Confederate War Department to name Reynolds to fill the anticipated vacancy in brigade command. Thus, as the Confederacy began to wilt, Reynolds continued to mature as a commander; toward the conclusion of the third year of war, he emerged as a leader in whom his men and fellow officers expressed considerable confidence and esteem.[4]

JANUARY 1, THURSDAY
Party at Mrs. Susan Read's.

JANUARY 2, 3, 4, 5, 6
About Lake Village and neighborhood. The United States Fleet passed up the River from Vicksburg, they having been badly defeated in attempting to capture Vicksburg. I am with Captain Jacob McConnell to start back to the army in Tennessee on tomorrow a.m.[5]

JANUARY 7
Left Lake Village and dined at Mrs. Read's and reached "Tecumseh Place" just at dark and stopped for the night with Mr. Dunn. Mr. Thomas Hunnicutt is taking us to Vicksburg in an ambulance.[6]

JANUARY 8
Went down the river until we reach Polk's place and went through by Capt. Bennett's and spent the night with Col. Ralph on the Macon Hills.[7]

JANUARY 9
Crossed Bayou Macon, which was in a bad condition, and after much trouble reached Mr. Goza's on Old River Lake in Louisiana. Took dinner with Mr. Goza; the Federals have paid him a visit and relieved him of some of his horses and household furniture. Spent the night with Mr. Govey Hood on Lake Providence, 3 miles from the town of that name.[8]

JANUARY 10
Reached Ballard's place, 2 miles from Goodrich's Store and 9 miles from Milliken's Bend. Roads very bad and a hard time we had of it.[9]

JANUARY 11
Reached Oak Grove Place on Walnut Bayou, 24 miles from Vicksburg, and spent the night with overseer named Bird. Only 3 miles from Milliken's Bend.[10]

JANUARY 12
Reached Vicksburg at 4 p.m. and stopped at Trowbridge House, decidedly a hard place. All quiet. No enemy near.[11]

JANUARY 13
Left Vicksburg at 1 p.m. Passed through Jackson at 6 p.m. and reached Meridian at 4 a.m. on 14th. The railroad is sadly out of repair. Met some old friends at Jackson.

JANUARY 14
Left Meridian at 9 a.m. and reached Mobile at 9 p.m. and stopped at the Battle House. Went to the theatre and saw the play of *Blue Beard*. Had plenty of fine oysters.[12]

JANUARY 15
Spent day on Mobile. At night went to the theatre; play was *"Metamora" or the Last of the Wampanoags*, and the farce *A Pretty Piece of Business*.[13]

JANUARY 16
Left Mobile at 7 a.m. and reached Montgomery at 10 p.m. and stopped at the Exchange Hotel.[14]

JANUARY 17
Spent the morning about town. Quiet, cold, and ground frozen. At 4 p.m. left for Atlanta, where we arrived at 7 a.m. on 18th. A cold and disagreeable night.

JANUARY 18
Spent the day in Atlanta, having arrived too late for the train going to Chattanooga. At 7½ p.m., we left for Chattanooga, night very cold and poor accommodations on cars.

JANUARY 19
Reached Chattanooga at daylight and at 7½ a.m. left for Tullahoma and on our way we learned that our command was at Shelbyville, where we arrived at 7 p.m. and found the regiment camped in a very muddy place 1½ miles south of town. Here we learned the details of a very hard fought battle at Murfreesboro on the 31st December 1862 in which the regiment lost 96 in killed,

wounded, and missing. Shortly after the battle our portion of the army fell back to this place where we have since been encamped, men living in their tents.[15]

January 20 and 21

At same camp, all quiet. I assumed command of the regiment. Col. Harper being absent at Richmond, Virginia, on business and Major Ramseur being severely wounded and at Murfreesboro, the regiment has for sometime been under command of Capt. Stone of Co. K.[16]

January 22

Still at same camp 1½ miles south of Shelbyville, nothing new during the day. Heard that my old friend and schoolmate Otho F. Strahl, Colonel of the 4th Tennessee volunteers, was camped not more than 500 or 600 yards from me.[17]

January 23

Went to see Col. Strahl and spent the day with him. Went to Shelbyville. Heard the report of the fall of the Post of Arkansas, but the report is not believed.[18]

January 24

Day wet and rainy and the camp quite muddy. Gen. McNair ordered me on duty as officer of the day and I did not report on account of being in command of the regiment. He called for my reasons and I referred him to paragraphs 552 and 592 of Article XXXVI *Army Regulations.*[19]

January 25, Sunday

Col. Williamson, Dr. Carrington, and Maj. Mulherrin, and myself went into the country some 4 miles on a ride. Col. Harper still absent.[20]

January 26, 27, 28

All quiet. No news from front. Camp very muddy and still have rain occasionally. Snow 4 inches on morning of 28th.

January 29 and 30

All quiet. Still in the same camp and very muddy.

January 31

An election was held in each company of the regiment while on dress parade for the non-commissioned officers and privates (one in each company) to receive the Badge of Distinction for gallant conduct in the battle of Murfreesboro, December 31, 1862, which resulted as follows:

Co. A, Pat Calahan; Co. B, Wm. Blakemore; Co. C, James Pearson; Co. D, C. Jenkins; Co. E, T. J. Underwood; Co. F, _____; Co. G, W. S. Colburn; Co. H, T. Thomson; Co. I, I. L. Caston; Co. K, [George B.] House.[21]

FEBRUARY 1, 2, 3, 4, 5, 6, 7, 8

Nothing worthy of note. Men in good health and fine spirits.

FEBRUARY 9

Gen. Joe E. Johnston reviewed the division and is said to have reported himself well pleased.[22]

FEBRUARY 10–26

Nothing worthy of note. At same camp. Skirmishing along the front. Rumor of peace armistice. Resolutions in Northwest, foreign intervention, etc. . . . kept alive some interest in camp. A great deal of rain during the time and roads very bad, the health of the army only tolerable but the spirits pretty good.[23]

FEBRUARY 27

Col. Williamson of the 2nd Arkansas Mounted Riflemen left for Arkansas and left his regiment in my charge, it being temporarily consolidated with the 1st Arkansas Mounted Riflemen and Col. Harper being in command of the brigade.

FEBRUARY 28

I mustered the 4th Arkansas regiment and 4th Arkansas battalion and Col. Thomas H. McCray mustered 1st and 2nd Mounted Riflemen.[24]

MARCH 1, 2, 3, 4

Lt. Henry left for Chicot on the 3rd, he is still suffering from his wound.

On 4th, fourteen Master Masons including myself made application for a *travelling warrant* or dispensation for our brigade. The lodge to be called "Harper Travelling Lodge," in honor of Col. R. W. Harper of the 1st Arkansas Mounted Riflemen. I was selected to be the first Worshipful Master of the Lodge and Capt. Hardwick, Senior Warden, and Colonel R. W. Harper, Junior Warden. I hope the application may be granted. There are many good masons among us who desire it.[25]

MARCH 5–31

Remained at same camps and but little of interest. I was sick from 8th to 20th. Much sickness in camps and some deaths. Men who are now in hospitals suffering from wounds received at Murfreesboro send back complaints of neglect on part of Surgeons and Assistant Surgeons.[26]

APRIL 1–12

Gen. Stewart has been placed in command of our division in place of Gen. McCown, who is now under arrest. Much attention given to drill. Regiment and brigade improving.[27]

APRIL 13–30

Changed camps to a point ¾ of a mile west of old camps and on the bank of Duck River. Men much improved by the changed water and camps much better. Still much attention given to drill. Col. Harper at Huntsville, Alabama, with his sick children and Col. McCray in command of the brigade. Gen. McNair on leave of absence in Arkansas. The regiment mustered on 30th by Lt. Colonel Eli Hufstedler of the 25th Arkansas regiment.[28]

MAY 1–7

Still at same camp on bank of Duck River on 6th. All the brigade except 1st and 2nd Arkansas Mounted Riflemen moved to a new camp 1¼ miles south from our present camp. Gen. McNair has returned from Arkansas and Colonel Harper from Huntsville.

MAY 8

Moved to our new camp 4 miles south of Shelbyville.

MAY 9

Officer of the day for first time since March 1862.

MAY 10

At ¼ before 1 a.m. received orders to hold ourselves in readiness to move by railroad at a moment's warning. At 1 a.m. received order to cook 3 days' rations at War Trace and send our baggage to Shelbyville to be sent by railroad at 8 a.m. We moved and passed through Shelbyville and reached War Trace at 1 p.m. and at 4½ p.m. went aboard the train for Chattanooga.

MAY 11

Reached Chattanooga at 7 a.m. and at 12 m. left for Atlanta.

MAY 12

At 7 a.m. reached Atlanta and at 1 p.m. left for West Point, where we arrived at 6 p.m. and had to lay over until 9 a.m. on tomorrow. Obtained leave and came on to Montgomery on the passenger train at 12 p.m.

MAY 13

Had a good time during day. Regiment arrived at 8 p.m. and immediately went on board a steamboat for Selma. Left Montgomery at 11 p.m. Left a detail to take charge of the baggage of the "United Regiments" and by order of Gen. McNair was to press on to Jackson, Mississippi, as rapidly as possible. Telegraphed to Selma to have cooked rations ready for us on our arrival.[29]

MAY 14

Reached Selma at 7 a.m. and immediately took cars after drawing 3 days' cooked rations and left Selma at 10½ a.m. and reached Uniontown and waited sometime for up train, then learned that it had run off the track 4 miles west of us. Took one carload of men and got broken cars out of our way, and we reached Demopolis at 12 p.m. and at 4 a.m. on 15th took boat to cross to McDowell. While at Demopolis we learned that the enemy had captured Jackson and the great necessity for us pursuing rapidly forward had ceased to exist.[30]

MAY 15

Took cars at 7 a.m. at McDowell and reached Meridian at 4½ p.m. and had an inspection of arms.[31]

MAY 16

At Meridian. Remainder of brigade arrived last night and all laid over here today. No news from Jackson. Gen. Gist has ordered us to be ready to leave on tomorrow at 7 a.m. with 5 days' rations, 3 being cooked owing to the great scarcity of transportation in the country near Brandon, and the fact that we will have to do on the very smallest amount, as it will all have to be pressed. We have determined to send all baggage that can be dispensed with to Selma, there to remain under guard. I only retain 3 shirts and other things in proportion; in fact 4 of us, my Commissary Adjutant and Sergeant Major and myself, carried our clothes in one knapsack. Col. Harper was left at Stevenson, Alabama, on our way here, sick.[32]

MAY 17, SUNDAY

The regiment left Meridian at 7½ a.m. destined for Jackson, having 3 days' cooked rations in our haversacks. I learned that the enemy had evacuated

Jackson on the 15th and was making his way back toward the Mississippi River and our forces were pressing on his rear. The regiment with the brigade camped near Brandon at 5 p.m. No news from the front this evening.

May 18, Monday

All quiet. At 7 a.m. the horses we drew at Meridian from Quartermaster to use until ours arrive reached us. Received orders to be ready at a moment's notice to leave on the cars in the direction of Jackson, Mississippi. Men in fine health and spirits. Remained in camp during day and night. Remainder of brigade went up to within 4 miles of Jackson. Not cars enough to carry us all at once.[33]

May 19, Tuesday

Left on train at 6 a.m. and reached brigade at 8 a.m. and at 10½ a.m. left for Jackson, having two wagons to the "United Regiments" carrying only cooking utensils. Reached Jackson and camped for the night. Orders to move tomorrow at daylight to join Gen. Johnston near Canton, Mississippi. The enemy have done much damage to the people of Jackson by burning and destroying property.[34]

May 20

Left camp at 6 a.m., the 4th Arkansas in advance; men's feet very sore from yesterday's march, but all in fine spirits. Reached a point 5 miles south of Canton at 2 p.m. and camped. In the morning from 2 to 6 o'clock we could distinctly hear the discharges of artillery, supposed to be at Vicksburg as the pieces were very heavy.

May 21

Remained in camp until 3 p.m. when we moved to a point 5 miles southwest of Canton and camped near a pond for water.

May 22

Remained in camp all day, men washed their clothing. We turned over our ox teams and received the promise of better teams. No news from Vicksburg but continual firing of heavy artillery during the morning.

May 23

Gen. Gist assumes command of all the forces in this vicinity by order of Gen. Johnston.[35]

MAY 24

Capts. Edwards and Jones and Dr. Sayle and myself went into the country and had a fine dinner.[36]

MAY 25

Gen. Walker placed in command of several brigades including ours.[37]

MAY 26

By invitation took dinner with a widow lady near camp. Had a very fine vegetable dinner.

MAY 27

At 4 p.m., the regiment was inspected by Capt. Crump of Gen. Walker's staff.[38]

MAY 28

At 5 a.m., left camp and moved to a point 2 miles southeast of Canton on Bear Creek. Water very poor and an indifferent camping place. From appearances will have plenty of snakes and mosquitoes.

MAY 29, FRIDAY

Orders to leave on tomorrow at daylight with three days' cooked rations in haversacks.

MAY 30

Left camp at daylight and passed through Canton and crossed Big Black River at Moore's Bluff on a newly constructed floating bridge and camped 9 miles from river on Yazoo City Road, just after dark.

MAY 31, SUNDAY

Left camp at daylight but halted and waited for two brigades (Gregg's and Ector's) to pass us, their place being in front. At 9 a.m., we halted 2 miles from Benton. Moved up to Benton about 12 m. and got water and moved on at intervals the rest of the day, and camped near Yazoo City after night. The whole march from Canton to this place has been worst conducted march that I have ever seen. About dark and some two miles from camp one of Walker's staff passed through our lines while at rest on the roadside and was requested not to ride so fast, whereupon he cursed and abused every one near and behaved in a disgraceful manner and also behaved very badly when he reported the same to me in a few minutes after. Walker and his staff seem to think we are a hard set of men and he and they are going to strengthen us up. They are, we know, a very contemptible set and they will have a hard time unless they keep on the right line. We know our rights and knowing dare maintain them.[39]

June 1

In camp today. Orders for men to bathe in Yazoo River. Capt. Edwards and myself went to the river north of town and took a bath. Can hear the guns at or near Vicksburg; they seem to be holding out there yet.

June 2

Moved to a point 2½ miles south of Yazoo City. Took division from early in the morning until late in the evening to make the move and get into camps, so poorly is the division managed under Gen. Walker. On the banks of the little brook, we get a pretty good camping ground and water plenty fair for Mississippi, though warm. Men have no soap to wash with and their clothes need it much.[40]

June 3

The charges I sent up against Gen. Walker's Aide-de-Camp were sent back by the general and says he will reprimand his Aide-de-Camp but this matter shall not stop here.[41]

June 4

At same camp until 4 p.m. when we were moved back to the camp we had occupied near town. We reached the old after dark and sent a detail of men to wagon train to cook up rations.

June 5

At 4 p.m. we moved to a point 3 miles south, which we reached after dark. Orders not to have any home sounded until further orders (some deserters).

June 6

At same camp, all quiet.

June 7, Sunday

At same camp. Nothing to note. Some rumors of Gen. E. Kirby Smith having crossed the Mississippi River etc. . . . . Rain much needed.

June 8

All quiet. Went to Yazoo City.

June 9

Rations have been scanty for sometime and much complaint.

June 10

Rained all the morning and occasionally during the day.

June 11

A pleasant day. Can distinctly hear cannonading at Vicksburg. We are anxious to move forward and relieve the place as soon as possible.

June 12

A beautiful morning. An occasional gun at Vicksburg. It has been several days since our men there had any rest as the shelling has been almost constant.

June 13

At daylight ready to move but did not get off until 12 m. and arrived at Big Black River at McNamara's Ferry at 8 p.m., having marched 20 miles. A hard day's march and many stragglers from division, but few from the 1st and 2nd Arkansas Mounted Riflemen. I have come to the conclusion that Gen. Walker is totally unfit to command a division or indeed a brigade. Camped in a cornfield.

June 14, Sunday

Remained near Big Black River until 3 p.m. Rumors of a repulse of the enemy at Vicksburg, no particulars. At 3 p.m., crossed river and moved to a point 1 mile south of Vernon and camped in a beautiful camp ground.

June 15

All quiet. A general desire in brigade to be transferred to some other division.

June 16

Occasional firing at Vicksburg.

June 17

Men in pretty good health and fine spirits.

June 18 and 19

Some firing at Vicksburg. Drill twice a day.

June 20

Heavy firing from 3 a.m. to 11 a.m. at Vicksburg.

JUNE 21, SUNDAY

At 1 a.m. a report in direction of Vicksburg as if an explosion of a magazine. Occasional firing at Vicksburg during the day. Rev. Snodgrass preached a sermon in camp at 5 p.m.[42]

JUNE 22

Received an order transferring our brigade to Maj. Gen. French. I obtained a 2 days' leave to go to Canton. Dr. Sayle goes with me. Brigade leaves tomorrow at 5 a.m. Left for Canton and stopped for the night at Mrs. Bowles, 8 miles west of Canton.[43]

JUNE 23

Went to Canton and could not get articles desired and concluded to go to Jackson. Went out nine miles toward Jackson and stopped for night with Mr. Home.[44]

JUNE 24

Went to Jackson and thence to Clinton, where we remained for the night.

JUNE 25

Reached camp, 6 miles from Livingston on the Brownsville Road.

JUNE 26, 27, 28, 29

All quiet at same camp, nothing to note.

JUNE 30

Mustered 26th and 31st Arkansas regiments. Lt. Colonel Hufstedler mustered 1st and 2nd Arkansas Mounted Riflemen. No blank muster rolls.

JULY 1

Moved to within 3 miles of Brownsville. Col. Harper came up and remained only 3 or 4 hours, still sick.

JULY 2

Left camp at 4 a.m. and moved to Mr. Birdsong's place 4 miles from Big Black River, one mile from road leading from Vernon to Edwards Depot.[45]

JULY 3

At same camp. No news of interest.

July 4

All quiet. Our pontoons near us but no news of a move.

July 5

Col. Williamson has returned from Arkansas and also Col. Smith, many officers will soon be here. The regiment will be separated.[46]

July 6

Regiments separated this morning. We received the news at 1 a.m. of the fall of Vicksburg. At daylight we commenced the retreat toward Jackson, camped 3 miles west of Clinton.

July 7

At 7 a.m., we were again on the move and reached Jackson at 5 p.m. All quiet during early part of the night. At 11 p.m. a few pickets were sent out.

July 8

All quiet during the day. At 9 p.m. the long roll was beaten in the brigade (Evans) next to us and pickets were sent out from it on the Raymond Road. Cooked rations for tomorrow.[47]

July 9

The regiment was sent out on picket on the Raymond Road and to its right. All quiet along our line but firing heard to our right.

July 10

At 3 a.m., firing of pickets and some artillery was heard on our right. During the forenoon, the pickets on our right were forced back and we compelled to swing around using our left as a pivot until we reached the Raymond Road, forming parallel to it to prevent the enemy from outflanking us. We moved forward on our new front and recovered all the ground we had lost. We charged the enemy and drove them back, captured some canteens etc. . . . , which they left in their flight, then we fell back and resumed our old line. In evening, we were relieved by the 4th Arkansas regiment. During the day, I lost one man killed and several wounded.

July 11

At 3 p.m. moved out and relieved the 4th Arkansas and held our old position during the night. In evening, the enemy opened a battery on us and fired several shots grape and canister. During the night could hear the enemy passing toward our left with artillery and infantry. I am expecting an attack on us early tomorrow morning. Went along our lines and urged men to hold position until ordered to fall back.[48]

July 12

At 6½ a.m., the enemy opened on us from 3 points with 10 or 15 pieces of artillery and gave us a terrible shelling. The men on our right and left gave way. We were near a row of Negro quarters and nearly every cabin was unroofed and shrubbery in yard was terribly cut up. After the shelling had slackened we fell back toward our fortifications, but not until we were placed under a cross fire of artillery, the enemy having advanced on our flanks, which were exposed by the retreat of those on our right and left. The shelling was the most terrible I have experienced at any time during the war. One half of the regiment had been sent into camp before daylight, the remainder fell back inside of our lines to support our men at the breastworks if necessary, but the enemy did not attack our works, but attacked Breckinridge on our left and were repulsed, we capturing 4 flags. At night, Capt. Parks' company was sent out on picket. Regiment held in readiness to move at a moment's warning. Capt. McConnell acting Lt. Colonel was wounded in left leg just below the knee just after daylight, a slight wound which will unfit him for duty for 6 or 8 weeks.[49]

July 13

Sent out two companies of skirmishers under Capt. Basham, drove the enemy's pickets back near their fortifications and 700 or 800 from our works. Regiment all relieved during the evening and early part of the night.

July 14

All moving on as usual for the last few days. Pickets firing from all parts of our line. Had a truce from 2 p.m. to 4 p.m. to bury the dead Yankees in front of Breckinridge's line, killed in the charge on the 12th. Pickets on both sides met in front of our brigade and agreed not to fire on each other during the remainder of the evening. The promise has been kept. Sent out 5 companies under Capt. Stone to relieve pickets in front of our brigade. Quiet in front of our brigade during night. Our line was on left of Raymond Road where it passes through our works.

July 15

My regiment was relived in evening by 4th Arkansas, but little firing in our immediate front, firing on every other part of our line. Strengthening our works every night by cotton baled and throwing up more dirt.

July 16

Maj. Eagle relieved 4th Arkansas at 5 p.m. At dark, we received orders to prepare to leave Jackson. The artillery was taken back from works by hand, then attached to the limbers and taken off. We commenced leaving town at 10 p.m. and by daylight on 17th the whole army had left. At 1 a.m. on 17th our pickets were relieved; not a gun was fired on us during the night by the enemy; indeed, so quietly did we get away that they actually shelled Jackson next morning when we were many miles away. Everything was done very quietly but very slowly.[50]

July 17

Daylight found us 3 miles west of Brandon. We camped 2½ miles east of Brandon, men much in need of rest and sleep.

July 18

Left camps at 5 a.m. for "Line Creek," 17 miles east of Brandon, where we arrived at dark in one of the hardest rains I have at any time witnessed. The road became one puddle of mud. The men were wet to the skin, though many were not able to get their clothes dry.

July 19

Changed camps a short distance and rested for the day. The whole army here came on different roads, French's division and Breckinridge's division on one road and Loring's and Walker's on another. Received orders at night to be ready to move at a moment's notice.[51]

July 20

At 12 m. left camp and moved 12 miles and camped 11 miles southeast of Forest Depot. Capt. Edwards gone to Meridian at Depot Commissary.

July 21

At same camp. Rained before dark, a heavy rain and men badly provided for it.

July 22

Had inspection of arms in evening and wrote a report of the engagements at Jackson from the 9th to 16th instant inclusive, our loss in regiment 2 killed and 20 wounded. Orders to go into a good camp, to drill etc. . . . , preparatory to offensive operations against the enemy in Mississippi.[52]

JULY 23

Moved to a new camp 5 miles distant, near line between Smith and Scott counties, the best running water I have seen in Mississippi. We are 12 miles from Forest railroad station.

JULY 24

Some talk of consolidation of regiments, for the purpose of permanently relieving one half of the officers of the regiments so united.

JULY 25

Question of consolidation submitted to the regiment and they required to give an answer on the morning of 26th. Col. Harper arrived and will assume command of the regiment soon, his health much improved. Orders to leave for Enterprise tomorrow morning.

JULY 26

Order to go to Enterprise countermanded. Question of consolidation answered in the negative.

JULY 27, 28, 29

At same camp, nothing of note. Drilling twice each day.

JULY 30

The regiment did today agree to permanently unite with the 2nd Arkansas Mounted Riflemen and to re-enlist for the war, if we can be remounted and sent west of the Mississippi River. "To unite if we can be remounted," the vote on the propositions was unanimous.[53]

JULY 31

All quiet about camp and men again in good spirits, were much depressed on and after retreat.

AUGUST 1, SATURDAY

At same camp. In p.m., several Master Masons met for the purpose of organizing a lodge, having received a dispensation from Grand Master of Masons of Arkansas for that purpose. Made necessary arrangements and I am to go to Mobile and buy the furniture.[54]

AUGUST 2

Inspection in a.m. and guns in fine condition.

AUGUST 3
Col. Harper officer of the day.

AUGUST 4 AND 5
Nothing to note.

AUGUST 6
Orders to move to Forest on tomorrow morning and take the cars for Meridian.

AUGUST 7
Left camp just after daylight and reached Forest at 11½ a.m. and at 2 p.m. left for Meridian, where we arrived at 8 p.m. and camped near town.

AUGUST 8
Camp at same place; obtained a leave of absence for 5 days from Col. Harper commanding brigade and left 9¼ p.m. with Capt. George S. Laswell.[55]

AUGUST 9
Arrived at Mobile at 8 p.m. and stopped at Battle House, room 110. Saw my young friend Harpin Davis.[56]

AUGUST 10
Spent day in selecting articles of furniture for Masonic Lodge, and at night went to the theatre and saw the play of "Hamlet" murdered.[57]

AUGUST 11, 12, 13
About city made purchase of Masonic jewels and got some stars made for myself etc. . . .[58]

AUGUST 14
At 4 p.m. left for Meridian.

AUGUST 15
Arrived at Meridian at 5 a.m. and found the regiment camped about one mile from depot. Called camp "Camp Bowen" in honor of Gen. Bowen of Missouri. Found all in fine health and spirits and at a good camp ground.[59]

AUGUST 16, SUNDAY
Harper Travelling Lodge met at 2 p.m. for the first time under its dispensation. Received orders to leave for Okolona at 4 p.m. on tomorrow.

August 17

Left camp at daylight and reached Okolona at sundown and camped about 150 yards east of the water tank.[60]

August 18, 19, 20

Spent time in looking about town, viewing the location, and putting up a few log breastworks for our pickets. Have no tools to entrench with, trying to get some axes, spades, and picks.

August 21

Fast day and no duty in our camp. The Rev. Mr. L. Eathe preached in camp at 10 a.m.[61]

August 22

Rumors of the enemy having captured Grenada. Some rain.[62]

August 23, Sunday

Command still at Okolona. I left at 8 a.m. for Montgomery and reached Meridian at 8 p.m. and went out to camps. We had left all our sick and disabled men and extra baggage at Meridian when we (our regiment and 25th Arkansas) went to Okolona. Remainder of brigade at Camp Bowen.

August 24

Left Meridian at 6½ a.m. and reached Selma at 4 p.m. and took steamboat (*Coquette*) for Montgomery. Left Selma at 5½ p.m.[63]

August 25

Reached Montgomery at 7 a.m. Stopped at Exchange Hotel down No. 83, a poor room but promise of better. Let me have room No. 43, a good room.

August 26

Went to theatre, a poor affair.

August 27

Dull day. Troops passing through from Johnston's army in Mississippi to Gen. Bragg near Chattanooga. Ector's Texas Brigade now passing. Went to theatre.

August 28, 29, 30, 31

Still at Montgomery but too unwell to leave though otherwise ready. No news from regiment since I left.

September 1, 2, 3, 4, 5, 6
Yet at Montgomery and not well enough to return to camp.

September 7
Still at Montgomery improving and hope to be able to be off, on tomorrow.

September 8
Advance of McNair's Brigade reached here just as I was on the eve of starting for Meridian to join my regiment. On the 7th I wrote an article for the *Advertiser* over the Letter X, and it appeared in this morning's paper, against emancipation as advocated in the *Mississippian* and in favor of placing slaves in the army as nurses, teamsters, sappers and miners, cooks, etc. . . . , but not to arm them, etc. . . . As the brigade is coming I have nothing to do but wait until it comes.[64]

September 9
Regiment reached Montgomery at 8 a.m. and had to lay over for want of transportation. Went to theatre, most of the regiment there.

September 10
Regiment left for Atlanta at 5 a.m., but being unwell, I did not go with it. During day 2nd Arkansas Mounted Riflemen arrived.

September 11
Left for Atlanta at 5 a.m. and reached Atlanta at 5 p.m. and joined the regiment 2 miles from town; it had reached there in the morning.

September 12
At 4 p.m. received orders to leave for Resaca at 5 p.m. Moved into town but did not get any of our baggage [from] regimental headquarters but went on nevertheless. Col. Harper joined us at the railroad depot and fortunately had some rations with him but neither of us had a blanket. We ran all night and reached Resaca at day on the morning of 13th all safe.

September 13, Sunday
Moved out to camps ½ miles west of town where we remained all day and night. Quite cold and we had to borrow blankets and board with the band; our servants as well as supplies and baggage behind.

September 14, 15

At same camp. No news from front. Troops arriving from Virginia army by way of Atlanta.[65]

September 16

At 2 a.m. received orders to be ready to leave at 4 a.m., but it was shortly after changed to 9 a.m., when we left for Ringgold. Arrived at the Chickamauga Creek where a bridge had been burned 2½ miles south of Ringgold, where we camped for the night beside the railroad in line of battle. Men in fine spirits. My health improving.

September 17

Moved over the creek in a.m. and camped and had our baggage brought over. At 4 p.m. got orders to move to Ringgold; moved over to and about one half mile up the road and camped for the night. The enemy having retreated from vicinity of Ringgold. Cooked two days' rations during the night and with two already on hand, making four days' rations including the 18th.

September 18

At 4 a.m. we left camp and moved up to Ringgold and there took the Lafayette Road and moved out some 3 miles and there took the road to Graysville and in the road formed a line of battle and moved against the enemy to the southwest and routed them. Only the troops on our left being engaged, except in skirmish, and then we lost but one man wounded. Crossed Chickamauga Creek at Reed's Bridge and moved up to within 10 or 11 miles of Chattanooga and ½ mile east of Chattanooga and Lafayette Road where we laid on our arms for the night.[66]

September 19

Gen. Bragg joined us during the night with Buckner's and D. H. Hill's Corps, and about 9 a.m. the fight opened about 1½ miles to the northwest of us on or near the Chattanooga Road. We were placed in line at daylight and up to 11½ a.m. (now) have not moved from our position. At 12 m., we moved forward to support Gregg's Brigade and were soon engaged with the enemy and being exposed to a front and flank fire on our right flank. We moved rapidly forward until we crossed the Chattanooga Road, when we were informed that our brigade had been flanked on the left and driven from the field, which we were prevented from seeing by an elevation of ground on the left of our regiment. In a few minutes, the enemy were on our left and in our rear and in our front and at the same time exposed to a flank fire from the right flank of artillery. When the enemy first appeared in our rear we were uncertain who they were, whether friend of foe, and before we could ascertain we had one man killed, one wounded, and one taken prisoner, Page of Company D, a gallant man. We then moved by the right flank and the enemy advanced and fired upon us a second time and then retreated. We then moved back to our position at the opening of the fight, joined the remainder of the brigade and drew ammunition, and moved into line again near the Chattanooga Road, where we remained in line of battle for the night and sent pickets to the front. Capt. Galloway, Lieutenants Green and Cravens, and Adjutant Prather were wounded and six men killed and a great many wounded. Our regiment captured the standard of the 8th Kansas regiment, a beautiful banner, an ambulance, and some prisoners, though we were in a very tight place ourselves. The regiment, brigade, and indeed the whole army seem to be in excellent spirits. Quiet along our lines during the night, except an occasional gun from a picket or the groans of wounded men. We lay on ground held by the enemy during the early part of the day and from which they were driven. The night was cold and men suffered, as they could not be permitted to build fires. All dreaming of and expecting the continuance of the great fight tomorrow. Tis a sad thought for the bravest of us.[67]

SEPTEMBER 20, SUNDAY

All quiet along the lines, except an occasional shot from a picket, until about 9½ a.m. when the firing commenced on our right and gradually extended toward us. Soon we moved forward and, when about 600 yards from the line we had left, we engaged the enemy, who yielded at the first volley but contested the ground inch by inch as they fell back. The brigade on our right (Brig. Gen. Brown's) fell back and was rallied and again fell back and again rallied; and in the meantime we were moving to the front, driving the enemy from behind his hastily constructed fortifications of logs, rocks, etc. . . . ; we crossed two roads leading toward Chattanooga, the first called the "Main Chattanooga Road," when we reached an open field through which the enemy were retreating in great confusion. We poured in on their retreating hosts a very distinctive fire, but their batteries in the field were soon in position and played upon us effectively. Here Col. Harper fell mortally wounded and died at 5½ p.m. The most of our brigade pressed on and took the artillery or rather a part of it, 9 pieces, and brought them off the field. A part of our regiment was badly cut up and scattered by the enemy's batteries. These, or the most of them, I soon collected and placed them on the right of Kershaw's Brigade, which was then approaching the field in which the artillery had just been captured; but, owing to the fact that the brigades on our right had fallen back, it was necessary for Kershaw's Brigade to form nearly at right angles to our former line as the enemy were advancing at right angles to their former line over the ground formerly occupied by our forces that had retired. Kershaw's Brigade with part of our regiment attached to his right was soon hotly engaged and were for a moment driven back, but rallied and drove the enemy into the timber on the opposite side of the field. It was at this time that Capt. Jacob McConnell fell dead while nobly discharging his duty; the ball entered his right temple and came out behind his left ear. He was a noble man. The part of the regiment soon joined the brigade which had fallen back to the log field works from which we had lately driven the enemy, in order to get more ammunition as many of our men were entirely out and others had but little. The contest had been severe, but the infirmary corps had been actively engaged and most of the wounded were removed. Details were at once sent out to gather cartridges from the dead and wounded, both friend and foe, and all ammunition taken from the prisoners who were being constantly carried by us; in this way we were soon nearly supplied, and the ammunition train arrived and we completed our supplies. Shortly after being supplied, the enemy opened on us with artillery at long range, and here Capt. Stone was mortally wounded by a cannon shot. After resting for a short time, we were carried forward to support B. A. Johnson's Brigade some 1½ miles to the left and in front of us. Soon after reaching our position, an attack was made on our lines and Johnson's Brigade broke and attempted to leave the field and were stopped by our brigade. We were at once ordered forward to drive back the enemy, who soon yielded a short distance but contested the ground stubbornly and soon made a determined stand; and here the contest was terrific; for nearly an hour, it was one continual roar of musketry, but the enemy finally yielded and fled from the field. Our line advanced some distance and then fell back a short distance and laid in line of battle for the night. It was a terrible night to us who lay on the field to hear the groans of the poor wounded Yanks as they lay between our line and that of the enemy. All who were near us were cared for. They had fought us and are trying to enslave us, but they are human (in form at least) and we rendered them all the assistance we could. It was cold and we could build no fires. Our loss, so far as we have been able to ascertain in our regiment on 18, 19, and today, is 14 killed, 76 wounded, and 16 missing. There will be some changes when we learn all particulars. Our men have acted nobly and are ready to renew the contest on tomorrow. I rode all day yesterday and until in the last charge today. Although quite unwell on 18th and 19th, the excitement has improved my health. All quiet along our lines, scarcely a single gun. Quite a contrast to the thunder and noise of today.[68]

SEPTEMBER 21

The enemy retreated during the night in direction of Chattanooga. We remained in line until 1 p.m. when we were ordered to move in direction of Chattanooga. We sent out details to gather up the arms on the battlefield, and also a detail to bury our dead. The dead of the regiment were all collected and buried on the ground fought over by us on Saturday and all their graves neatly and plainly marked. At 1 p.m. we moved about a mile and halted and remained during remainder of day and night.

September 22

Moved up and camped near the Red House Ford of Chickamauga Creek on Chattanooga and Ringgold roads 9 miles from Ringgold; in the morning just after starting to move received orders to proceed to Mississippi without delay. I am quite unwell, hardly able to ride.[69]

September 23

Moved down to our old camp 2½ miles south of Ringgold and had our baggage carried to the railroad to be ready for transportation at any time and had a detail to cook rations for men. Have been quite unwell today, with considerable fever. Hope I will be better soon, am quite bilious, am tired and worn out.

September 24

Took care at 10 a.m. and reached Atlanta at 6 a.m. on 25th. Am no better, but still in command.

September 25

Left Atlanta at 8½ a.m. and reached West Point at 6 p.m. and rested for the night.

September 26

Left West Point at 9 a.m. and reached Montgomery at 8 p.m. I went to hotel, being very unwell. Drew two days' rations. Men slept at Montgomery and Mobile railroad depot.

September 27, Sunday

Left for Mobile at 8 a.m. and reached Pollard at 6 p.m. Here we had to wait till 10 p.m. for an engineer, when we proceeded on our way and reached Blakely Station over the Bay from Mobile at 9 a.m. on 28th.[70]

September 28

Came across the bay in steamboat *Natchez No. 2* and teams were ready to transport our baggage to the Mobile and Ohio Railroad depot. At 5 p.m. the troops left for Meridian (my own regiment and 4th Arkansas being under my command), where they arrived on morning of 29th and moved out and camped in old camp "Bowen" 1 mile southwest of Meridian. I was so unwell

that I remained at Mobile for thirty hours. I had laid on a pallet in the cars all
the way from Chickamauga to Mobile, but am worse now than on 24th but
owing to fatigue I suppose. I wrote letters.[71]

September 29
Left for Meridian at 5 p.m. and reached Meridian on 30th at 4 a.m.

September 30
Remained quietly in camps in charge of brigade; remainder of the brigade
arriving.

October 1
Remained in camps until p.m. and came out to Mr. Burwell's 4 miles from
camps to stay a few days or until I get well. A good quiet place.[72]

October 2 and 3
Spent time in making out a report of the late battle of Chickamauga and
in writing letters to send to Arkansas.[73]

October 4, Sunday
Went to camp and found everything moving along quietly. I returned to
Mr. Burwell's at night.

October 5, 6, 7, 8
At Mr. Burwell's and my health much improved.

October 9
Came into camps and found everything in good order. I am now able to
remain in camps.

October 10
Went with Col. Smith [and] Capt. Wilburn to Sage Village Lodge No. 86
and saw three men initiated and attended to some other business.[74]

October 11
Harper Travelling Lodge met at 1 p.m.; had pleasant meeting.

October 12, 13, 14, 15, 16, 17, 18
Received orders on 18th to send train to Brandon and also the horses of
brigade and be ready to leave tomorrow by 12 m. President Davis arrived at
Meridian on night of 17th. Wrote to Arkansas by Capt. Nat Jones. Received a

supply of provisions from Post or Depot Commissary and from Uniontown, Alabama.[75]

OCTOBER 19

Left Meridian at 12 m. and reached Brandon about 2 a.m. on 20th. We had a hard time on the trip; the car in which we rode had some loose cotton in it and it took fire while we were under way and we had difficulty in getting the cars stopped. Fortunately, no one was hurt seriously. Col. Smith and Alex W. Jones jumped off or fell off. I lost nothing as my things were in the end of the car that did not take fire.[76]

OCTOBER 20

Moved to where the Canton Road crossed the railroad and camped on same ground occupied by us when here last May.

OCTOBER 21, 22, 23, 24, 25, 26, 27, 28, 29, 30, 31

Still at same camp and men all in fine health, and reports say that our wounded all doing very well and many of them are returning to duty. On 31st, I mustered 2nd Arkansas Mounted Riflemen and Maj. Noles mustered my regiments.[77]

NOVEMBER 1, SUNDAY

Still at same camp. Masonic Lodge met today. No news.

NOVEMBER 2, 3, 4

Nothing to note. $400 and letters from home.

NOVEMBER 5

Received orders to be ready to leave for Meridian as soon as transportation can be had for us.

NOVEMBER 6

At 8 p.m. sent off 4 companies to Meridian under charge of Capt. Laswell.

NOVEMBER 7

At 8 p.m. with remainder of regiment and the 4th Arkansas I left for Meridian, where we arrived at 9 p.m. and got some wagons and moved out to old camp ground; left my companies and 4th Arkansas at depot.

NOVEMBER 8

Remainder of regiment came out to camps. At 2 p.m. Harper Travelling Lodge met.

NOVEMBER 9, 10

Rumors that we may build winter quarters here.

NOVEMBER 11

Col. Bunn, Maj. Eagle, and myself laid off the ground for winter quarters and the men have commenced the work of building.

NOVEMBER 12–25

Men busy in erecting log cabins for winter quarters. Owing to the fact that tools are scarce, it is a very tedious job; but in a few days, every man will be comfortably housed. During this time, the men have drawn blankets and some clothing and are now pretty well to do for the winter. There has been but little sickness and that mostly of a chronic character. The men are in fine condition. We are all anxious to go to Arkansas, but as yet no indications are to be seen that we will likely move in that direction.

NOVEMBER 26–30

Most of the men have completed their cabins and the camp is in fine condition. Senator Mitchel passed through on his way to Arkansas from Richmond and made a speech to the brigade, telling them that the Secretary of War had determined that we could not be spared from this side of the Mississippi at this time, and urged the men to stand by their colors and not to desert etc. . . . Harpin Davis passed through Meridian on his way to Mobile. He left Chicot on the 20th; all well at home then. I moved into my cabin on 29th; a nice cabin, about 14 feet square, mostly of Magnolia logs ("Magnolia Hall"), lined on the inside with oak boards and have a good chimney. I fear we may not stay here long as we are too comfortably fixed up. The men are all in fine health and many of those wounded at Chickamauga are returning to duty.[78]

DECEMBER 1, 2, 3, 4, 5

Time passing pleasantly. Some complaint about poor rations.

DECEMBER 6, SUNDAY

Received orders to leave for Brandon on morning of 7th, and are now making preparations to move.

DECEMBER 7

Left camp at 3 a.m. and at 4½ a.m. got aboard the cars and at 4 p.m. arrived at the camps 2½ miles east of Brandon, where we have to drink pond water.

December 8

Assisted Col. Bunn, Maj. Noles to lay off camps. My regiment still on the right, some talk of putting 39th North Carolina on the right. I will object.

December 9

Rode around the country to hunt a better campground but decided on none, a hard day's ride.

December 10

Made another search and laid off camps near railroad and some ½ mile east of depot and on north side of track near and on the ground occupied by part of brigade in November, where we could find excellent water and tolerable ground to camp on.

December 11

In evening received orders to move to a camp 2½ miles south of Brandon where all the field officers of the brigade had determined not to occupy, but it has been ordered by Maj. Gen. French, who is as little capable of commanding a division as a rogue is of becoming an honest man.[79]

December 12

At 6 a.m. we were on the move for new camps, where we arrived at 10 a.m. Col. Coleman placed his regiment on the right of brigade, but as I contended for my position he yielded and my regiment resumed its old place. The camps were laid off at once by Col. Bunn and myself, and the men commenced to clear up the ground. Only about one half of the regimental baggage has arrived. The water here is very poor.[80]

December 13, Sunday

Remainder of regiment arrived and camped. Gen. McNair arrived from Meridian on his way to Arkansas and came out to camps to see us all. I went into town to see Maj. Elstner. All the field officers of the Arkansas portion of the brigade signed a memorial to the Secretary of War asking that I be appointed a brigadier general and assigned to command this brigade. I wrote to Gen. Churchill by Gen. McNair. Col. Coleman said the memorial was all right and proper, but as he was my senior officer, he could not sign it. He aspires to the position himself.[81]

December 14

Went to town early to see Gen. McNair. He had written a letter to Hon. R. W. Johnson, our senator in Congress, urging him to try and secure my appointment as brigadier general. Col. Coleman called a meeting of the officers who had signed the memorial and myself. He becomes satisfied that the signers had no idea of reflecting on him. I wrote to Senator Johnson, forwarding the memorial and letter of Gen. McNair. The men are cleaning up camps and some are building. I am only building up 4 or 5 logs high to put my tent on. This my birthday. I am this day 31 years old (thirty-one). Had I spent all my days as I should have done, I might at this time be able to render my country much more valuable services than it is now possible for me to do. How much I do regret the time I have spent in idleness. Let the past be a warning to me in future and I will try and improve my times to better advantage.[82]

Camp McNair's Brigade
December 12th, 1863
Hon. J. A. Seddon,
Secretary of War

We as field officers and commandants of the several regiments composing McNair's Brigade, in view of the probable promotion of our present commander, Brig. Gen. McNair, while expressing our deep regret at the loss of the superior council and command of such an officer as immediate commander and while we can but feel that he is eminently worthy of additional honor and if entrusted with higher offices will administer them with credit to himself and honor to his state and profit to the country at large.

We would most respectfully ask, in the event that we are to be separated from Gen. McNair, that he may be succeeded by an officer from our own state, and as one long tried and peculiarly fitted both by nature and experience for the position we have the honor to mention Col. Daniel H. Reynolds of the 1st Arkansas Mounted Rifles, who we feel assured if favored with Executive confidence will fully and faithfully discharge the trust. Hoping that his Excellency the President may favorably consider and our honorable Senate favorably advise in the premises.

We are with great respect,
Obedient Servants
H. G. Bunn, Col. 4th Arkansas (Maj. J. B. McCulloch absent)
J. T. Smith, Lt. Col. 2nd Arkansas Mounted Riflemen
(Col. J. A. Williamson and Maj. J. P. Eagle absent)
Geo. L. Laswell, Maj. 1st Arkansas Mounted Rifles
(Lt. Col. L. M. Ramseur absent)
J. A. Ross, Maj. 4th Arkansas Battalion[83]
Eli Hufstedler, Lt. Col. 25th Arkansas
L. L. Noles, Maj. 25th Arkansas (Col. Turnbull absent)

All the field officers of McNair's Brigade present with their commands have signed the foregoing, except Col. D. Coleman of the 39th North Carolina regiment and he declines as it would be promoting a junior officer over him.

J. A. Ross, Maj. 4th Arkansas Battalion
Hdqs. Brigade Brandon, Miss.
December 14th, 1863
Hon. Robert W. Johnson,
Richmond, Va.
Sir:

It is with great pleasure that I recommend to your favorable consideration for the appointment of brigadier general Col. D. H. Reynolds, of the 1st Arkansas Mounted Rifles (dismounted).

He has been in the service upward of two years and during that time has proven himself worthy of the trust and confidence reposed in him. There is not a more gallant and efficient officer in the service as his deeds on the battlefields of Oak Hills, Missouri; Elkhorn, Arkansas; Farmington, Mississippi; Richmond, Kentucky; Murfreesboro and Chickamauga will attest. I feel justified in saying that no one could fill the position with more credit than himself, nor any appointment give more general satisfaction. This officer has won a reputation for cool and gallant daring on every battlefield that will be fondly remembered by every Arkansian.
I am very respectfully,
Your Obedient Servant,
E. McNair

Camp McNair's Brigade
December 14th, 1863
Senator Johnson:
Dr. Sir:

Enclosed you will find a memorial to the Secretary of War and a letter from Gen. McNair to you.

As these papers will show the Arkansas portion of the brigade represented by their field officers present have unanimously recommended me for the position of brigadier general and to be assigned to the command of this brigade instead of Gen. McNair, who is about to be separated from it permanently.

I entered the army as Senior Captain of Churchill's regiment in June 1861. Have served with it ever since and am now its Colonel. Was in command of my regiment through the Kentucky campaign under E. Kirby Smith, when the regiment was highly complimented by that officer for gallantry at the battle of Richmond, Kentucky. Since have commanded it at the engagement around Jackson, Mississippi, and after the fall of Col. Harper at the battle of Chickamauga.

Having received the approval and endorsement of all the Arkansas portion of the brigade (there is but one other regiment in the brigade, the 39th North Carolina, and its colonel is seeking promotion), I feel highly complimented and am anxious to obtain the position. I could at this time ask no greater honor than to command a brigade that has won such a reputation and that too with their entire approval and at their solicitation and being as I am its junior colonel.

Should it meet with your approval and you will present the application for me, I will be under many obligations to your and you will confer a favor upon a body of tried Arkansas soldiers.

Respectfully etc. . . .

D. H. Reynolds

December 15

Men working slowly as it is probable that we will change camps again in a day or two.

December 16

Completed my "half cabin and half tent" house and am tonight (8 p.m.) comfortably seated by a nice fire brightly blazing. It is a rainy bad night. I just completed my work in time. Dr. Mitchell, Acting Adjutant Belt, and Sergeant Major Ferguson are visiting me tonight.[84]

December 17–31

Remained at old camp until 27th and then moved to a camp ½ mile to northeast where many of the men had built new houses. During Christmas here, had a tolerable time. Have been officer of the day every third day for two or three weeks. Am protesting it and will have order changed.

On morning of 31st, we had a very heavy hailstorm. I think the largest hail I ever saw fall; rained during the day and tonight (31st). It is raining hard occasionally and very windy and disagreeable. The regiment inspected and mustered by Gen. French and his inspectors. The health of the troops very good.

The year will soon close, as it is now 11 p.m. I wonder how many years will close before our cruel enemies will cease a hopeless war and acknowledge our independence. We have suffered many hardships and we are able to bear and will bear many more rather than to yield. Anything is preferable to submission, even death itself. I am in hopes that 1864 may see the close of the war and our brave and suffering soldiers returned to their homes and our country beginning to recover from the great burdens that are now weighing her down. Our independence once gained and our future will be glorious and prosperous. As a people, we have all the elements of greatness. If we are true to ourselves, we will be a beacon light to guide the oppressed of other nations in future times. May we all have the wisdom and manhood necessary to enable us to struggle on until we succeed in our great contest, remembering that future generations are alike interested with us in the result.

FOUR

1864

THE MOST TERRIBLE FIGHTING
I HAVE SEEN DURING THE WAR

The fortunes of the Confederacy turned from grim to desperate by the fourth season of the war, particularly in the Western Theater. Unable to save the vital rail line at Chattanooga in late 1863, the South's defensive line shrank back on Atlanta and braced for the commencement of total warfare, while Union armies focused their attentions as much against the resources and sagging morale of Confederate civilians as the Rebel armies in the field.

The internal squabbles that long characterized the Army of Tennessee also magnified late in the war. More a reflection of professional rivalry and personal ideology than critical strategic issues, such schisms continued to exact a negative toll on the army's morale and effectiveness. For Reynolds and the First Arkansas Rifles these conflicts came to fruition in 1864. In January, Samuel Gibbs French ordered Reynolds arrested on charges of disobedience of orders and conduct prejudicial to good order and military discipline. Although quickly cleared, the "frivolous" charges signaled the end of an already strained relationship with this "narrow minded and contemptible creature" and paved the way for the regiment's second transfer in less than a year.[1]

The uproar with French, however, did nothing to impede the trajectory of Reynolds's career. In March, he received the much-anticipated promotion to brigadier general. Shortly thereafter, Reynolds and his brigade transferred to the division of Maj. Gen. Edward Cary Walthall, with whom he quickly developed a more amiable relationship.[2]

In the aftermath of these changes, some hard feelings lingered between Reynolds and David Coleman, the brigade's senior colonel and disappointed aspirant for promotion. To eliminate the tension, Reynolds exchanged Coleman's 39th North Carolina Infantry for the 9th Arkansas Infantry of Matthew D. Ector's Brigade during operations in northern Georgia. With this adjustment "Reynolds's Arkansas Brigade" assumed its final composition, as it shared in the sanguine tableaus of the Army of Tennessee through the harsh autumn of the war.[3]

With each defeat or strategic setback, hopes of ultimate victory receded as well. Even Reynolds's previously steadfast hopes for Confederate independence displayed their first signs of vulnerability at this time. Like a resilient but tired farmer whose harvest has been devastated by the forces of nature, who yet retains a desperate hope to salvage a small portion of the original crop, Reynolds was forced to realize, with the fall of Atlanta, that the ineffectual "Chicago Platform" represented terms "as good as we could expect" in relation to southern independence.[4]

Despite the decline in Confederate prospects, Reynolds and his men continued to sacrifice on behalf of the South. In the fall, they marched northward with John Bell Hood toward near destruction at Franklin, Tennessee. In the aftermath, four of the six Confederate generals killed on that field lay stretched out on the lower back porch of the Carnton Plantation, including Reynolds's old Wesleyan classmate—Otho French Strahl. Thereafter, the husks of the western Rebel army continued northward toward another major defeat at Nashville, effectively ending Confederate hopes in the Western Theater and severely reducing their prospects for the war in general. Marked by such tragedy and defeat, the year closed as the remnants of the Army of Tennessee—along with the rest of the Confederacy—nursed wounds that would soon prove fatal.[5]

January 1, 2, 3, 4, 5, 6, 7

At same camp and men in very good health. Are getting our cabins or winter quarters nearly completed, and judging from our experience, we will have to move soon. The only indications of a move are that we are getting comfortably fixed. The roads are getting so bad in Mississippi that it is certainly almost impossible for an army to move; and hence I conclude we may stay sometime, notwithstanding the old rule, which has governed us so long.

January 8

Received orders to cook two days' rations and be ready to leave on the cars for Meridian at 7 a.m. on tomorrow. Our baggage is being carried to the railroad depot tonight, so it seems that the old rule still governs us. The weather has been very cold for the last 10 days and the ground is now frozen.

January 9

Left camp at 5 a.m. Very cold, reached depot at 6 a.m. and about 9 a.m. left for Meridian. Reached Meridian at 7 p.m. and moved out to old camp. Found many of our cabins unroofed and some entirely gone. "Magnolia Hall," my cabin, still standing but ill-treated. The men of course felt much outraged at such treatment and they made a cavalry company fairly fly from our camp.

January 10, 11, 12, 13, 14, 15, 16, 17, 18, 19

Still at same camp; men repairing cabins and getting some more from Missouri camp nearby that has just been left. On the 15th received orders for all the officers to go before an examining board. Much dissatisfaction about it.

On 16th the Quartermaster, Acting Paymaster of this department, refused to turn over money to pay my regiment full cavalry pay. I made application to go to Richmond to see about the matter and was refused by the brigade, division, and department headquarters. I then took a new paper and it was approved at brigade and division headquarters, and after being placed in the office of the Adjutant General at department headquarters, it was followed and taken out by brigade and division commanders and the endorsement changed, the approvals being erased and disapprovals placed on it. Made a speech to my regiment on dress parade. On the 18th I protested against the order ordering all the officers before the Examining Board. On the 19th, saw Gen. Polk and prepared a statement of the claim of my regiment to full cavalry pay; received my protest and sent it to Department Headquarters; are doing all in their power to prevent my appointment as brigadier general and no means are too base for them to use.[6]

January 20–31

The claim of the regiment for full cavalry pay has not yet been decided by Gen. Polk. Maj. Elstner has gone to Richmond in my place to see about it, as I could not go. He left camps on the 24th.

My protest was returned from department headquarters and the application not granted and I have forwarded same to Richmond in a letter addressed to Hon. A. H. Garland. I am in hopes the Secretary of War may consider the matter differently.[7]

I was tried on 27th before the Military Court of Department at Enterprise, Mississippi, on two charges: 1st Disobedience of orders, 2nd Conduct prejudicial to good order and military discipline. From indications, the trial was a mere farce; the court deeming the charges frivolous. I may be mistaken; I will soon hear. On 31st, 5 days after my trial, I was (for the first time since my entry into service) put in arrest by the division commander to await the decision of the court in my case. This [is] the reason given, but is not the true reason. The true reason is to annoy me and prevent me from interfering with him, while he is engaged in his disgraceful and disorganizing acts.[8]

The weather for the latter part of the month has been quite pleasant and the troops in good health, but much dissatisfaction at the manner they are treated by the narrow minded and contemptible creature who commands the division.

Some of the North Carolina troops of this brigade have been furloughed and the same privilege has been denied to the Arkansas troops, and leaves of absence have been granted to officers to go to Arkansas and been denied to the enlisted men. Our officers are illegally brought before a board to relieve the army of disabled, disqualified, and incompetent officers. This treatment added to other causes I fear will cause the Arkansas troops to desert and will destroy my regiment along with the brigade. I have great confidence in my regiment, but injuries and insults are heaped on it by the contemptible creatures who command the brigade and division. The division commander has been despised by all the troops he has ever commanded and is an injury to our cause every day he is in command. God grant that we may soon be relieved from such a commander for he has already done the army great injury.

FEBRUARY 1 AND 2

Received orders on night of 1st to have 3 days' rations cooked and be ready to leave for Jackson at a moment's notice. Preparations are progressing.

FEBRUARY 3

Still at same camp.

FEBRUARY 4

The 2nd Arkansas Mounted Riflemen left at 5 a.m. and my regiment with remainder of brigade left at 10½ a.m. and reached a point one mile east of Jackson at 2 a.m. on 5th and remained on cars.[9]

FEBRUARY 5

At an early hour unloaded our baggage and camped by the road side. Could hear the enemy's cannon early in the day. About 10 a.m., we put our baggage on the cars and commenced the retreat on foot toward Brandon; we moved back six miles and halted, and rested, and at 9 p.m. moved again and arrived at a point ½ mile from Brandon where we remained until nearly day-light on the 6th. Temporarily relieved from arrest and placed in command of my regiment.[10]

FEBRUARY 6

At 5½ a.m., we left for some indefinite point east of Brandon. My regiment acting as a rear guard. Passed through Brandon and camped 17 miles from Brandon and 5 miles from Morton. My regiment and 25th Arkansas acting as picket. The remainder of the division one mile further east.

FEBRUARY 7

Remained at same place quietly. The enemy reported to have taken procession of Brandon at 11 a.m. today. On the 5th, when we were about to leave Jackson on the retreat, I was, at the request of Colonel Bunn, released from arrest by Gen. French; and my regiment has been placed in the rear, the position of honor on a retreat.

FEBRUARY 8

11½ a.m. still finds us at same place and our cooking utensils sent to Morton and two companies one mile in the rear to act as skirmishers should the enemy advance. At 1 p.m., we left for Morton in rear of the army; —— of my companies and 2 from 4th Arkansas some distance in rear of my regiment as skirmishers. A line of battle was formed at Morton, and some heavy skirmishing between the enemy and the 5 companies, but no result except that the enemy were detained. At 8 p.m., we again moved on the retreat toward Hillsboro next to the Missouri Brigade, which was in front of the army.

FEBRUARY 9

Reached Hillsboro at 4 a.m. and rested until 1 p.m., and again moved on in direction of Newton Station, and at 9½ p.m. halted 12 miles from Newton Station and after resting two hours again moved on.

FEBRUARY 10

Reached Newton Station at 6 a.m. and at 11 a.m. took cars for Meridian, where we arrived at 7 p.m. and at 10 p.m. left for Mobile on some cars. While at Meridian, I sent out to camps and had my baggage brought and put on train and also had other baggage looked after.[11]

FEBRUARY 11

Daylight found us at Enterprise 20 miles from Meridian. Reached Mobile at 7 p.m. and camped near the depot.[12]

FEBRUARY 12

At 1 p.m. moved out to camp at Halls Mills 11 miles from Mobile on Pascagoula Road. Left our baggage behind for want of transportation. Reached camp at 7 p.m. and had no blankets with me and passed a very unpleasant night of it. It being quite cold and no one had blankets to spare.

FEBRUARY 13

Moved camp ½ mile near a spring. A tolerable campground. Troops had been camped here 2 years ago.

February 14, Sunday

I rode out to Fowl River and saw for the first time pine trees prepared to yield turpentine and rosin. At 2 p.m. received orders to move to the factory on Dog River 6 miles from Mobile. We reached the place at 8 p.m., my baggage and the baggage of the regiment still behind. Am living very hard indeed as my cook and mess box are both at railroad depot yet. Camped 150 yards from Dog River and ½ mile below the factory, or rather where the factory was. It was burned some two years ago.

February 15

At same camp. Had some of the baggage of the regiment brought out.

February 16–21

At same place. Have had baggage brought out and camp laid off and policed. Can hear occasional firing at Fort Powell by Farragut's fleet.[13]

February 22

At dress parade, I made a call upon the regiment to re-enlist for the war and directed all those who were in favor of so doing to step forward six paces and dress on the colors, at which more than nine tenths of the regiment stepped forward. The regiment adopted the following resolutions:

1. Resolved—That we renew our pledge to our country and re-enlist for the war.
2. Resolved—That we will hail with delight the return of peace, if ladened with blessings of Independence; that we prefer war with all its evils to an ignominious peace based on submission to our enemies.
3. Resolved—That we send to our friends in Arkansas, overrun by the foe, this our determination, and beg them to continue to resist the enemy and await an honorable peace, which will secure to them their honor and liberties.[14]
4. Resolved—That, having re-enlisted in August last for the war, on condition that we should be remounted, we now re-enlist without conditions (except to remain as cavalry) but hope that the government may remember our just claims.
5. Resolved—That a copy of these resolutions be sent to the President of the Confederate States, to the Governor of Arkansas, and to our Department Commander and that they be published in the Mobile *Register and Advertiser* for publication.[15]

FEBRUARY 23–29

Time spent in camp. Men in fine health and spirits. Occasional firing at Fort Powell.

MARCH 1–12

At same camp. Received orders to move to Pollard, Alabama, on the 13th at 9 a.m.

MARCH 13

At 9 a.m. left camp for Mobile. Took cooking utensils; tents etc. . . . to come after us. At 1 p.m. the boat [left] the wharf, and at 6 p.m. the cars left the railroad depot on Tensas River for Pollard, where we arrived at 11½ p.m. and got off the cars at depot and built fires and remained for the night.[16]

MARCH 14

Remained at depot during day and night.

MARCH 15

Moved out ½ mile and camped. Remainder of baggage arrived at depot in night.

MARCH 16

Moved out remainder of baggage. Had tents put up etc. . . . Capt. Slaughter and Lt. Lane spent day with me.[17]

MARCH 17

Part of regiments moved to new campground 4½ miles from Pollard.

MARCH 18

I moved to new camp with remainder of regiment.

MARCH 19

All quiet. Received a letter from Hon. A. H. Garland.

MARCH 20, SUNDAY

All quiet. Letters from home. Threatening rain.

MARCH 21–31

About 26th, I received my appointment as brigadier general dated March 12th and taking rank from March 5th; on 31st I assumed command of the brigade. On evening of 26th the band and men of the brigade, on hearing of my promotion, serenaded me. I take charge of the brigade with the good will of nearly every man in it.[18]

APRIL 1–20

Remained in camp 4 miles northeast of Pollard. Nothing worthy of note to record.

APRIL 21

Moved to Pollard and assumed command of the East Division District of the Gulf, having in addition to my own brigade about 1,000 cavalry and two batteries.[19]

APRIL 22–30

Two regiments (1st and 2nd) at camp, one (25th) on railroad, one (4th) at Gonsulia, Florida, and one (39th North Carolina) on Blackwater River, Florida. Nothing worthy of note.

MAY 1, 2, 3

Nothing worthy of note except that on 2nd executed a member of 39th Mississippi regiment for the crime of desertion.

MAY 4

Received orders to move with my brigade to Dalton, Georgia, and report to Gen. Johnston. Several dispatches urging the movement to be made as expeditiously as possible.[20]

MAY 5

Two regiments (1st and 2nd) left for Dalton at 5 a.m. and am busy making preparations for others to be sent forward as fast as they can be brought to Pollard. At 8 p.m., I left for Dalton with part of my staff, leaving others to hasten forward the remainder of brigade.

MAY 6

Reached Montgomery at 6 a.m. and at 7½ a.m. left for West Point. Reached Atlanta at 11½ p.m.

MAY 7

Left for Dalton at 7 a.m. and reached Resaca at 3 p.m., where I found orders to stop with the remainder of my brigade. Two regiments having already reached Dalton.[21]

MAY 8, SUNDAY

I remained at Resaca. The two regiments at Dalton (1st and 2nd) had a fight at Dug Gap and repulsed the enemy with considerable loss. Capt. Henry and Lt. Preston of 1st regiment killed; 28 killed and wounded in the two regiments.[22]

MAY 9

A considerable skirmish at Resaca. The enemy were repulsed. Cantey's Brigade lost some 70 men killed, wounded, and prisoners. I lost none from my brigade; none of it engaged. One regiment, 25th, was on the skirmish line but to the left of where the attack was made, and two regiments, 4th Arkansas and 39th North Carolina, arrived shortly after the skirmishing commenced and were taken from the cars and placed in line of battle, but were not called on to fire a gun. My left rested on the Oostenaula River.[23]

MAY 10, 11, 12

All quiet in our immediate front. The enemy some 3 or 4 miles distant on the Villanaw Road. On the night of 12th, our forces evacuated Dalton. A portion of Walker's division passed over the bridge at Resaca.

MAY 13

The enemy advanced on our front about 1 p.m. and from that time to 7 p.m. the skirmishing was incessant; our loss was small. The two regiments (1st and 2nd) from Dalton joined me. I have command of the line from the Resaca and Villanaw Road to the river about 1,000 yards. I have about 800 men in addition to my own brigade's brave, slight works and am repairing them and making embrasures for artillery; men all in fine spirits.[24]

MAY 14

Skirmishing commenced at daylight and up to this time 8 a.m. continued. The enemy have been using artillery for about two hours and we have not yet replied but are ready and at the proper time will be heard from. Skirmishing continued until 4 p.m. when the enemy advanced and droved in our line and the division commander ordered out 3 small regiments one at a time and without any concert of action, and we drove the enemy back some distance but failed to recover all the lost ground. The fighting continued until after dark and we established our line some 200 yards in rear of old line. I lost in my brigade some 130 in killed and wounded. A. W. Belt Aide-de-Camp mortally and H. Waldrop slightly wounded. Colonel Williamson severely wounded. Heavy skirmishing on our right.[25]

May 15, Sunday

Skirmishing from early in the morning throughout the entire day. Some heavy fighting on our right. Made preparations to evacuate early at night. My brigade was on extreme left and the right withdrew first, which left me to fall in rear of all except Gen. Vaughan's Brigade on my immediate right. All the troops had crossed, the skirmishers were withdrawn and crossed the bridge after it was set on fire. The enemy discovered our departure just as the last of the column had crossed and opened fire on the bridge from one gun. My skirmishers, some 400 men, crossed the bridge under this fire without any casualties. We crossed the bridge at 4 a.m. on the 16th. I remained and crossed with the rear as the greater part of my brigade was on the skirmish line.[26]

May 16

Moved on [toward] Calhoun and formed a line of battle one mile south of Calhoun, where we remained for the night.

May 17

Left camp at 5 a.m. and reached Adairsville at 11 a.m. and camped near town. At 7 p.m. moved in direction of Cassville and travelled all night. All suffered for want of sleep. All in good spirits.

May 18

Reached Cassville at 6 a.m. and camped for the day. At night, we moved into line of battle and remained quiet all night. Ector's Brigade reached here.

May 19

Orders from army headquarters notifying the army that we were about to meet the enemy in battle. Preparations were made to advance on the enemy but learning that he was advancing from Kingston instead of Adairsville our line was changed to meet them and we assumed the defensive. Skirmishing commenced about 5 p.m., pretty heavy and our cavalry was driven in and just after dark the enemy advanced into Cassville. The pickets on my right came in and thus the enemy occupied a part of the town and my men the other part and the pickets' line being at nearly right angles to my line of battle. My skirmishers on the right being near the line so as to connect with those on my right and my left being several hundred yards advanced. During the early part of the night we commenced moving our wagons and building field works.[27]

May 20

At 2 a.m., the army commenced withdrawing and retreating in direction of Etowah Bridge thru Cartersville, leaving men along the works to keep up the appearance of working and left our skirmishers at their posts, with orders to leave at daylight. We reached Cartersville at daylight and crossed the R. K. Bridge at 7 a.m. and moved out and camped 4½ miles southeast of the railroad bridge. The workmen and skirmishers left behind came and reported that they all withdrew in safety and that after they commenced the retreat and were some distance off, the enemy commenced firing on our works very briskly. The bridges across the river were all burned.[28]

MAY 21

At same camp. Our trains moving back toward Marietta. The men all in fine spirits notwithstanding the retreat. All are satisfied that Gen. Joe E. Johnston knows best and all feel that when we do turn upon the enemy all will be well, that victory will certainly crown our arms and that we will have the enemy a long way from his base of supplies and works and will be able to reap more fruits from a victory.[29]

MAY 22

Remained at same camp. Fired off and cleared up wet guns. Men enjoying their rest.

MAY 23

At 10 a.m. moved in southwesterly direction and encamped 12 miles from Marietta and about same distance from Dallas.

MAY 24

Moved at 3 a.m. in a southern direction. Moved some ten miles and camped for night. Rained during the night.

MAY 25

Moved at 5 a.m. in direction of Dallas. The morning cloudy but has the appearance of clearing up. At 3 p.m. moved into position on the Dallas and Marietta roads. Some 2½ miles from New Hope Church. Here the 9th Arkansas regiment was placed in my brigade. It is an excellent regiment and under the command of Col. I. L. Dunlop. It is given to me in place of the 39th North Carolina regiment, which was sent to Ector's Brigade just before going into position here. At 5 p.m., we moved over near New Hope Church to re-enforce Gen. Hood. We arrived after dark and just as the fight closed and we remained on the roadside. Hood had a sharp little fight in which he suffered but little and injured the enemy considerably.[30]

MAY 26

Moved into position at 6 a.m. as reserve, Canty's Brigade being in our front. Some skirmishing in our front and to our right. Some of Hardee's Corps has been moved from the left to the right of the army. Report says that Wheeler burned some 300 wagons at Cassville and the enemy perhaps as many more and that he (W) brought in some 1,200 mules.[31]

MAY 27

Continued firing during the night, but no demonstration. The firing on our right seemed to be some 5 or 6 miles, and that on our left some 10 miles distant. Hardee's troops moved back to the left again before daylight. Up to this time, ¼ before 1 p.m., nothing has been done except skirmishing on our left and some cannonading on the Resaca Road. Men all in fine spirits and anxious for the enemy to attack us here. At 3 p.m. moved to a point some 2½ miles southwest and went into line just about sunset, a little skirmishing in our front.[32]

MAY 28

At 1 a.m. moved over and took position front line near New Hope Church, relieving Gen. Stewart's Division. Some skirmishing on our line; left a line of skirmishers to hold the position we left this morning.

MAY 29, SUNDAY

Skirmishing along the line, some fighting on my left, Gen. Bate's Division I learn. Skirmishers left behind on yesterday came in; some firing to my right and left just after dark but no movement by either party.[33]

MAY 30

Skirmishing along our line. No part of the army engaged today except in skirmish.

MAY 31

Both parties in same position as yesterday. A few men are wounded daily on the lines.

JUNE 1

At 11 p.m., the brigade moved back behind a 2nd line, which now becomes the front line. My right resting on New Hope Church. Left a good line of skirmishers in the old works; destroyed old works.

June 2

Made a new reserve line at night; relieved my skirmishers, the 4th Arkansas, with the 1st Arkansas.

June 3

Relieved skirmishers at 12 p.m. Lost 2 men killed on the skirmish line today from 1st Arkansas.

June 4

At 10:40 p.m. left our line of works and moved back to Lost Mountain. The mud was very deep and it was a terrible night's march, but my men can bear almost anything and be cheerful.

June 5

Reached Lost Mountain at 8 a.m. and moved north near two miles and rested for the day and had an issue of whiskey. At 8 p.m., we moved back to Lost Mountain and took a position on the right of Ector's Brigade, my left resting on the summit of the mountain.

June 6

At 10 a.m., the Missouri Brigade moved over on Ector's right and I moved to the right of the Missouri Brigade (placing 3 of the finest brigades in the army side by side, to wit: Ector's, Cockrell's, and my own). We commenced on our works as soon as we got into position and soon had tolerable works of logs and stone.[34]

June 7

At 7 a.m., we got some tools and soon had good strong works by adding dirt to our legs etc. . . . At 11½, we received orders to move to the right 12 m. We moved to the right of Cheatham's division and one mile south of Pine Mountain and commenced another line of work. My left connecting with Cheatham's right in the timber and my center and right in an open field.[35]

June 8

During last night, my brigade made a splendid line of works and during the day they have cut down the brush in front of the line and made arbors along that part of the line in the old field.

June 9

Still occupy the same line and all quiet in our front today.

JUNE 10

Remained at same place until 5 p.m. when we moved some 500 yards to the right, Gen. Cheatham closing on us again.

JUNE 11

Moved about 100 yards further to the right, Gen. Cheatham again closing on us.

JUNE 12

At same place. Men suffering from laying on cold damp ground.

JUNE 13

Very little firing on any part of the lines and none in our immediate front.

JUNE 14

At 1 a.m. received orders to be ready to move to the right at daylight. At daylight we moved to the right, our division taking position across the railroad and between French on left and Loring on right. My right resting on a battery about 150 yards west of the railroad; our line being about 1½ miles in front of Kennesaw Mountain. We are in works without reserves and Gen. Hood is on our right without works and Hardee on our left in works. Bates' division is on Pine Mountain in front of our line (to our left). Gen. Polk was killed on Pine Mountain at 11½ a.m. by a cannon shot from a rifle gun, the shot passing through both arms above the elbow and thru his body. His loss is severely felt at this time. He was a noble man and an excellent officer. Generals Johnston and Hardee were near him when killed. At 2 p.m., we had rumors of an advance of three lines of infantry in our front but they did not reach us. At night, we sent out and relieved the skirmishers in our front. All quiet on our part of the line during the night.[36]

JUNE 15

Skirmishing on our right but none in our front. The fire of the enemy's artillery crosses my line and to the right of my line, but has not resulted in any casualties.

JUNE 16

Skirmishing on our lines but so far no casualties in my brigade. Cannonading by the enemy on the greater part of the lines, ours not replying.

JUNE 17

Skirmishing along the lines during the day. At 10 p.m., left the works and moved back to the top of Big Kennesaw. I left the 9th Arkansas behind to bring up the rear. I placed my men in one rank and connected my left with Ector's right between Big and Little Kennesaw. I made my headquarters on the south face of Big Kennesaw and about 50 yards from the summit.

JUNE 18

Placed my men in line some 50 yards below the crest of mountain and commenced to fortify with rocks, etc. . . . Could get no tools to work with. Shortly after daylight the enemy moved up and occupied our old works and advanced nearer the mountain. At 9 a.m., they opened on us with a Parrott gun but did no harm, though the shots fell near us, some passing entirely over the mountains.

JUNE 19

Enemy shelled our line today. But one casualty in brigade. At 11 p.m., got some tools and the men worked busily the remainder of the night on their works. On yesterday and today could see nearly all the movements and dispositions of the enemy. We have a good telescope, several field glasses, and have an excellent view of all the country for miles around the mountain on every side, including both armies and Marietta. A locomotive and two cars came down the railroad to Harrison Station. Our artillery fired some shots at them but did them no harm.

JUNE 20

Strengthened our lines today. At 9 p.m., we moved by the left flank and occupied the line just vacated by Ector's Brigade, between the mountains, and at 11 p.m. relieved his skirmishers and spent remainder of night in strengthening our works, still in one rank.

JUNE 21

Skirmishing on our line but no casualties.

JUNE 22

Skirmishing on our lines. Some fighting on our left, on Hardee's lines and Hood's also, in which we gained the advantage.

JUNE 23

Some fighting on Hood's and Hardee's fronts and skirmishing continued on our lines.

JUNE 24

Occasional firing on Hood's and Hardee's lines. Nothing of interest at any point.

JUNE 25
Much as on yesterday.

JUNE 26
Quiet during the day. Almost 5 p.m., the enemy put some 2,000 or 3,000 more men in the trenches in our immediate front. There seems to be a movement of the enemy to our left.

JUNE 27
The enemy placed some 3,000 men or more in front of French's division (on Little Kennesaw) and in full view of our lines. Many indications go to show that the enemy intend to make an attack on our left today or soon at least. At 9½ a.m. the enemy advanced on my front and to my right and left. My skirmishers repulsed them. A part of my skirmish line was driven in but was soon re-established. Maj. Noles of 25th Arkansas was killed on the skirmish line by the enemy's advance. Heavy skirmishing on the front of Featherston's line (on our right) and on French's line (on our left) and also along the front of our (Walthall's) division. Some fighting on Hood's and Hardee's fronts during the forenoon and to Hood's left with the cavalry. There has been little or no change in any part of our lines, and things become comparatively quiet before night. Today's fighting has not been to the enemy's advantage in any respect. From my position I could view the fighting on all parts of the lines.[37]

JUNE 28
But little change in any respect. The enemy seem to be taking care of their wounded from yesterday's fighting.

JUNE 29
The operations here have assumed the character of a siege. Some new batteries open from the enemy's lines occasionally. The shelling and skirmishing, though not heavy, is almost incessant.

JUNE 30
Shelling and skirmishing as usual has been the order of the day. But little change in the position of Sherman's forces.[38]

JULY 1
Usual shelling and skirmishing until about 5 p.m. when they opened an unusually heavy fire of artillery on Big and Little Kennesaw but principally on the gorge between them occupied by my brigade. The fire was by battery and

then by vollies from over 40 pieces of artillery and was truly terrific, [reminding] one of the line, "Then shook the hills with thunder riven etc. . . ." After shelling a short time, the infantry raised a shout and fired off their guns and demonstrations as if they intended to charge, but they did not come. They would sound the bugle then shout and fire off their guns. This they did three times but did not move out of their works. We were being shelled all the time by their batteries. My men were ready and anxious for them to come, but they did not. The shelling continued until 9 p.m. and afterward an occasional shot during the remainder of the night.

JULY 2

Shelling commenced in front of the mountains at 3½ a.m. and gradually extended along almost the entire line of both armies and was very heavy. From my position, I could see the firing from all parts of both lines. Our left was some 5 miles from the mountain and there was some cavalry still fighting further to the left. Pretty heavy infantry firing on Hardee's front. For some time I looked for an assault to be made on some part of our line, but by 8 a.m. it became evident they had no such intention at that time. The firing gradually ceased and by 9½ a.m. it had assumed the usual firing which amounted to several hundred shots (from 700 to 1,400) daily over the line occupied by my brigade in the gorge and some, tho not so much, on other parts of the line. At 5 p.m. received order to evacuate the mountain at 10 p.m., leaving our skirmishers, and they to withdraw at 1 a.m. on 3rd. The shelling commenced very briskly about 6 p.m. and continued until about 8 p.m. and with occasional shots until 9 p.m., when it ceased entirely and there was no more firing of artillery until we had left the mountain. There was but little skirmish firing, which was very favorable for us as it enabled us to withdraw without loss. We moved off very slowly as it was difficult to come down from the mountain owing to its being so rough. We reached Marietta about midnight.[39]

JULY 3, SUNDAY

We reached a point some 5 miles south of Marietta by daylight and by 9 a.m. we had formed a line of battle some six miles from Marietta and at once commenced to fortify. Skirmish pits were prepared before our arrival on the line. At 3 p.m. the enemy commenced skirmishing with the skirmishers of the brigade on my left and shortly after with a rifle gun and continued to shell us occasionally all night. We were busy preparing our works.

JULY 4

My skirmishers became engaged about 8 a.m., and those on their left giving way, all fell back, and the enemy occupied our skirmish line, and my skirmish line was formed nearer our works. We expected the enemy would charge us but they concluded to stop and fortify. They kept up a continual fire on us all day from their skirmish line, which was returned by our skirmishers. There is great cheering in the Federal camps tonight as if applauding some "4th of July orators." I presume they have had an extra issue of whiskey and they all feel patriotic. At 11 p.m., we received orders to fall back to a position near the river.

JULY 5

At 1 a.m., we left our works. Daylight found us only 1¾ miles from the works we left. We moved to our position on the railroad and commenced to fortify. At 2 p.m., the enemy opened on us with artillery, completely enfilading my line, and in a few minutes I had 8 men wounded. But fortunately the enemy were not aware of the execution they were doing and soon ceased firing, and the men worked with great zeal to make traverses and works for protection. I went out in my front and examined the ground, recommended a change of line to a point some two hundred yards in advance.

JULY 6

I again examined the ground in my front and reviewed my application to change my line and urged the division commander to insist on the change, which we had also been urging. Having obtained permission, at 2 p.m. I moved the brigade and took the new position in front of the railroad and at once commenced the work of fortifying. The pickets or skirmishers were advanced some 250 yards and fortified.

JULY 7

Daylight showed my line of works very strong and nearly complete with traverses as the line could be enfiladed. My skirmishers not yet engaged except with a small scout of five, 3 of whom were wounded.

JULY 8

At 2:40 a.m., received order to be ready to move at daylight and to follow Gen. Quarles, who would move by the right flank. We were soon ready and at daylight were moving and crossed on a bridge above the railroad bridge and moved up the river to the Pace's Ferry Road and some mile from the river. We bivouacked and rested. I in company with generals Wheeler, Walthall, and Quarles rode out to view the river in our front etc. . . . We returned at 1 p.m. and I was very tired and hungry, as I had not eaten breakfast. On our trip, we found the cavalry posted along the river and some artillery in position. At points, we have the advantage, and at others, it is with the enemy. The men are cleaning up their guns and are anxious to go to the train and get clean clothes or wash what they have on, but owing to the fact that the enemy may at any-time try to force a crossing, no leaves can be granted even for a few hours. We rested quietly all night.[40]

July 9

At 8 a.m., received orders to hold ourselves ready to move at a moment's notice to meet the enemy at any point he may attempt to cross the river.

July 10

At 3 a.m., the brigade moved back (with division) in the direction of Atlanta and camped 4 miles north of the city. The whole army crossed to the south side of the river this morning at daylight and burned the bridges.

July 11

Army resting quietly and but little skirmishing on the river.

July 12

Men washing clothes and resting. Rumors of successes to our arms in Virginia, Maryland, and Arkansas. The army is in excellent spirits.

July 13

All quiet and no orders to move. Men much improved in appearance by their clean clothes. Had an inspection of arms and clothing and find all in good condition.

July 14

At 1 p.m., I went in company with generals Walthall and Quarles to Gen. Stewart's headquarters to meet Gen. Bragg. He seems to be in fine health and spirits. At 6 p.m., I moved my brigade to the bridge over Peachtree Creek on the Pace's Ferry Road. I placed a picket at the bridge and also at the forks of the road ½ mile from the bridge, one road leading to the ferry (Pace's) and one to Buckhead. In taking out the picket, I was in a very heavy rain and with the pickets got a complete drenching. The remainder of the brigade were pretty well protected by blanket etc. . . . [41]

July 15

All quiet last night. Today I went to see Gen. Wheeler and learned from him that the 4th, 16th, and 23rd corps of the enemy have crossed the river and that the 14th is crossing. This evening I was placed in charge of the bridge over the creek and ordered to be ready to destroy it at any time when necessary.[42]

JULY 16

All quiet on our line and but little firing in our front.

JULY 17, SUNDAY

Went to Commissary train and while there at 1 p.m. heard that the cavalry in my front was being pressed back. I hastened to the brigade and found there was no cause for alarm. That our cavalry had fallen back a short distance but were in a position to hold for the night unless pressed by a heavy force, and the enemy did not seem disposed to press.

JULY 18

Cavalry in our front engaged in skirmishing and at 12 m. were driven back to within ½ mile of the bridge. At 2 p.m., the cavalry came across the bridge, and my detail for the purpose set the bridge on fire. Shortly afterward the enemy came up to the creek bank on the opposite side and we opened fire on them with small arms and artillery and continued skirmishing during the night.[43]

JULY 19

At 2 a.m., I received orders to move to the left and unite with Loring, when I should be relieved by another brigade. I moved my reserve line back some 800 yards from the creek and weakened my line on the right of the road and strengthened it on the left and thus matters stood at 6½ a.m. My skirmishers on the left being connected with those of Adam's Brigade and on my right with Vaughan's Brigade. At ___½ p.m. my brigade except 80 men was relieved by Gen. Gist's Brigade. I moved down to near Moore's Mill, my left reaching 300 yards from the mill from which point to Gist's left being some 3,000 or 3,500 yards. There was a gap of 500 or 600 yards between my former left and Adam's right. I relieved part of Adam's Brigade with 25th and 9th regiments, placing them some 10 paces apart. The remainder of the brigade was resting behind the old gap on the road. I visited my former left, but what was now my right, preparatory to extending a line across the gap, which was in great part an open field. While on the line I saw the enemy passing to the left rapidly. It occurred to me that the enemy were massing in front of the gap in the skirmish line. I started back to place my men in position as soon as possible, but before I reached them the enemy raised a shout and charged, covering the whole gap and extending to the right and left. My skirmish line was compelled to fall back. I moved that portion of brigade not on line at a double quick in front of and to the left of the gap and met the 9th regiment and halted but a moment to form the line and advanced to meet the enemy who were advancing on me and were then not 200 yards distant. The brigade advanced in fine style and drove the enemy back some distance, capturing two flags and 80 or 90 prisoners. I sent for the 15th Mississippi regiment that I had relieved to join me on the left as the enemy were outflanking me. After great delay and sending for it four times (and after it had fortified with rails a line at right angles with and some 500 or 600 yards from my flank) it was formed on my left and ordered to keep dressed to the right, by this time the enemy far outnumbering me had pushed back both my flanks. The center of my line was in an open field and in a good position behind a fence but could not advance. I now ordered the center to remain stationary and both flanks to advance; the enemy were pressed back some distance and suffered greatly from the attacking force and the center of the line, which poured an enfilading fire on them as they retired. I recaptured most of the lost ground, but was compelled to yield a part of it again owing to the greatly superior force of the enemy. At dark I still held a part of my old line and was at no point more than 150 or 200 yards retired. During the night, I cared for my wounded and strengthened my works. We gathered up 102 guns from the front of our lines and could only get those near the line as the enemy's line was not more than 250 yards from us and they would fire on anyone they could see; we also gathered up some of their wounded. (It was a cloudy night and the moon would shine occasionally thro the clouds.) Along the immediate front of the 2nd and 9th regiments 60 dead bodies were counted. I feel satisfied that my brigade alone killed, wounded, and captured more than its number in the short space of 4 hours. With scarcely 400 men I defeated and held in check for nearly 4 hours the whole of Jeff C. Davis' Division of the Federal army and was then helped by the 15th Mississippi regiment. After dark I reformed my line; Gen. Quarles having sent me the 1st Alabama regiment of his brigade, I relieved the Mississippi regiment with it and then extended my line to the Pace's Ferry Road by deploying the remainder of my brigade, except the 9th Arkansas regiment; in some parts of the line the men were 20 paces apart and a part of the line guarded by scouts. Some temporary defenses were placed along nearly the entire line. Gen. Gist's Brigade fell back from the creek, and a considerable force of the enemy were extending up the creek and across the Pace's Ferry Road and fortifying. Thus, matters stood at midnight; every man was on duty and there was no sleeping in the brigade. I lost in the engagement 8 killed, 48 wounded, and 3 missing. Maj. Eagle and Lt. Kirkpatrick of the 2nd are among the wounded. In the charge the line came upon the Yankees lying behind a fence, and they were so surprised at finding themselves charged where they scarcely expected any resistance that they could offer no resistance; many of them were captured and more killed perhaps.[44]

July 20

The enemy continued to fire during the night and until 9 a.m. when I was relieved by Gen. Quarles' brigade. The enemy showed no disposition to advance. I moved the brigade except the 9th Arkansas into the works just beyond, occupied by Gen. Quarles, and placed the 9th regiment on the skirmish line. At 12 m. Gen. Walthall informed me that we would advance on the enemy at 1 p.m. and that my brigade would be on the extreme left of the attacking portion of the army. At 1¾ p.m. we moved to the Pace's Ferry Road and at 2¼ p.m. moved out of the works by the right of companies to the front and at the skirmish line formed into line of battle and at once advanced my right, resting on the Pace's Ferry Road. My brigade drove back the enemy and captured part of his works when, as was anticipated, the enemy came down on our left flank and compelled the line to fall back a short distance (about 100 yards). I directed Major Preston, Chief of Artillery for division, to place Selden's Battery into position and open on the enemy who were pressing my left flank. He did so and soon drove them off, and my brigade continued to hold its position, although the brigade on its right had fallen back and leaving both flanks exposed, until after night when it was ordered to withdraw and the whole army went inside the works. We had been on duty for 7 days and for two nights had not slept; after moving inside the works we stacked arms and, supperless, laid down to take some much needed sleep. My casualties today were 6 killed, 52 wounded, and 9 missing. The brigade as usual acquitted itself with credit, being the only one who held its position until ordered out. So far as I can learn.[45]

July 21

At daylight we were ordered to fall in and move to the right, extending the line in one rank and at intervals. We passed some distance to the right of the Pace's Ferry Road and returned to it and then let the left of my brigade rest some 400 yards to the left of that road. Gen. French's division extending over the ground occupied by the whole corps, except 400 yards. About 4 p.m., the skirmishers on my left were driven in, but the enemy did not seem disposed to advance. At dark, we withdrew and went into position near the city between some redoubts and some 1,500 yards west of the Atlanta and Chattanooga Railroad. My men were placed in 1½ ranks and we commenced the work of fortifying after midnight.[46]

July 22

Daylight found my men pretty well entrenched and all were busy. I soon had a good skirmish line and good abates in front of my line and traverses dug to protect against any enfilading fire. At this writing, the men are in the ditches under arms and ready for offensive or defensive movements. There has been heavy firing on the right of the army for the last hour; it has just ceased. During the early part of the night, I was moved to the right some 400 yards and remained near the ditches all night.

July 23

Moved by the left flank; let my right rest near where my left rested on yesterday. Gen. Ector moving to the left to make room for us. We occupy 216 yards or steps as stepped by Harpin Davis. Still at work on our fortifications to make them strong.

July 24, Sunday

Strengthening our lines by abates and also our picket lines. In response to a call from Gen. Hood the whole army is busy at work. But little firing on our lines. My skirmishers have reduced in number to 66 (11 pits). I have lately been furnishing from 100 to 150 daily.

July 25

Still strengthening our works, which are now almost impregnable against any direct assault. Youngblood's Battalion of Mechanics from Macon and Columbus, Georgia, joined me today. They are 167 strong.[47]

July 26

At 3 p.m., moved by the left flank some 2½ miles to the Lick Skillet and [Pace's] Ferry Road and become the extreme left of our army except the cavalry. We fortified during the night.

July 27

Continued to work on main line and also established and fortified a skirmish line. At 4 p.m., Gen. Bates informed me that he would move to the right the length of one brigade and that the cavalry in our front were being forced back. Also received notice from army headquarters that from indications the enemy intended to attack our left. I held my brigade in readiness for an attack at any time and pressed my work rapidly forward. I allowed the gap in the main line to remain but connected the skirmishers, making a very long skirmish line. Messrs. Trawick and Wages from Chicot came to see and gave me many items of news, the first from Chicot since Smith's Raid. Ruffin and James Hunt and Wiley and John Jones came to see me.[48]

July 28

Continued to strengthen our works during the forenoon. About 1 p.m. Gen. Gholson's Brigade, dismounted cavalry 450 strong under Col. McGuirk, was attached to my brigade; and shortly after we were ordered with the division out on the Lick Skillet Road some mile and a half and formed in line at the Poor House and ordered to charge the enemy who [was] to the north of the house; we did so and drove him inside his works and could drive him no further. We held our position some 2½ hours and then were ordered back. We moved back in good order to the road and then by the left some 300 or 400 yards and built a line of field works out of rails etc. . . . on the road and on the extreme left of all. We remained here until 10½ p.m. when we withdrew inside of our works. The fight today was very heavy and my loss great. I only had in my brigade proper some 400 men (the others being left on the skirmish line) and my loss was 167 killed and wounded. Youngblood's Battalion, 150 strong, only lost nine wounded. In Gholson's Brigade, 450, they lost 144 killed and wounded. Of my brigade Lt. Col. James F. Smith (of 2nd), Lt. Col. Eli Hufstedler (of 25th) were killed and Col. Bunn (of 4th) and Lt. Col. Galloway (of 1st) were wounded and considerable number of company officers killed and wounded. We camped in line behind our old works, leaving them for other troops.[49]

JULY 29

Commenced to fortify reserve line in a.m., when we received orders to move back and occupy the old position in the main line. My brigade was placed in reserve to support the militia who occupied our old line. Sent to hospital to hear from wounded and to have the ball cut out of my horse "Robert's" head. He was wounded yesterday about 3 inches above the left nostril. I have ridden him at Richmond, Kentucky; Jackson, Mississippi; Chickamauga, Moore's Mill, and Peachtree Creek, and on yesterday, and this is his first wound.[50]

JULY 30

About 10 a.m. the skirmishers to our right some distance on the railroad were driven in, which enabled the enemy to place artillery so as to enfilade my line. I at once ordered a new one to be dug, with traverses to protect from shots coming from this new position. The day has been very hot, yet the men all work with spirit. Rumors of a victory in the valley of Virginia.[51]

JULY 31, SUNDAY

Working on our line and its traverses. Occasional firing by the enemy's batteries. Two or three shots were fired at us, completely enfilading our line.

AUGUST 1

Firing from various portions of the lines but no advance of the enemy.

Large working party from my brigade tonight. Making a reserve line across the Chickamauga Railroad. Marietta Road in rear of main line.

AUGUST 2
Light skirmishing along the line. The enemy busy working on his lines in our front.

AUGUST 3
Usual skirmish firing. Continue to send out working parties at night.

AUGUST 4
Some heavy firing on the skirmish line to our left. No particulars.

AUGUST 5
Skirmishing at the salient on the Marietta Road. Are ready to move to assistance of our line if necessary. Being the only brigade in reserve near on this part of our line, we will be called at any point where assistance may be needed.

AUGUST 6
Gen. French's division made a demonstration in our front today. Some firing of artillery by the enemy, doing little or no execution.

AUGUST 7, SUNDAY
Went to cook train southeast of town for clean clothes etc. . . . Borrowed $500 from Maj. Mulherrin. Returned to brigade and at 5 p.m. rode around a portion of our line. The day very quiet. Fighting on our left tonight, may be caused by lightning bugs.

AUGUST 8
But little firing along the lines. Rained during day and prospects good for rain tonight. Working parties every night to work on forts and reserve lines.

AUGUST 9
No change in our front today. Usual working parties.

AUGUST 10
No changes to note.

AUGUST 11
At daylight the enemy drove back the videttes in our front and established a skirmish line. Continued to work with a heavy detail on reserve line in rear

of salient on Marietta Road and ordered to move to this reserve line as soon as I can sufficiently complete it. Heavy firing by enemy last night. Our guns have been firing some today on working parties of the enemy.

AUGUST 12

At 4 a.m. moved to the reserve works in rear of the salient. My right rest on the Marietta Road. From early in the morning until 10½ a.m. shelled the position just left by us, our guns replying slowly. We are busily engaged in fixing up in our new homes. Our position is comparatively safe from a direct fire but it may be enfiladed by artillery. We are making traverses. Called on Brig. Gen. A. W. Reynolds and helped eat a watermelon etc. . . .[52]

AUGUST 13

Strengthening our works.

AUGUST 14, SUNDAY

The enemy continued to shell our lines and the town the greater part of the day.

AUGUST 15

Are making a covered way so as to pass to the right or left as we may be needed. Very little firing on part of the enemy. Our cavalry have gone to their rear, but no news from them yet.

AUGUST 16

Had my horse "Robert" appraised by Board of appraisers and valued at $3,800. But little firing today.

AUGUST 17

Comparatively quiet. Still in the reserve line.

AUGUST 18

At 10 a.m., moved over and took place of Cantey's Brigade in main line. I found his works wretchedly constructed and at once commenced to repair them. Continued to work until 11 p.m., when we received orders to be ready to move at 3 a.m. tomorrow, leaving Gholson's Brigade.[53]

AUGUST 19

At 3 a.m., moved down to a point on West Point Railroad, where Whitehall Street crosses the railroad, where we camped at daylight. At 10 a.m., Gen. Walthall rode up to my camp and informed me that he had a little job for me, that the enemy were making a raid on our railroads in our rear and that my brigade had been called for to go and assist in repelling it. As 160 of my brigade were on picket, the 48th Tennessee, 160 strong, were ordered to report to me, making my whole force about 460 effective. Gen. Walthall ordered me to have the troops formed at once and to call at his headquarters and he would go with me to Gen. Hood's headquarters to receive orders and directions. I went to Gen. Hood's headquarters and he informed me that the enemy had already cut the West Point Railroad at Fairburn and were moving on the Macon Railroad, that he could give me no definite instructions but that I must be governed by circumstances and that I should report to Brig. Gen. W. H. Jackson, commander of cavalry. I left Atlanta at 10½ a.m. for East Point and reached Jonesboro at 1 p.m., and there was ordered by Gen. W. H. Jackson to move on down the railroad and that he would keep me advised of the movements of the enemy. On reaching Lovejoy's, I learned that the enemy were tearing up the railroad track 4 miles below us. We could distinctly see the smoke. I at once put some 25 men on two platform cars and fortified them with crossties and sent them on in advance under charge of Capt. Waldrop and I followed with the main train. About 2 miles below Lovejoy's the scouts reported to me that about 1,000 of the enemy had just crossed the railroad in my front and that they were then only a short distance off. I moved down some 300 yards further, and while moving the enemy opened fire on us. I stopped and got the men off the cars and in line as soon as possible. The enemy after firing a few shots retreated in the direction of Fayetteville, and Gen. Armstrong came up with his brigade in a few minutes and followed them. I placed my men on the cars and proceeded to Bear Creek Station, and found that the enemy had torn up some 400 or 500 yards of railroad track and burned a lumber train. I here received orders to return to Jonesboro, as the enemy were pressing that point. The train moved up toward Jonesboro, Gen. Jackson on the train with us. When within four miles of Jonesboro saw the smoke from the burning town and met straggling cavalry who informed us that the enemy were in the town. Ran the train up to within 2 miles of town and then moved up on foot to within 800 yards of town, where I formed a line, having my skirmishers some 200 yards in advance. My right extending across the railroad and my left across the Lovejoy Road. Scarcely had I taken this position when the enemy were driven back, losing some of their men and horses. I at once had my lines fortified with rails etc. . . . . About 11½ p.m., it rained very hard and during the rain the enemy crept up near my pickets and with a shout opened fired on my line and their main line cheered them lustily and my men answered by deliberate firing from the pickets' line only and soon repulsed them. During the firing, my men would call on the enemy, telling them "to come on" etc. . . . . During remainder of the night there was only an occasional gun fired. My loss in all, 3 wounded and one missing.[54]

August 20

About 2 a.m., Gen. Jackson reported to me that the enemy were entirely surrounded and could not leave town without being fired on. And I was ordered to hold myself in readiness to advance as soon as they soon attempt to leave town, or I should hear heavy firing on any of the roads leaving from town. At daylight, I moved into town and found that the enemy had retreated on the Decatur Road. Gen. Ferguson having failed to fire on them as they passed, as it was understood he should do so. I captured six men who had been left asleep. Gen. Jackson then ordered me to move across the break in railroad (through town) some 600 yards wide and be ready to take the cars to return to Atlanta, he supposing the enemy would at once retire to their lines. Before the train could arrive for us from Atlanta I received orders to re-cross the railroad break and take the cars and move at once to Lovejoy's. I arrived Lovejoy's about 12 m. and in 20 minutes was deployed in single rank at open order and advancing to meet the enemy, who were reported to be rapidly advancing on the depot. When about 600 yards from the depot the enemy raised a shout and charged me. I at once ordered a charge and my men sent up a cheer and dashed forward, routing the enemy and driving them over ¾ of a mile, they making their escape by cutting their way through Ross Texas Brigade. The enemy's line was so much longer than mine (he having some 3,000 or 3,500 men and I having only 460) that he outflanked several hundred yards on right and left, but he was so sorely pressed in the center that he could not use his advantage. Getting short of ammunition and fearing the enemy would discover my real strength, I called a halt and fell back a short distance and threw up some rails and replenished my ammunition. When the order was given to fall back a part of my line was within 75 yards of a battery, two guns, but I feared such success as the battery was in an open field and to take it would expose my strength and also give the enemy the advantage of an open field in which to use his cavalry. The enemy lost 28 killed and quite a number wounded and some 20 prisoners, among them three Captains. My loss was 8 killed and 4 wounded. We also captured some horses and equipment, and 50 or 60 Spencer rifles (7 shooters). This fight shows the immense superiority of infantry over cavalry. After cutting his way through Ross's Brigade, Kilpatrick retreated in direction of McDonough, followed by Armstrong, who came up some hour after the retreat commenced. We gathered up our dead and wounded, and buried some of the dead and placed the others on the cars, and we took cars to be ready to move back to Jonesboro if the enemy should turn in that direction. At dark, we moved toward Jonesboro, where we arrived at 9 p.m., and having placed out pickets and scouts, the greater part of the brigade were permitted to sleep. The wounded were placed in the hospitals.[55]

August 21, Sunday

Found Engineer troops at work on railroad and others fixing up the telegraph. Telegraphed to Gen. Hood for two days' rations, having had none since 19th, and told him of our success. He soon answered that the rations would be sent and for me to stay until recalled. The men got some corn and roasted it and some fruit and potatoes and made out very well until 1 p.m. when rations arrived. Had our wounded cared for and our dead buried and turned our prisoners over. The railroad was completed by 12 m. and my train sent to Macon for supplies. It being ascertained that the enemy had returned inside his lines we, at 9½ p.m., received orders to return to Atlanta; we were soon off and arrived at our camps on railroad and went into camps by 1 a.m. on 22nd and all at once retired to sleep, having slept but little for four nights.[56]

August 22

Left late. Remainder of brigade, 160 men left on picket, rejoined brigade and the working details from other brigades returned to camps. Gen. Quarles and others called to congratulate us on our recent victory, for all were interested and all felt grateful (all our rations come over that railroad). Gen. Hood congratulated me and seemed very much pleased at our success. All look upon the late fight as quite a success on our part. The 48th Tennessee was engaged in the fight and acted nobly as did all who were engaged.[57]

August 23

Sent 100 men to work on fortifications and 30 men to cut brush for abates. Resting quietly. Visited Gen. Quarles.

August 24

Sent some details as yesterday. No important news from any part of our lines.

August 25

No details. All resting. Not much firing on right of our lines.

August 26

Not working any today. The men are having preaching and prayer meetings day and night. At 7½ p.m received orders to move over to the fort on Marietta Street. The understanding is that the enemy have all left in front of our lines from the right as far arrived as Gen. French's lines, or about the center of our lines and about 1½ miles southwest of where the Marietta Road crosses our works. After arriving near fort on Marietta Street we rested for the night. Gen.

Quarles sent out one regiment as a picket on the Marietta Road. The Militia are still in works. Generals French and Loring were to make a demonstration on their fronts at 11 p.m. but from some cause failed to do so.[58]

August 27

With Gen. Walthall rode out toward the river on Marietta Road to within short distance of our former line and then returned on account of rumors of a large force in front of our left. Gen. Quarles went with his brigade in sight of railroad bridge across river. Skirmished a little with the enemy but suffered no casualties. From Gen. Quarles and Col. Young and scouts it is pretty well ascertained that the enemy have moved, then left back across the river at the railroad bridge, and their trains across for some 2 or 3 miles down the river. They seem to be few if any of the enemy on south bank of river and east of railroad bridge. Troops resting; 200 men on picket today and 75 tonight.[59]

August 28, Sunday

Quiet in the morning and no indications of a charge. Went cooking, then to change clothes etc. . . . , took dinner with Major Mulherrin. Just as dinner was over learned that the brigade was at the railroad near Gen. Hood's headquarters, ready to take the cars (except 75 of 4th on picket; the brigade had been specially called for by Gen. Hood); went rapidly to town and saw Gen. Hood. He told me a raid was looked for and I must go to Jonesboro and protect the railroad. Went to railroad and put troops on train and sent horses by dirt road; left Capt. Wilburn to bring up those on picket. Reached Jonesboro about 3½ p.m. and bivouacked on the Fairburn Road near depot and sent Capt. Waldrop back to assist in bringing up rations and the troops. Road around town and vicinity to look at it with reference to defense. Gen. Lewis arrived after night with his brigade. My rations and pickets still behind.[60]

August 29

Uncertainty as whether or not the enemy would move on this place. Viewed the vicinity of the town with Gen. Lewis and Engineer. At 2 p.m., rumor that enemy were within 8 miles of town, and the line having been determined on, we commenced placing troops in position. Gen. Lewis on the right, his right resting on the railroad above the depot some 200 yards and extending around the town, his left near the Fairburn Road and my right connecting with his left and left resting on the railroad in southern part of the town, making a line some 1¾ or 2 miles long. Lewis was deployed at 2 paces and I at from 2 to 4, nearly all at 4. Spent evening in making skirmish pits.

August 30

During the forenoon strengthened our works. At 2½ p.m. I sent a party of 50 men under Maj. Bratton to guard the ford on the river on the road running from the Fayetteville Road near town to the Fairburn Road, the ford being about one mile from town. Lewis was to guard the ford on the Fairburn road and to destroy the bridge when our cavalry should cross. About 3½ p.m. the enemy approached the river on the Fairburn Road following Armstrong's and Ross' brigades and soon were across the river, our forces retreating without destroying the bridge, and I was shortly after ordered to withdraw my force from the river as the enemy were across and moving forward rapidly. I sent at once to withdraw my force from the ford. Lewis also informed me that he had closed up to the right and left about 400 yards between his left and my right. I prepared to move to the right at once to fill this place and while moving by the flank the enemy commenced firing on me and almost immediately afterward and before I was in position, although moving at a double quick; they charged me but were repulsed. They made two or three more efforts but failed, thus matters rested for the night and we continued to work on our lines and the enemy to mass in force in our front. During the night Gen. Hardee and Jackson arrived and Hardee's and Lee's Corps [are] looked for.[61]

August 31

About 3 a.m. learned that Hardee's and Lee's Corps had run into the enemy's lines and had to take another road and would not arrive before 5 or 6 a.m. When they arrived Hardee was placed on the left and Lee on the right. Lewis closed his brigade to the right on Lee and I closed on the Lewis and Tyler's Brigade on my left. Rode around the line with Gen. Hardee to look at ground on which the new line was to be placed. An attack was to be made on the enemy as soon as our troops were in position. Through my scouts, I had reported to Gen. Hardee that the enemy had cavalry on his right and that his infantry line extended a short distance south of the Fairburn Road and was being rapidly fortified. The plan of attack as proposed was for our left to swing round and thus drive their cavalry back on their infantry and strike their infantry at right angles to their main line. At 1 p.m., the skirmishers on the left advanced and the enemy opened on them and they retired and the enemy (cavalry) withdrew across the river at the ford. Soon after an order for a general advance along the whole line was given. My brigade moved forward and took the enemy's skirmish line in our front and held it until after dark; the brigades on our right and left withdrew except some few men who remained with my brigade. Hardee's Corps (we were with it) suffered but little as most of it did not strike the enemy as he (the cavalry) had withdrawn across the river. Lee on our right suffered more, though the whole loss was very slight. In fact, it was a weak effort and we failed. My loss was 3 killed and 23 wounded. After dark, I was withdrawn and ordered to report to Gen. Hardee, and he ordered me to proceed to Lovejoy Station to guard his rear against cavalry raids etc. . . . and to be ready to leave at anytime after midnight. I let the brigade rest in the streets of Jonesboro and saw Col. McMicken, Chief Quartermaster of the army, and he informed that the train to take me to Lovejoy would be ready for me at midnight. At midnight the train was ready and the troops were moving to get on it when the order was countermanded and I was ordered to Lt. Gen. Lee, and he ordered me to move on the road toward Atlanta to be shown me by a guide, and when I should reach the Flat Shoals Road I should picket that until his corps had passed.[62]

SEPTEMBER 1

Moved at 3 a.m. and after some difficulty and having a part of the brigade to take the wrong road, I arrived at the Flat Shoals Road just after daylight and put out pickets as directed and remained until 3 p.m. when Lee's Corps had passed; I then moved toward Atlanta and by order camped between Lee's Corps and Atlanta. Some 6 miles from town, I saw on the road some indications of an approaching evacuation of the city. Shortly after dark, I learned that Atlanta was being evacuated and that I would be left to bring up the rear of the army on my road. I as well as my men were completely worn down and we laid down to rest for the night.[63]

SEPTEMBER 2

We were up before daylight and at daylight moved down the road some ½ mile to take our place in rear of the army as soon as it should move into the road. Two pieces of Capt. Douglas' Texas Battery were ordered to report to me. All wagons and ambulances were placed in my front and I brought up the rear left in front in the following order. The 25th Arkansas to keep the road cleared of stragglers, etc. . . . , then the 9th, then two pieces of artillery, then some 200 yards to the rear, 8 companies of the 1st regiment and some 150 yards farther to the rear the two remaining companies of the 1st Rifles. We moved down the Atlanta and McDonough Road, being exposed to an attack at any time on our flank as the enemy were not more than 2 or 3 miles from our road for many miles. All moved wretchedly slow and just before dark an advance train came into our road and delayed us till long after night, and I halted and let the men sleep for one hour to give the train time to get well in advance. I then moved and soon overtook the train again and passed it; but shortly after, learning that the enemy had been very near the road at that point just before dark, I halted and sent back for the train and ordered it forward and remained until it had passed, which took some two or three hours, and then pushed forward again.[64]

September 3

Just at daylight I overtook Gen. Johnston's Division in camp and received orders to take my place in the center of his division and were again soon on the march without having any much needed rest. When within 9 miles of McDonough I received orders to join my division that had gone to Lovejoy. I moved out on the Lovejoy Road about one mile and let the men rest and sleep for two hours and then moved on and joined division about 1½ miles from Lovejoy, where we camped for the night. Rained during afternoon and night. The enemy are shelling the left of our line, some shots falling in our camp.[65]

September 4

At 7½ a.m. moved across the railroad near the depot, passing over the battle ground of 20 August, and moved out on the "Cul-bank Ford Road" and then took the "Glass Hedge Road" and camped some 2 miles from Lovejoy, where we remained quietly. Sent out 100 men to picket my front, the other brigades being in my rear; nothing but cavalry of the enemy in my front. Saw the Chicago Platform; like it very much. Think it as good as we could expect.[66]

September 5

At same place, relieved my pickets with others. Sent out 50 men on horseback to find out position of the enemy in front of our left as our cavalry could not be relied on to give the information. Rained during p.m. and evening. No news worthy of note.

September 6

Remained in camp quietly. The enemy retreating toward Atlanta. Some of our forces moved up to Jonesboro.

September 7

Moved camp in evening. Some 600 yards west to a good place. A good spring near by and other conveniences and not too close to other brigades.

September 8, 9, 10

Spent time and fixing up camp and making ourselves comfortable. Need money etc. . . . , very much. All enjoying our rest.

SEPTEMBER 11, SUNDAY

A day of rest and religious services in camp and at Gen. Stewart's headquarters by Bishop Lea.[67]

SEPTEMBER 12

Ten days' truce commenced at daylight this morning to let Sherman send the women and children out of Atlanta. Drills etc. . . . the order of the day.

SEPTEMBER 13

Bishop Lea held religious service in camp today.

SEPTEMBER 14

French reviewed his division in a.m. and Loring in p.m. Settled with quartermaster and drew pay to August 1, 1864.

SEPTEMBER 15

Day of fasting, humiliation, and prayer in Georgia and the Army of Tennessee. No duties performed except brigade dress parade.[68]

SEPTEMBER 16

Gen. Hood reviewed our corps at 10 a.m.; all passed off quietly and orderly. Gen. Young to dinner with me.[69]

SEPTEMBER 17

Orders to move tomorrow.

SEPTEMBER 18, SUNDAY

Left camp at 12 m. taking the road to Fayetteville. Commenced raining just as we left camp, occasional showers during evening. Camped one mile west of Fayetteville. No stragglers from brigade. My brigade in front and left in front.

SEPTEMBER 19

Left camp at 5 a.m. My brigade in rear left in front. Loring 1st, Walthall 2nd, and French 3rd. Camped 3 miles northwest of Palmetto for the night, made a long march, but all in good condition and no stragglers.

SEPTEMBER 20

At 5 a.m., moved on Pumpkin Town Road. Halted about 10 a.m. and were shortly after placed in line, the center of my brigade crossing the Pumpkin Town Road. Commenced putting up a line of breastworks, the brigade in single rank. Make a salient angle near the center of my brigade, brigade on the extreme left our line.

SEPTEMBER 21

Fortifying. Rained during day.

SEPTEMBER 22

Rained all day and night. Fortifying.

SEPTEMBER 23

Works complete.

SEPTEMBER 24

Moved into camp about ½ mile southwest of our works.

SEPTEMBER 25, SUNDAY

Regimental inspection, condition of arms etc. . . . , good except clothing which is bad. President Davis arrived at army headquarters.[70]

SEPTEMBER 26

The President informally reviewed the army at 11 a.m.[71]

SEPTEMBER 27

Called on the President at 3½ p.m.

SEPTEMBER 28

No move. No news.

SEPTEMBER 29

Moved at 1 p.m. and halted at works to let Loring pass. Crossed the river at Pumpkin Town and camped 3 miles from the river on the Powder Springs Road.

SEPTEMBER 30

Moved at 6 a.m. and at 12 m. halted on Powder Springs Road 7 miles from Powder Springs.

OCTOBER 1

It is now 12 m. and we remain in camp. A council is in session at army headquarters; at 5 p.m. we called at division headquarters by order and men in fine spirits and eager for an advance of our forces.

October 2, Sunday

Moved at 9 a.m. and at 2½ p.m. we camped 4 miles southeast of New Hope Church and near where we camped on night of 20 or 21 of May last. Rained during night.

October 3

Moved at 5 a.m. and reached the forks of the road leading to Ackworth and Big Shanty, 4½ miles from each place, at 12 m., and at 3 p.m. reached Big Shanty, just captured by Featherston's Brigade, and was at once formed to south of town to resist a reported advance of the enemy from direction of Marietta. The report was unformed and I was then ordered to proceed to Moon Station on railroad 2 miles from Big Shanty (north) and was informed that it was garrisoned by some 60 men. Reached the station just before dark, and before I was aware we were so near it, my skirmishers became engaged. I sent forward 9th and 25th regiments and they moved forward and captured a stockade and 84 prisoners. My loss was 1 killed and 6 wounded. Sergeant Major John Tim Walton of 9th regiment was killed, he was an excellent soldier. Took a good many oil clothes and blankets and a small quantity of rations and commissary. Sent prisoners to Big Shanty and after placing out pickets commenced tearing up railroad track. Rained during night but men worked right manfully.[72]

October 4

Continued work in direction of Ackworth, tearing up railroad. Burned water tank and stockade. At 2 p.m. moved down to Big Shanty and then out toward Lost Mountain and camped 3 miles from mountain. Road very muddy.[73]

October 5

Moved at 6 a.m. nearer Lost Mountain and late in p.m. took position on top of Lost Mountain facing Kennesaw Mountain. Rained during the night.

October 6

Moved at 5 a.m. on New Hope Road and passed New Hope and camped 15 miles from Van Wert. Rained in a.m. but cleared up in p.m. Showing signs of coming fair weather.

October 7

Left camp at 6 a.m. and at 3 p.m. camped 2 miles north of Van Wert. Fair day.

October 8

Left camp at daybreak and had to go 2 miles out of our way to cross a creek that could not be bridged for the troops, and then taking Cedar Town Road we reached camp 1 mile northeast of town. Cool day.

October 9, Sunday

According to orders, prepared for a 10 or 15 days' campaign, leaving barefooted men and baggage and artillery behind. Each brigade carrying one ordnance wagon, one tool wagon, and ambulances. I traded for a two horse wagon for an ambulance having none. One battery to a division and horses selected. Our corps moved at 12 m., French 1st, Walthall 2nd, and Loring 3rd. My brigade in front and left in front. Took the road to Van's Valley Post Office and camped near the post office after dark. Gen. Beauregard reached the army today. We learn that he is in command of this department and Department of Mississippi and East Louisiana. All are well pleased at his arrival. Hood has been gaining the confidence of the troops very much in the last few days. Our destination is so far kept a secret.[74]

October 10

Moved at 7 a.m. with five days' rations of bread. At 4 p.m. crossed the Coosa River ½ mile from Coosaville and some 10 miles from Rome. Army crossed on one pontoon bridge. Cheatham went in direction of Rome and we took the road to Texas Valley. Men in fine spirits.[75]

October 11

Moved at daylight, passing through Texas Valley, and at 4 p.m. camped one mile from Dirt Town, having marched 14 or 15 miles. French 1st, Walthall 2nd, and Loring 3rd, and Quarles, Reynolds 2, and Cantey 3.

October 12

Moved at 6 a.m. and at 8½ p.m. camped 2½ miles West of Resaca. 2nd regiment on picket. Our division guarding train and artillery. French and Loring tearing up railroad north of Resaca. 2nd division of Lee's Corps before Resaca and made a demand for its surrender and demand refused. Rained a little.[76]

October 13

A beautiful morning. Some firing of artillery at Resaca but quiet elsewhere at this time, 8 a.m. At 9 a.m. we moved and struck the railroad between Tilton and Dalton and commenced tearing it up. Gen. French's Division captured Tilton. Cleburne's Division between us and Dalton, and Brown's Division took Dalton with 300 white and 800 Negro soldiers. Continued destroying railroad until 10 p.m., then moved up and camped near Dalton. Men out of rations.[77]

October 14
Moved at 5 a.m. and, passing through Dug Gap, camped ½ mile north of Villa. Now at 4½ p.m.

October 15
Moved at 7:45 a.m. and camped at 5 p.m. 8 miles northeast of Summerville.

October 16, Sunday
Moved at 7 a.m. and, passing through Summerville, camped 1½ miles from town on Chattanooga Road at 11:45 a.m. Am having moccasins made for bare-footed men out of raw hides. It is said they will do very well. I will see. No news from Dixie of a late date, all with us are in fine spirits. Hood is becoming more popular daily.[78]

October 17
Moved at 2 a.m. and, passing through Summerville, stopped at daylight on roadside where we camped for day and night. At 10½ a.m. Federal prisoners passed and camped near us. Saw prisoners to hear from Major Laswell's relative. Learned some news from Wapello, Iowa.

October 18
Moved at 6:30 a.m. and marched 18 miles, camping 3 miles southwest of Galesville, Alabama.

October 19
Left camp at 7:30 a.m. and moved 3 miles on Blue Pond Road and then took road toward Blue Mountain and camped for night 13 miles from Galesville.

October 20
Moved at 2 a.m. and at 12 m. camped 4 miles from Gadsden on Cartersville Road. The whole army to travel same road. Our Corps in advance and our division in front.

October 21
Remained in camp at 8 p.m. Judge U. M. Rose visited us. 72 men in my brigade barefooted and 182 nearly so.

October 22

At 3 a.m. shoes etc. . . . arrived and issue commenced and it was completed at 6 a.m. and at 7 a.m. the division moved. Camped 21 miles from Gadsden on Decatur on Warrenton Road on top of Sand Mountain. Judge Rose left us at 6 a.m.

October 23, Sunday

Moved at 6 a.m., marched 16 miles on Decatur Road 7, camped at 4½ p.m.

October 24

Continued the march on Decatur Road. Camped one mile east of Summit.

October 25

Moved early and camped ½ mile west of Summerville, Alabama, at 2 p.m.

October 26

Moved early. It commenced raining at 2 a.m. and continued until 3 p.m. Came to within 2 miles of Decatur. Gen. Loring was engaged in driving in the enemy's pickets. We used some artillery and the enemy replied. We bivouacked in timber 2 miles from Decatur. Furnished the 4th regiment as pickets or skirmishers who with others from division were to go up near the enemy's works and entrench a skirmish line.

October 27

Relieved 4th by 1st regiment. Maj. Eagle officer of the day. Rode with Gen. Walthall to examine in front of enemy's works etc. . . . , our skirmish line within 500 yards of their works. Capt. Fryer of 1st regiment was killed on the skirmish line today. He was an excellent officer and one of the best hearted men I ever knew. The loss of such a man and officer is irreparable. Moved in p.m., letting left rest on Darwill Road near Gen. Hood's headquarters. Loring occupies between Summerville Road and river. Walthall between Summerville and Danville Road and French between Danville and Moulton Roads and Cheatham on his left.[79]

October 29

Relieved 1st with 9th at 3 a.m.; left of 9th on Danville Road. Clear and cool morning and discharges of artillery reverberate through the woods for miles. No movements on the line.

OCTOBER 30, SUNDAY

Moved at sunrise and camped ½ mile east of Leighton. Troops marched on railroad and train moved on dirt road.

OCTOBER 31

Moved at daylight on dirt road north side railroad, and train on south side of railroad, reached Tuscumbia at 12 m. and camped ¾ mile southwest of town; the quartermaster train that left us at Cedar Town has just arrived. It is reported that 2 divisions of S. D. Lee's Corps have crossed the river at Florence.[80]

NOVEMBER 1, TUESDAY

In camp, making preparations to cross the river. We will travel very light.

NOVEMBER 2

Preparations going forward. J. C. Dugan arrived from Chicot.

NOVEMBER 3

Saw Major Moore and Gen. Walthall on some business. Moved camp one mile to east in good camp.[81]

NOVEMBER 4

Orders to be ready to move tomorrow and to keep two days' cooked rations on hand until further orders.

NOVEMBER 5

Waiting for supplies to come up from Corinth and below.

NOVEMBER 6, SUNDAY

All quiet in camp.

NOVEMBER 7

Heavy rains, creeks up, etc. . . . Heard of death of Senator Mitchel and election of Hon. A. H. Garland to succeed him.[82]

NOVEMBER 8

Rains and terrible roads the order of the day. Supplies detained.

NOVEMBER 9

No movement. No news.

NOVEMBER 10 AND 11
Quiet weather. Cold and windy.

NOVEMBER 12
Reviewed at 11 a.m. by Beauregard.[83]

NOVEMBER 13, SUNDAY
Inspection of brigade at 9 a.m. and orders to be ready to move.

NOVEMBER 14
Moved at sunrise and passing through Tuscumbia. Camped in sight of Florence ½ mile from river.

NOVEMBER 15 AND 16
Working on fortifications.

NOVEMBER 17
Forrest's Cavalry crossing the river. He is in command of all the cavalry in this army. Rumors of the evacuation of Atlanta by the enemy. Went to Florence to see my old friend and schoolmate Gen. Strahl, who commands a brigade in Cheatham's old division.[84]

NOVEMBER 18 AND 19
Our trains and supplies are crossing the river.

NOVEMBER 20, SUNDAY
Moved at sunrise and, passing through Florence, camped 4 miles from town on Lawrenceburg Road at 1 p.m. Road in terrible condition and still raining slowly. No signs of good weather except that it has been bad so long that a change may be expected soon.

NOVEMBER 21
An issue of shoes and blankets and corn. Marched at 12 m., moving 5 miles. The day very cold and some snow.

NOVEMBER 22
Moved at sunrise and camped after marching some 10 miles. Crossed the Tennessee state line.

NOVEMBER 23
Moved 8 miles. Supply trains and artillery behind. 4th Ark. with artillery.

November 24

No rations of head and men living on parched corn. The trains will be up tonight and all will be well again.

November 25

Moved 12½ miles and camped one mile northeast of Henryville. A pleasant day. Trains etc. . . . all up. Rumor of a great victory over Grant at Richmond.

November 26

Moved at sunrise. Camped 2 miles from Mt. Pleasant on Columbia Road. Trains all up. Report that enemy are in force at Columbia.

November 27, Sunday

Moved to within 4 miles of Columbia, then left the pike going to the east until we took up a position 2 miles south of town. Sent out 110 men on skirmish line. My brigade sent out to build works for a battery and also some rifle pits on the left of Pulaski Pike.

November 28

Went to skirmish line before daylight and shortly after moved into town and found that the enemy had evacuated and were on north side of Duck River. Moved men back into camp. Lee's Corps had possession of town and guards were placed over stores, and a niggardly game was being played, so I was informed. Orders at 12 m. to move during p.m. Moved a short distance and returned to camp for the night.

November 29

Moved at daylight and crossed the river 3 miles above town and moved so as to strike the pike at Spring Hill. A long and tiresome march as the roads were in wretched condition. Stopped about 1½ miles from Spring Hill in rear of Cheatham's line. Cheatham and Forrest had a little fight during the p.m. The enemy retreated toward Franklin during the night. We should have by all means thrown some of our forces across the pike early in the night. Then the only escape of the enemy would have been by the Carter's Creek Pike and he would necessarily lose much time and material and men. A great chance lost.

November 30

Moved in pursuit of the enemy at daylight about 1½ miles in their rear. Came up with enemy strongly posted near Franklin at 10 a.m. and after wasting much valuable time attacked him with Cheatham's and Stewart's Corps.

My brigade in reserve for our division. Loring's right resting on Harpeth River. Our line was that of a semicircle and was pressed forward against the enemy's works near town. In pressing forward the line necessarily lapped. Our men moved forward in gallant style and dashed up against the enemy's works and were broken and driven back in wild confusion. I was ordered forward with my brigade and met the retreating forces. I never saw my brigade in finer trim, and when they met the retreating mass they cheered and tried to induce them to return, moving steadily on until within some 15 or 20 steps of main line near the gin house with not an organized force on my right or left. Here the fire became so terrible that we were forced to fall back. As we went out we met the Missouri Brigade going in and they too were soon repulsed. This was the last fighting until late at night when part of Lee's Corps fought further to the left than where we struck. We fell back some 1,000 yards and collected the men and sent a picket line back to the first line of works which we had carried and still held. We rested for the night. The other troops fell still further before re-forming. Many men of the army stopped in the ditch in front of the enemy's work and in their outer line and kept up a fire until late at night. My friend Gen. Strahl and all his staff were killed. Our loss was very heavy; the enemy's not so great. We lost in general officers 6 killed and 7 wounded and one captured. Several other general officers were struck or had horses killed under them. It was the most terrible fighting I have seen during the war. During the night gathered up and cared for our wounded. About 11 p.m., received orders to be ready to renew the attack tomorrow morning. All the artillery of the army, some 70 pieces, were to be placed in position and at 7 a.m. were to open and each fire rapidly 100 rounds and then another assault to be made.[85]

DECEMBER 1

About 1 a.m, the enemy retreated. After daylight Lee's Corps crossed the river passing through town. The remainder of the army lying in line and engaged in burying their dead and caring for their wounded. My loss was ____ killed and ____ wounded, of these ____ commissioned officers. It is now 10½ a.m. and I am in hopes every exertion will be made to press the enemy. Moved at 3 p.m. and crossed the river one mile above town and camped for the night. Gen. Quarles brigade is attached temporarily to mine. Gen. Quarles was severely wounded yesterday.[86]

DECEMBER 2

Moved up to within 4½ miles of Nashville, where we arrived after dark and camped. Rained during night. On Granny White Pike.

December 3

All quiet around our lines up to this writing, 9 a.m. Moved at 10 a.m. and joined our lines near Mr. Gale's house, where we rested until after night, when we went into position with my left resting at northeast corner of the ruins of Montgomery's house, where we fortified during the night.[87]

December 4, Sunday

Was shelled during the day and had 3 men wounded. Corps, division, and brigade commands of this corps visited Gen. Hood by request. He spoke of the failure to cut off the enemy at Spring Hill and said that we ought to and could have destroyed their army and showed by his remarks that he had ordered some one to strike the enemy there and went on to say that if ever such another chance occurred he desired the first troops that should arrive at the point to commence the attack. Also spoke of the fight at Franklin and of clothing and making comfortable our men etc. . . .

December 5

At 2¾ a.m., received orders that French would move from his position on our left and that we would fill up his works. The movement to commence at 3 a.m. At nearly 5 a.m., the movement commenced and was soon completed and had out skirmishers etc. . . . The enemy shelled by line considerably with little loss. At night built traverses and put abatis in front of works. The enemy can nearly or quite enfilade my line from a battery on my left.

December 6

As we anticipated, my line was enfiladed but without injury. At 10 p.m., we left trenches and moved back some half mile. Loring taking our place.

December 7

At this writing, 10 a.m., all quiet on our lines. Same all day. No news from Murfreesboro.

December 8

Made a demonstration with my brigade on our left. Went to within 500 or 600 yards of the river, was shelled a little at one point and I compelled them to re-enforce the skirmish line in front of some of their works. A long and tiresome march, reached camp just after sunset.

December 9

Sent 250 men in p.m. to work on fortifications on Hillsboro Pike. Worked four hours and returned to camp. Sleeted and snowed during the day and we are suffering with cold. I have 100 men who are nearly and some 40 who are entirely destitute of shoes.

DECEMBER 10

At 5 a.m., sent out 50 men on skirmish line and at 8 a.m. 125 men to work on fortifications near Hillsboro Pike. Snow on ground and very cold. At dark moved my available force to a new point on the line on east side of and near the Hillsboro Pike. A wretched place and it is very cold.

DECEMBER 11, SUNDAY

Visited my line and found that the men had been working some notwith-standing the severe cold. Snow still on the ground and not warm enough to melt. Went to cook train to have horse shod and see after the shoe-shop, which I found under way, and I hope to be able to shoe all my barefooted men in a few days. The men are all quiet, cheerful under the circumstances. Men who can bear up under the present difficulties will endure any hardships that my fall to their lot. They deserve and will win their liberties.

DECEMBER 12

Day milder than yesterday. Sent 4th regiment under Ross to William's on Harding Pike "to support the cavalry there." No changes in front of my line.

DECEMBER 13

Strengthening works.

DECEMBER 14

Some of regiment have their works completed. Major Ross rejoined brigade at 4 p.m. with 4th regiment. This is my birthday, am 32 years old today and ought to have been a much more useful man than I have been.

DECEMBER 15

Moved camp some 500 yards and into the woods near Compton's house, and visited Gen. Walthall early and while there was notified that the enemy were moving on our cavalry on our left near the Harding Pike and was ordered to put my men under arms at once and be ready to move with brigade to the hill north of Compton's house and west of the end of our for-tified line, and about 12 m. was placed behind the stone fence on east side of pike, my right resting behind and a little south of the fort or earth work, with Quarles and Shelley on my left. About 1 p.m., I was ordered over to the left in the timber near Compton's house, facing the other brigades. The enemy by this time had taken the hill southwest of Compton's house, were attacking the hill west of the Compton house. I moved rapidly as possible to the works northeast of Compton's and found the enemy there and drove them back, but shortly after they advanced in greater force and, having carried the hill west of Compton's, turned batteries from both hills on men. I had a gap on my right of some 400 yards and on my left of 300 yards. Soon the force on my left gave way and we were soon compelled to fall back, but not until the enemy were in 40 yards of us. Our whole division and part of Johnson's was now falling rapidly back, and it soon became a run and all commands became mixed up and in confusion and many men throwing away their guns, but I am glad to say that but few if any of my brigade was guilty of so disgraceful an act. The run continued across the Granny White Pike. Here Loring joined the route, but nearly all were rallied ½ mile east of the Granny White Pike. Just after crossing the pike I collected all my flags and quite a number of my men and moved on by the flank behind Gen. Stevenson's line, where we stopped just at night about ¾ mile east of Granny White Pike. The enemy pressed us very hard after our line gave way, firing upon us rapidly until after we had crossed the Granny White Pike. About 10 p.m. we moved across the Granny White Pike, near Mrs. Bradford's house (south of it), and formed with Quarles and Shelley on my right and Sears on my left. Quarles' right on the Granny White Pike and Sears' left at foot of hill. Here we commenced to fortify. I lost during day ____ killed and ____ wounded and ____ prisoners. Capts. Mercer and Koouse killed; Capt. Ralston wounded; Major Ross and Capt. Lavender prisoners.[88]

DECEMBER 16

Shortly after daylight I went on the hill to my left occupied by Bate's Division and could distinctly see the enemy in my front in strong force. I could not from my position see either end of their line. The remainder of Cheatham's Corps was on left of Bate. Soon it was apparent that the enemy were trying to turn our left; they soon succeeded so far as to get in our rear and placing their right across the Granny White Pike and still extending their right to the east, evidently making for the Franklin Pike, and were doubling our left back upon us. About 3 p.m., I was taken from the line by order of Gen. Hood for the purpose of trying to check their extreme right. When I reached a grassy field on north face of the hill and some 300 yards to east of Granny White Pike I halted to rest and close up my command etc. . . . , get specific orders from Gen. Stewart. The enemy attacked our whole line in front and to the right and left of which I had been in the main line and were being repulsed along the greater part of the line when, to the surprise of every one, the division of Bate on the hill gave way, and as he occupied the key to the whole line, the whole line from right to left a once gave way and became one fleeing mass of men, and the enemy pressing in hot pursuit. Our line was [at] time of the attack much in shape of a fishhook, the left the point being thrown back and resting on a range of hills that extended toward the Franklin Pike; to the east of our left was a gorge in the mountain ridge, and through this it was necessary for all of Cheatham's Corps to left of Bate's division to pass, and our main line or works just given up on east of Granny White Pike was nearer the gorge than Cheatham's men who had to pass through it. The enemy seeing this pressed across the main line and re-formed and endeavored to cut Cheatham off. I immediately formed in the little grassy field and threw up some rails for protection and drove the enemy back and thus enabled Cheatham to withdraw in safety. I then moved back to the gap and, leaving the 1st regiment in north end, formed remainder across south end and held for some ½ hour and until Cheatham and Ector had formed and moved off. I followed, leaving 1st as rear guard, and when some ¾ mile from gap and just as we had passed a hill that had been covering our right, the enemy were coming down on the road we were travelling and were not more than 800 yards distant, and as my rear regiment came up the enemy charged down upon it and fired a volley after demanding its surrender; fortunately there were no casualties. The regiment returned the fire and moved rapidly on amid the shouts of the enemy, calling on them to surrender and asking, "Johnny Rebs are you going all the way tonight," etc. . . . etc. . . . . I formed the brigades some 600 yards further on a hill round which the road wound and determined to check the enemy if possible and save my rear regiment. The regt. soon came up and the enemy also came pressing on at this time; their cavalry came up on us, and we drove them back. The sun was now down. I left the 2nd regiment to hold for a short time and pressed on some ½ mile further and rested to allow some ordnance wagons to pass and for my rear regiment to come up, and then leaving the 9th regiment behind, I again moved. I moved some ½ mile and came into a road running diagonally across my path, for I was not in any road, and I was at a loss to know whether to take the road or not; but fortunately I had a pocket compass and by the dim twilight I was just able to see the needle and found the road was running northeast and southwest and, as southwest was my direction, I crossed it and moved on. Shortly after crossing the road, I heard artillery in a northeast direction, and it must have been on the pike near where this road entered it. I moved very slowly as my men were near worn down, and when within some ¾ mile of Brentwood I could hear a great noise in my front not unlike that of the runners of hotels at railroad depots, thousands of voices were calling the different commands of the army. I was fearful that we had got so far behind as to be cut off from the pike, so I sent Lt. Cahal forward to learn if I could reach the pike and halted to wait. While waiting we discovered that there was a picket line on our left extending from us. Soon firing commenced from this line, but we were unable to determine the direction of the firing, most contending that the firing was in direction of the noise; if so, it must be the enemy. While talking, the firing commenced some mile to our right, then the firing on picket line ceased and we could see men passing the little picket fires and going in direction of the noise, and soon a dark line could be seen between us and the noise. It was an anxious time. I sent out some scouts in direction of this dark line, but before they returned Lt. Cahal came up and informed me the route was clear and I moved on and struck the pike at Brentwood, where I arrived just as the last of our pickets came in, and moved on in direction of Franklin. Save Ector's, mine was the only organized brigade that was near the left and almost the only one in the army. When within 4 miles of Franklin I halted and rested for 3 hours, until 1 a.m. on 17th. The men were very much exhausted from the day's work and marching through the deep mud. My loss during the day was _____ killed and _____ wounded and _____ prisoners. It was a most shameful and disgraceful route and the first one I had ever seen; it was impossible to stop the men until they got entirely out of sight of the enemy and some of them not then. Bate's division was the cause; after they gave way the other parts of the line could not be held and could not be withdrawn in order. My brigade behaved finely and did themselves credit and the country great service in holding the enemy in check long enough for our men to get behind them and then covered the retreat. We had been given up as captured by Gen. Walthall and others, and we thought several times we would be after we got so far behind all before us; it has taught us never to despair under any circumstances.[89]

December 17

At 1 a.m., we moved and, passing through Franklin, encamped at 4 a.m. one mile southeast of town and near where we formed before making attack at Franklin. Rested until 11 a.m., then moved and reached Spring Hill just at dark, and my brigade was sent out on picket on the road leading to Carter's Creek Pike. My brigade being the only one in division in condition for such duty. Men waded a small swollen stream that was knee deep, but soon had good fires and were quite comfortable.

December 18, Sunday

Moved at daylight and at 12 m. reached the river opposite Columbia and went into position with my left some 350 yards from the river (I was on the left), occupying some works made by Van Dorn in 1862 which we are repairing. Raining during p.m. and night.

December 19

It being believed that the enemy would be on us soon, every one was at work by daylight and by 11 a.m. had excellent works and abatis in front of them, Stewart's Corps only in line. Rained all day and night. Ordered to be ready to move at 11 p.m. but did not move; other troops and wagons occupied more time than was anticipated. The crossing is very bad.

December 20

Crossed Duck River at 3 a.m. and camped where we did the first night before Columbia some 3 weeks ago. At 4 p.m. moved to within 1½ miles of Columbia on Pulaski Pike. Left pickets behind in the works when we crossed the river, and as they failed to get across before the bridge was taken up, I fear they have been captured. Went to Columbia with Gen. George D. Johnston and took supper at Dr. Bryan's.[90]

December 21

No change of camp. Went to Columbia again with Gen. Johnston and called on Misses B. and W. Returned to camp and spent a very disagreeable night as I have no blankets and it is very cold.[91]

December 22

At daylight pickets from my brigade and Ector's were relieving pickets along the river in front of Columbia when the enemy, who had crossed a force above them, opened fire on them, as also did those on opposite bank of river, and compelled our men to withdraw, leaving ____ killed, ____ wounded, and ____ prisoners. I was ordered to form my command, my own and Ector's Brigades, and shortly after the whole moved down Pulaski Pike and camped 13 miles from Columbia, my brigades in rear. On 20th, eight brigades had been selected to cover the retreat of the army and were ordered to report to Gen. Forrest; these brigades were under command of Gen. Walthall. The brigades were Ector's, Reynolds', Quarles', Strahl's, Maney's; Smith's, Palmer's, and Featherston's.[92]

December 23

Formed on hill occupied by me last night, myself and Palmer on left and field on right of Pike. Enemy not disposed to press us.

December 24

Forces moved, my command in rear, and when 4 miles from Pulaski formed on bank of Richland Creek. Other troops some ½ mile in our rear. At

6 p.m. we moved back to hills near Pulaski and halted in Yankee works. Night very cold.

December 25, Sunday

At daylight passed through Pulaski, and Featherston and Palmer formed line 4 miles from Pulaski and repulsed the enemy, capturing one piece of artillery and several horses. In meantime with my own command (Ector's and Reynolds'), Feild's, Maney's, and Strahl's Brigades. I found a line some 3 miles in rear and threw up rails etc. . . . , was ordered back to reinforce our advance troops and moved back some 3 miles and was again ordered to my own. I halted with my own (E and R) brigades and the other troops passed us and it was a dark and dreary night. We reached and camped on Sugar Creek late at night. A number of stragglers on the road, some worn down, some barefooted, and some few "playing out." Here we strike the rear of Lee's wagon train.[93]

December 26

The wagon train commenced moving at an early hour and by daylight had almost entirely gone. The troops were ordered to form a stack arms and rest. They were very much scattered. I was ordered to remain in rear with my command and Col. Feilds; to remain on creek until 4 p.m. and then follow the other troops. While receiving the orders from Gen. Forrest, he received news that the enemy were pressing back the cavalry. I at once moved my force back some ½ mile and formed them near creek bank. Ector on right, then Reynolds, Maney, and Strahl. Col. Coleman commanding E and R. Part of Ross' cavalry still in my front; it was soon withdrawn and put on my right and in rear that he might protect my flank and charge the enemy as soon as I should route him. It was very foggy, so much so that we could not see more than 200 yards. The other troops were drawn up some ½ mile in our rear. Shortly after everything was ordered to move and all was in motion except my command, and I was just ready to move it when the enemy opened fire on us. I waited a few minutes, then returned the fire, the enemy continuing to advance. I then ordered my men to charge forward to a ravine some 150 yards in their front; this they did, routing the enemy, killing and wounding several men and horses. Gen. Ross returned with 2 regiments. I then ordered Ector's Brigade forward and again drove the enemy, and Ross charged them. We captured 16 prisoners, 20 horses, and killed and wounded a number of the enemy, a great many of his horses. I withdrew Ector's Brigade from pursuit and soon took up line of march. My loss was 1 killed and 6 wounded. We camped two miles south of Lexington, my command (E and R) being in rear of all except one brigade of cavalry. At 4 p.m. the enemy had not crossed Sugar Creek. We tamed them a little.[94]

December 27

Moved at daylight, leaving some of the other troops in our rear. The enemy had not crossed Sugar Creek at daylight this morning. Crossed Shoal Creek and formed line on south bank with all the "Old Guard." After dark all were withdrawn except my brigade, and I picketed the creek.

December 28

Half an hour before daylight received orders to move my brigade to the river and my pickets to follow at daylight. Near the river I passed Ector's pickets and his brigade and soon reached river and found that nearly all the troops were over. E and R being in rear, crossed in following order, Reynolds's Brigade, Ector's Brigade, Ross's pickets, Ector's pickets; and when they had passed, followed by a few stragglers, the bridge was cut loose from north bank and swung round to south bank. Two regiments of Ector's Brigade formed on south bank, and brigades moved out one mile and rested until 12 m. and then moved to within 2½ miles of Tuscumbia and rested for the night.

December 29

Moved at sunrise, passed through Tuscumbia, and camped one mile east of Cherokee Station. Day cold and barefooted men suffering very much.

December 30

Moved at sunrise and went into camp ½ mile east of Big Bear Creek at 12 m. Road blocked with wagons and troops. Pontoons not down when we arrived, but were put in shortly after and then trains moved in following order, Cheatham's, Lee's, and Stewart's.

December 31

At daylight trains were still moving and at 10½ a.m. the troops moved and camped ½ mile north of Iuka, troops marched on the railroad. Roads bad and trains got in late. The day very cold.

1865

THE WAR IS OVER AND WE FAILED

By the spring of 1865, all realistic hopes for Confederate independence lay as withered as dried fruit. Joseph E. Johnston, popular as ever among the rank and file in spite of the unkind assessments of Jefferson Davis, returned to command the Army of Tennessee in February. Even Johnston's strategically conservative approach, however, could not overcome the destruction suffered at Franklin or the dwindling resources of the South. Thus, the final campaign in the Western Theater played out in the Carolinas, as Johnston retreated and maneuvered against a backdrop clouded by smoking ruins in the wake of William Tecumseh Sherman's juggernaut.[1]

Determined to see his cause through to the end, Reynolds led his brigade for the final time in the gray army's unsuccessful stand at Bentonville, North Carolina. Severely wounded early in the battle, he lost his left leg to amputation above the knee and spent the final weeks of the war in painful convalescence—awaiting news from the protracted peace negotiations between Johnston and Sherman at Bennett Place.[2]

Although the surrender clearly pained Reynolds as deeply as the loss of his leg, he reluctantly accepted the destruction of the Confederate government and agreed to abide by the laws of the United States. In accordance with the terms of surrender, he signed a parole at Greensboro, North Carolina, on May 2, 1865, and began his long journey home. Traveling by steamboat and rail across much of the war-torn South, he arrived in Lake Village by the middle of June.[3]

With the question of military defeat settled, Reynolds nursed his physical and psychological wounds but wasted little time wallowing in self-pity. During his trip home, Reynolds commented in brief but dark tones about the anticipated nature of race relations and Federal restrictions on former Confederates during the upcoming period of Reconstruction. When possible, however, he tried to find solace in defeat; in addition to expressions of defiant pride in services rendered, Reynolds voiced a resolute hope that sacrifices endured by his fellow Confederates might sustain the Southern people in the uncertain days that lay before them. With these frank thoughts, Reynolds closed his wartime diary and prepared ground for the crops whose harvest would distinguish the next season of his life—Confederate veteran, postwar planter, attorney, and elder statesman of Chicot County.

January 1, Sunday

Remained in camp at Iuka. At night sent my barefooted men, 160, to depot to be taken on cars to Corinth; cars did not come. Very little to remind one of New Year's Day. Men enjoying their much needed rest. Made application to have my brigade furloughed for sixty days to go home.

January 2

Train commenced moving at daylight and troops at 8 a.m. and at 12 m. camped at Burnsville. Barefooted men could not get on train and are making their way here on foot.

January 3

Started barefooted men to Tupelo under charge of Capt. Cooke. Maj. Estes of Ector's Brigade in charge of all from our division. Barefooted men have 3 days' rations and am preparing 3 for brigade from tomorrow a.m.[4]

January 4

Moved at sunrise and passed through Jacinto and camped 8 miles from town on Tupelo Road.

January 5

Moved at sunrise, marched 15 miles, and camped 29 miles from Tupelo.

January 6

Moved 10 miles and found the road almost impassable in 20 Mile Creek Bottom. The greater part of the bottom had to be bridged.

January 7

Moved at 8 a.m. and camped 7 miles from Tupelo on the bank of a small creek.

January 8, Sunday

Moved at sunrise, Loring in front. Camped ½ mile west of Priceville and within 600 yards of where we camped on 8th day of June, 1862, 31 months ago.

JANUARY 9
Moved at 9 a.m. through Tupelo and camped on Pontotoc Road 4 miles from Tupelo. Rainy and disagreeable day.

JANUARY 10
Raining still. Branch between camp and town swimming.

JANUARY 11
Gen. Walthall, Col. Earp, and myself visited Gen. Hood to learn whether or not the Trans-Mississippi troops would be furloughed. Hood could not answer until he could see Gen. Beauregard and hear from War Department.[5]

JANUARY 12
Inspected the brigade; guns in tolerable condition. Several who have joined us since coming out of Tennessee from hospitals etc. . . . , without guns. Most of men have good shoes drawn yesterday, but other clothing deficient.

JANUARY 13
Moved at sunrise and camped 1½ miles southwest of Verona depot.[6]

JANUARY 14–26
Remained in camp, drew a little clothing. Furloughed 79 men and 10 officers under General Orders No. ____, Headquarters Army of Tennessee, dated January 15. Not allowed to furlough whole brigade as I desired. Did not have as many officers as order allowed me to furlough. So in companies that had two officers I granted leave to one and none to field officers; only two with me, Galloway, and Eagle.[7]

JANUARY 27
Moved at sunrise in direction of West Point, troops marching on railroad and sending trains empty. Camped on railroad 2 miles south of Okolona.

JANUARY 28
Moved at sunrise, Loring in front as on yesterday. Camped 2 miles south of Prairie Station on Ewing's Place.[8]

JANUARY 29, SUNDAY
Moved at sunrise and at an early hour camped one [mile] northwest of West Point. Baggage arrived on cars in time and we were soon fixed up at brigade headquarters and brigade drew hardtack etc. . . .

January 30 and 31

In same camp, waiting transportation to Meridian.

February 1

Sent all horses of brigade except four to Marion Station, Mississippi, by dirt road.

February 2

All the infantry except my brigade and 29th Alabama gone below, also generals Stewart, Loring, Walthall, and all our horses to go by railroad. James Shell in charge of my horse Robert.[9]

February 3

Moved command to depot and put them on cars and at 9:54 a.m. left for Marion Station. Passed Marion Station, stopped a few minutes at Meridian, and then without changing cars moved on toward Mobile. Rained yesterday and last night and had a terrible time getting men to West Point depot to take cars.[10]

February 4

Reached Mobile at 3 p.m. and placed command in warehouse west of depot and had baggage that was stored during campaign divided among troops. We have much extra baggage as we lost so many men on late campaigns. Went to theatre with Gen. Walthall and heard the play of *La Tour de Nesle;* Hamilton as Capt. Buridan. Talked with Gen. Stewart in regard to battles near Nashville.[11]

February 5

Remained in Mobile for want of transportation. French's division remains here and we must separate from the "Chubs" and "Jakes" again.[12]

February 6

Left Mobile at 7 a.m. and reached Pollard at dark and have to lay over until morning. Changed all except horses. Left them on same car.

February 7

Left Pollard at 5 a.m. and at 5½ p.m. reached Montgomery. Camped troops at fairgrounds and separated baggage to be left from that to be carried with us.

February 8

Left Montgomery at 8:15 a.m. Left Lt. Hart and 10 men to store baggage of brigade and to follow the command. No rain but a little snow. Reached

Columbus, Georgia, at 7½ p.m. and received a supper given by ladies of Columbus and vicinity. At 10 p.m. left for Macon.[13]

February 9
Reached Macon at 9 a.m. and Midway, 2 miles from Milledgeville, at 4:30 p.m. and camped near railroad depot.[14]

February 10
Remained at Midway. Went to Milledgeville and got 4 yards grey cloth from quartermaster department at $30 per yard.

February 11
Quartermaster arrived and issued clothing to troops, and at 2 p.m. Command moved and camped 6 miles from town on Sparta Road.

February 12, Sunday
Moved at sunrise and passed through Sparta and camped 2 miles from town, having marched 20 miles.

February 13
Moved at 6 a.m. Reached Mayfield at 10:30 a.m., took cars for Camack and sent horses by dirt road and left baggage to be bought by detail. Reached Camack at 2 p.m., horses at 2½ p.m., and baggage at 8 p.m. At 11½ p.m. took cars for Augusta. Gen. Walthall having gone in advance and caused a train to be sent for us. No arrangements had been made for us at Camack. Things are terribly out of joint and no one seems disposed to try and get things right. Most of the officers are now absent, when all should be present.[15]

February 14
Passed through Augusta before daylight and at 8 a.m. reached Graniteville, South Carolina, and camped. Cheatham's Corps is here and will move tomorrow.[16]

February 15
Notice that we may move tomorrow and 5 days' rations have been issued.

February 16
For want of wagons we could not move without leaving cooking utensils etc. . . . behind; but having received preemptory orders, we moved at 3 p.m. Moved 1½ miles, leaving a guard with cooking utensils etc. . . . , to be brought up by wagons on way from Augusta. The movement is considered dangerous

by Gen. Hill. No cavalry to cover our flank. Gen. Walthall is putting himself in communication with Cheatham, who is nearly two days in advance of us.[17]

FEBRUARY 17
Moved 18 miles on Columbia Road by Norris's Store. Camp 7 miles from store. Notice that our army has crossed to north side of river Columbia and that the enemy are on our road at Lexington.[18]

FEBRUARY 18
Moved 27 miles and camped ½ mile from McNary's Ferry on Saluda River. Report that enemy are between us and railroad on north side of river. During night ascertained the report to be untrue.[19]

FEBRUARY 19, SUNDAY
At 2 a.m. received orders to cross the river, my brigade in rear, but owing to delay in Loring's division we did not get over until just at daybreak, and then we moved out one mile and waited for the crossing of our wagons and artillery. Then at 8 a.m. took up march for Frog Level on the railroad. When within 3½ miles of Frog Level we took the road to Newberry and camped at 4 p.m., one mile from Newberry, having marched some 17 miles. Have a pleasant camp.

FEBRUARY 20
Remained at Newberry Courthouse and had 5 days' rations cooked. Went to concert at courthouse given by band of Govan's Brigade. Find the people here very clever and glad to see us here, are disposed to give the men any vegetables etc. . . . they have to spare.[20]

FEBRUARY 21
Moved at 6:30 a.m. taking road to Union Courthouse. Marched 18 miles. Cheatham's Corps just in front of us. Camp 7 miles from Jones' Ferry on Enoree River.[21]

FEBRUARY 22
At daylight took up march on our return to Newberry Courthouse and at 2 p.m. camped 1½ miles north of town.

FEBRUARY 23
Took cars at 6 a.m. and ran down to Pomaria, 15 miles. Camped ½ mile from depot. Wagons and artillery came [by] dirt road. Rumors of enemy's scouts near Cheatham's Corps here.[22]

February 24
Quiet in camp. No news.

February 25
Had 3 days' rations cooked.

February 26, Sunday
Moved at 12 m. and camped in Columbia and Buncombe Road 12 miles from Pomara. Troops had to wade a creek near camp. Recent rains have made roads very muddy.

February 27
Moved at daylight and reached Jones's Ferry on the Enoree River at 3 p.m. Not able to cross this evening.

February 28
Crossed the brigade about 4½ p.m. but I remained behind to see the wagons and artillery of division over the river. The ferryboat got loose last night and was lost and they are now making a new one, which must be completed before we can cross the river. Received pay to November.

March 1, Wednesday
Remained in camp until late in p.m. and moved down to the river with wagons and artillery, but did not get them over till after dark. It was 11 p.m. when I reached camp 1 mile from river and where brigade camped last night. Brigade moved to Union Courthouse, leaving camp at 10 a.m.

March 2
I moved with artillery and train at sunrise and reached camp near Union Courthouse at 3 p.m. Command are cooking. Are to have four days' [rations] from tomorrow morning.

March 3
Moved at sunrise, crossed Broad River, and camped 3 miles from river and 15 miles from Chester Courthouse. The roads are and have been for several days past in a wretched condition and still raining. The portion of country through which we have passed in South Carolina is very much worn out, but the people seem to be in good circumstances and are all in fine spirits. They feel that the country is being overrun by the enemy, but they have confidence in our ability to conquer an honorable peace with Independence as no peace could be honorable without separation.

March 4

Moved at sunrise. My brigade in front of our whole force of Stewart's and Cheatham's Corps. Reached Chester at 1 p.m. and camped ½ mile south of the town.

March 5

At 2½ p.m. took train for Charlotte, North Carolina. Rain occasionally and slowly during the night.[23]

March 6

Reached Charlotte at 4 a.m. and at 11½ a.m. left for Salisbury. It is slow business travelling on (train) railroad.[24]

March 7

Reached Salisbury, North Carolina, at 3½ a.m. and drew and cooked five days' rations of meal and bacon, including yesterday.

March 8

At 11 a.m., sent 1st and 4th regiments on toward Raleigh. I remained with the balance of the brigade. Gen. Walthall went on with 1st and 4th and the other brigades. Two brigades now in one.

March 9

Took train at 11 a.m. with balance of brigade, being the rear of Stewart's Corps. Lt. A. G. Moore gave us a splendid basket supper at the station at Thomasville.[25]

March 10

Reached Raleigh at 5 p.m. and moved on same train in direction of Goldsboro, North Carolina.[26]

March 11

Reached Goldsboro at 4 a.m. and were ordered into camp to wait for the command to join us from Kinston as they are now retreating toward this place. Are removing stores etc. . . . from Goldsboro to Raleigh. Gen. Bragg in town. Hampton defeated Kilpatrick near Fayetteville on yesterday. Had a little fighting at Kinston on yesterday. My regiment not in time to be in it. Not much fighting.[27]

March 12, Sunday

A beautiful day and order and quiet being in Goldsboro at this 9 a.m. The troops of our corps arrived at 12 m. and went into camp west of the town. The removal of stores still continues. Nearly all good.

MARCH 13
At 4 p.m., marched toward Smithfield. Marched 8 miles. Lee's Corps first and ours next.

MARCH 14
Moved at 7½ a.m. and at 2½ p.m. camped near railroad depot 3 miles north of Smithfield. The country poor, roads pretty good.

MARCH 15
At 4 p.m., moved through Smithfield and camped on a road leading to Raleigh, though not the direct one, and some 3 miles from town. Gen. Johnston passed us while on the march and before we arrived at Smithfield. He seems and says he is in excellent health. The troops cheered him as he passed. It is the first time we had seen him since his removal in July last. It has been raining during p.m. and continues tonight.[28]

MARCH 16 AND 17
Had three days' rations cooked and in haversacks. Weather clearing.

MARCH 18
Shortly after 8 a.m. moved, and reached Bentonville at 5½ p.m. Orders to make no noise in camp. The enemy are near us.

MARCH 19
At 8 a.m., moved out some 2½ miles from town, where we were just in the act of going into position in line of battle when I was wounded by a cannon shot. It entered my horse's breast and came out under my left leg, cutting away my stirrup and breaking my leg just below the knee and tearing off a great part of the calf of the leg, and then killed a horse standing next to mine. My horse reared up, and taking my right foot out of the stirrup, with my hands I threw myself out of the saddle, falling on the dead horse, the blood from my horse's side spurting over me, and fearing my horse would fall on me, I, by aid of a bush, got out in front of him, the noble animal still standing though a stream of blood larger than my arm was gushing from his breast. Fearing he might fall forward on me, I called for help, but it was already there; my litter bearers, seeing me fall, had come running, and putting me on a litter, carried me a short distance, and then put me on an ambulance and carried me to Bentonville. Here had my leg amputated just above the knee, the operation

was performed by Dr. John T. Darby, Medical Director, Army of Tennessee, assisted by my own surgeons and others. My orderly, V. King, got my saddle and bridle and brought them off the field. During p.m., the brigade with other parts of the army engaged the enemy and drove him back some distance, driving him out of works. The brigade acted with great gallantry and won the praise of all who beheld the charge. The brigade went in with 178 guns and the loss was 41 killed and wounded.[29]

MARCH 20
At 8 a.m., was placed in an ambulance to be carried to Smithfield Railroad Depot. The roads were wretchedly bad and I had a terrible day of it. I reached the depot shortly after dark and was at once placed on cars for Raleigh at 11½ p.m., and after some delay was taken to the officer's hospital in Dr. Haywood's house on Capitol Square. It was 1½ a.m. on 21st before I was taken from my litter and placed on a bed. It was a day of great suffering to me.[30]

MARCH 21
After I got on my bed I took a short nap and felt a little refreshed in the morning. Had my wound dressed for the first time. It was quite painful.

MARCH 22–31
Citizens kind and attentive. Wound frequently very painful but is doing very well. Was quite unwell for four or five days but am in good health now. Have a great many invitations to go to private houses as soon as I am able to be moved. Gen. Beauregard has visited me, and many of the people and officers of the town, in fact I received every attention I could desire. Dr. Price, Capt. Ragland, and Vol. King are with me.[31]

APRIL 1
Nothing of note.

APRIL 2
Doing very well. Wound painful but healing rapidly.

APRIL 3–7
No changes. My wound doing well but quite painful at times.

APRIL 8–12
Remained in hospital. Very kindly treated by citizens. Preparation going forward indicating an evacuation of Raleigh soon. On 9th my brigade was

consolidated into one regiment. Bunn, Eagle, and Wells being the field officers. Our army commenced retreating from Smithfield in direction of Raleigh on 10th in p.m. and passed through Raleigh on the 11th with the advance. On 12th I was placed on cars to be carried west. Left Raleigh at 3 p.m. and run up to Morrisville and "laid over" until 13th as the engine had to return to Raleigh to bring up another train.[32]

APRIL 13

At 12 m., after threats were made to kill the conductor if we should fall in hands of the enemy and when the enemy were within one mile of us, we were moved on in direction of Greensboro. My wound doing tolerable well. We moved up to within five miles of Hillsboro and "laid over."[33]

APRIL 14

Reached Hillsboro at 8 a.m. and was put on a car by myself, having only my party with me. We passed Haw River and Mr. Thomas Hole brought me out a very nice lunch and a bottle of fine brandy. We passed "Company Shops" and "laid over" again 8 miles from Greensboro.[34]

APRIL 15

Reached Greensboro at 12 m. and was taken to the house of Maj. James E. Sloan, [P.]A.C.S. My trip has irritated my wound a little, but it is still doing very well, and I am gaining strength. Russ Evans came in to see me and I learned that my grey team was near town and that he also had an ambulance; these I ordered him to bring to me, that I may be ready to go on with the army tomorrow; by 10 p.m. wagon and ambulance were ready.[35]

APRIL 16, SUNDAY

Army resting, camps near Greensboro, North Carolina, and Gen. Johnston gone to Hillsboro to meet Gen. Sherman. Many rumors afloat in regard to surrender of the army etc. . . . etc. . . . All in the dark yet.

APRIL 17

Army still in camp. Rumors more rife, if possible, than on yesterday. My wound is doing very well and I am very kindly treated by Mr. Sloan and family.

APRIL 18

Army resting and rumors flying and some few men leaving. Nothing definite yet; suspense painful.

April 19

Gen. Johnston returned. A truce agreed upon. Negotiations for peace pending. Lincoln's death by assassination announced by Sherman in orders etc. . . . Things more quiet but much anxiety as to what may become of us.[36]

April 20

Major Generals Walthall, Anderson, and Brown called to see me and told me of the terms of settlement between the U.S. and C.S. as proposed by generals Sherman and Johnston. Rumors are not rife as during the past few days and things are becoming quiet, and all seemed disposed to wait patiently to see what will be done by the two governments. I had a terrible spell with my wound this evening; the muscles commenced contracting and for more than an hour the pain was so intense that I was compelled to yield to "cries of pain"; later in the night it got more quiet and I slept well. Maj. Elstner, my old quartermaster, arrived. He has been transferred to the Trans-Mississippi Department.[37]

April 21

Nothing worthy of note.

April 22

Gen. Joseph E. Johnston called to see me. He looks to be in good health and spirits. Did not speak of public affairs.

April 23, Sunday

Nothing worthy of note.

April 24

My old brigade came into town on its way to Jamestown to guard some stores etc. . . . Many of them called in to see me. Just after night, I heard that Gen. Johnston had received notice that the truce would terminate at 11 a.m. on the 26th inst. It was quite a surprise as all had settled in the conclusion that we would have peace. Serenaded.[38]

April 25

Army getting ready to move. I still have my wagon and ambulance but have concluded to remain here as I would no doubt suffer very greatly in attempting to travel in an ambulance. Many views of opinions as to cause of the rejection of peace terms and as to what is to be in store for this people in future. Counsel at army headquarters.

April 26

After 11 a.m., the troops moved through town and camped on southwest side some four miles from town. Gen. Johnston has gone to have another interview with Gen. Sherman. Rumor of an extension of truce and that further negotiations are pending. Gen. Walthall called to see me.[39]

April 27

It has been creditably announced that terms have been agreed upon by generals Sherman and Johnston. Terms not generally known but will be published to the army soon.

April 28

Arrangements going on to carry out the terms of the Military Convention between generals Sherman and Johnston. Artillery being packed etc. . . . etc. . . .

April 29

Sent my headquarters wagon to regiment to be used in hauling baggage etc. . . . Sent off all my baggage except trunk, blankets, and overcoat. Am waiting to know when army will be paroled and move etc. . . . I obtained money from my old brigade. They had been omitted by someone when estimate was made for the brigade to which it is attached.

April 30, Sunday

My wound is doing finely and is almost healed up. I hope to be able to get on my crutches this coming week. Some Yankee officers came up and were billeted on the citizens.

May 1, Sunday

Paroling of the army commenced on today. Weather fine. Some rumors of our paroled officers in Virginia being grossly mistreated by the Yankee government. I hope it is not so. Our distracted country needs some repose.

May 2

Paroling continued. The troops will move soon. One regiment of Yankees arrived to garrison this town.

Greensboro, North Carolina

May 2nd, 1865

In accordance with the terms of the Military Convention entered into on the twenty-sixth day of April 1865 between General Joseph E.

Johnston, commanding the Confederate Army, and Major General W. T. Sherman, commanding the United States Army in North Carolina, Brig. Gen. D. H. Reynolds, P.A.C.S., has given his solemn obligation not to take up arms against the Government of the United States until properly released from this obligation; and is permitted to return to his home, not to be disturbed by the United States authorities so long as he observes this obligation and obey the laws in force where he may reside.

M. H. Cofer, Colonel, C.S.A.,[40]

Commanding.

Wm. Hartsuff,[41]

Brevet Brig. Gen. and A.I.G.

U.S.A. Special Commissioner.

MAY 3

The army took up its march to their respective states preparatory to being disbanded, and all the unfinished business of the army is being dispatched as rapidly as possible that all may return to their once happy homes.

MAY 4

Officers of the army leaving, nearly all the army gone. My wound doing very well.

MAY 5

Am doing very well but am getting lonesome. Dr. Price gone to Danville.[42]

MAY 6

All moving on quietly. Am disgusted with the way the U.S. troops conduct themselves, especially the cavalry.

MAY 7

Wound doing well. It is seven weeks today since I was wounded.

MAY 8

Improving. Commenced walking on my crutches. Only took a few steps. Am very weak yet and had a person near me to prevent my falling.

MAY 9

Continued my walking and feel somewhat improved. Dr. Price returned. Cool and pleasant today.

May 10

Saw Kilpatrick, the Yankee general that I defeated at Lovejoy Station, Georgia, on August 20th last. Walked through the house several times and then out through the yard twice and down to the garden, walking in all some 700 yards or more.

May 11, Thursday

Improving rapidly in strength and walking etc. . . . Had set 15th instant as the day on which we will start home.

May 12

Walked some half mile or more and am gaining strength daily. Think will be able to stand my coming trip finely. My wound is almost entirely healed, only one abscess that still runs a little.

May 13

A fine morning, had an excellent night's rest last night. We are now in the midst of the "cold spell in May" and fires are quite comfortable.

May 14, Sunday

I walk a little daily and find I am getting strength very rapidly. Weather is quite pleasant today.

May 15

At this writing, 10 a.m., am ready to take the cars for Danville, Virginia, on my way to Arkansas. Get off at 4 p.m. At 5½ p.m., left Greensboro and reached Danville at 11:30 p.m. and then went into cars on the R.L.D. Railroad.[43]

May 16

At daylight found we were in wrong car and changed and at 5:20 a.m. left and reached Burksville at 12 m. and 6 p.m. left for Richmond. Was in much anxiety for some time for fear our car would not be taken, and we could not find out for certain until late in p.m. It was amusing to watch those interested in our train going. We are in the same car that President Davis occupied when he left Richmond at the evacuation.

May 17

Reached Manchester across the Prairie River from Richmond at 3 a.m. Put up at the "Powhatan House."[44]

May 18, Thursday

Left Richmond at 6 a.m. and reached Chadwell 3 miles from Charlottesville at 3 p.m. and then rode to town in a wagon. The railroad bridge over Ruaima River has not been rebuilt since it was destroyed by the enemy some 8 weeks ago. Went with Dr. Price to his sister's (Miss Nancy), who is living at the University, having been compelled to leave home by the Yankees.[45]

May 19

Spent the day at Miss Nancy's. Rained some during day.

May 20, Saturday

At Miss Nancy's. Showers during day. Several ladies came in p.m. and we had music etc. . . . , time is passing away very pleasantly. I am anxious to know my fate, so far as it is to be decided by the Federal government. I hear that President Johnson has under consideration a new Amnesty Proclamation. Will I be included or excluded is the important question. Negroes free by proclamation in Virginia.[46]

May 21, Sunday

The day has been showery and warm. The crops are growing finely. The University grounds and the surroundings are beautiful.

May 22–28, Sunday

Spent the week at the house of Miss Nancy. Went to table at the Jefferson Hall on evening of 23rd. A nice affair. Intended to start home on tomorrow.[47]

May 29

Left Charlottesville early and reached Richmond at 5 p.m. and stopped at the "Powhatan House."

May 30

Left Richmond at 6 a.m. on *M. Martion* and reached Fortress Monroe at 2 p.m. and at 5 p.m. left for Baltimore on the steamer *Louisiana*. Richmond sightseers on board, from Boston.[48]

May 31

Reached Baltimore at 6 a.m. and stopped at the Fountain House and at 4:25 p.m. took cars for Philadelphia, which place we reached at 9:30 p.m. and took rooms at the Continental Hotel, room No. 230.[49]

June 1, Thursday

The day set apart by President of U.S. for fasting, humiliation, and prayer, on account of the death of the late President of the U.S., Mr. A. Lincoln.[50]

June 2

Went to see Dr. Palmer and engaged an artificial leg from him. He is to send it by Express to Memphis. I paid him for it ($150) one hundred and fifty dollars. Dr. Price went with me. The leg to be done in a month or six weeks.[51]

June 3

Left Philadelphia at 6 p.m. for New York, where we arrived at 10½ p.m. and stopped at St. Nicholas Hotel, room B.[52]

June 4, Sunday

Visited Central Park; it is a beautiful place. Many people in park. Fine turnouts, etc. . . . , etc. . . . At night wrote some letters.

June 5

At 6 p.m. left on New York and Erie Railroad for Dunkirk. Could not get into sleeping cars, all taken. Fare from New York to St. Louis $35.90.[53]

June 6

Reached Burghampton at daylight. Here Maj. Smith stopped over to see some relatives.[54]

Reached Dunkirk at 1:30 p.m. and took cars for Cleveland, where we arrived at 9:30 p.m. and took cars for Crestline.

June 7

Reached Crestline at 1:30 a.m. and took the Indianapolis train. Reached Indianapolis at 1:30 p.m. and left for Terre Haute. Reached Terre Haute at 6 p.m. and without a change of cars went on to St. Louis.

June 8

Reached St. Louis at 1:30 a.m. and stopped at Lindell Hotel, room 295. A fine hotel but poorly kept. Weather quite warm.[55]

June 9

At 3½ p.m. took passage on *Belle Memphis* for Memphis, fare $17. Smith has not overtaken us yet.[56]

At 5 p.m. the steamer left the wharf. A sorry looking set of passengers, reminding me of birds of prey hunting down the now prostrate South. The

Negro deck hands sung a song as the flag of U.S. was raised when the boat started out. The Negroes are fit supporters for the flag that is now an emblem of tyranny and oppression.[57]

JUNE 10

Moved slowly down the river and at 12 m. reached Cairo, where we remained until 6 p.m.

At New Madrid my friend and surgeon Dr. R. A. Price parted with me. He had remained with me from time I was wounded and had done all in his power as a surgeon and friend. God bless him.

JUNE 11

Arrived at Memphis at 8 p.m. and owing to rain etc. . . . , I remained on steamer all night.

JUNE 12

Breakfast on steamer and then went to Gayoso House, room 282. Met some old friends and acquaintances and heard from Chicot County.[58]

JUNE 13

Number of friends called on me. At 4 p.m. went on steamer *Bostonia* and at 6 p.m. left Memphis on her for Chicot County.[59]

JUNE 14

The country on both sides of the river has been desolated by the U.S. forces. Reached Sunnyside, Chicot County, about 11 p.m. Mr. C. W. Saunders came on steamer with me. I rested on some sacks of oats and corn; sat off by the boat for a time, waiting for conveyance.[60]

JUNE 15

Mr. C. W. Saunders went up to Caughey's (the Sunnyside House) and got a wagon and sent for his buggy. I went home with Mr. Saunders (to the Bass Place) and slept during the a.m. and at 3 p.m. came up to Mr. Diamond's (the Robinson place) and about sundown crossed over to Lake Village.[61]

Today is the anniversary of my arrival in Lake Village to settle in 1858; just seven years and to me some of them very eventful. I stopped with Mr. [John] Hunnicutt, who was keeping hotel and with whom I boarded before leaving for the army.[62]

The war is over and we failed. I have many things to regret and many things to be proud of, but of none am I prouder than that of having commanded

"Reynolds's Arkansas Brigade" and nothing do I regret so much as the loss of our cause. We lost many noble men, but those who did their duty like men will ever be held in grateful remembrance by their relatives and friends, and by the friends of constitutional liberty everywhere. Peace to their ashes.

APPENDIX

Camp near Greensboro,
    May 3, 1865
My dear General,

    I am about to move and have to go without seeing you. I expected to see you yesterday, but was so occupied I could not do so, though I went to town mainly for that purpose. I had a thousand things to do after I got there and found I had staid my time out without getting through. I hope you may soon be restored, and that you will write to me from time to time how you are getting on. I will always feel great interest in you wherever you may be, and trust you will not fail to write to me.

    I write in haste mainly to say goodbye.

    Your friend truly and sincerely,

    E. C. Walthall

NOTES

INTRODUCTION

1. D. H. Reynolds describes his reaction to the end of the war and service with the Arkansas Brigade in his entry for June 15, 1865. *Biographical and Historical Memoirs of Southern Arkansas* (Chicago: Goodspeed Publishing Company, 1890), 1084.

2. Born in 1771 in Loudon County, Virginia, Reynolds's paternal grandfather, William Reynolds, died in 1824 in Knox County, Ohio. Born in 1773 in Loudon County, Virginia, his paternal grandmother, Rebecca (Harris) Reynolds, died in 1840 in Knox County. Born in 1783 in Baltimore County, Maryland, his maternal grandfather, James Houck, died in 1833 in Knox County. Born on October 2, 1784, in Frederick County, Virginia, his maternal grandmother, Sarah (Shadley) Houck, died in Knox County sometime in the 1860s. Born on January 16, 1801, in Loudon County, Virginia, his father, Amos Reynolds, died in Knox County on March 26, 1850. Born on April 25, 1808, in Muskingum County, Ohio, his mother, Sophia (Houck) Reynolds, died in Knox County on September 14, 1849. In 1820, Amos Reynolds lived in Huron County, Ohio, and James Houck lived in Knox County. By 1840, Amos Reynolds lived in Hillar Township in Knox County with his wife, Sophia, five sons and two daughters. Reynolds-Wallace Genealogy, Daniel Harris Reynolds Papers, University Libraries, Fayetteville, Box 1, Folder 6, Item 115 (hereafter cited as DHR Papers); Bureau of the Census, *Fourth Census of the United States, 1820* (Washington, DC: National Archives and Records Administration, 1820), M33–88, 82A, and 94; Bureau of the Census, *Sixth Census of the United States, 1840* (Washington, DC: National Archives and Records Administration, 1840), M704–406, 262; *Biographical and Historical Memoirs of Southern Arkansas,* 1062; Robert Patrick Bender, "Daniel Harris Reynolds," in *Arkansas Biography: A Collection of Notable Lives,* ed. Nancy A. Williams and Jeannie M. Whayne (Fayetteville: University of Arkansas Press, 2000), 239–40.

3. No graduation record exists for Reynolds or Strahl, but the Registrar's Office at Ohio Wesleyan University lists both men in its records for 1850 through 1854. Reynolds joined Hiram Lodge No. 18 in 1853 and attained the rank of thirty-third-degree Mason. He moved to Louisa County, Iowa, in 1854 and to Somerville in Fayette County, Tennessee, in 1857. Beth Beach (Registrar's Office, Ohio Wesleyan University) to Robert Patrick Bender, July 16, 2009, in possession of the editor; *Biographical and Historical Memoirs of Southern Arkansas,* 1062, 1083–85; Bender, "Daniel Harris Reynolds," 239–40.

4. Bureau of the Census, *Eighth Census of the United States, 1860* (Washington, DC: National Archives and Records Administration, 1860), M653–38, 919; *Biographical and Historical Memoirs of Southern Arkansas,* 1062, 1083–85; Bender, "Daniel Harris Reynolds," 239–40; Willard B. Gatewood, "The Arkansas Delta: The Deepest of the Deep South," in *The Arkansas Delta: Land of Paradox,* ed. Willard B. Gatewood and Jeannie M. Whayne (Fayetteville: University of Arkansas Press, 1996), 15; Donald Holley, "The Plantation Heritage: Agriculture in the Arkansas Delta," in *The Arkansas Delta,* 244–45.

5. Reynolds made at least nine public speeches between January 12 and 25, 1861, at "Lake Village, P. P. Bunch's estate, the Masonic Hall, Grand Lake, Lynch's estate, Jesse Hill's estate, Columbia, Gaines Landing, and Mrs. Bowie's estate." Isaac H. Hilliard, a North Carolina–born planter who lived in Louisiana Township in Chicot County and owned 125 slaves in 1860, served as the county's sole delegate. After the war, Reynolds recounted his antebellum political beliefs and activities in applications for presidential pardon. Reynolds to Andrew Johnson, August 21, 1865, and January 15, 1866, DHR Papers, Box 1, Folder 5, Items 108 and 109; *Chicot Press* (January 17, 1861), 2; *Eighth Census,* M653–38, 948; Bureau of the Census, *Eighth Census of the United States, 1860, Agriculture Schedule and Slave Schedule* (Chicot County, Arkansas), M653, Roll 53, 92.

6. In an article published in the *Chicot Press* on January 17, 1861, two anonymous authors urged the county's planters to provide financial support for the fledgling military company known as "the Chicot Rangers" in order to defend the county's plantation economy. "Brief History of the 1st Regiment of Arkansas Mounted Riflemen (Dismounted)," DHR Papers, Box 1, Folder 6, Item 112; *Chicot Press,* (January 17, 1861), 2.

7. For a discussion of the internal conflicts within the hierarchy of the Army of Tennessee see Thomas Lawrence Connelly, *Autumn of Glory: The Army of Tennessee, 1862–1865* (Baton Rouge: Louisiana State University Press, 1971), 18–23, 69–92, 123–24, 153–62, 189–90, 235–78, 430, 440–48, 455–56, 502–3, 517–18.

8. In addition to citations in official reports, enlisted men and fellow officers praised Reynolds. Edward C. Walthall expressed high regard on May 3, 1865, and expanded upon these sentiments on August 1, 1865. Dr. Robert H. Dacus, who served as a private in Company H of the 1st Arkansas Mounted Rifles and authored a small memoir, assessed the regiment's officers as "cool-headed, brave and determined men, from General Reynolds down." Dr. W. L. Gammage of the 4th Arkansas Infantry also respected Reynolds. Reynolds's Brigade earned a reputation for hard fighting. Edward Cary Walthall to Daniel Harris Reynolds, August 1, 1865, DHR Papers, Box 1, Folder 5, Item 107; Daniel Harris Reynolds Diary, DHR Papers, Box 1, Folder 8, Item 131, Page 140; Robert H. Dacus, *Reminiscences of "Company H," First Arkansas Mounted Rifles* (Dardanelle, AR: Post-Dispatch Printing, 1897), 8; W. L. Gammage, *The Camp, the Bivouac, and the Battle Field: Being a History of the Fourth Arkansas Regiment, from Its First Organization Down to the Present Date* (Little Rock: Arkansas Southern Press, 1958), vii, 46, 82–83; *Biographical and Historical Memoirs of Southern Arkansas,* 1084–85.

9. Walthall submitted his application on July 18, 1865. In addition to Murphy, Reynolds received endorsements from W. D. Snow, U.S. district attorney Orville Jennings, and former Union general George W. Morgan. Edward Cary Walthall to Andrew Johnson, July 18, 1865, DHR Papers, Box 1, Folder 5, Item 106; Edward Cary Walthall to Daniel Harris Reynolds, August 1, 1865, DHR Papers, Box 1, Folder 5, Item 107; Reynolds to Andrew Johnson, August 21, 1865, DHR Papers, Box 1, Folder 5, Item 108; Reynolds to Andrew Johnson, January 15, 1866, DHR Papers, Box 1, Folder 5, Item 109; National Archives and Records Service, Case Files of Applications from Former Confederates for Presidential Pardons: ("Amnesty Papers") 1865–1867; James L. Douthat, comp., *Special Presidential Pardons of Confederate Soldiers: A Listing of Former Confederate Soldiers Requesting Full Pardon from President Andrew Johnson* (Signal

Mountain, TN: Mountain Press, 1999), 1:173; J. T. Dorris, "Pardoning the Leaders of the Confederacy," *The Mississippi Valley Historical Review* 15, no. 1 (June 1928): 3–21.

10. Reynolds argued two cases before the U.S. Supreme Court. *New Orleans Canal and Banking Company, et al v. Reynolds, et al* (1893) involved settlement of Francis Griffin's estate. He also served with Augustus H. Garland and H. J. May as counsel for the appellant in *Halliday v. Stuart* (1894), which involved competing claims to Chicot County lands previously owned by Horace F. Walworth. Edward Cary Walthall to Andrew Johnson, August 1, 1865, DHR Papers, Box 1, Folder 5, Item 107; *Biographical and Historical Memoirs of Southern Arkansas,* 1063, 1083–85; William N. Sessions, "History of Lake Village, Chicot County, Arkansas," in *A Tribute to Chicot County, Arkansas,* ed. Sheila Ferrell Brannon (Dermott, AR: Brannon, 2000), 1:172; Robert Desty, ed., *Supreme Court Reporter: Cases Argued and Determined in the United States Supreme Court,* vol. 14, *October Term 1893* (St. Paul: West Publishing Company, 1894), 302, 1150.

11. The 1870 federal population census lists Martha Jane Reynolds as "Mattie." Reynolds established his law office next to "Lakeside." The office no longer exists. Kate Reynolds married Joseph Morrison Hill on November 19, 1890. Robert Wallace Reynolds married Julia Ryland Bagby on July 9, 1898. He served as a first lieutenant with the 13th U.S. Cavalry and died at the U.S. Army hospital at Hot Springs on September 2, 1905, from disease contracted in the Philippines. Eleanor Reynolds broke off an engagement to a local planter and never married. She died on January 8, 1915. Ruth Reynolds married A. B. Duncan in 1899, but he died later that year. She later married Francis Dane (Frank) Bull, assistant cashier of the Chicot Bank. Daniel H. Reynolds Jr. attended Ouachita Baptist College but suffered a breakdown that required institutionalization. He never married. After the general's death, Mattie Reynolds lived with Ruth and Eleanor and granddaughters Isabel and Eleanor Bull and rented rooms to boarders. She died on March 23, 1924, and received burial in Lake Village Cemetery. Currently owned by Richard and Connie Cox, the Reynolds family home still stands on Lakeshore Drive in Lake Village. Reynolds-Wallace Genealogy, DHR Papers, Box 1, Folder 6, Item 115; "D. H. Reynolds lands in Chicot," DHR Papers, Box 1, Folder 7, Item 117; Isabel P. Hill to "Dear Joan and Sam," September 24, 1955, Richard and Connie Cox Collection, used by permission; Virginia Hurst to "Dear Joan," January 31, 1977, Richard and Connie Cox Collection, used by permission; Bureau of the Census, *Ninth Census of the United States, 1870* (Washington, DC: National Archives and Records Administration, 1870), M593, RG29–49, 128; Bureau of the Census, *Thirteenth Census of the United States, 1910* (Washington, DC: National Archives and Records Administration, 1910), T624–45, 4A; *Biographical and Historical Memoirs of Southern Arkansas,* 1062, 1082–85; J. W. McMurray, "Mrs. D. H. Reynolds, Member of County Pioneer Family," *A Tribute to Chicot County,* 1:48–49, 160; Dallas T. Herndon, ed., *Centennial History of Arkansas* (Chicago: S. J. Clarke Publishing Company, 1922), 1: 916; Bender, "Daniel Harris Reynolds," 239–40; Lawrence L. Hewitt, "Daniel Harris Reynolds," in *Confederate General,* ed. William C. Davis and Julie Hoffman (Harrisburg, PA: National Historical Society, 1991), 5:84–85.

12. "From General D. H. Reynolds," *Confederate War Journal* (April 1894), 2:45.

13. Isabel P. Hill to "Dear Joan and Sam," September 24, 1955, Richard and Connie Cox Collection, used by permission; Virginia Hurst to "Dear Joan," December 1, 1972, Richard and Connie Cox Collection, used by permission; Virginia Hurst to unknown, February 20, 1979, Richard and Connie Cox Collection, used by permission; *Arkansas Democrat* (March 14, 1902), 1.

14. *Arkansas Democrat* (March 14, 1902), 1; *Confederate Veteran* 11:3 (March 1903) : 130; Leona Brasher, "An Historical Manuscript of Chicot County," in Brannon, *A Tribute to Chicot County, Arkansas,* 1:39.

ONE

1. In February 1861, Arkansas residents voted 27,412 to 15,826 in favor of a state secession convention. Analysis indicates 23,626 votes for Unionists and 17,927 votes for Secessionists. Editors of the *Arkansas Gazette* applauded Virginia's "conservative counsels" as a bulwark against the "mad fanaticism" of other southern states. *Arkansas Gazette* (March 2, 1861), 3; *Arkansas Gazette* (March 9, 1861), 2; Jack B. Scroggs, "Arkansas in the Secession Crisis," *Arkansas Historical Quarterly* 12, no. 3 (Autumn 1953): 185, 188–92, 197, 199, 208; James M. Woods, *Rebellion and Realignment: Arkansas's Road to Secession* (Fayetteville: University of Arkansas Press, 1987), 113–32.

2. The editors of the *Arkansas Gazette* eventually supported secession as a necessary counter measure to Lincoln's call for troops. On May 6, 1861, Arkansas seceded by a vote of 65 to 5. The final vote changed to 69 to 1 when H. H. Bollinger, John Campbell, T. M. Gunter, and Samuel Kelley changed their votes as a gesture of unity. Isaac Murphy remained the lone vote of opposition. *Arkansas Gazette* (May 4, 1861), 2; *Arkansas Gazette* (May 11, 1861), 2; Scroggs, "Arkansas in the Secession Crisis, 219–24; Woods, *Rebellion and Realignment,* 153–65.

3. Several prominent leaders in Chicot County, including R. M. Gaines, Isaac H. Hilliard, Samuel R. Walker, and William B. Streett, joined Reynolds in support of secession as early as January 1861. In response to Gov. Henry M. Rector's call for the enrollment of county militia units, Reynolds recruited the Chicot Rangers about the same time as the call for the first state secession convention. The *Chicot Press* (January 17, 1861), 1–2; *Arkansas Gazette* (May 11, 1861), 2; *Arkansas Gazette* (June 1, 1861), 2; Orville W. Taylor, *Negro Slavery in Arkansas* (Durham: Duke University Press, 1958), 51–52, 98; Willard B. Gatewood, "The Arkansas Delta: The Deepest of the Deep South," in *The Arkansas Delta: Land of Paradox,* ed. Willard B. Gatewood and Jeannie M. Whayne (Fayetteville: University of Arkansas Press, 1996), 15.

4. A grand public gathering occurred at St. John's College on May 28, 1861, in honor of Col. Thomas J. Churchill's regiment. On behalf of the women of Little Rock, Miss Mattie Faulkner presented the regiment with a flag. Smaller events marked the arrival of the remaining companies. Company commanders drew for position on May 31, 1861. On May 23, 1861, Confederate secretary of war LeRoy P. Walker informed Ben McCulloch that, once organized and armed for service, Churchill's regiment should proceed to Fort Smith for muster by Capt. James McIntosh. Walker also informed McCulloch of a shortage of rifles. In reply, McCulloch mentioned some reluctance

within Churchill's regiment to enlist beyond 12 months. Reynolds's rank as captain of the Chicot Rangers dated from June 14, 1861. Other captains elected at this time included John S. Pearson (Company B, "the Des Arc Rangers"), replaced by John B. Hardwick after the battle of Oak Hills; Oliver Basham (Company C, "the Johnson Rifles"); Charles Matlock (Company D, "the Augusta Guards"), replaced by Lee M. Ramseur after election to lieutenant colonel; Zachariah P. McAlexander (Company E, "the Lawrence County Rifles"); Morton G. Galloway (Company F, "the Pulaski Rangers"); John L. Porter (Company G, "the Napoleon Rifles"); Thomas J. Daniels (Company H, "the Yell County Rifles"); Robert W. Harper (Company I, "the McCulloch Rangers"), replaced by George S. Laswell after election to major; William S. Gibbs (Company K, "the Independence County Rifles"). "Brief History of the 1st Regiment Arkansas Mounted Riflemen (Dismounted)," Daniel Harris Reynolds Papers, University Libraries, Fayetteville, Box 1, Folder 6, Item 112 (hereafter cited as DHR Papers); "Appointments," DHR Papers, Box 1, Folder 7, Item 127; U.S. War Department, *War of the Rebellion: Official Records of the Union and Confederate Armies* (Washington, DC: Government Printing Office, 1880–1901) (hereafter cited as *OR* or *Official Records*), 1:3, 581–83; *Arkansas Gazette* (June 1, 1861), 2.

5. See the entry of June 29, 1861, for reference to the accidental death of Private Daniel Robinson and desertion of privates Martin Worthington and Columbus Simpson, all of Company A. See the entry of July 22, 1861, for reference to the murder of Private William Finnerty of Company G by Lt. David A. Alexander Jr. of the same company.

6. This report does not appear in the *Official Records.*

7. Born in Alabama about 1831, A. C. Wells lived in the Conway County town of Lewisburg with his 21-year-old wife, Harriet, a daughter, and mother-in-law. In 1855, he opened a grocery store. In 1860, he owned $1,000 in real estate and a personal estate valued at $5,000. The grocery closed early in the war but re-opened afterwards. Wells moved his business to Morrilton in 1880 and is listed in a postwar publication as a "retired merchant and planter" and one of "very few" veterans of Carroll's Arkansas Cavalry in Conway County by the 1890s. Wells enlisted as a private in Company B on October 11, 1862, but went absent without leave on October 19, 1863. Wells applied for a special presidential pardon, due to violation of the wartime amnesty offer of December 8, 1863. Endorsed by Gov. Isaac Murphy, Wells received a pardon on November 9, 1865. Born in Pennsylvania about 1813, William H. Sutton lived in Old River Township with his 40-year-old wife, Mary, and three sons. Sutton served as county and probate judge for Chicot County between 1838 and 1840. By 1861, he practiced law with W. W. Edwards in Lake Village. After the war, Sutton owned "Belle Island" plantation in partnership with Reynolds and a man named McGinnis. Born in Kentucky about 1820, Joshua M. Craig lived in Oden Township with his 36-year-old wife, Elizabeth. In 1860, he owned $59,342 in real estate and a personal estate of $91,000, as well as 159 slaves. The Craig family owned adjacent plantations, "Bellvue" and "Yellow Bayou," five miles north of Lake Village. Exempt from the general amnesty of May 29, 1865, due to personal wealth of more than $20,000, Craig applied for a special presidential pardon. Endorsed by Gov. Isaac Murphy and U.S. district attorney Orville Jennings, Craig

received a pardon on October 28, 1865. Born in Kentucky about 1804, Benjamin P. Gaines lived in Railroad Township with three daughters and developed "Gaines Landing" plantation with R. M. Gaines and William H. Gaines. In 1860, Benjamin P. Gaines owned $48,000 in real estate and a personal estate of $39,000, as well as 77 slaves. U.S. War Department, Compiled Service Records of Confederate Soldiers Who Served in Organizations from the State of Arkansas, National Archives, Microcopy 376, Roll 24 (hereafter cited as CSR with microfilm and roll numbers; these numbers are individual service records); Bureau of the Census, *Eighth Census of the United States, 1860* (Washington, DC: National Archives and Records Administration, 1860), M653–39, 446; *Eighth Census,* M653–38, 923; *Eighth Census,* M653–38, 952, 956; Bureau of the Census, *Eighth Census of the United States, 1860, Agriculture Schedule and Slave Schedule* (Chicot County, AR), M653–53, 99B–100B, 107B; *Chicot Press,* January 17, 1861, 1; *Biographical and Historical Memoirs of Western Arkansas* (Chicago: Goodspeed Publishing Company, 1891), 15, 30, 32, 24, 122; *Biographical and Historical Memories of Southern Arkansas* (Chicago: Goodspeed Publishing Company, 1890), 1062, 1064–65; James L. Douthat, comp., *Special Presidential Pardons of Confederate Soldiers* (Signal Mountain, TN: Mountain Press, 1999), 1:169, 174; Orville W. Taylor, *Negro Slavery in Arkansas* (Durham: Duke University Press, 1958), 78, 100, 146, 212.

8. Born in Kentucky about 1802, America J. Bowie lived in Railroad Township with her 23-year-old son, James W. Bowie, and 16-year-old daughter, May A. Bowie. In 1860, she owned $34,000 in real estate and a personal estate of $7,000. Born in Arkansas about 1837, James W. Bowie served as Chicot County sheriff from 1860 to 1862 and mustered in as major in the 12th Arkansas Cavalry (also known as Wright's Arkansas Cavalry) on November 10, 1863. His regiment saw action at Poison Springs and Marks's Mills and participated in Sterling Price's 1864 Missouri Raid. Born in Georgia about 1815, William F. Trippe lived on a Railroad Township farm with his 34-year-old wife, Mary, three sons, and three daughters. In 1860, he owned $35,000 in real estate and a personal estate of $20,000. "Mr. Cheer" may refer to D. B. Chairs, who owned property in Desha County but does not appear in the 1860 census. Born in Tennessee about 1827, Watson Webb lived in Jefferson Township in Desha County with his 35-year-old wife, F. J. Webb, and served as overseer for D. B. Chairs. Born in Alabama about 1816, Jacob M. Prewitt lived in the Drew County township of Bartholomew with his wife, N. P. Prewitt, three sons, and one daughter. In 1860, he owned $11,000 in real estate, a personal estate of $17,000, and 26 slaves. Prewitt also owned property in Desha County. Born in Tennessee about 1819, D. P. Phillips served as Prewitt's overseer in Desha County, where he managed $24,000 in real estate, a personal estate of $20,000, and 36 slaves. CSR, M376, Roll 3; *Eighth Census,* M653–38, 961; *Eighth Census,* M653–41, 32, 120, 241; *Eighth Census, Slave Schedule* (Desha County, Arkansas), M653–53, 220; *Biographical and Historical Memoirs of Southern Arkansas,* 1062.

9. Richard J. Shaddock and Abner Gaines mustered in with Company A of the 1st Arkansas Mounted Rifles at Fort Smith on June 15, 1861. Richard J. Shaddock mustered in as first lieutenant. Captured at Elkhorn Tavern on March 8, 1862, he remained a prisoner at Camp Chase until exchanged on May 25, 1862. He enlisted in Company A of the 39th Arkansas Infantry (also known as Cocke's Regiment) at Lake Village on October

8, 1862, earned promotion to third lieutenant on March 28, 1863, and to captain later in
1863. Captured again on July 4, 1863, at Helena, Arkansas, he remained at Johnson's
Island until exchanged at New Orleans on January 9, 1865. Born in Mississippi about
1834, Abner Gaines practiced law and lived in Old River Township with his 21-year-old
wife, Sallie, one son, and one daughter. In 1860, he owned $6,000 in real estate and a
personal estate of $3,000, as well as 6 slaves. He mustered in as second lieutenant on
June 15, 1861, but resigned on September 20, 1861. On March 27, 1862, he enlisted as a
corporal in Company G ("the Chicot Guards") of the 23rd Arkansas Infantry. Elected
captain on April 26, 1862, Gaines resigned on July 28, 1862. Born in Baltimore,
Maryland, on December 11, 1836, William B. Streett graduated from St. Mary's College
in 1856. He moved to Arkansas in 1857 and passed the bar in 1858. In 1860, Streett lived
in Old River Township at the Parker House and owned $3,000 in real estate. Streett ran
unsuccessfully for a seat in the first Arkansas secession convention. Streett is not listed
with the 1st Arkansas Mounted Rifles. Streett enlisted in Cocke's Regiment on
September 13, 1862. In 1863, he earned promotion to major and acting commissary of
subsistence on the staff of Alexander Travis Hawthorn. In 1865, he married Julia Reid of
Louisiana, fathered three sons, and purchased Chicot County lands in partnership with
Reynolds. Streett died at Lake Village on April 9, 1899. Cason, Wills, Ferguson, and
Estill all mustered in with Company A of the 1st Arkansas Mounted Rifles on June 15,
1861, at Fort Smith. Born in Kentucky about 1832, Frank Cason lived in Oden Township
and worked as a grocer. He mustered in as first sergeant. Born in Kentucky about 1834,
Eli T. Wills lived in Oden Township and worked on the plantation of H. H. Collins. He
mustered in as second sergeant and survived a wound at Oak Hills. Reduced to private
on August 18, 1861, he received a discharge due to disability on March 26, 1862. Wills
served as county clerk for Chicot County between 1862 and 1864. Charles C. Ferguson
mustered in as third sergeant but earned promotion to sergeant major in 1862.
Captured on April 30, 1864, while on courier duty in Arkansas, Ferguson remained a
prisoner at Camp Chase until exchanged at City Point, Virginia, in March 1865. Born in
Arkansas about 1835, Frank Estill lived in Old River Township and worked as a
mechanic on the farm of David K. Oursler. He mustered in as sergeant on June 15, 1861.
Wounded at Oak Hills, he received a discharge for disability at Pond Spring, Missouri,
on August 23, 1861. He enlisted in Company G of the 23rd Arkansas Infantry on May 13,
1862. Born in South Carolina about 1831, George Emett lived in Prairie Township in
Drew County with his 25-year-old wife, Mary, one son, and one daughter. CSR, M376,
Roll 21; M376, Roll 22; M376, Roll 8; U.S. War Department, Index to Compiled Service
Records of Confederate Soldiers Who Served in Organizations Raised Directly by the
Confederate Government and of Confederate General and Staff Officers and Non-
Regimental Enlisted Men, National Archives, Microcopy 818, Roll 23, (hereafter cited as
CSR with microfilm and roll numbers); M376, Roll 4; M376, Roll 25; M376, Roll 7;
Eighth Census, M653–38, 919, 920, 926, 950, 954; *Eighth Census*, M653–41, 149; *Eighth
Census, Slave Schedule* (Chicot County, Arkansas), M653–53, 102; *Chicot Press*, (January
17, 1861), 1; *Biographical and Historical Memoirs of Southern Arkansas*, 1065, 1086.

10. Born in Elbert County, Georgia, on October 20, 1808, Madison Tate McGehee
married Lucy Cosby Meriwether of Oglethrope, Georgia, on May 14, 1835, and fathered

ten children. McGehee settled near Pine Bluff and farmed along the Arkansas River. In 1860, he owned $60,000 in real estate and a personal estate of $75,000. Two of his sons served in Company G of the 2nd Arkansas Infantry, including Capt. Valentine M. McGehee. Born in Haysboro, Tennessee, on August 27, 1800, William Selby Harney received a direct commission into the U.S. Army in 1818. He served in several antebellum Indian campaigns and the Mexican War, where he earned a brevet promotion to brigadier general. While in command of the Department of the West, he agreed not to engage the Missouri State Guard if they made no direct action against the Federal government. For this dubious action, authorities relieved him of command and placed him on the retired list in 1863. Nonetheless, he received a brevet promotion to major general at the end of the war. Afterwards, he lived at Pass Christian, Mississippi, and St. Louis. He died on May 9, 1889, in Orlando, Florida, and received burial at Arlington National Cemetery. Harney did not attempt to attack Randolph County or Little Rock. *Eighth Census,* M653–38, 485; "Bible Record of Francis Madison McGehee," transcription in possession of Carolyn Golowka, used by permission; Howard M. Ingham, "Captain Valentine Merriwether M'Gehee," in *Publications of the Arkansas Historical Association* (ed. John Hugh Reynolds) 4 (1917): 140–41; Ezra J. Warner, *Generals in Blue: Lives of the Union Commanders* (Baton Rouge: Louisiana State University Press, 1964), 208–9.

11. In 1860, James A. Hudson lived just southwest of Pine Bluff in Talledaga Township in Jefferson County. Born in Georgia in January 1817, Hudson moved to Memphis in 1830. He married Nancy Gillespie in Tennessee and fathered four sons and four daughters by 1860, plus two more prior her death in 1867. Hudson fathered one child with his second wife, Mary R. Ingraham. He settled in Jefferson County in 1844, served in the 1860–1861 state legislative sessions and again in 1878. In 1860, he owned $10,000 in real estate and a personal estate of $20,000. His son James M. Hudson served under Madison Tate McGehee's son (Capt. Valentine M. McGehee) as second lieutenant of Company G in the 2nd Arkansas Infantry. *Eighth Census,* M653–44, 725; *Biographical and Historical Memoirs of Pulaski, Jefferson, Lonoke, Faulkner, Grant, Saline, Perry, Garland and Hot Springs Counties Arkansas* (Chicago: Goodspeed Publishing Company, 1889), 147, 180–81; Ingham, "Captain Valentine Merriwether M'Gehee," 140–41.

12. Built in 1841 by Nicholas Peay, Anthony House stood at the corner of Markham and Scott Streets. Joseph Anthony took over operation after Peay died in 1842. Anthony House served as headquarters for Elisha Baxter's faction during the 1874 "Brooks-Baxter War" and burned on September 21, 1875. Theatre Hall hosted early patriotic activities during the war. In May 1861, an association of Little Rock women converted the hall into a manufactory of Confederate uniforms. In December 1861, Theatre Hall hosted "the Darkies Ball" as a benefit for sick Confederate soldiers. *Arkansas Gazette* (May 4, 1861), 2; *Arkansas Gazette* (June 1, 1861), 2; *Arkansas Gazette* (December 14, 1861), 2; Dallas T. Herndon, *Centennial History of Arkansas* (Chicago: S. J. Clarke Publishing Company, 1922), 836; John Gould Fletcher, *Arkansas* (Chapel Hill: University of North Carolina Press, 1947), 109, 268; Earl F. Woodward, "The Brooks and Baxter War in Arkansas, 1872–1874," *Arkansas Historical Quarterly* 30 (Winter 1971): 315–36.

13. Chartered through the Masonic Order on December 31, 1850, St. John's College first offered classes in the fall of 1859 on a campus located on present-day MacArthur

Park in Little Rock. In addition to its use as a campground for in-coming companies of the 1st Arkansas Mounted Rifles, the college served as a hospital several times during the war. On January 8, 1864, the campus served as the execution site for convicted Confederate spy David O. Dodd. Classes resumed in the fall of 1867. In 1874, Joseph Brooks used the campus as his headquarters during the "Brooks-Baxter War" and the school's cadets as his bodyguard. "Brief History of the 1st Regiment of Arkansas Mounted Riflemen (Dismounted)," DHR Papers, Box 1, Folder 6, Item 112; *Arkansas Gazette* (June 1, 1861), 2; Aaron B. Pierce, "St. John's College," *Pulaski County Historical Review* 36 (Summer 1988): 39–44; Fletcher, *Arkansas,* 133, 154, 173, 187, 266; Herndon, *Centennial History of Arkansas,* 309, 570–71, 961, 1009.

14. Companies for Churchill's regiment arrived in Little Rock throughout late May and camped on the grounds of St. John's College. Within days, each company marched to Fort Smith. Part of the regiment left on Friday, May 31, with the remainder expected to depart in a day or two. Morton G. Galloway mustered in as captain of Company F ("the Pulaski Rangers") of the 1st Arkansas Mounted Rifles on June 15, 1861. Promoted to lieutenant colonel, he left active duty due to a wound received at Murfreesboro on December 31, 1862. Born in Williamson County, Tennessee, on July 25, 1808, Thomas Bradley moved to Crittenden County in 1847 and lived on a plantation in Wappanocca Township with his 40-year-old wife, Jane. In 1860, he owned $42,500 in real estate and a personal estate valued at $118,000. In 1861, he represented Crittenden County as a Unionist delegate at the state secession convention. Nonetheless, he accepted the outcome and joined the Confederacy. He briefly commanded the Eastern Division of the Arkansas Militia with rank of brigadier general, until removed in the first year of the war due to general ineffectiveness and a lack of confidence in his leadership. He died in Memphis in September 1864. His papers are located at the Tennessee State Library and Archives in Nashville. Prominent Chicot County attorney and planter Richard M. Gaines established "Gaines Landing" plantation with Benjamin P. Gaines, Junius W. Gaines, and William H. Gaines. He represented Chicot, Ashley, and Drew Counties in the state senate between 1856 and 1859 and owned 85 slaves in 1860. In January 1861, he ran unsuccessfully as a candidate to the state secession convention on a platform that supported immediate secession by individual slave states and the creation of a southern Confederacy. The title of "General" appears to be honorary. Born in Kentucky about 1823, J. C. Ray lived in Little Rock with his 32-year-old wife, A. T. Ray, and one son. In 1860, Ray worked as a merchant tailor and owned a personal estate of $6,000. Jacob McConnell worked as a merchant when he mustered in as third lieutenant in Company A on June 15, 1861. He earned promotions to second lieutenant and captain and served until killed at Chickamauga on September 20, 1863. "Brief History of the 1st Regiment of Arkansas Mounted Riflemen (Dismounted)," DHR Papers, Box 1, Folder 6, Item 112; CSR, M376, Roll 8; M376, Roll 15; *Eighth Census,* M653–49, 72; *Eighth Census,* M653–40, 839; *Eighth Census, Slave Schedule* (Chicot County, Arkansas), M653, Roll 53, 101; *Chicot Press* (January 17, 1861), 2; *Arkansas Gazette* (June 1, 1861), 2; *Biographical and Historical Memoirs,* 1061–63; Bruce S. Allardice, *More Generals in Gray* (Baton Rouge: Louisiana State University Press, 1995), 41.

15. Born in the District of Columbia, Daniel Hines lived in Chicot County and worked as a plasterer. He mustered in as a private in Company A of the 1st Arkansas

Mounted Rifles on June 15, 1861. He received a discharge for disability at Big Eagle, Kentucky, on September 19, 1862. The only identifiable Arkansas soldier named "B. F. Allen" served as a private in Capt. William Hart's Battery of Arkansas Light Artillery. Benjamin F. Danley served as sheriff and jailor of Pulaski County. In response to the 1857 Dred Scott decision Danley signed a petition, along with state supreme court justice and future governor Henry M. Rector and future Confederate generals Thomas J. Churchill and Albert Pike, which sought expulsion of all free Negroes from Arkansas. On July 29, 1861, Danley mustered in as captain of Company D ("Danley's Rangers") of the 3rd Arkansas Cavalry. Elected lieutenant colonel on November 1, 1861, he received a discharge after he failed to gain reelection in May 1862. CSR, M376, Roll 1; M376, Roll 11; M376, Roll 6; Taylor, *Negro Slavery in Arkansas*, 69, 256.

16. Born in Arkansas about 1826, Dr. William L. Menefee lived in the Conway County township of Welborn with his 28-year-old wife, Mary, one son, and one daughter. He farmed and practiced medicine, but listed no assets in 1860. Born in Arkansas, Andrew Acker lived in the Old River Township household of Isaac Sumner. He enlisted as a private in Company A of the 1st Arkansas Mounted Rifles on June 15, 1861. *Eighth Census*, M653–38, 920; *Eighth Census*, M653–39, 458; *Eighth Census*, M376, Roll 1.

17. Born in Boone County, Kentucky, in 1807, Peter Hanger moved to Arkansas in 1834 and engaged in plantation commerce along the Red River. He settled in Chicot County later that year, established a general mercantile at Gaines's Landing in 1838, and served in the state legislature. After a failed attempt to establish a mercantile in Van Buren, Hanger moved to Little Rock in 1848 and purchased stage mail contracts between Little Rock and Fort Smith and between Little Rock and Hot Springs. He married Matilda Cunningham on June 18, 1850, and fathered seven children. In 1860, he owned $30,000 in real estate and a personal estate of $30,000. The war interrupted his enterprise in 1862. Afterward, he became a planter. After Matilda Hanger died in 1865, he married Ann M. Gaines. Born in Nassau, Germany, in 1826, John Kurtz lived as a bachelor farmer in the Conway County township of Welborn. In 1860, he owned $11,000 in real estate as well as a personal estate of $11,000. Point Remove Bayou flows out of the Boston Mountains and joins the Arkansas River near the border between Conway and Pope Counties. *Eighth Census*, M653–49, 67; *Eighth Census*, M653–39, 452; *Biographical and Historical Memoirs of Pulaski, Jefferson, Lonoke, Faulkner, Grant Saline, Perry, Garland and Hot Springs Counties, Arkansas* (Chicago: Goodspeed Publishing Company, 1889), 458–59; *Biographical and Historical Memoirs of Western Arkansas*, 195.

18. Born in Pennsylvania around 1804, Kirkbridge Potts moved to Arkansas from New Jersey and founded the Pope County town of Pottsville in 1828. In 1860, he resided in Illinois Township with his 49-year-old wife, Pamela, seven sons, and one hired laborer. At that time, he owned $8,860 in real estate and a personal estate valued at $29,005. He worked as an Indian agent and postmaster and owned a station on the Butterfield Stage between Little Rock and Fort Smith. His background in such frontier business ventures probably accounts for a clever and frugal reputation. In 1864, the 33rd Iowa Infantry camped on Potts's property. Andrew F. Sperry, who served in Company G of the 33rd Iowa and authored the regimental history, described Potts as "an ardent old rebel." According to Sperry, Potts lived in "a large white house, with big

barns and granaries" at the foot of Carrion Crow Mountain. *Eighth Census*, M653–48, 724; Gregory J. W. Urwin and Cathy Kunzinger Urwin, eds., *History of the 33d Iowa Infantry Volunteer Regiment, 1863–66* (Fayetteville: University of Arkansas Press, 1999), 126, 301 n.11.

19. Born in North Carolina about 1826, Sidney Bumpass Cozort lived in the Johnson County township of Pittsburg with his 29-year-old wife, Martha, four sons, and one daughter. In 1860, Cozort owned $7,000 in real estate and a personal estate valued at $9,000, as well as 6 slaves. *Eighth Census*, M653–44, 977; *Eighth Census, Slave Schedule* (Johnson County, Arkansas), M653–53, 4B.

20. Dr. McGehee could not be identified. Born in Maryland about 1820, Charles G. Scott lived with his 31-year-old wife, Caroline, three sons, and three daughters in Van Buren. He inherited considerable property and slaves in 1855 from his father-in-law, John Drennen, including property above Lake Village later owned by Reynolds, George Read, and John G. B. Simms. In 1860, Scott owned $30,000 in real estate and a personal estate valued at $46,000, as well as 29 slaves (including 13 from the Drennen estate). *Eighth Census*, M653–40, 611; *Eighth Census, Slave Schedule* (Crawford County, Arkansas), M432–25, 166B-167; *Eighth Census, Slave Schedule* (Chicot County, Arkansas), M653–53, 104; *Biographical and Historical Memoirs of Southern Arkansas*, 1065.

21. The "Half Way House" at Van Buren, Arkansas, could not be identified. Charles H. Matlock mustered in as lieutenant colonel of the 1st Arkansas Mounted Rifles on June 9, 1861. Captured on August 31, 1863, while on furlough in Augusta, Arkansas, Matlock died at Johnson's Island on December 9, 1864. Born on November 11, 1811, in Rutherford County, Tennessee, Ben McCulloch participated in the Texas War for Independence and the California Gold Rush. Commissioned as a brigadier general in May 1861, he commanded troops in the Trans-Mississippi Department until killed at Elkhorn Tavern on March 7, 1862. He received burial at the State Cemetery in Austin, Texas. CSR, M376, Roll 15; M818, Roll 16; Thomas W. Cutrer, *Ben McCulloch and the Frontier Military Tradition* (Chapel Hill: University of North Carolina Press, 1993), 3–7, 27–175, 194–218, 245–309, 313.

22. Located south of Fort Smith, Massard Prairie served as an early campground for portions of the 1st Arkansas Mounted Rifles. On July 27, 1864, Massard Prairie witnessed a sharp engagement between Texas and Native American cavalry under Richard Gano and dismounted Union troops of the 6th Kansas Cavalry. This small but decisive Confederate victory set the stage for an unsuccessful attack on the Union garrison at Fort Smith on July 31, 1864. Eaton Tatum moved from Missouri to Sebastian County in 1843 and settled near Massard Prairie in the "Jenny Lind" community. Born at Fort Brooke, Florida, in 1828, James McQueen McIntosh graduated last in the West Point class of 1849 and served on the frontier until he resigned in May 1861. He served as a captain and aide to Ben McCulloch until promoted to colonel of the 2nd Arkansas Mounted Rifles. Promoted to brigadier general in January 1862, he commanded a division when killed at Elkhorn Tavern on March 7, 1862. He received burial at the State Cemetery in Austin, Texas. Robert H. Dacus, *Reminiscences of Company "H," First Arkansas Mounted Rifles* (Dardanelle, AR: Post-Dispatch Printing, 1897), 1; *History of*

Benton, Washington, Carroll, Madison, Crawford, Franklin and Sebastian Counties Arkansas (Chicago: Goodspeed Publishing Company, 1889), 692; Anne Bailey, "James McQueen McIntosh," in *The Confederate General,* ed. William C. Davis and Julie Hoffman (Harrisburg, PA: National Historical Society, 1991), 4:124–25; Frank Arey, "'The Place is Well Fortified . . .': Massard Prairie and the Confederate Attack on Fort Smith," *Journal of the Fort Smith Historical Society* 27 (April 2003): 3–9.

23. Stedman, Lyerly, and Mathis all mustered into service with Company A of the 1st Arkansas Mounted Rifles on June 15, 1861. Born in Mississippi about 1838, Henry W. Stedman lived in Louisiana Township and worked as a clerk. He mustered in as a private. Promoted to sergeant major on March 16, 1862, he transferred to the Trans-Mississippi. Born in Alexander County, Illinois, James B. Lyerly lived in Chicot County and worked as a carpenter. He mustered in as a farrier, but provided Thomas Woods as a substitute and received a discharge on October 2, 1861. On February 26, 1862, he enlisted as a sergeant in Company B ("the Chicot Rebels") of the 8th Arkansas Infantry Battalion. Wounded at Corinth, Mississippi, on October 5, 1862, and captured at Port Hudson, Louisiana, on July 9, 1863, he received parole on July 13, 1863. Born in Mississippi about 1830, Boelfield W. Mathis lived on a Vaugine Township farm in the Jefferson County town of Pine Bluff with his 26-year-old wife, Martha, a son, and daughter. In 1860, he owned $18,000 in real estate and a personal estate of $25,000, as well as 1 slave. He mustered in as a private, survived a wound at Wilson's Creek, and received a discharge in 1862. On November 10, 1863, he enlisted in Company F of the 12th Arkansas Cavalry. Initially elected as first lieutenant, he earned promotion to captain on December 17, 1863. CSR, M376, Roll 22; M376, Roll 14; 376, Roll 25; M376, Roll 15; *Eighth Census,* M653–38, 948; *Eighth Census,* M653–44, 821; *Eighth Census, Slave Schedule* (Jefferson County, Arkansas), M653–53, 398.

24. Mr. Madison could not be identified.

25. Robinson, Worthington, and Simpson all mustered into service with Company A of the 1st Arkansas Mounted Rifles on June 15, 1861, at Fort Smith. Daniel Robinson mustered in as a private and died in a fall from his horse on June 29, 1861. Martin V. Worthington mustered in as a private but deserted on June 29, 1861. Returned under guard on July 28, 1861, he participated in the battle of Oak Hills. He survived a wound at Chickamauga but deserted again at Dalton, Georgia, and took the oath of allegiance at Chattanooga, Tennessee, on May 19, 1864. Columbus Simpson mustered in as a private and deserted on June 29, 1861. CSR, M376, Roll 20; M376, Roll 26; M376, Roll 21.

26. Born about 1832 in Tennessee, William W. Wair farmed in Prairie County's White River Township with his 30-year-old wife, Morgan, and family. In 1860, he owned $16,500 in real estate and a personal estate valued at $10,000, as well as 9 slaves. He mustered in as first lieutenant of Company B in the 1st Arkansas Mounted Rifles on June 9, 1861, and later earned promotion to captain. CSR, M376, Roll 24; *Eighth Census,* M653–48, 974; *Eighth Census, Slave Schedule* (Chicot County, Arkansas), M653–54, 26.

27. Officially known as "the Cherokee Nation–Arkansas Line Road," the "Line Road" ran north to south along the western border of Arkansas. Emmet Starr, *History of the Cherokee Indians and Their Legends and Folk Lore* (Oklahoma City: Warden Company, 1921), 113.

28. Col. De Rosey Carroll commanded the 1st Arkansas State Cavalry, which served in the Trans-Mississippi Department from June until September 1861. Disbanded in September, it formed the nucleus of the 1st Arkansas (Carroll's) Cavalry organized at Fort Smith in October 1862 under Col. Charles A. Carroll. The regiment served until reorganized under Col. Anderson Gordon in December 1863 as the 4th (Gordon's) Arkansas Cavalry. Captain William Edward Woodruff commanded Woodruff's Battery (also known as Marshall's Battery, Woodruff's-Marshall's Battery, the Pulaski Artillery, and the 3rd Arkansas Field Battery), which mustered at Little Rock in July 1861. The battery served in the Trans-Mississippi at Oak Hills, Elkhorn Tavern, Prairie Grove, Helena, and Bayou Fourche and ended its service as part of the Reserve Battalion at Marshall, Texas, under command of Capt. John G. Marshall. On April 1, 1863, Woodruff became chief of artillery for Sterling Price, with the rank of major. Woodruff wrote an important memoir of his service in the Trans-Mississippi. Born in Prince Edward County, Virginia, on September 20, 1809, Sterling Price served in the U.S. Congress and in the Mexican War and was governor of Missouri. Price supported secession after the incident at Camp Jackson and commanded troops throughout the Trans-Mississippi. He refused to surrender and lived in exile in Mexico and Venezuela before ill health influenced his return to Missouri. He died in St. Louis on September 29, 1867, and received burial at Bellefontaine Cemetery. *OR,* 3: 38–39; CSR, M376, Roll 4; M818, Roll 26; M818, Roll 19; W. E. Woodruff, *With the Light Guns in '61–'65: Reminiscences of Eleven Arkansas, Missouri and Texas Light Batteries, in the Civil War* (Little Rock: Central Printing Company, 1903), 29–30; United States War Department, *List of Staff Officers of the Confederate States Army, 1861–1865* (Washington, DC: Government Printing Office, 1891), 183; *Biographical and Historical Memoirs of Western Arkansas,* 15; Albert Castel, *General Sterling Price and the Civil War in the West* (Baton Rouge: Louisiana State University Press, 1993), 3–7, 13–15, 81–84, , 92–93, 271, 277–78; Albert Castel, "Sterling Price, in *Confederate General,* ed. Davis and Hoffman, 5:58–63; Joseph H. Crute Jr., *Units of the Confederate States Army* (Midlothian, VA: Derwent Books, 1987), 61.

29. Born in Jefferson County, Kentucky, on March 10, 1824, Thomas James Churchill studied law at Transylvania University and served with the 1st Kentucky Rifles during the Mexican War. He moved to Little Rock and served as postmaster in 1861, when he recruited the 1st Arkansas Mounted Rifles. Churchill mustered in as colonel on June 9, 1861, and commanded the regiment until promoted to brigadier general on March 4, 1862. He served in the Kentucky campaign, commanded Arkansas Post during the Vicksburg campaign, and earned promotion to major general on March 18, 1865. Exempt from the general amnesty, due to rank as a Confederate general officer, Churchill applied for a special presidential pardon. Approved by U.S. attorney general James Speed, he received a pardon on October 19, 1865. Churchill served as state treasurer from 1874 to 1880 and as governor in 1880. He died in Little Rock on May 14, 1905, and received burial in Mount Holly Cemetery. Captain Charles A. Carroll commanded Company A of the 1st Arkansas State Cavalry, which left Van Buren on May 25, 1861. On July 5, 1861, Carroll's men and six companies of the 1st Arkansas Mounted Rifles made a coordinated attack on a small garrison of Union troops at Neosho, Missouri. Under

overall command of James M. McIntosh, they captured Capt. Joseph Conrad's Company B of the 3rd Missouri (Union) Infantry. In his report to Col. Franz Sigel, Conrad estimated Confederate strength at 1,200 to 1,500. Conrad and his men remained prisoners in the courthouse until July 8, 1861. Although Conrad reported fair treatment from Confederate officers, he claimed abuse by enlisted Rebels. The theft of canteens, however, is the only specific issue of mistreatment mentioned in his report. After their release, local civilians threatened to kill them. *OR*, 1:3, 38–39; CSR, M376, Roll 5 and M818, Roll 5; M376, Roll 4; Douthat, *Special Presidential Pardons*, 1:22; Anne Bailey, "Thomas James Churchill," in *The Confederate General*, ed. William C. Davis and Julie Hoffman (Harrisburg, PA: National Historical Society, 1991), 1:186–87; F. Clark Elkins, "Thomas James Churchill, 1881–1883," in *Governors of Arkansas: Essays in Political Biography*, ed. Timothy Paul Donovan, William B. Gatewood, Jr., and Jeannie M. Whayne (Fayetteville: University of Arkansas Press, 1995), 72–76; Clara B. Eno, *History of Crawford County, Arkansas* (Van Buren: Press-Argus, 1951), 240, 248–51.

30. Claiborne Fox Jackson narrowly won election as governor of Missouri in 1860. Under his direction, the state legislature met at Neosho and passed an ordinance of secession despite the lack of a legal quorum. On July 5, 1861, Jackson and Sterling Price led a combined force of 6,000 Missouri State Guard troops against 1,000 Federals under Col. Franz Sigel at Carthage. Weary from a series of long marches, with no cavalry to protect his flanks, Sigel's troops withdrew toward Springfield. Along the way, they repulsed a series of Confederate charges. Afterward, both sides claimed victory. Union forces extracted most of their troops and inflicted heavier casualties on a numerically superior foe, but the Confederates defended valuable lead mines in southwestern Missouri. After the battle of Elkhorn Tavern, Jackson led a government-in-exile from Camden, Arkansas. He died in Little Rock from tuberculosis and stomach cancer on December 7, 1862, and received burial in the Sappington Cemetery near Arrow Rock, Missouri. The term "Dutch" served as a derogatory description of German-American Unionists. Already engaged in bitter factional conflict with Unionist neighbors, the slave-owning secessionists of western and southern Missouri welcomed Price's troops as they moved through the state in 1861. William Monks, *A History of Southern Missouri and Northern Arkansas: Being an Account of the Early Settlements, the Civil War, the Ku-Klux, and Times of Peace* (West Plains, MO: West Plains Journal Company, 1907), 42–46; Christopher Phillips, *Missouri's Confederate: Claiborne Fox Jackson and the Creation of Southern Identity in the Border West* (Columbia: University of Missouri Press, 2000), ix, 212, 230–73; Wolfgang Hochbruck, "Battle of Carthage," in *Encyclopedia of the American Civil War: A Political, Social, and Military History*, ed. David S. Heidler and Jeanne T. Heidler (Santa Barbara: ABC-Clio, 2000), 1:368; Stephen D. Engle, "German-Americans," in *Encyclopedia of the American Civil War*, ed. Heidler and Heidler, 2:822–24; T. J. Stiles, *Jesse James: Last Rebel of the Civil War* (New York: Alfred A. Knopf, 2002), 67–71.

31. Scott's Mill is located in southwestern Missouri, 18 miles west of Cassville. James F. (Frank) Whitten mustered in as a private in Company A of the 1st Arkansas Mounted Rifles on June 15, 1861. He transferred to Company B of the 2nd Arkansas Cavalry on May 27, 1862. *OR*, 1:13, 979; CSR, M376, Roll 25.

32. Born about 1833 in Dallas County, Alabama, James Shaddock lived and worked on the Old River Township property of Susan Neale. He mustered into Company A of the 1st Arkansas Mounted Rifles as a private on June 15, 1861. He received a discharge at Camp Pickens, Missouri, on October 19, 1861. *Eighth Census,* M653–38, 925; CSR, M376, Roll 21.

33. Alex McKissick lived southwest of Bentonville, Arkansas. McKissick's land, along "McKissick's Creek," served as one of two main encampments for divided Union forces prior to the battle of Elkhorn Tavern. William L. Shea and Earl J. Hess, *Pea Ridge: Civil War Campaign in the West* (Chapel Hill: University of North Carolina Press, 1992), 56.

34. Born in 1814 to a prominent southern family, William Lowndes Yancey received his education in New York. He settled in Alabama, practiced law, and served in the state legislature and the U.S. House of Representatives. Yancey defended states' rights and secession and refused to adjust his stance in relation to the South's national needs. He died of kidney disease on July 27, 1863, and received burial at Oakwood Cemetery in Montgomery. Eric H. Walther, *William Lowndes Yancey and the Coming of the Civil War* (Chapel Hill: University of North Carolina Press, 2006), 1–37, 74–127, 229–73, 369–76.

35. Born in Virginia about 1797, John C. Bush lived on a farm in Mill Creek Township in Drew County with his 50-year-old wife, Mary W. Bush. In 1860, he owned $8,000 in real estate and a personal estate valued at $8,000. *Eighth Census,* M653–41, 85.

36. Born in Arkansas about 1839, David A. Alexander Jr. lived in Wilkinson Township of Desha County and worked as a deputy clerk in the sheriff's office. In 1860, he owned a personal estate of $50. His father, a prominent Desha County planter, lived in Island Township. In 1860, the elder Alexander reported $18,500 in real estate and a personal estate of $39,000, as well as 45 slaves. David A. Alexander Jr. mustered in with Company G on June 15, 1861. Elected second lieutenant on June 16, 1861, he killed Private William Finnerty of Company G on June 28. Arrested on July 1, 1861, tried and convicted of murder on July 24, and dismissed from the regiment, Alexander returned home. He lived with his wife, Josephine, on a Wilkerson Township farm and worked as a sheriff's clerk. In 1870, he owned $2,400 in real estate and a personal estate of $1,000. Born about 1837, William Finnerty mustered in as a private in Company G of the 1st Arkansas Mounted Rifles on June 15, 1861. Born in Maryland about 1834, Robert W. Harper lived his 23-year-old wife, Laura, a son, and his brother James (who also served in the 1st Arkansas Mounted Rifles). Harper farmed and practiced law in Welborn Township in Conway County. In 1860, he owned $16,000 in real estate and a personal estate of $32,000. Harper mustered in as captain of Company I of the 1st Arkansas Mounted Rifles on June 6, 1861. Elected as major on June 15, and colonel in April 1862, Harper served until killed at Chickamauga on September 19, 1863. CSR, M376, Roll 1; M376, Roll 8; M376, Roll 10; *Eighth Census,* M653–39, 450; *Eighth Census,* M653–41, 16, 18; *Eighth Census, Slave Schedule* (Chicot County, Arkansas), M653–53, 4; Bureau of the Census, *Ninth Census of the United States, 1870* (Washington, DC: National Archives and Records Administration, 1870), M593–52, 548; "Brief History of the 1st Regiment of Arkansas Mounted Riflemen (Dismounted)," DHR Papers, Box 1, Folder 6, Item 112 .

37. A native of Chicot County, Thomas N. Lambe worked as a farmer. He mustered

in as a private in Company A of the 1st Arkansas Mounted Rifles on June 15, 1861. He
received a discharge for disability while at Camp Bragg on July 24, 1861, but reenlisted
at Camp Lee, Missouri, on September 19, 1861. Lambe died at Fayetteville, Arkansas, on
December 22, 1861. CSR, M376, Roll 13.

38. "Boy Monroe" appears to be a slave attendant for Thomas N. Lambe but could
not be identified. See Sterling Price's report of operations and movements from July 25
to August 11, 1861, in relation to the battle of Wilson's Creek. U.S. War Department,
War of the Rebellion: Official Records of the Union and Confederate Armies (Washington,
DC: Government Printing Office, 1881), 1:3, 98–103 (hereafter cited as *OR* or *Official
Records*).

39. Ambrose Hundley Sevier Jr., youngest child and only son of a prominent territorial congressman and antebellum U.S. senator for Arkansas, served as first lieutenant
and aide-de-camp to Thomas J. Churchill from August 12, 1861, to January 18, 1864. He
served thereafter as assistant adjutant general on the staff of Edmund Kirby Smith,
with rank as captain to date from May 13, 1864. In his report for Wilson's Creek,
Churchill cited Sevier for a wound received while rallying troops. *OR*, 1:3, 110; CSR,
M818, Roll 21; Joseph H. Crute Jr., *Confederate Staff Officers, 1861–1865* (Powhatan, VA:
Derwent Books, 1982), 36–37; James M. Woods, "Ambrose Hundley Sevier," in *Arkansas
Biography: A Collection of Notable Lives,* ed. Nancy A. Williams and Jeannie M. Whayne
(Fayetteville: University of Arkansas Press, 2000), 259–60.

40. Basham, Daniels, Gaines, Griffin, and Hardesty all mustered in with the 1st
Arkansas Mounted Rifles at Fort Smith. Oliver Basham mustered in as captain of
Company C on June 6, 1861. Born in Tennessee about 1828, Thomas J. Daniels owned
a farm in Magazine Township in the Yell County town of Dardanelle, where he lived
with his 26-year-old wife, Mary, three sons, and three daughters. In 1860, he owned
$2,400 in real estate and a personal estate of $15,000. He mustered in as captain with
Company H on June 9, 1861. Born in Tennessee about 1827, Ruben B. Griffin lived in
the Conway County town of Lewisburg. In 1860, he worked as a merchant and owned
$3,000 in real estate and a personal estate of $10,000. He mustered in as second lieutenant in Company I in June 1861 and received a discharge in May 1862. Born in
Kentucky about 1832, T. A. Hardesty lived in the household of Sheriff S. C. Clayton in
the Desha County town of Napoleon. In 1860, Hardesty worked as a deputy sheriff and
owned $200 in real estate and a personal estate of $1,000. He mustered in as second
lieutenant with Company G on June 15, 1861, and sustained a wound at Oak Hills. *OR*,
1:3, 106; CSR, M376, Roll 2; M376, Roll 6; M376, Roll 8; M376, Roll 9; M376, Roll 10;
Eighth Census, M653–52, 1051; *Eighth Census,* M653–39, 443; *Eighth Census,* M653–41.

41. On July 28, 1861, Lt. William P. Campbell of Capt. Lee M. Ramseur's Company D
led 25 men in a skirmish against 75 to 80 Union troops near Flat Creek, Missouri.
According to Private Thomas Jefferson Jobe of Company B, Campbell's force killed 17
Federals and suffered no casualties. This skirmish represented the first armed conflict
in Barry County. The Union force may have consisted of Home Guard. Robert Allen
Campbell, *Campbell's Gazetteer of Missouri* (St. Louis: R. A. Campbell, Publisher, 1875),
51; Desmond Walls Allen, *First Arkansas Confederate Mounted Rifles* (Conway: Arkansas
Research, 1988), 29.

42. McCulloch's Brigade, with six companies of cavalry as advance guard and three companies of infantry as flankers, marched toward Springfield, Missouri, on July 31, 1861, as part of the Army of Arkansas. The First Division followed the advance. The Second Division marched out of Cassville on August 1, followed by the Third Division on August 2. Born in Madison County, Mississippi, Andrew W. Mabry worked as a farmer. He mustered in as a private with Company A of the 1st Arkansas Mounted Rifles on June 15, 1861, and received a discharge for disability on December 12, 1861. Mr. McCult could not be identified. *OR,* 3: 102–3; CSR, M376, Roll 15.

43. H. G. Wilson mustered in on June 9, 1861, as regimental quartermaster with the 1st Arkansas Mounted Rifles. CSR, M376, Roll 25.

44. John I. Smith lived near the Cassville Road, 35 miles south of Springfield, and owned a stop on the Butterfield Stage route in northeast Barry County. He died later in the war, due to his Unionist loyalties. Kim Allen Scott, ed., *Loyalty on the Frontier or Sketches of Union Men of the South-West with Incidents and Adventures in Rebellion on the Border* (Fayetteville: University of Arkansas Press, 2003), 63; Emory Melton, "Civil War Days in Barry County," *White River Historical Quarterly* 5, no. 1 (Fall 1973): 8–9.

45. Lyon engaged Missouri State Guard troops under James S. Rains at Dug Springs on August 2 in an incident known as "Rains's Scare." Poor performance by the Missouri State Guard produced a negative impression among fellow Confederates. On August 3, Lyon renewed contact and drove the Rebels toward the community of Curran Post Office, where Churchill's regiment fell back in an apparent attempt to draw Lyon's force toward Crane Creek. Lyon pursued as far as the McCullah farm and store but broke contact by late afternoon and called a council of war that evening. William Garrett Piston and Richard Hatcher III, *Wilson's Creek: The Second Battle of the Civil War and the Men Who Fought It* (Chapel Hill: University of North Carolina Press, 2000), 141–44.

46. The 1st Arkansas Mounted Rifles marched with the cavalry column, along with Col. De Rosey Carroll's 1st Arkansas State Cavalry, the 2nd Arkansas Mounted Rifles, Col. Elkanah Greer's 3rd Texas (South Kansas–Texas) Cavalry and General Sterling Price's command. In accordance with General Orders No. 24, issued on August 4, 1861, the cavalry column marched behind the infantry column. *OR,* 1:3, 107–8.

47. Price described this movement and encampment in his report for operations from July 25 through August 11, 1861. Born in Tennessee about 1826, Susan Dixon lived on a Porter Township farm in Christian County, Missouri, with her 47-year-old husband, John, four sons, and two daughters. In 1860, the Dixons owned $9,200 in real estate and a personal estate of $31,095. Positioned east of Wire Road, near the confluence of Terrell and Wilson Creeks, the Dixon farm lay south of the main battlefield and Joseph Sharp's stubble field. *OR* 1:3, 99; *Eighth Census,* M653–613, 459; Piston and Hatcher, *Wilson's Creek,* 154, 221, 249, 256, 257, 259.

48. The 1st Arkansas Mounted Rifles came under Union artillery fire while preparing breakfast. With no Confederate artillery available, Churchill ordered his men to fall back toward a patch of woods. While following the road to Springfield, Churchill met Price's aide, who placed them on the left of General Slack, where they fought for 3 or 4 hours under fire by Totten's Battery. The 1st Arkansas Mounted Rifles engaged U.S.

regulars and the 1st Iowa Infantry, led by Nathaniel Lyon. Churchill reported that
Reynolds's horse threw him. Churchill reported 42 killed, including regimental
Adjutant James Harper, and 155 wounded, including Sgt. Maj. N. T. Roberts and volun-
teer aide Ambrose H. Sevier. *OR*, 1:3, 109–10, 121; W. H. Tunnard, *A Southern Record:
The History of the Third Regiment Louisiana Infantry* (Fayetteville: University of
Arkansas Press, 1997), 52.

49. No company-level report exists for the Chicot Rangers at Wilson's Creek.
Stephenson, Knighton, Beakes, Dugan, Stuart, Harmon, Mathias, Thurman, Cable,
Yuill, Lynch, P. J. Smith, and Frank Smith all mustered into Company A of the 1st
Arkansas Mounted Rifles on June 15, 1861. Born in Kentucky about 1834, David S.
Stephenson worked as a carpenter and lived on the Planters Township property of
Henry Robb. He mustered in as a private and served until reported missing after
Wilson's Creek. Born in Louisiana about 1828, Josiah Knighton lived in Bayou Mason
Township and worked as an overseer for James D. Clanton. He mustered in as a pri-
vate. Promoted to sergeant on May 1, 1862, he received a discharge on June 4, 1862. Born
in Arkansas about 1842, Abraham J. Beakes lived on his father's Mill Creek Township
farm in Drew County and mustered in as a private. He died on August 12, 1861, of
wounds received at Wilson's Creek. Born in Knox County, Tennessee, Jasper C. Dugan
worked as a farmer in Chicot County and mustered in as a private. Wounded at
Wilson's Creek, he received a discharge for disability at Camp Bragg, Arkansas, on
March 26, 1862. Born in Saratoga, New York, Samuel S. Stuart worked as a farmer in
Chicot County. He mustered in as a private, survived wounds at Wilson's Creek and
Chickamauga, and transferred to the Confederate Invalid Corps on August 26, 1864.
He remained hospitalized at Meridian, Mississippi, until March 25, 1865. Born in South
Carolina about 1833, Leander Harmon lived in Old River Township and worked as a
carpenter. He mustered in as a corporal. Wounded at Wilson's Creek, he died of fever
at Sarcoxie, Missouri, on September 14, 1861. Robert Mathias mustered in as a private.
He survived a wound at Wilson's Creek and transferred to Company G on February 1,
1862, with which he served until presumed dead at Elkhorn Tavern. Born in Ashley
County, Richard Thurman worked as a farmer and mustered in as a private. Wounded
at Wilson's Creek, he received a discharge for disability at Camp Bragg, Arkansas, on
March 26, 1862. Born in Franklin County, Ohio, Frank Cable lived in Chicot County
and worked as a grocer when he mustered in as a private. Wounded at Wilson's Creek,
he received a discharge for disability at Baldwin, Mississippi, on June 4, 1862. Born in
New York about 1821, James A. Yuill worked as a laborer in Railroad Township and
mustered in as a private. Wounded at Wilson's Creek, he received a discharge for disability in 1862. Nelson M. Lynch mustered in as a private. He survived a wound at
Wilson's Creek and earned promotion to third corporal in 1862. Reduced to private
in 1863, he disappeared after October 31, 1863. Born in Mississippi about 1830, Peter J.
Smith lived in Old River Township and worked as an overseer when he mustered in
as a private. He survived a wound at Wilson's Creek and received a discharge on
September 27, 1862. Born in Texas about 1842, Benjamin F. (Frank) Smith lived in
Magnolia Township in Columbia County and worked as a laborer for his father. He
mustered in as a private and survived a wound at Wilson's Creek. Captured at

Nashville on December 16, 1864, and confined at Camp Douglas, Illinois, he took the oath of allegiance on May 13, 1865. Smith died on October 27, 1878. McCulloch reported a Confederate force of 5,300 infantry, 15 artillery pieces, and 6,000 cavalry and a Union force of 12,000. McCulloch reported 800 Federal soldiers killed, 1,000 wounded and 300 prisoners, and the capture of 6 Federal cannon and 700 small arms. McCulloch reported 265 killed, 800 wounded, and 30 missing. The Union Army of the West reported 223 killed, 721 wounded, and 291 missing, for an aggregate of 1,235 casualties. *OR*, 3:72, 104–7, 109–10; CSR, M376, Roll 22; M376, Roll 13; M376, Roll 2; M376, Roll 7; M376, Roll 22; M376, Roll 10; M376, Roll 15; M376, Roll 23; M376, Roll 4; M376, Roll 26; M376, Roll 14; M376, Roll 21; *Eighth Census*, M653–38, 923, 925, 932, 943, 962; *Eighth Census*, M653–41, 80; *Eighth Census*, M653–39, 356.

50. Beakes died from his wound on August 12, 1861. CSR, M376, Roll 2.

51. Confederates established initial field hospitals close to the battlefield but moved their wounded to Springfield on August 11. Both armies used public and private buildings near Springfield as hospitals. The specific Christian church could not be identified, as many area churches served as hospitals. Missouri State Guard troops engaged in considerable celebration and pillage. William Garrett Piston, "'Springfield Is a Vast Hospital': The Dead and Wounded at the Battle of Wilson's Creek," *Missouri Historical Review* 93, no. 4 (July 1999): 353, 356–57.

52. Medical care initially varied but improved after word spread of need for supplies and volunteers. Dr. William A. Cantrell of the 1st Arkansas Mounted Rifles described the amount of medical staff as insufficient. Although Confederate confidence swelled with the Union withdrawal, the battle-weary southerners could offer no pursuit. Piston, "'Springfield Is a Vast Hospital,'" 353, 356–58; Piston and Hatcher, *Wilson's Creek,* 305, 308.

53. Due to a lack of medical preparations, and the hasty Union retreat, many Federal casualties became prisoners. Generals Nicholas Bartlett Pearce of the Arkansas State Militia and Ben McCulloch visited Union wounded in Springfield. Many Springfield Unionists fled the area before the battle or immediately after the Federal defeat. Piston, "'Springfield Is a Vast Hospital,'" 349–50, 353, 356–58.

54. Born in Florida about 1828, A. C. Wellborn resided in Franklin Township in 1860. Unmarried, he owned $25,000 in real estate and a personal estate of $46,800. The title of "Colonel" appears to be honorary. *Eighth Census*, M653–38, 963; *Eighth Census, Slave Schedule* (Chicot County, Arkansas), M653, Roll 53, 90.

55. In accordance with the "Articles of Transfer of Arkansas Volunteers to the Confederate States" issued on July 15, 1861, the following Arkansas regiments, battalions, companies, and detachments were transferred to the command of William J. Hardee: the 1st, 2nd, 3rd, 4th, 5th, 6th, and 7th Arkansas Infantry regiments; 1st Arkansas Cavalry regiment; 1st Arkansas Cavalry Battalion; Pulaski Artillery Battery (Woodruff's Battery); Clarke County Artillery; McCown Artillery; Trigg's Artillery, and an independent artillery company attached to Pearce's command. Born in Knoxville, Tennessee, on January 28, 1828, Thomas Carmichael Hindman practiced law in the Phillips County town of Helena, where he lived with his 23-year-old wife, Mary, and two daughters. In 1860, he owned $15,000 in real estate and a personal estate of $2,000.

He served as colonel of the 2nd Arkansas Infantry but earned promotion to brigadier general on September 28, 1861 and to major general on April 14, 1862. Hindman commanded the Trans-Mississippi Department at Prairie Grove but served the rest of the war with the Army of Tennessee. He went to Mexico but returned by 1868 to oppose Reconstruction. An unidentified assassin murdered him on September 28, 1868. He received burial in Helena at Maple Hill Cemetery. Born on October 12, 1815, in Camden County, Georgia, William Joseph Hardee graduated from West Point in 1838 and earned two brevets for gallantry during the Mexican War. He resigned on January 31, 1861, and received an appointment as a brigadier general on June 17, 1861. He earned promotion to major general on October 7, 1861, and lieutenant general on October 10, 1862. He served with the Army of Tennessee for most of the war. Afterward, he owned a plantation in Selma, Alabama. He died in Wytheville, Virginia, on November 6, 1873, and received burial in Live Oak Cemetery in Selma. *Eighth Census,* M653–47, 396; *OR,* 1:3, 609–10; Diane Neal and Thomas W. Kremm, *Lion of the South: General Thomas C. Hindman* (Macon, GA: Mercer University Press, 1997), 1–20, 65–86, 197–242; Bobby L. Roberts, "General T. C. Hindman and the Trans-Mississippi District," *Arkansas Historical Quarterly* 32 (Winter 1973), 297–311; Nathaniel Cheairs Hughes Jr., *General William J. Hardee: Old Reliable* (Baton Rouge: Louisiana State University Press, 1992), 74–76; Richard M. McMurry, "William Joseph Hardee," in *Confederate General,* ed. Davis and Hoffman, 3:58–61; Edwin C. Bearss, "Thomas Carmichael Hindman," in *Confederate General,* ed. Davis and Hoffman, 3:106–9.

56. Mr. Emanuel could not be identified.

57. "Mr. Woods" of Mount Vernon may refer to John B. Woods or his father, Oliver Woods. Born in Tennessee around 1812, John B. Woods lived on a Mount Vernon Township farm in Lawrence County, Missouri, with his 46-year-old wife, Martha, three sons, two daughters, and his elderly father. In 1860, John B. Woods owned $10,000 in real estate and a personal estate of $2,300. Born in Kentucky around 1784, Oliver Woods may have reflected the strong Unionist sentiments that characterized his generation and native state. The derogatory term "black Republican" referred to any individual who expressed support for abolitionism or the Lincoln administration. Born in Tennessee about 1832, David H. White lived in Holly Springs Township in Dallas County and worked as a carpenter. In 1860, he owned $3,000 in real estate and a personal estate of $500. He mustered in as a private in Company A of the 1st Arkansas Mounted Rifles on June 15, 1861. He received a discharge for disability at Pond Spring, Missouri, on August 23, 1861. Born in Maryland about 1838, James Harper lived in the household of his brother Robert W. Harper and practiced medicine in Welborn Township in Conway County. He mustered in as adjutant with the 1st Arkansas Mounted Rifles on June 9, 1861, and served on Churchill's staff until mortally wounded at Wilson's Creek. Harper died on August 18, 1861. *Eighth Census,* M653–28, 885; *Eighth Census,* M653–40, 1020; *Eighth Census,* M653–39, 450; CSR, M376, Roll 25; M376, Roll 10; Webb Garrison, *The Encyclopedia of Civil War Usage: An Illustrated Compendium of the Everyday Language of Soldiers and Civilians* (Nashville: Cumberland House, 2001), 28.

58. Born in Arkansas about 1840, Oscar Lee Mathis lived on his father's farm in Planters Township. He mustered in as a private on June 15, 1861. Discharged for disabil-

ity on December 12, 1861, he enlisted as a corporal in Company G of the 23rd Arkansas Infantry on May 13, 1862, at Corinth, Mississippi. Captured at Port Hudson, Louisiana, on July 9, 1863, he received parole the next day. CSR, M376, Roll 15; *Eighth Census,* M653–38, 932.

59. Sappington and Coulter enlisted in the company of the 1st Arkansas Mounted Rifles on June 15, 1861, at Fort Smith. Born in Louisiana about 1839, John H. Sappington lived and worked on the Eudora property of Warren J. Philips. He mustered in as a private and died of disease in 1862. Born in Tennessee about 1825, O. H. Coulter worked as an overseer in Chicot County. In 1860, he reported a personal estate of $15,000. He served as regimental butcher from August 14, 1861, until discharged for disability on October 25, 1862. CSR, M376, Roll 20; M376, Roll 5; *Eighth Census,* M653–38, 929, 935.

60. Located in southeastern Missouri on the border with Kansas, Jasper County consisted of two-thirds fertile prairie and one-third timber with deposits of limestone, lead, and zinc. Joplin, Carthage, and Sarcoxie comprised part of the county. In 1860, Jasper County totaled 6,607 residents. Nathan Howe Parker, *The Missouri Handbook: Embracing a full description of the State of Missouri* (P. M. Pinckard: St. Louis, 1865), 114–15.

61. Isaac Newton mustered in as a private and flag bearer in Company A of the 1st Arkansas Mounted Rifles on June 15, 1861. He died at Richmond, Mississippi, on June 27, 1862. CSR, M376, Roll 17.

62. While waiting to link with McCulloch to counter Lyon's potential movements against Springfield, Price camped north of Joplin at Cowskin Prairie, in southeastern Missouri, and organized the Missouri State Guard. Eugene Morrow Violette, *A History of Missouri* (New York: D. C. Heath and Company, 1918), 359.

63. The Crouch family operated the Butterfield Stage stop between Neosho and Cassville, Missouri. Their loyalties are unknown. Melton, "Civil War Days in Barry County," 9.

64. De Witt C. Hopkins owned a farm near Price's encampment at Cowskin Prairie, which Price used as his headquarters in June. Hopkins secretly observed and reported Confederate movements to Union commanders. He continued these activities during the Pea Ridge campaign, until captured on April 27, 1862. Initially sentenced to death as a spy, Confederate authorities exchanged him on August 2, 1862. Thereafter, he served as a scout and captain of Company I in the 1st Arkansas (Union) Cavalry. U.S. War Department, Compiled Service Records of Confederate Soldiers Who Served in Organizations from the State of Arkansas, National Archives, Microcopy M383, Roll 2 (hereafter cited as CSR with microfilm and roll numbers); Scott, *Loyalty on the Frontier,* 89–100.

65. Gibbs, Jones, Thompson, and Campbell all served in the 1st Arkansas Mounted Rifles and mustered in at Fort Smith. Born in Kentucky about 1831, William E. Gibbs practiced law in Ruddell Township in the Independence County town of Batesville. He mustered in as captain with Company K on June 9, 1861. He received a discharge on May 1, 1862. Born in Georgia about 1822, Dr. J. J. Jones practiced medicine in Wilkinson Township in the Desha County town of Napoleon. He lived with his 38-year-old wife, Catharine, two sons, and a daughter. In 1860, he owned a personal estate of $2,500. He

enlisted as a 1st lieutenant in Company G on June 15, 1861, but received a commission as captain by August 15, 1861. Jones resigned on May 1, 1862. Born in Alabama about 1838, Lycurgus L. Thompson lived in Big Rock Township in Pulaski County with his 25-year-old wife, Elizabeth, a son, and a hired farm hand. In 1860, Thompson owned $15,000 in real estate and a personal estate of $6,500. Thompson mustered in as 1st lieutenant in Company I in June 1861 and received a discharge in May 1862. Born on August 28, 1838, in Muhlenburg County, Kentucky, William P. Campbell settled in Arkansas in 1854 and operated a pharmacy in Augusta until 1860, when he studied law. He mustered in as third lieutenant in Company D ("the Augusta Guards") on June 9, 1861, and survived wounds at Wilson's Creek and Murfreesboro, with amputation of his left leg. Captured at Murfreesboro, he remained a prisoner for four months. He returned home, married Virginia C. Davies in October 1863, and fathered four daughters and five sons. Campbell rejoined the regiment that fall and served as commissary until February 1865. After Bentonville, he became major of the consolidated 1st Mounted Rifles. He farmed in Woodruff County, served as county clerk, operated a mercantile business, and served as clerk of the Arkansas Supreme Court. CSR, M376, Roll 9; M376, Roll 13; M376, Roll 23; M376, Roll 4; *Eighth Census,* M653–43, 12; *Eighth Census,* M653–41, 7; *Eighth Census,* M653–49, 160; *Biographical and Historical Memoirs of Pulaski, Jefferson, Lonoke, Faulkner, Grant, Saline, Perry, Garland, and Hot Spring Counties, Arkansas* (Chicago: Goodspeed Publishing Company, 1889), 427–28.

66. "Mr. Gray" probably refers to John Gray of Osage Township in Benton County, near Bentonville. Born in Kentucky about 1829, Gray owned $450 in real estate in 1860. He lived with his 26-year-old wife, Sarah, one son, and one daughter. *Eighth Census,* M653–37, 246–47; B. Clay Shannon, *Still Casting Shadows: A Shared Mosaic of U.S. History* (Lincoln, NE: iUniverse, 2006), 66.

67. Born in Kentucky about 1836, John Brawner lived at the Buckhorn Hotel in Old River Township and worked as a mechanic. He mustered into the 1st Arkansas Mounted Rifles on June 15, 1861. He died at Lauderdale Springs, Mississippi, on October 20, 1863, of wounds received at Chickamauga. *Eighth Census,* M653–38, 921; CSR, M376, Roll 3.

68. Alonzo Griffith mustered in as a private in Company A of the 1st Arkansas Mounted Rifles on June 15, 1861. He died of measles in Newton County, Missouri, on September 20, 1861. Martin V. Worthington returned to duty with Company A due to good conduct at Wilson's Creek. CSR, M376, Roll 9; M376, Roll 26.

69. The term "Jayhawker" originated in the 1850s as a derogatory moniker for anti-slavery settlers in Kansas territory. During the war, the term referred to pro-Union guerrillas on the Missouri-Kansas frontier. Michael Fellman, *Inside War: The Guerrilla Conflict in Missouri during the American Civil War* (New York: Oxford University Press, 1990), 167–70; Garrison, *Encyclopedia of Civil War Usage,* 127.

70. Born in Kentucky about 1831, P. E. Bush lived on a farm in Mill Creek Township in Drew County with his 22-year-old wife, V. L. Bush, and three sons. He mustered in as a private in Company A of the 1st Arkansas Mounted Rifles on June 15, 1862. *Eighth Census,* M653–41, 79; CSR, M376, Roll 4.

71. MacLean, Stamps, and Talbot all joined Company A of the 1st Arkansas Mounted Rifles at Fort Smith on June 15, 1861. Born in Scotland, John MacLean mus-

tered in as a private and brigade pioneer. He earned promotion to lieutenant on
September 24, 1861, and received a discharge on May 1, 1862. Born in Mississippi about
1847, Hiram C. Stamps lived in Railroad Township with his 33-year-old mother, Elvira
Stamps, a brother, and four sisters. He mustered as a 15-year-old musician and received
a discharge in 1862 due to his youth. Born in Georgia on December 12, 1806, Stand
Watie received his education through mission schools. He lived as a planter, published
a Native American newspaper, and signed the controversial 1835 agreement to cede
Cherokee tribal lands in Georgia and relocate to the Indian Territory. He served as
colonel of the 1st Cherokee Mounted Rifles, which he commanded at Wilson's Creek
and Elkhorn Tavern and on raids in the Indian Territory. On May 6, 1864, he earned
promotion to brigadier general. He surrendered on June 23, 1865, and resumed his
business and planting interests. He died at Honey Creek in Indian Territory on
September 9, 1871, and received burial in the Old Ridge Cemetery. Mr. Cockerel could
not be identified. The Texas and Missouri Road ran between Gibson and Cabin Creek
in the Indian Territory. Watie attacked Federal supply convoys along this route.
Thomas A. Talbot mustered in as a private. Discharged due to age, he died at Okolona,
Mississippi, in 1862. CSR, M376, Roll 15; M376, Roll 22; M818, Roll 25; M376, Roll 23;
Eighth Census, M653–38, 958; *OR,* 1:41 (Part 1), 782; Benjamin E. Snellgrove, "Stand
Watie," in *Confederate General,* ed. Davis and Hoffman, 6:110–11. For a full discussion
of Stand Watie and the Cherokee Nation during the Civil War see Clarissa W. Confer,
The Cherokee Nation (Norman: University of Oklahoma, 1997); Frank Cunningham,
General Stand Watie's Confederate Indians (Norman: University of Oklahoma Press,
1998).

72. Neo Woodard could not be identified. Captain Buzzard commanded Company
A of the 1st Cherokee Mounted Rifles until killed near Fort Gibson in Indian Territory
on May 20, 1863. Captain Robert Calvin Parks commanded Company B of the 1st
Cherokee Mounted Rifles until promoted to lieutenant colonel. Dan C. Carey operated
a ferry across the Grand River in Delaware County in Indian Territory. CSR, M818, Roll
4; M818, Roll 18; George H. Shirk, *Oklahoma Place Names* (Norman: University of
Oklahoma Press, 1987), 45; Annie Heloise Abel, *The American Indian as Participant in
the Civil War* (Cleveland: Arthur H. Clark Company, 1919), 126, 192.

73. Gilstrap's Ferry crossed the Grand River in Indian Territory near the Neosho
and Spring Rivers. "Ferries," Vertical File, Research Division, Oklahoma Historical
Society, Oklahoma City; John McCorkle, *Three Years with Quantrill: A True Story Told
by His Scout* (New York: Buffalo-Head Press, 1966), 98; for a discussion of the Cherokee
alliance with the Confederacy see Laurence M. Hauptman, *Between Two Fires:
American Indians in the Civil War* (New York: Free Press, 1995), 27–28, 45–48.

74. Born in Alabama about 1814, James D. Latimer lived in Oden Township with his
47-year-old wife, Louisa, and two daughters. He worked as a mechanic and owned
$1,800 in real estate and a personal estate of $300. He mustered into the 1st Arkansas
Mounted Rifles on June 4, 1861, as a captain and assistant quartermaster. *Eighth Census,*
M653–38, 950; CSR, M376, Roll 14.

75. Mathis, Robb, Wilson, Phillips, Carpenter, and Hurley all served in Company A
of the 1st Arkansas Mounted Rifles. Born in Arkansas about 1843, Dudley M. Mathis
lived on his father's farm in Planters Township. He mustered in at Camp Lee, Missouri,

as a private on September 29, 1861, and received a discharge in 1862. Born about 1844 in Coahoma County, Mississippi, William H. Robb lived on his father's farm in Planters Township and mustered into Company A as a private on September 19, 1861. He earned promotion to fourth corporal on March 1, 1862, and first corporal on May 1, 1862. Demoted to private on September 23, 1862, he received a discharge at Loudon, Tennessee, on November 4, 1862. Born in Arkansas about 1836, Thomas J. Wilson lived on his father's farm in De Bastrop Township in the Desha County town of Hamburg. In 1860, he owned $1,000 in real estate and a personal estate of $260. He mustered in as a private in Company A on September 19, 1861, at Camp Lee. He received a discharge in 1862. Born in Jasper County, Georgia, William D. Phillips lived on his father's farm in Planters Township in Eudora. He mustered in as a private on September 19, 1861, at Camp Lee. Wounded and captured at Murfreesboro, he lost his right arm while imprisoned at Camp Morton, Indiana. Exchanged at City Point, Virginia, on April 12, 1863, he received a discharge for disability at Shelbyville, Tennessee, on May 3, 1863. Born in Arkansas about 1843, James Carpenter lived on the Bayou Mason Township farm of his 40-year-old mother, Julia. He enlisted at Camp Lee as a private on September 19, 1861. Captured at Elkhorn Tavern on March 8, 1862, Carpenter received a discharge after exchange. He later enlisted as a private in Company G of the 36th Arkansas Infantry and earned promotion to corporal. Thomas Woods mustered in with Company A of the 1st Arkansas Mounted Rifles as a private and substitute for James B. Lyerly at Camp Lee on October 2, 1861. He received a discharge on September 19, 1862. Arrested on February 15, 1864, at Skippers Point, Mississippi, he took the oath of allegiance at Camp Chase on April 22, 1864. Born in Arkansas about 1841, John H. Hurley lived in Fort Smith and studied law. On June 15, 1861, he mustered in as a private but earned promotion to third corporal on October 1, 1861, and second corporal on September 23, 1862. Hurley deserted on July 15, 1863, at Jackson, Mississippi. CSR, M376, Roll 15; M376, Roll 20; M376, Roll 25; M376, Roll 18; M376, Roll 4; M376, Roll 26; M376, Roll 12; *Eighth Census,* M653–38, 932, 935, 944; *Eighth Census,* M653–37, 110; *Eighth Census,* M653–50, 1141.

76. The son of former South Carolina governor Andrew Pickens, Francis Wilkinson Pickens advocated states' rights in the U.S. House of Representatives until the 1850s and then shifted toward moderate cooperation with the national Democratic Party. He initially argued against secession but followed popular opinion and won election as governor by December 1860. While governor, he urged the use of force against Fort Sumter. His term ended in December 1862. He lost most of his fortune during the war and died in 1869. David S. Heidler and Jeanne T. Heidler, "Francis Wilkinson Pickens," in *Encyclopedia of the American Civil War,* ed. Heidler and Heidler, 3:1517.

77. Born in England about 1834, Edward Molero lived at the Parker House hotel in Old River Township. He worked with his older brother William as a plasterer and cistern builder. Molero mustered in as a private in Company A of the 1st Arkansas Mounted Rifles on June 15, 1861. He earned promotion to sergeant on August 1, 1862. Captured on September 8, 1864, near Decatur, Georgia, and confined at Camp Douglas, Illinois, he took the oath of allegiance on May 16, 1865. CSR, M376, Roll 17; *Eighth Census,* M653–38, 919; *Chicot Press* (January 17, 1861), 1.

78. McCulloch and Price clashed repeatedly after Wilson's Creek. Price wanted to exploit the victory by moving into the Missouri River Valley to threaten Lexington, while McCulloch wished to create a secure supply base for a raid into Kansas. Price captured the Lexington garrison on September 20, but failed to secure sufficient arms for his new, undisciplined recruits. McCulloch postponed his operation in order to aid Price, who suddenly abandoned their agreed-upon plan to attack Fremont near Springfield and instead fell back on McCulloch's force at Neosho. Price's movements allowed Fremont to occupy Springfield and threaten McCulloch's base at Fayetteville. This circumstance forced McCulloch to establish a defensive position at Cross Hollows, 20 miles below the Missouri-Arkansas border. Cutrer, *Ben McCulloch,* 258–60; Piston and Hatcher, *Wilson's Creek,* 310–16; Shea and Hess, *Pea Ridge,* 2–3, 46–48.

79. Mack P. J. Smith refers to Peter J. Smith. George E. Young enlisted in Company A of the 1st Arkansas Mounted Rifles as a private on May 15, 1862, in Corinth. He survived a wound at Chickamauga but disappeared after August 31, 1864. CSR, M376, Roll 26.

80. Alexander Winchester Dinsmore resided near Cave Springs, Arkansas. He owned six slaves and five mercantile stores near Bentonville. His son, Hugh Anderson Dinsmore, served as U.S. minister to Korea from 1887 to 1890 and in the U.S. House of Representatives between 1892 and 1905. Scott, *Loyalty on the Frontier,* 136; F. P. Rose, "Hugh Anderson Dinsmore," *Arkansas Historical Quarterly* 11 (Spring 1952): 69–78.

81. "Greasy Bill" Smith could not be identified.

82. Born in Warren County, Virginia, in May 1826, Thomas Alexander Harris moved to Hannibal, Missouri. He entered West Point in 1843 but withdrew in 1845. He received a direct commission as a second lieutenant during the Mexican War but saw no action, and then served in filibuster expeditions in Cuba and Central America. He practiced law, edited a newspaper, married the sister of future Union admiral David Dixon Porter, and served in the Missouri House of Representatives. Appointed as a brigadier general in the Missouri State Guard in June 1861, he served at the siege of Lexington. Thereafter, he served in the Confederate House of Representatives, where he advocated promotions for Sterling Price and opposed the Davis administration. Harris lost his seat in 1864 and sold contraband at the end of the war. Captured in Florida on May 17, 1865, and held at Fort McHenry, he received a special presidential pardon on September 2, 1866. He worked as a life insurance agent and newspaperman in Louisville, Kentucky, and represented Oldham County in the Kentucky House of Representatives. He died in Louisville on April 9, 1895, and received burial in Cave Hill Cemetery. Clayton E. Jewett, ed., *Rise and Fall of the Confederacy: The Memoir of Senator Williamson S. Oldham, CSA* (Columbia: University of Missouri Press, 2006), 209n5; Ezra J. Warner and W. Buck Yearns, eds., *Biographical Register of the Confederate Congress* (Baton Rouge: Louisiana State University Press, 1975), 109–10; Douthat, *Special Presidential Pardons,* 1:118; Allardice, *More Generals in Gray,* 121–22.

83. Born on October 11, 1825, in Paris, Tennessee, Elkanah Brackin Greer served under Jefferson Davis in the Mexican War and settled in Marshall, Texas, as a planter and merchant. In July 1861 he received a commission as colonel of the 3rd Texas Cavalry (also known as the "South Kansas–Texas Mounted Volunteers"), which he led

at Wilson's Creek and Elkhorn Tavern. On October 8, 1862, he earned promotion to brigadier general and chief of the Bureau of Conscription for the Trans-Mississippi Department. He commanded the department's reserve forces in 1864. He died at his sister's home in DeValls Bluff, Arkansas, on March 25, 1877, and received burial in Elmwood Cemetery in Memphis. Greer's regiment served in the Trans-Mississippi Department until after Elkhorn Tavern, when it transferred east of the Mississippi River. U.S. War Department, Compiled Service Records of Confederate Soldiers Who Served in Organizations from the State of Texas, National Archives, Microcopy M227, Roll 14 (hereafter cited as CSR with microfilm and roll numbers); M818, Roll 10; *OR*, 3: 717–18; Crute, *Units of the Confederate States Army,* 323–24; Anne Bailey, "Elkanah Brackin Greer," in *Confederate General,* ed. Davis and Hoffman, 3:34–35.

84. "Crenshaw" may refer to L.A.D. Crenshaw. Born in Tennessee about 1823, Crenshaw and his 30-year-old wife, Mary, owned a farm in Wilson Township in Greene County, Missouri, with two sons and a daughter. In 1860, Crenshaw owned $20,000 in real estate and a personal estate valued at $20,000. *Eighth Census,* M653–621, 177.

85. Born in Kentucky in 1806, David Walker settled in Fayetteville, Arkansas, in 1830 and practiced law. He served in the state senate until selected to the Arkansas Supreme Court. He chaired the state's first secession convention as a delegate from Washington County. He served as chief justice of the Arkansas Supreme Court after the war and died in Fayetteville on September 30, 1879. Exempt from the general amnesty, due to personal wealth greater than $20,000, Walker applied for a special presidential pardon. Endorsed by Gov. Isaac Murphy and U.S. district attorney Orville Jennings, he received a pardon on October 9, 1865. Douthat, *Special Presidential Pardons,* 1:174; Ted J. Smith, "Mastering Farm and Family: David Walker as Slaveholder," *Arkansas Historical Quarterly* 58, no. 1 (Spring 1999): 61–79; John Hugh McReynolds, *Makers of Arkansas History* (New York: Silver, Burdett and Company, 1905), 139–42; Joseph S. Utley, "Graves of Eminent Men," in *Publications of the Arkansas Historical Association,* ed. John Hugh McReynolds (Little Rock: Democrat Printing and Lithographing Company, 1908), 2:265; Jeannie M. Whayne, "Henry Massie Rector," in *Arkansas Biography: A Collection of Notable Lives,* ed. Nancy A. Williams and Jeannie M. Whayne (Fayetteville: University of Arkansas Press, 2000), 235.

86. Morgan Buck owned a farm 23 miles south of Fayetteville, Arkansas. On November 13, 1863, Col. M. La Rue Harrison of the 1st Arkansas (Union) Cavalry reported Buck as providing the only source of food for retreating Confederates within 67 miles. Exempt from the general amnesty for violation of his oath, Buck applied for a special presidential pardon. Endorsed by Gov. Isaac Murphy and Col. J. W. Johnson, he received a pardon on September 5, 1865. "Mr. Mills" may refer to Archibald Mills, a 25-year-old farmer with an 18-year-old wife, Mary, who owned a farm south of Fayetteville in West Fork Township in Washington County. *OR*, 1:22 (Part 1), 749–51; Douthat, *Special Presidential Pardons,* 1:169; *Eighth Census,* M653–52, 793.

87. Bots are a common species of gadfly that deposit their eggs on horsehair by means of a glutinous fluid. The eggs hatch in a few days and release a small worm, which the horse ingests when it licks the affected area. Once ingested, the worm attaches to the cuticular portion of the stomach and feeds on the host animal's stom-

ach mucus through winter. Once mature, it detaches in the spring and moves into the villous portion of the stomach, where it passes out with the chyme and evacuates with the dung of the host animal. The larva lay buried for a few weeks, transform into a chrysalis and then a fly. The females lay their eggs in the hair of the host animal and the process repeats. In the mid-nineteenth century, no effective treatment existed other than to collect expended larva as they built up around the host animal's tail or to wash the eggs off the hairs with warm water. William Youatt and Walter Watson, *The Horse: With a Treatise on Draught* (London: Longmans, Green, 1880), 224–25.

88. The 1st Arkansas Mounted Rifles remained in winter quarters at Spadra Bluffs, opposite Clarksville near the Arkansas River, until February 1862. Outbreaks of smallpox occurred between Clarksville and Fort Smith in the winter of 1861–1862. Dacus, *Reminiscences,* 2; William Oates Ragsdale, *They Sought a Land: A Settlement in the Arkansas River Valley, 1840–1870* (Fayetteville: University of Arkansas Press, 1997), 76.

89. Dr. William M. Lawrence mustered in as assistant surgeon with the 1st Arkansas Mounted Rifles on June 20, 1861. In 1860, three farmers with the surname "Bryant" owned property within 25 miles east of Van Buren in Mulberry Township in Franklin County. Born in Missouri about 1834, E. B. Bryant lived with his 22-year-old wife, Elizabeth, a son, and Bryant's 45-year-old mother. He owned $1,235 in real estate and a personal estate of $8,100. Born in Alabama about 1835, J. M. Bryant lived with his 22-year-old wife, Elizabeth, a daughter, and two hired laborers. He owned $500 in real estate and a personal estate of $500. Born in South Carolina about 1830, H. J. Bryant lived with his 33-year-old wife, April, three sons, and a daughter. He owned $180 in real estate and a personal estate of $280. Given the difference in their estates, it seems likely that Reynolds stayed with E. B. Bryant. CSR, M376, Roll 14; *Eighth Census,* M653–41, 309–11.

90. Hiram Brodie owned the Planter's Hotel of Van Buren. "Capt. Stuart" seems to refer to Capt. James T. Stuart, who commanded "the Crawford Artillery." Unable to acquire horses, the battery reorganized as Company I of the 3rd Arkansas Infantry (State Troops). Dr. John H. Carroll served as a surgeon with the 1st Arkansas Mounted Rifles. Between April 25, 1863, and September 21, 1864, Carroll served as a surgeon on the staff of William L. Cabell. CSR, M376, Roll 22; M376, Roll 4, and M818, Roll 5; Crute, *Confederate Staff Officers,* 30; *History of Benton, Washington, Carroll, Madison, Crawford, Franklin and Sebastian Counties* (Chicago: Goodspeed Publishing Company, 1889), 530; Clara B. Eno, *History of Crawford County, Arkansas* (Van Buren: Press-Argus, 1951), 261.

91. Dr. John Williams operated a drug store in Aurora, Arkansas, near War Eagle Creek. *History of Benton, Washington, Carroll, Madison, Crawford, Franklin and Sebastian Counties,* 461.

92. "Mr. Garrett" may refer to E. W. Garrett. Born in Georgia about 1824, E. W. Garrett lived in White Oak Township in the Franklin County town of Ozark with his 27-year-old wife, Ruth, one son, and one daughter. In 1860, Garrett worked as a wheelwright and owned a personal estate of $20. *Eighth Census,* M653–41, 265.

93. "P. G. Smith" should be listed "P. J. Smith." Bateman and Graham mustered into Company A of the 1st Arkansas Mounted Rifles on June 15, 1861, at Fort Smith. Born in

England about 1840, Thomas J. Bateman lived at the Buckhorn Hotel in Old River
Township and worked as a bricklayer. He mustered in as a second corporal. Reduced to
private in December 1861, he transferred to Rivers's Arkansas Battery (also known as
Provence's Arkansas Battery and Humphrey's Arkansas Battery) in November 1862.
He deserted this unit on November 21, 1864. Captured by Federal troops on November
25, 1864, he remained a prisoner at Old Capitol Prison in Washington, D.C., until he
escaped on February 2, 1865. Born in Arkansas about 1841, Moses Graham lived in
Planters Township in the household of his brother Jonathan. He mustered as a private
but earned promotion as corporal in December 1861. Reduced to private on March 1,
1862, he regained the rank of corporal on May 1, 1862. He survived wounds at
Murfreesboro and Chickamauga and received parole at Jamestown, North Carolina,
on April 30, 1865. CSR, M376, Roll 2; M376, Roll 9; *Eighth Census*, M653-38, 921, 936.

TWO

1. The 1st Arkansas Mounted Rifles served variously in the Army of Mississippi,
the Army of Kentucky, and the Army of Tennessee. For a full discussion of the signifi-
cance of Forts Henry and Donelson and the battle of Elkhorn Tavern, see Benjamin
Franklin Cooling, *Forts Henry and Donelson: The Key to the Confederate Heartland*
(Knoxville: University of Tennessee Press, 1987); William L. Shea and Earl J. Hess, *Pea
Ridge: Civil War Campaign in the West* (Chapel Hill: University of North Carolina
Press, 1992).

2. See Reynolds's entry of April 14, 1862, for comments about reluctance to serve
dismounted. Confederate authorities issued the order to dismount on April 13, 1862.
Twelve members of Company F briefly laid down arms on June 14, 1862, in protest over
dismounted service. According to Robert H. Dacus, the regiment dismounted at
DeValls Bluff, Arkansas, and proceeded to Memphis with a promise that their horses
would follow in 60 days. Robert H. Dacus, *Reminiscences of Company "H," First
Arkansas Mounted Rifles* (Dardanelle, AR: Post-Dispatch Printing, 1897), 2.

3. Reynolds ranked as major from April 14, 1862, and lieutenant colonel from May
1, 1862. "Appointments," Daniel Harris Reynolds Papers, Special Collections,
University Libraries, Fayetteville, Box 1, Folder 7, Item 127 (hereafter cited as DHR
Papers).

4. Thomas Lawrence Connelly, *Autumn of Glory: The Army of Tennessee, 1862–1865*
(Baton Rouge: Louisiana State University Press, 1971), 4–5, 13–29.

5. *Biographical and Historical Memoirs of Southern Arkansas* (Chicago: Goodspeed
Publishing Company, 1890), 1085.

6. During the Pea Ridge campaign the 3rd Louisiana Infantry, Dandridge McRae's
15th Arkansas Infantry (also known as the 21st Arkansas Infantry and the Northwest
Arkansas regiment), and Evander McNair's 4th Arkansas Infantry served in Louis
Hebert's Brigade. Hebert's Brigade included the 14th, 15th, 16th, and 17th Arkansas regiments, as well as the 1st and 2nd Arkansas Mounted Rifles and the 4th Texas Cavalry
Battalion. Born in Baldwin County, Alabama, on October 10, 1829, Dandridge McRae
graduated from South Carolina College in 1849. He practiced law in Searcy, Arkansas,

and served as clerk of the county and circuit courts. He served as colonel of the 15th Arkansas Infantry at Wilson's Creek and Elkhorn Tavern and earned promotion to brigadier general on November 5, 1862. He remained in the Trans-Mississippi but resigned in 1864. He returned to Searcy and practiced law. Exempt from the general amnesty of May 29, 1865, due to his rank as a Confederate general officer, he applied for a special presidential pardon. Endorsed by W. Byers, H. C. Coldwell, U.S. district attorney Orville Jennings, and Gov. Isaac Murphy, McRae received a pardon on August 8, 1865. He died on April 23, 1899, and received burial in Searcy. Born in Laurel Hill, North Carolina, on April 13, 1820, Evander McNair moved to Mississippi in 1830. He served in the 1st Mississippi Rifles under Jefferson Davis during the Mexican War, settled in Washington, Arkansas, and operated a mercantile business. He served as colonel of the 4th Arkansas Infantry at Wilson's Creek and Elkhorn Tavern. Promoted to brigadier general on November 4, 1862, he survived a wound at Chickamauga and remained in the Trans-Mississippi Department. Exempt from the general amnesty of May 29, 1865, due to his rank as a Confederate general officer, McNair applied for a special presidential pardon. Endorsed by U.S. district attorney Orville Jennings and W. D. Snow, he received a pardon on December 12, 1865. He settled in Mississippi and died in Hattiesburg on November 13, 1902. He received burial in Magnolia, Mississippi. U.S. War Department, Compiled Service Records of Confederate Soldiers Who Served in Organizations from the State of Arkansas, National Archives, Microcopy 376, Roll 16 (hereafter cited as CSR with microfilm and roll numbers); U.S. War Department, Index to Compiled Service Records of Confederate Soldiers Who Served in Organizations Raised Directly by the Confederate Government and of Confederate General and Staff Officers and Non-Regimental Enlisted Men, National Archives, Microcopy 818, Roll 16 (hereafter cited as CSR with microfilm and roll numbers); Henry G. Bunn, "Gen. Evander McNair," *Confederate Veteran* 11 (1903): 265–66; James L. Douthat, comp., *Special Presidential Pardons of Confederate Soldiers: A Listing of Former Confederate Soldiers Requesting Full Pardon from President Andrew Johnson* (Signal Mountain, TN: Mountain Press, 1999), 1:23, 171; Joseph H. Crute Jr., *Units of the Confederate States Army* (Midlothian, VA: Derwent Books, 1987), 45, 51; Shea and Hess, *Pea Ridge,* 23; Ezra J. Warner, *Generals in Gray: Lives of the Confederate Commanders* (Baton Rouge: Louisiana State University Press, 1959), 205–6.

7. The Union troops at Cross Hollows, Sugar Creek, and Elm Springs represented the lead elements of the Army of the Southwest during the Pea Ridge campaign, commanded by Samuel R. Curtis. Two runaway slaves informed Curtis of the position and movement of Confederate forces in the area. Shea and Hess, *Pea Ridge,* 50–52.

8. Reynolds is probably referring to companies of the 4th Texas Cavalry Battalion. Shea and Hess, *Pea Ridge,* 23.

9. Born in North Carolina about 1835, George M. Henry lived in Old River Township at the Parker House hotel and practiced law. He mustered in as a private in Company A of the 1st Arkansas Mounted Rifles on June 15, 1861. He earned promotion to third lieutenant and quartermaster on April 14, 1862, and first lieutenant on May 1, 1862. He survived a wound at Murfreesboro and earned promotion to captain on September 20, 1863. Henry died at Dug Gap, Georgia, on August 31, 1864. CSR, M376,

Roll 11; Bureau of the Census, *Eighth Census of the United States, 1860* (Washington, DC: National Archives and Records Administration, 1860), M653–38, 919.

10. James McIntosh commanded a brigade at Elkhorn Tavern, consisting of the 3rd, 6th, 9th, and 11th Texas Cavalry regiments, the 1st Texas Cavalry Battalion, and the 1st Arkansas Cavalry Battalion. Born on March 13, 1820, Louis Hebert graduated third in the West Point class of 1845. He served as colonel of the 3rd Louisiana Infantry until captured at Elkhorn Tavern. Hebert earned promotion to brigadier general on May 26, 1862. Capt. John J. Goode commanded Goode's Company, Texas Light Artillery State Troops (also known as Douglas's Company of Texas Light Artillery and the Dallas Light Artillery). Comprised of two 50-man companies from Dallas and Smith Counties, the battery mustered in June 1861 and fought at Elkhorn Tavern, Corinth, the Kentucky campaign, Murfreesboro, Nashville, and Mobile. Capt. William Hart commanded Hart's Arkansas Battery. At Elkhorn Tavern, Hart's Battery lost two guns and its colors. As a result, Van Dorn officially censured the battery and ordered it disbanded. Cleared by a court of inquiry, the battery reorganized on August 1, 1862, and served in the Trans-Mississippi. Capt. David Provence commanded Provence's Battery of Arkansas Light Artillery (also known as Rivers's Battery). Organized in the spring of 1861, with recruits from Fort Smith, this battery fought at Elkhorn Tavern, the Kentucky campaign, Murfreesboro, Chickamauga, and Chattanooga under captains David Provence, John T. Humphreys, and John W. Rivers. Born in Tennessee about 1830, Henry Hayes lived in Old River Township at the Buckhorn Hotel. In 1860, he owned $4,500 in real estate and a personal estate of $500. Hayes served as probate judge for Chicot County between 1860 and 1866. Due to disproportionate land-based wealth, the South lacked sufficient liquid assets to finance its war effort. As a result, the Confederate Congress passed a direct tax on real and personal property in August 1861. State collection proved ineffective as most states paid their quota with nearly worthless state notes or loans rather than collect payments from individual residents. U.S. War Department, *The War of the Rebellion: A Compilation of the Official Records of the Union and Confederate Armies* (Washington, DC: Government Printing Office, 1902), 1:8, 728 (hereafter cited as *OR* or *Official Records*); U.S. War Department, Compiled Service Records of Confederate Soldiers Who Served in Organizations from the State of Louisiana, National Archives, Microcopy M378, Roll 13 (hereafter cited as CSR with microfilm and roll numbers); M818, Roll 11; U.S. War Department, Compiled Service Records of Confederate Soldiers Who Served in Organizations from the State of Texas, National Archives, Microcopy M227, Roll 14 (hereafter cited as CSR with microfilm and roll numbers); M376, Roll 10; M376, Roll 19; *Biographical and Historical Memoirs of Southern Arkansas,* 1062; *Eighth Census,* M653–38, 921; Terry L. Jones, "Louis Hebert," in *Confederate General,* ed. William C. Davis and Julie Hoffman (Harrisburg, PA: National Historical Society, 1991), 3:82–83; Glenn Dedmondt, *The Flags of Civil War Arkansas* (Gretna, LA: Pelican Publishing Company, 2006), 46–47; Crute, *Units of the Confederate States Army,* 63, 344; CSR, M376, Roll 19; Shea and Hess, *Pea Ridge,* 23, 109; James M. McPherson, *Battle Cry of Freedom: The Civil War Era* (New York: Oxford University Press, 1988), 437–39.

11. In late February, Confederate troops under McCulloch gathered supplies at Fayetteville, Arkansas. The endeavor degenerated into general ransacking of private

households. McCulloch ordered the destruction of all provisions not taken by his troops, which magnified problems for civilians. Shea and Hess, *Pea Ridge,* 48–49.

12. Born on February 3, 1805, Samuel Ryan Curtis graduated from West Point in 1831. Appointed as a brigadier general on May 17, 1861, Curtis earned promotion to major general on March 21, 1862. He commanded the Department of the Missouri, the Department of Kansas, and the Department of the Northwest. He died at Council Bluffs, Iowa, on December 26, 1866, and received burial at Oakland Cemetery in Keokuk. The movements ordered by Van Dorn on March 5 and 6 proved crucial to Elkhorn Tavern. Van Dorn blamed a slow march for a lost opportunity to defeat Sigel's forces. *OR,* 1:8, 283; Warner, *Generals in Blue,* 107–8; Shea and Hess, *Pea Ridge,* 62–65.

13. In the spring of 1862, McCulloch's staff consisted of Lt. Frank C. Armstrong (assistant adjutant general), 1st Lt. Edward Dillon, Dr. J. J. Gaenslen (surgeon), Capt. Dr. T. L. Hunter (assistant surgeon), 2nd Lt. Manning M. Kimmel (ordnance officer), Maj. William Montgomery (assistant quartermaster), Capt. W. S. Pemberton (assistant commissary of subsistence), and Ben Johnson (volunteer aide-de-camp). Born in Boston, Massachusetts, on December 29, 1809, and appointed as a brigadier general on August 15, 1861, Albert Pike negotiated an alliance between the Confederacy and the Cherokee Nation. At Elkhorn Tavern, he commanded a brigade that included a regiment of Cherokee. Exempt from the general amnesty of May 29, 1865, due to his rank as a Confederate general officer, commissioner, and district judge, Pike applied for a special presidential pardon. Endorsed by 113 individuals, Pike received a pardon on April 23, 1866. Born on September 17, 1820, Earl Van Dorn graduated near the bottom of his 1842 West Point class and earned two brevet promotions for gallantry in the Mexican War. He resigned on January 31, 1861. Appointed as a brigadier general on June 5, 1861, he earned promotion to major general on September 19, 1861. Van Dorn commanded Confederate cavalry during the Vicksburg campaign, until murdered by a jealous husband on May 7, 1863. He received burial at Wintergreen Cemetery in Port Gibson, Mississippi. The capture of Louis Hebert magnified the loss of leadership on the Confederate right flank. The 1st Arkansas Mounted Rifles entered the battle in reserve near the 2nd Arkansas Mounted Rifles. *OR,* 1:8, 281, 284; Dacus, *Reminiscences,* 2; Douthat, *Special Presidential Pardons,* 1:23; Arthur B. Carter, *The Tarnished Cavalier: Major General Earl Van Dorn, C.S.A.* (Knoxville: University of Tennessee, 1999), 1–12, 22, 34, 44–64, 76–78, 186–90; Joseph H. Crute Jr., *Confederate Staff Officers, 1861–1865* (Powhatan, VA: Derwent Books, 1982), 137–38; Shea and Hess, *Pea Ridge,* 88–206; Walter Lee Brown, *A Life of Albert Pike* (Fayetteville: University of Arkansas Press, 1997), 383–94; Warner, *Generals in Gray,* 130–31, 240–41.

14. During the second day of fighting, the 1st Arkansas Mounted Rifles took position southwest of Elkhorn Tavern, near the intersection of the Ford Road and Telegraph Road, north of Ruddick's Field. Col. Henry Little commanded the First Missouri Brigade, which consisted of the 1st Missouri Cavalry and two artillery batteries. Col. Frank A. Rector commanded the 17th Arkansas Infantry. Born near Franklin, Tennessee, on March 11, 1818, John Wilkins Whitfield served in the Mexican War and lived in Missouri and Kansas, where he supported slavery as a territorial delegate to the U.S. Congress. He moved to Texas and served as colonel of a unit known as Whitfield's Legion and Whitfield's 4th Texas Cavalry Battalion prior to its designation as the 27th Texas Cavalry regiment (known, in turn, as the 1st Texas Legion). Organized in the

spring of 1862, Whitfield's unit drew recruits from Daingerfield, Clarksville, and Paris, as well as Titus County. Praised at Elkhorn Tavern and Iuka, Whitfield earned promotion to brigadier general on May 9, 1863. Although Whitfield was popular with his troops, Joseph E. Johnston and Stephen D. Lee favored Lawrence Sullivan Ross for brigade command. On extended leave for the rest of the war, Whitfield signed a parole at Columbus, Texas, on June 29, 1865, settled in Lavaca County, and served in the state legislature. Whitfield died in Hallettsville, Texas, on October 27, 1879, and received burial in Hallettsville Cemetery. Col. John Q. Burbridge commanded the 2nd Missouri Infantry of the First Missouri (Confederate) Brigade. Van Dorn blamed his defeat and withdrawal on insufficient ordnance, rather than his poor management of available ordnance. Born in New York, Peter Van Winkle owned a sawmill in Benton County. In 1860, he reported $2,500 in real estate and a personal estate of $35,600. Forced from the area after the battle due to his Confederate sympathies, he moved to Texas. The mill fell into disrepair, but Van Winkle returned after the war and regained his prosperity. Van Dorn initially estimated his losses at 800 to 1,000 killed and wounded and 200 to 300 captured. He adjusted these figures to 600 killed and wounded, plus 200 men and 1 cannon captured. He originally estimated Union losses at 800 killed, 1,000 to 1,200 wounded, plus 300 men and 2 batteries captured. He adjusted these figures to 700 men killed, 700 wounded, and 300 captured. Samuel R. Curtis reported 203 killed, 980 wounded, and 201 missing, for an aggregate of 1,384 Union casualties. *OR*, 1:8, 206, 281–85; CSR, M376, Roll 19; M227, Roll 39; U.S. War Department, Compiled Service Records of Confederate Soldiers Who Served in Organizations from the State of Missouri, National Archives, Microcopy M380, Roll 2 (hereafter cited as CSR with microfilm and roll numbers); *Eighth Census*, M653–37, 387; Dacus, *Reminiscences*, 2; Shea and Hess, *Pea Ridge*, 23, 159, 207–60, 270; Judith Ann Benner, *Sul Ross: Soldier, Statesman, Educator* (College Station: Texas A&M University Press, 1983), 89–97; Anne Bailey, "John Wilkins Whitfield," in *Confederate General*, ed. Davis and Hoffman, 6:130–31.

15. The retreating Confederates carried three days' rations but would not see commissary trains for twelve days. Robert H. Dacus described the terrain as "a sparsely settled, mountainous country." Russell Ward mustered in as a private in Company A of the 1st Arkansas Mounted Rifles on June 15, 1861. He served as regimental butcher from October 15, 1861, until June 4, 1862, when he received a discharge due to age. Born in Kentucky about 1838, Cyrus Hanks worked as a clerk and lived in the Oden Township household of merchant Jacob McConnell in 1860. Hanks later served as postmaster for Chicot County. CSR, M376, Roll 24; *Eighth Census*, M653–38, 953; Dacus, *Reminiscences*, 2; Shea and Hess, *Pea Ridge*, 261–68.

16. John W. Lawrence served as captain of Company K in the 16th Arkansas Infantry. Col. John T. Hill commanded the 16th Arkansas during the spring of 1862 as part of Hebert's Brigade in McCulloch's Division of the Army of the West. Samuel R. Curtis reported on March 20, 1862, that Benton and Hill's Confederate regiments disbanded after Elkhorn Tavern, but the 16th Arkansas saw service at Iuka and Corinth prior to capture at Port Hudson. Capt. William Gipson mustered in as captain of Company A (the "Booneville Rifles") in the 2nd Arkansas Mounted Rifles on July 18, 1861, at Bentonville. He served through the Pea Ridge campaign but did not gain

reelection at the reorganization in May 1862. *OR*, 1:8, 628, 746; CSR, M376, Roll 14; M376, Roll 11; M376, Roll 9.

17. Benjamin T. Embry mustered in on July 15, 1861, at Bentonville and served as captain of Company B ("the Galla Rangers") of the 2nd Arkansas Mounted Rifles before election to colonel. Embry did not win reelection at the May 1862 reorganization. CSR, M376, Roll 7.

18. Erwin and Cooke both mustered into the 1st Arkansas Mounted Rifles on June 15, 1861. W. A. Erwin mustered in as a private in Company G and earned promotion to second lieutenant. R. G. Cooke mustered in with Company F as first sergeant and earned promotion to second lieutenant. CSR, M376, Roll 7; M376, Roll 5.

19. Born in Arkansas about 1840, Henry C. West worked as a farm laborer on the Fourche Township farm of W. S. Huggins in Pulaski County. On June 15, 1861, he mustered in as a private in Company G of the 1st Arkansas Mounted Rifles and earned promotion to first lieutenant. "Mr. Stillwell" may refer to John Stillwell. Born in Kentucky about 1821, Stillwell lived in Cole Township in Sebastian County with his 36-year-old wife, Nancy, five sons, and two daughters. In 1860, Stillwell owned $2,000 in real estate and a personal estate of $500. Born in Arkansas about 1838, David Oscar Bowles lived on his father's farm in Franklin Township. He mustered in as a private in Company A of the 1st Arkansas Mounted Rifles on October 25, 1861, at Camp Stephens. Captured at Elkhorn Tavern on March 8, 1862, Bowles remained a prisoner at Alton, Illinois, until exchanged on May 17, 1862. He transferred to the Signal Corps after two months and served in Company A of Carlton's Arkansas Cavalry. He signed a parole at Memphis, Tennessee, on June 19, 1865. In 1860, Bowles's father owned 36 slaves. CSR, M376, Roll 24; M376, Roll 3; *Eighth Census*, M653–49, 198; *Eighth Census*, M653–50, 1017; *Eighth Census*, M653–38, 963; *Eighth Census, Slave Schedule* (Chicot County, Arkansas), M653–53, 44.

20. After Elkhorn Tavern, Curtis and Van Dorn negotiated an exchange of prisoners. This exchange included 12 Union officers and 224 enlisted soldiers. The exact number of Confederate prisoners exchanged cannot be determined, as most went to St. Louis, and it took several more weeks to finalize their exchange. Shea and Hess, *Pea Ridge*, 285–86.

21. Born in Bradfordsville, Kentucky, on March 5, 1834, Uriah Milton Rose graduated from Transylvania University and married Margaret T. Gibbs in 1853. Rose settled in Batesville's Ruddell Township and practiced law. In 1860, he reported $2,500 in real estate and a personal estate valued at $5,000. Kept out of military service due to poor health, he accepted an assignment to compile a roster of all Arkansas Confederate soldiers. A Richmond warehouse fire at the end of the war destroyed these records. After the war, he established the Rose Law Firm in Little Rock. Rose died at the age of 79 on August 12, 1913, and received burial in Oakland Cemetery in Little Rock. *Eighth Census*, M653–43, 12; Allen W. Bird II, "U. M. Rose: Arkansas Attorney," *Arkansas Historical Quarterly* 64 (Summer 2005): 171–205; Allen W. Bird II, "U. M. Rose," in *Arkansas Biography: A Collection of Notable Lives,* ed. Nancy A. Williams and Jeannie M. Whayne (Fayetteville: University of Arkansas Press, 2000), 250–51.

22. The Latin phrase "sine die" means to adjourn a court indefinitely. *The American Heritage Dictionary* (New York: Dell Publishing Company, 1985), 637.

23. Col. B. Warren Stone commanded the 6th Texas Cavalry after Lawrence Sullivan Ross earned promotion to brigadier general. With recruits drawn primarily from Dallas, McKinney, Waco, Austin, and Lancaster, as well as Bell County, the 6th Texas Cavalry mustered into service at Dallas in September 1861. They served in the Indian Territory and at Elkhorn Tavern prior to a transfer east of the Mississippi River. William C. Young commanded the 11th Texas Cavalry, which organized in May 1861 at Camp Reeves in Grayson County, Texas. After service in the Indian Territory and Arkansas, they transferred east of the Mississippi River and served dismounted at Richmond and Murfreesboro. Once remounted, they served in John Wharton and Thomas Harrison's Brigade at Chickamauga, Knoxville, Atlanta, Savannah, and the Carolinas. Col. William B. Sims commanded the 9th Texas Cavalry, which organized in the summer of 1861 with recruits from Clarksville, Sherman, Mt. Pleasant, Avinger, and Paris. They served in the Indian Territory prior to a transfer east of the Mississippi River in the spring of 1862. Elijah Gates served as colonel of the 1st Missouri Cavalry, which consolidated with the 3rd Missouri Cavalry after the Vicksburg campaign. On March 19, 1862, Dabney H. Maury issued orders from Van Dorn for Churchill to prepare a secret cavalry raid against Federal stores in and around Springfield, Missouri. Maury instructed Churchill to gather supplies at Horse Head, send his baggage toward Pocahontas by way of Jacksonport, and be underway no later than March 23. Maury further instructed Churchill to approach Springfield by way of Forsyth, Missouri, and proceed immediately to Pocahontas, Arkansas, after the raid. *OR*, 1:8, 791–92; CSR, M227, Roll 35; M227, Roll 41; M227, Roll 33; M380, Roll 6; Crute, *Units of the Confederate States Army*, 326, 328, 330.

24. The largest tributary of the Buffalo River, Hudson's Fork is now known as the Little Buffalo River. The Buffalo River flows into the White River near Buffalo City, Arkansas. Edward T. Smith mustered in as a private in Company A of the 1st Arkansas Mounted Rifles on June 15, 1861. He signed a parole at Jamestown, North Carolina, on April 30, 1865. In 1860, 24-year-old William W. Kilburn lived in the Masona Township household of Chicot County planter Thomas C. Horner. The Massachusetts-born dentist enlisted as a private in Company A of the 1st Arkansas Mounted Rifles on June 15, 1861, and served until discharged on September 9, 1862. CSR, M376, Roll 21; *Eighth Census*, M653–38, 930; Kenneth L. Smith, *Buffalo River Handbook* (Fayetteville: University of Arkansas Press, 2006), 186, 417.

25. Born in 1844 in South Carolina, John Anderson lived on his father's plantation in Masona Township in the town of Lake Village. His father, John P. Anderson, owned one slave in 1860. Anderson mustered into Company A as a private on January 15, 1862, at "Camp Bragg." He received parole at Jamestown, North Carolina, on April 30, 1865. *Eighth Census*, M653–38, 927; *Eighth Census, Slave Schedule* (Chicot County, Arkansas), M653–53, 95; M376, Roll 1.

26. Born in North Carolina about 1800, Dr. A. R. Stevenson lived in Cove Township in Searcy County with his 59-year-old wife, Ann, a son, and an apparent daughter and grandson. In 1860, Stephenson owned $1,200 in real estate and a personal estate valued at $1,500. Originally established in 1856 by Littleton Baker, J. W. Gray, and Jack Marshall, and named for N. B. Burrow, the town of Burrowville changed its name to

Marshall when it incorporated on January 13, 1884, as the county seat of Searcy County. *Eighth Census*, M653–50, 938; Dallas T. Herndon, ed., *Centennial History of Arkansas* (Chicago: S. J. Clarke Publishing Company, 1922), 1:805.

27. Born in Tennessee about 1811, Page Hatchett owned $480 in real estate and a personal estate valued at $1,200 in 1860. He and his 40-year-old wife, Thankford, lived on a farm in Hartzogg Township in Van Buren County with four daughters, three sons, and Hatchett's mother. *Eighth Census*, M653–51, 360.

28. During the Confederate retreat from Elkhorn Tavern, Price ordered Stone's 6th Texas Cavalry to cover the withdrawal of the infantry and trains toward the Boston Mountains. *OR*, 1:8, 302–4.

29. Andrew J. Little enlisted on June 14, 1861, and served as assistant commissary sergeant on the staff of the 1st Arkansas Mounted Rifles. CSR, M376, Roll 14.

30. M. J. Schnebley enlisted in Company B of the 1st Arkansas Mounted Rifles on October 10, 1861, at Des Arc. He earned a promotion to corporal and survived a wound at Murfreesboro on December 31, 1862, but deserted on July 3, 1864. CSR, M376, Roll 21.

31. The movement to Memphis preceded a move to join the Army of Mississippi at Corinth. Dacus, *Reminiscences*, 2–3; Malcolm Muir and Timothy B. Smith, "Army of Mississippi," in *Encyclopedia of the American Civil War: Political, Social, and Military History*, ed. David S. Heidler and Jeanne T. Heidler (Santa Barbara: ABC-Clio), 1:83–85.

32. Built in 1861 in Jeffersonville, Indiana, and originally known as the *Mary T.*, the *J. A. Cotton* carried four guns and served as a Confederate cotton-clad gunboat until seized on the Red River in early 1863. In February 1867, the *J. A. Cotton* sank in Pittsburgh due to ice damage. In April 1862, Churchill's staff consisted of Capt. Breckinridge Blackburn (assistant inspector general), Capt. James M. Butler (assistant adjutant general), Capt. Benjamin S. Johnson (assistant adjutant general), First Lt. N. T. Roberts (adjutant), and Lt. A. H. Sevier (aide-de-camp). Crute, *Confederate Staff Officers*, 36–37; Frederick Way Jr., comp., *Way's Packet Directory, 1848–1994: Passenger Steamboats of the Mississippi River System since the Advent of Photography in Mid-Continent America* (Athens: Ohio University Press, 1994), 229; Paul H. Silverstone, *Civil War Navies, 1855–1883* (New York: Routledge, 2006), 2:184.

33. Built in 1852 in New Albany, Indiana, the *H.R.W. Hill* worked the New Orleans to Memphis trade and served as a Confederate steamer until captured on June 6, 1862. Thereafter, it served in the Western Gunboat Flotilla as a dockside commissary boat for the garrison at Cairo, Illinois. Built in Elizabeth, Pennsylvania, the *Victoria* worked the Missouri River between Jefferson City and St. Joseph, Missouri, and saw use as a Confederate steamer until captured at Memphis on June 6, 1862. Thereafter, it served as an auxiliary quartermaster vessel named *Abraham*. Sold after the war and renamed *Lexington*, it returned to commercial use. It was damaged in a hurricane at Vicksburg, Mississippi, on April 14, 1868; it burned at Algiers, Louisiana, on February 3, 1869. The steamboat *Means* could not be identified. Between December 1857 and June 1858, the Mississippi River experienced four high rises collectively known as the flood of 1858. Estimates place the high-water mark for the flood of 1862, regarded as one of the river's most severe floods, at least one foot higher than that of 1858. Way, *Way's Packet Directory*, 204, 284, 469; Charles Dana Gibson and E. Kay Gibson, comp., *Dictionary of*

Transports and Combatant Vessels Steam and Sail Employed by the Union Army, 1861–1868 (Camden, ME: Ensign Press, 1995), 141, 325; Emerson W. Gould, *Fifty Years on the Mississippi; or, Gould's History of River Navigation: Containing a History of the Introduction of Steam as a Propelling Power on Ocean, Lakes and Rivers* (St. Louis: Nixon-Jones Printing Company, 1889), 259–60.

34. After the Union army captured Memphis in 1862, seven regiments of U.S. Colored Troops served at Fort Pickering and numerous refugee slaves settled near the fort. Designed for use as an ordnance and commissary depot as well as an earthen work fortification, and constructed largely by hired black labor, Fort Pickering stood below the occupied city and above the steep riverbanks on the southern edge of Memphis. Shortly after the war, Z. B. Tower, inspector general of fortifications for the Military Division of the Mississippi, described the ground in front as "broken." Born in Ireland about 1831, James F. Robinson lived in Old River Township with his 23-year-old wife, Mary, and one son. In 1860, Robinson practiced law and owned $70,000 in real estate and a personal estate valued at $45,000. He mustered in as captain of Company G of the 23rd Arkansas Infantry on March 27, 1862, at Jacksonport and gained election as major on April 25, 1862. *OR*, 1:49 (Part 2), 899–901; CSR, M376, Roll 20; *Eighth Census*, M653–38, 920; Hannah Rosen, *Terror in the Heart of Freedom: Citizenship, Sexual Violence, and the Meaning of Race in the Post Emancipation South* (Chapel Hill: University of North Carolina Press, 2008), 29–30; Edward F. Williams and Ted Williams, *Early Memphis and Its River Rivals* (Memphis: Historical Hiking Trails, 1968), 33.

35. The Overton Hotel served as a hospital during the capture of Memphis. Administered by the Western Sanitary Commission, Overton Hospital accommodated 700 patients in nine wards. Jacob Gilbert Forman, *The Western Sanitary Commission: A Sketch of its Origins, History, Labors for the Sick and Wounded of the Western Armies, and Aid Given to Freedmen and Union Refugees, with Incidents of Hospital Life* (St. Louis: R. P. Studley and Company, 1864), 56, 75.

36. The Memphis and Charleston Railroad connected at Corinth, Mississippi, with the Mobile and Ohio Railroad. Alexander M. Haskell served as a lieutenant and staff ordnance officer for Earl Van Dorn. On January 28, 1862, Haskell earned promotion to major and served as assistant adjutant general. From June 26 until an unspecified date in July 1862, he served as assistant inspector general. Thereafter, he served as major in the 6th Texas Infantry. CSR, M818, Roll 11; M227, Roll 16; J. C. Swayze, *Hill and Swayze's Confederate States Rail-Road and Steam-Boat Guide, Containing the Time-Tables, Fares, Connections and Distances on all the Rail-Roads of the Confederate States; also, the Connecting Lines of Rail-Roads, Steam-Boats and Stages. And will be Accompanied by a Complete Guide to the Principal Hotels, with a Large Variety of Valuable Information* (Griffin, GA: Hill and Swayze, 1862), 48–49; Joseph H. Crute Jr., *Confederate Staff Officers, 1861—1865* (Powhatan, VA: Derwent Books, 1982), 198.

37. Born in Virginia about 1833, Charles J. Turnbull lived as a "gentleman" in Hot Springs with no assets or dependents. He served as colonel of the 30th Arkansas Infantry, renamed as the 25th Arkansas Infantry after Stones River. Henry K. Brown mustered in with the 2nd Arkansas Mounted Rifles on July 24, 1861. Elected to the rank

of captain on July 27, 1861, he earned promotion to lieutenant colonel on August 26, 1861. *Eighth Census,* M653–42, 910; CSR, M376, Roll 23; M376, Roll 3; Crute, *Units of the Confederate Army,* 55.

38. Approved on April 16, 1862, and published on April 28, Confederate General Orders No. 30 required three years of military service by all white male residents of Confederate states between the ages of 18 and 35. This act also extended existing enlistments to three years. Article VI, paragraph 13, allowed units originally enlisted for 12 months to reorganize and elect new officers. After expiration of the original one-year enlistments, new enlistments lasted for "three years or during the war." Lee M. Ramseur mustered in as captain of Company D of the 1st Arkansas Mounted Rifles on June 9, 1861, and survived a wound at Oak Hills. Wounded and captured at Murfreesboro, he succeeded Reynolds as lieutenant colonel after Chickamauga. Although he was promoted to colonel after Reynolds advanced to brigade command, lingering effects from his Murfreesboro wound kept him from assuming command. Ramseur practiced law in Augusta, Arkansas, served one term in the state legislature, and served as Woodruff County judge from 1874 until 1876. Ramseur died on August 14, 1881. Born in Louisiana about 1840, John W. Turner lived at Gaines Landing when he mustered in as a corporal in Company A on June 15, 1861. Promoted to sergeant on December 9, 1861, and second lieutenant on May 1, 1862, Turner served until killed at Chickamauga on September 20, 1863. Abner J. Maxey served as Chicot County surveyor in 1860. He mustered into Company A as a private on October 25, 1861. Promoted to third lieutenant on May 1, 1862, he survived a wound at Murfreesboro and earned promotion as first lieutenant to date from September 20, 1863. Arrested and court-martialed on April 10, 1864, he received a sentence of six months' suspension from duty. He is sometimes listed "Abner G. Maxey." According to Robert H. Dacus, the reorganization occurred on May 25, 1862. The 1st Arkansas Mounted Rifles served in the same brigade with the 2nd Arkansas Mounted Rifles (Williamson), 4th Arkansas Infantry (McNair), and 25th Arkansas Infantry (Hufstedler). *OR,* 4:1, 1094–1100; "Appointments," DHR Papers, Box 1, Folder 7, Item 127; CSR, M376, Roll 19; M376, Roll 11; M376, Roll 23; M376, Roll 15; *Eighth Census,* M653–45, 91; *Biographical and Historical Memoirs of Southern Arkansas,* 1062; Dacus, *Reminiscences,* 1–3; Bobby Roberts and Carl Moneyhon, eds., *Portraits of Conflict: A Photographic History of Arkansas* (Fayetteville: University of Arkansas Press, 1987), 224–25.

39. Located 5 miles southeast of Corinth, Mississippi, the town of Farmington hosted a battle on May 9, 1862. Although present, the 1st Arkansas Mounted Rifles did not participate. Dacus, *Reminiscences,* 3; James Willis, *Arkansas Confederates in the Western Theater* (Dayton, OH: Morningside House, 1998), 224.

40. The Mobile and Ohio Railroad operated a 328-mile route between Mobile, Alabama, and Corinth, Mississippi. Swayze, *Rail-Road and Steam-Boat Guide,* 48–49.

41. Born on February 28, 1824, in Hawkins County, Tennessee, John Creed Moore graduated from West Point in 1849 and served in the Seminole War. He resigned in 1855 and taught in Texas. He served as colonel of the 2nd Texas Infantry until promoted to brigadier general on May 26, 1862. Moore was captured and exchanged at Vicksburg and then commanded the Eastern and Western Districts of the Department of the Gulf

during the defense of Mobile. Moore resigned on February 3, 1864, and returned to Texas. He died in Osage on December 31, 1910, and received burial in Osage Cemetery. Swayze, *Rail-Road and Steam-Boat Guide,* 38–40, 49; CSR, M227, Roll 26, and M818, Roll 17; Earl J. Hess, *Banners to the Breeze: The Kentucky Campaign, Corinth, and Stones River* (Lincoln: University of Nebraska Press, 2000), 148, 160–63, 169; Arthur W. Bergeron Jr., "John Creed Moore," in *Confederate General,* ed. Davis and Hoffman, 4:180–81.

42. Born in North Carolina about 1835, Benjamin F. Danley lived on the Cache Township farm of his brother in Green County. In 1860, he owned $300 in real estate and a personal estate of $425. He served as colonel of the 3rd Arkansas Cavalry. Capt. Jack Wharton commanded Company E in Stone's 6th Texas Cavalry. Harper suffered frequent bouts of poor health while in command of the 1st Arkansas Mounted Rifles. *Eighth Census,* M653–42, 564; M227, Roll 39; M227, Roll 35.

43. Born on August 19, 1815, in Sevierville, Tennessee, John Porter McCown graduated from West Point in 1840. He earned two brevet promotions for gallantry during the Mexican War and resigned his commission on May 17, 1861. He received a commission as a brigadier general on October 12, 1861, and earned promotion to major general on March 10, 1862. He assumed temporary command of the Army of the West in June 1862. Braxton Bragg charged him with disobedience of orders after Stones River and he served thereafter in obscure commands. He taught school in Knoxville after the war but soon moved to Magnolia, Arkansas, where he owned a farm. He died in Little Rock on January 22, 1879, and received burial in Magnolia. Lawrence L. Hewitt, "John Porter McCown," in *Confederate General,* ed. Davis and Hoffman, 4:114–15.

44. Opposition to the Confederate conscription law resulted in significant criticism and several lawsuits. In the spring of 1862, Gov. Henry M. Rector of Arkansas threatened to remove the state from the Confederacy due to conscription. Albert Burton Moore, *Conscription and Conflict in the Confederacy* (Columbia: University of South Carolina Press, 1996), 246; Mark E. Neely, *Southern Rights: Political Prisoners and the Myth of Confederate Constitutionalism* (Charlottesville: University of Virginia Press, 1999), 57.

45. Born in Arkansas about 1827, David P. Black lived on a farm in Demun Township in Randolph County with his 28-year-old wife, Ann, two sons, and a daughter. He owned $5,000 in real estate and a personal estate of $1,200. He mustered in as a second sergeant with Company B of the 1st Arkansas Mounted Rifles on June 9, 1861, and later served as captain and assistant quartermaster. *Eighth Census,* M653–49, 248; M376, Roll 3.

46. The Montgomery and West Point Railroad made 22 stops on the 88-mile journey between Montgomery, Alabama, and West Point, Georgia. Swayze, *Rail-Road and Steam-Boat Guide,* 43.

47. The Atlanta and West Point Railroad made 11 stops on its 87-mile journey between West Point and Atlanta, Georgia. Swayze, *Rail-Road and Steam-Boat Guide,* 42.

48. The Western and Atlantic (State) Railroad made 23 stops on the 138 miles between Atlanta and Chattanooga. Born on December 16, 1825, Henry Heth graduated last in the West Point class of 1847. He received a commission as a brigadier general on

January 6, 1862. Heth transferred to the Army of Northern Virginia in February 1863 and earned promotion to major general on February 17, 1864. After the war, he worked in the insurance business. Heth died in Washington, D.C., on September 27, 1899, and received burial in Richmond's Hollywood Cemetery. Born on January 1, 1827, in Danville, Virginia, William Lewis Cabell graduated from West Point in 1850. He resigned in 1861 and served on the staffs of Beauregard and Joseph E. Johnston. After a transfer to the Trans-Mississippi Department, he earned promotion to brigadier general on January 20, 1863. Captured during Price's 1864 Missouri Raid, he remained a prisoner until August 1865. Afterward, he studied law in Fort Smith and settled in Dallas, where he served as mayor, U.S. marshal, and vice president of the Southern Pacific Railroad. He died in Dallas on February 22, 1911, and received burial in Greenwod Cemetery. Swayze, *Rail-Road and Steam-Boat Guide,* 41; Robert E. L. Krick, "Henry Heth," in *Confederate General,* ed. Davis and Hoffman, 3:88–91.

49. Born in South Carolina about 1818, James H. May lived on a farm in South Fork Township in Montgomery County with his 35-year-old wife, Caroline, a son, and three daughters. He owned $2,500 in real estate and a personal estate of $1,500. He mustered in as major of the 4th Arkansas Infantry regiment on August 17, 1862, and later earned promotion to lieutenant colonel. He resigned on August 8, 1863. *Eighth Census,* M653–46, 851; M376, Roll 15.

50. Born on May 16, 1824, in St. Augustine, Florida, Edmund Kirby Smith graduated from West Point in 1845. He earned two brevet promotions in Mexico and served on the Texas frontier. He resigned on April 6, 1861, served under Joseph E. Johnston in the Shenandoah Valley, and survived a wound at First Manassas. He earned promotions to brigadier general on June 17, 1861, major general on October 11, 1861, lieutenant general on October 9, 1862, and full general on February 9, 1864. He commanded the Trans-Mississippi Department until he surrendered on May 26, 1865. Afterward, he served as a college professor and administrator and died in Sewanee, Tennessee, on March 28, 1893. He received burial in Sewanee in the University of the South Cemetery. Anne Bailey, "Edmund Kirby Smith," in *Confederate General,* ed. Davis and Hoffman, 5:162–71. For a full discussion of the life of Edmund Kirby Smith, see Joseph Howard Parks, *General Edmund Kirby Smith, C.S.A.* (Baton Rouge, Louisiana State University Press, 1954).

51. George Washington Morgan commanded approximately 10,000 Federal troops that withdrew from the Cumberland Gap. Born in Kentucky about 1814, A. E. Pogue lived near the Cumberland Gap with his 45-year-old wife, Mahala, and one daughter on a farm near Barbourville in Knox County. In 1860, Pogue owned $10,000 in real estate and a personal estate valued at $14,240, as well as five slaves. *Eighth Census,* M653–380, 37; *Eighth Census, Slave Schedule* (Knox County, Kentucky), M653–404, 7; E. Polk Johnson, *A History of Kentucky and Kentuckians: The Leaders and Representative Men in Commerce, Industry and Modern Activities* (Chicago: Lewis Publishing Company, 1912), 3:1551; Hess, *Banners to the Breeze,* 7; Warner, *Generals in Blue,* 333–34.

52. Benjamin S. Johnson served as captain and assistant adjutant general to Thomas J. Churchill, with rank from October 14, 1862. He earned promotion to major on May 13, 1864, and served as assistant adjutant general on the staff of Edmund Kirby Smith.

Capt. Breckinridge F. Blackburn served as assistant adjutant general on Churchill's staff, with rank from June 26, 1862. In September 1862, Blackburn became assistant inspector general on Churchill's staff. He resigned on August 1, 1864. Col. John C. Cochran commanded the 14th Kentucky (Union) Infantry. Col. Daniel W. Lindsey commanded the 22nd Kentucky (Union) Infantry. George W. Gallop served as lieutenant colonel of the 14th Kentucky (Union) Infantry. William H. Burton served as captain of Company H in the 14th Kentucky (Union) Infantry. The two surgeons could not be identified. "Lt. Montgomery" probably refers to Robert Montgomery, who served as second lieutenant in Company C of the 22nd Kentucky (Union) Infantry on the staff of George W. Morgan. Born on September 20, 1820, in Washington City, Pennsylvania, George Washington Morgan served in the War for Texas Independence and entered West Point as a cadet in 1841 but soon withdrew. He served in the Mexican War, practiced law, and served as U.S. consul in France and U.S. minister in Portugal. On November 12, 1861, he received a commission as brigadier general of volunteers, in command of the 7th Division in the Army of the Ohio at Cumberland Gap. Faced with capture or annihilation after the Confederate invasion of Kentucky cut him off from supply or reinforcement, Morgan conducted a skillful but controversial withdrawal. He resigned on June 8, 1863. Thereafter, he practiced law, ran an unsuccessful campaign as a Democratic candidate for governor of Ohio, and served in Congress. In the fall of 1866, he endorsed Reynolds's application for special presidential pardon. Morgan died in Fortress Monroe, Virginia, on July 26, 1893, and received burial in Mound View Cemetery in Mount Vernon, Ohio. CSR, M818, Roll 13; M818, Roll 3; U.S. War Department, Compiled Service Records of Confederate Soldiers Who Served in Organizations from the State of Kentucky, National Archives, Microcopy M386, Roll 5 (hereafter cited as CSR with microfilm and roll numbers); M386, Roll 16; M386, Roll 10; M386, Roll 2; M386, Roll 19; Warner, *Generals in Blue,* 333–34; Crute, *Confederate Staff Officers,* 36–37, 177; Hess, *Banners to the Breeze,* 7, 31, 47–53.

53. Born in Ireland on March 17, 1828, Patrick Cleburne immigrated to Arkansas in 1849. In 1860, Cleburne practiced law in Helena, where he owned $20,000 in real estate and a personal estate of $2,000. Cleburne served as colonel of the 15th Arkansas Infantry. He earned promotion to brigadier general on March 4, 1862, and major general on December 13, 1862, and commanded a division in Edmund Kirby Smith's Army of Kentucky. Killed on November 30, 1864, at Franklin, Tennessee, he received burial in Maple Hill Cemetery in Helena. Col. John S. Scott of the 1st Louisiana Cavalry commanded a cavalry brigade known as "the Kirby Smith Brigade" that consisted of the 1st Louisiana Cavalry (Lt. Col. James O. Nixon), 1st Georgia Cavalry (Col. J. J. Morrison), the "Buckner Guards" (a Kentucky cavalry company commanded by Captain W. L. Garrett), and the 3rd Tennessee Cavalry (Col. J. W. Starnes). On August 29, Scott conducted reconnaissance that located the enemy 3 miles from Richmond, Kentucky, and reported to Cleburne in command of the advance division. The term "rice bird artillery" appears to be slang for mountain howitzers, although its usage does not appear to be common. For a description of Federal units involved in this action, see the report of Mahlon D. Manson in *OR,* 1:16 (Part 1), 910–16; *OR,* 1:15, 937–39, 944–46, 1162; *Eighth Census,* M653–47, 394; M378, Roll 26; Lawrence L. Hewitt, "Patrick Ronayne

Cleburne," in *Confederate General,* ed. Davis and Hoffman, 1:198–201. For a full discussion of Cleburne's life and career, see Craig L. Symonds, *Stonewall of the West: Patrick Cleburne and the Civil War* (Lawrence: University of Kansas, 1997).

54. Evander McNair commanded the 2nd Brigade of the 3rd Division under Thomas J. Churchill. McNair praised his officers and men but did not submit casualty figures or details of the engagement on August 30, 1862. Reynolds's description of the engagement agrees with the report submitted by Churchill. *OR,* 1:16 (Part 1), 940–41, 943.

55. Ordered by Edmund Kirby Smith to move west of Richmond and secure the Lexington and Lancaster Roads leading to Lexington, Scott's force of approximately 850 ambushed a Federal force of approximately 5,000 as they retreated from the field at Richmond. According to Scott, the size of his force and dark conditions allowed many prisoners to escape. Nonetheless, he reported the capture of approximately 3,500 Federals, including Mahlon D. Manson. He turned over his prisoners to Col. Preston Smith in command of the 1st Brigade, 4th Division, Army of Kentucky. *OR,* 1:16 (Part 1), 938–39.

56. Edmund Kirby Smith and Mahlon D. Manson both claimed to be outnumbered during the battle of Richmond. Smith reported 400 killed and wounded, as well as the capture of 5,000 Union troops, 9 pieces of artillery, and 10,000 small arms. The 1st Arkansas Mounted Rifles suffered the heaviest losses within the 2nd Brigade, 3rd Division, Army of Kentucky, with 8 killed and 18 wounded, for an aggregate of 26 casualties. The Army of Kentucky reported 78 killed, 372 wounded, and 1 missing, for an aggregate of 451. The Union reported 206 killed, 844 wounded, and 4,303 captured or missing, for an aggregate of 5,353 casualties. *OR,* 1:16 (Part 1), 909, 935–36.

57. Born in 1828 near the town of Jonesborough in Washington County, Tennessee, Thomas Hamilton McCray moved to Arkansas and operated a Little Rock mill but moved Texas about 1856 to establish a manufacturing business. He returned to Arkansas and served as a lieutenant and adjutant with the 5th Arkansas Infantry but received a detached assignment as mustering officer under William Hardee. In this capacity, McCray recruited the 31st Arkansas Infantry Battalion, which he commanded as major by January 25, 1862. McCray won election as colonel in May 1862, when the 31st Arkansas reorganized as a regiment, and earned praise for his command of the 1st Brigade of Thomas J. Churchill's 3rd Division in the Army of Kentucky at Richmond. His command consisted of the 10th Texas Cavalry (Dismounted), the 11th Texas Cavalry (Dismounted), the 14th Texas Cavalry (Dismounted), the 15th/32nd Texas Cavalry (Dismounted), and McCray's Arkansas Regiment of Sharpshooters. McCray, however, did not receive promotion to brigadier general. That promotion went to Matthew Ector of Texas. Soon thereafter, the 31st Arkansas consolidated with the 4th Arkansas Infantry and McCray transferred to Arkansas. After a short stay in Mexico, he returned to his Arkansas farm and became a merchant for the McCormick Reaper Company of Chicago. He died in Chicago on October 19, 1891, and received burial in an unmarked grave in Cook County Cemetery in Dunning, Illinois. Edmund Kirby Smith sent a force toward Cincinnati in order to give the people of Kentucky time to organize. According to Smith's report, Heth commanded the Confederate advance at

Cynthiana, Kentucky, with orders to threaten the town of Covington. *OR*, 1:16 (Part 1), 933, 941–43; CSR, M376, Roll 15; Bruce S. Allardice, *More Generals in Gray* (Baton Rouge: Louisiana State University Press), 158–59.

58. Edmund Kirby Smith accepted the surrender of Lexington on September 2, 1862, and ordered Reynolds and the 1st Arkansas Rifles to serve as guards during the occupation. W. L. Gammage, *The Camp, the Bivouac, and the Battlefield: Being a History of the 4th Arkansas Regiment* (Little Rock: Arkansas Southern Press, 1958), 46; Hess, *Banners to the Breeze*, 44.

59. The *Official Records* contain no reference to Reynolds as military governor of Lexington. George William Brent served on Beauregard's staff as major and assistant inspector general, but later served as assistant adjutant general and acting chief of staff. By the summer of 1862, he served as acting chief of staff for the Western Department with the rank of lieutenant colonel, as well as adjutant and inspector general on the staff of James Edward Slaughter. During the Kentucky campaign, he served as inspector general for the Army of Kentucky and chief of staff and assistant adjutant general for Braxton Bragg. He earned promotion to colonel on August 8, 1863, and returned to Beauregard's staff as assistant adjutant general in October 1864. Edmund Kirby Smith cited Brent, along with other staff officers, for "active assistance" at Richmond. *OR*, 1:16 (Part 1), 935; CSR, M818, Roll 3; U.S. War Department, *List of Staff Officers of the Confederate States Army, 1861–1865* (Washington, DC: Government Printing Office, 1891), 19; Hess, *Banners to the Breeze*, 44.

60. Born on October 4, 1800, in Scott County, Kentucky, James F. Robinson graduated from Transylvania University in 1818 and practiced law in Georgetown. Elected to the state senate as a Whig in 1851, Robinson became Arkansas Senate Speaker in 1862 as a part of a deal to facilitate the resignation of Gov. Beriah Magoffin, who refused to send troops to either the Union or Confederate armies. Robinson succeeded Magoffin as governor on August 18, 1862, and supported the Union but remained critical of Lincoln's use of martial law and suspension of the writ of habeas corpus. On September 1, 1863, Robinson retired to his estate, "Cardome," and eventually supported George B. McClellan in the presidential election of 1864. Ron Payne could not be identified. John David Smith, "James F. Robinson," in *Kentucky's Governors*, ed. Lowell H. Harrison (Lexington: University Press of Kentucky, 2004), 89–92.

61. Heth conducted an extremely slow advance toward Covington, Kentucky. Confronted by a large but essentially untrained body of Ohio militia, he retreated from Florence after a brief skirmish on the night of September 11, 1862. Hess, *Banners to the Breeze*, 46–47.

62. Article VIII, paragraph 16, of the Confederate Conscription Act allowed the discharge of any soldier in a 12-month regiment under 18 and over 35 years of age, provided the regiment retained the maximum number of troops required by the act. *OR*, 4:1, 1099.

63. Born in Kentucky about 1820, Sidney Thomson lived on a farm in District Number 1 of Georgetown in Scott County, Kentucky, with his mother, Sallie Thomson. In 1860, Thomson owned $57,000 in real estate and a personal estate valued at $6,000. *Eighth Census*, M653-394, 993.

64. The regiment would link up with forces under Braxton Bragg at Frankfort, Kentucky. Dacus, *Reminiscences,* 5.

65. Born in Caroline County, Virginia, on February 6, 1797, Richard Hawes moved to Kentucky in 1810, practiced law, and married Hetty Morrison Nicholas. He served in the state House of Representatives and U.S. House of Representatives, joined the Democratic Party following the demise of the Whigs, and supported John C. Breckinridge in 1860. Hawes favored recognition of the Confederacy and strongly opposed Federal coercion of states, but also favored compromise over secession. He served briefly as a major and brigade commissary under Humphrey Marshall and succeeded George W. Johnson as governor, but followed the army out of the state after Perryville and struggled to maintain a state government. After the war, he obtained a presidential pardon and served as Bourbon County judge and master commissioner of the Circuit and Common Pleas Courts. Hawes died on May 25, 1877. Hess, *Banners to the Breeze,* 82–83; Lowell H. Harrison "Richard Hawes," in *Encyclopedia of the American Civil War,* ed. Heidler and Heidler, 2:949.

66. Born in Huntsville, Alabama, on June 1, 1825, John Hunt Morgan graduated from Transylvania College, served in the Mexican War, settled in Lexington, and manufactured hemp. He served under Simon B. Buckner but earned promotion to colonel of the 2nd Kentucky Cavalry on April 4, 1862, and to brigadier general on December 11. During the Kentucky campaign, Morgan led diversionary raids against railroads and outposts and joined Edmund Kirby Smith's command after the surrender of Lexington. He led raids throughout Kentucky and Tennessee and invaded Ohio in 1863. Captured during the Ohio raid, Morgan escaped and took command of the Department of Southwestern Virginia. Killed at Greeneville, Tennessee, on September 3, 1864, he received burial in Lexington Cemetery. Born in Warren County, North Carolina, on March 22, 1817, Braxton Bragg graduated from West Point in 1837 and served in the Seminole and Mexican wars. He resigned in 1856 and became a planter in Louisiana. Appointed as a brigadier general on March 7, 1861, he earned promotion to major general on September 12, 1861, and full general on April 6, 1862, and commanded the Army of Tennessee during the Kentucky invasion. Defeated at Chattanooga, he served the rest of the war as an advisor to Jefferson Davis. Afterward, he served as chief engineer for Alabama and then migrated to Texas. He died in Galveston on September 27, 1876, and received burial in Magnolia Cemetery in Mobile, Alabama. Born in Madison County, Alabama, on January 12, 1814, Jones Mitchell Withers graduated from West Point in 1835, served on the Kansas frontier, and resigned in 1836 to pursue business interests as a cotton broker. He married in 1837 and fathered ten children. He served as a colonel in the U.S. Regulars during the Mexican War and served in the Alabama state legislature, the U.S. House of Representatives, and as mayor of Mobile. Commissioned as colonel of the 3rd Alabama Infantry on April 28, 1861, he received promotion to brigadier general on July 10. He earned promotion to major general on April 6, 1862. Withers briefly resigned on July 13, 1863, but accepted command of the District of North Alabama in the Department of Alabama, Mississippi, and East Louisiana and commanded the Alabama Reserves at the end of the war. He received parole at Meridian, Mississippi, on May 11, 1865. He resumed his law practice and

served once more as mayor of Mobile. He died on March 13, 1890, and received burial in Magnolia Cemetery in Mobile. Joshua W. Sill commanded the column on its way to join Union troops at Perryville. Hess, *Banners to the Breeze*, 12, 24, 92–105, 107; James A. Ramage, *Rebel Raider: The Life of General John Hunt Morgan* (Lexington: University Press of Kentucky, 1986), 40–133; Lawrence L. Hewitt, "Braxton Bragg," in *Confederate General,* ed. Davis and Hoffman, 1:112–17; Lowell H. Harrison, "John Hunt Morgan," in *Confederate General,* ed. Davis and Hoffman, 4:184–89; Terry L. Jones, "Jones Mitchell Withers," in *Confederate General,* ed. Davis and Hoffman, 5:154–55. For a full discussion of the life and career of Braxton Bragg see Grady McWhiney and Judith Lee Hallock, *Braxton Bragg and Confederate Defeat,* vol. 2 (Tuscaloosa: University of Alabama Press, 1991).

67. Located on the northern Garrard County farm of Kentucky Unionist Richard M. Robinson, "Camp Dick Robinson" served as a Union recruiting and training ground as early as August 1861. Viewed by Confederates as a violation of Kentucky's neutrality policy, the camp provided Leonidas Polk with justification to occupy Columbus, Kentucky, in September 1861. The camp served as a Union supply depot until replaced by "Camp Nelson" in late 1862. Confederates occupied Robinson during the Perryville campaign. Susan Lyons Hughes, "Camp Dick Robinson," in *The Kentucky Encyclopedia,* ed. John E. Kleber (Lexington: University Press of Kentucky, 1992), 157–58.

68. Born in Fredericksburg, Virginia, on September 17, 1817, Carter Littlepage Stevenson graduated from West Point in 1838. Dismissed June 25, 1861, due to suspicions about his loyalties, he served as colonel of the 53rd Virginia Infantry. Promoted to brigadier general on February 27, 1862, he forced George W. Morgan to withdraw from Cumberland Gap. Stevenson earned promotion to major general on October 10, 1862. He signed a parole at Greensboro, North Carolina, on May 1, 1865, and worked as a civil engineer in Caroline County, Virginia, until his death on August 15, 1888. He received burial in the Confederate Cemetery at Fredericksburg. Lowell L. Hewitt, "Carter Littlepage Stevenson," in *Confederate General,* ed. Davis and Hoffman, 6:8–9.

69. Reynolds left this space blank. For a description of the Confederate retreat out of Kentucky, see Hess, *Banners to the Breeze,* 106–20.

70. Born in Alabama about 1840, Andrew J. Little lived in the household of Little Rock merchant John H. Newbern and worked as a clerk. In 1860, he owned $2,500 in real estate and a personal estate of $200. He mustered in as a sergeant with Company F of the 1st Arkansas Mounted Rifles on June 14, 1861, and served as assistant commissary of subsistence until relieved. *Eighth Census,* M653–49, 23; M376, Roll 14.

71. Robert H. Dacus reported twelve to fifteen inches of snow and sleet near the regiment's position at Cumberland Gap on October 26. Dacus, *Reminiscences,* 5.

72. John Kincaid lived in Campbell County, Tennessee, near Big Creek Gap, Kentucky. A staunch Confederate sympathizer, he owned 54 of the 61 slaves in Campbell County in 1860. On January 28, 1865, two veterans of the 1st East Tennessee (Union) Infantry murdered Kincaid in a dispute over lands acquired by Kincaid while the original owners served in local Union regiments. Gregory K. Miller, *The Civil War and Campbell County Tennessee* (Jacksboro, TN: Action Printing, 1992), 1–2, 14–15.

73. The East Tennessee and Georgia Railroad operated between Knoxville and Dalton with stops at Loudon and Cleveland, Tennessee. At Dalton, it connected with the Western and Atlantic (State) Railroad, with a stop at Kingston, Georgia. Kingston is located 41 miles and 5 stops after Dalton on the route to Atlanta. Swayze, *Rail-Road and Steam-Boat Guide,* 37, 41.

74. Marietta, Georgia, is located 39 miles and 8 stops from Kingston on the Western and Atlantic (State) Railroad. Kendrick could not be identified. Built in 1846 and located at the lower end of the passenger depot, Washington Hall accommodated passengers coming through Atlanta. The building did not survive the war. Swayze, *Rail-Road and Steam-Boat Guide,* 3, 41; Robert S. Davis Jr., ed., *Requiem for a Lost City: Sallie Clayton's Memoir of Civil War Atlanta* (Macon: Mercer University Press, 1999), 81.

75. Augusta's "Southern States Hotel" hosted many public events. On January 25, 1861, it hosted a concert to celebrate secession. *Daily Constitutionalist* (January 26, 1861), 3.

76. Built by Otis Mills and later owned by Thomas S. Nickerson and Joseph Purcell, the "Mills House" hotel stood at the southwest corner of Meeting and Queen Streets in Charleston, South Carolina. The fortifications mentioned by Reynolds defended Charleston and its harbor. Situated on an island at the mouth of the Cooper River, about one mile from the city, Castle Pinckney later served as a prisoner-of-war facility. Hostilities began in April 1861 with the bombardment and surrender of Fort Sumter, located on an island near the middle of the harbor entrance between Morris Island and a peninsula that extends from Sullivan's Island. Reynolds's reference to a "new fort to the right of Fort Sumter and nearer Charleston" may indicate the heavy battery set up at Cumming's Point just prior to the bombardment. Situated on Morris Island, to the right of Fort Sumter (but not actually closer to the city), the battery at Cummings Point served as home for the Palmetto Guard during the bombardment. Located to the left of Fort Sumter, on the Sullivan's Island peninsula, Fort Moultrie guarded the mouth of the harbor. Located on James Island at the mouth of the Ashley River, to the right of Fort Sumter, Fort Johnson served primarily as a barrack and storage area. In 1861, Confederates fired the signal to begin the bombardment of Fort Sumter from Fort Johnson. *The Southern Business Directory and General Commercial Advertiser* (Charleston: Steam Power Press of Walker and James, 1854) 1:346–47; Swayze, *Rail-Road and Steam-Boat Guide,* 3; David Detzer, *Allegiance: Fort Sumter, Charleston, and the Beginning of the Civil War* (New York: Harcourt, 2001), 29–31, 48, 101–7, 198, 272.

77. The South Carolina Railroad operated a 127-mile route between Charleston, South Carolina, and Augusta, Georgia. Swayze, *Rail-Road and Steam-Boat Guide,* 10–11.

78. The Georgia Railroad operated a route between Augusta and Atlanta. Swayze, *Rail-Road and Steam-Boat Guide,* 8.

79. The East Tennessee and Georgia Railroad operated the 82-mile journey from Loudon, Tennessee, to Chattanooga. Swayze, *Rail-Road and Steam-Boat Guide,* 37.

80. The Nashville and Chattanooga Railroad ran between Chattanooga and Bridgeport, Alabama. The regiments of Matthew D. Ector's Texas Brigade served alongside the 1st Arkansas Mounted Rifles until difficulties between Reynolds and French forced a reorganization of the division. "Job's Comforters" appear to provide

consolation, but actually enhance an affliction. Swayze, *Rail-Road and Steam-Boat Guide*, 38; E. D. Hirsch, Joseph F. Kett, and James S. Trefil, *The New Dictionary of Cultural Literacy* (New York: Houghton Mifflin Harcourt, 2002), 12.

81. Born in Alabama in 1827, Dr. Washington Lafayette Gammage moved with his wife to Cherokee County, Texas, in the 1850s. He enlisted on May 1, 1861, in Francis M. Taylor's "Lone Star Defenders" company but transferred to the 4th Arkansas Infantry to serve as regimental surgeon. In 1862, he became brigade surgeon on the staff of Evander McNair and staff surgeon for Edward Cary Walthall on June 19, 1864. He published a memoir in 1864 and died in a train accident in Mobile while in route home after the war. Born in Tennessee about 1835, W.A.C. Sayle graduated from medical school in Louisville, Kentucky, and settled in Lewisburg, Arkansas, in 1859. In 1860, he owned a personal estate valued at $500. Sayle mustered in as assistant surgeon of the 2nd Arkansas Mounted Rifles on August 1, 1861. Federal troops captured Sayle at home in October 1863. Mr. French could not be identified. CSR, M376, Roll 8; M376, Roll 20; M376, Roll 20; *Eighth Census*, M653–39, 443; Gammage, *The Camp, the Bivouac, and the Battlefield*, v–vi, 41–50; *Historical Reminiscences and Biographical Memoirs of Conway County, Arkansas* (Little Rock: Arkansas Historical Publishing Company, 1890), 22, 24, 26, 32, 34; Crute, *Confederate Staff Officers*, 140, 203.

82. The East Tennessee and Georgia Railroad ended at Dalton, Georgia. The Western and Atlantic (State) Railroad operated between Dalton and Atlanta. The Atlanta and West Point Railroad operated between Atlanta and West Point, Georgia. The Montgomery and West Point Railroad operated between Montgomery, Alabama, and West Point. Swayze, *Rail-Road and Steam-Boat Guide*, 37, 41–43.

83. The Alabama and Florida Railroad connected Montgomery to Mobile by way of the Mobile and Great Northern Railroad at Pollard, Alabama. Built in 1852 on a headquarters used by Andrew Jackson during the War of 1812 and owned by F. H. Chamberlain and Company, the Battle House enjoyed a stellar reputation. Swayze, *Rail-Road and Steam-Boat Guide*, 5, 44, 46–47.

84. The Mobile and Ohio Railroad operated a 134-mile route between Mobile and Meridian. The Southern (Mississippi) Railroad connected Meridian to Vicksburg by way of Jackson. Meridian served as the terminus for both the Southern and the Alabama and Mississippi Rivers Railroads. Swayze, *Rail-Road and Steam-Boat Guide*, 48–50.

85. Owned by T. McMackin, the Washington Hotel stood three blocks east of the Mississippi River on Washington Street in Vicksburg and served as a hospital during the siege. *A General Directory for the City of Vicksburg* (Vicksburg: H. C. Clarke, 1860), 56; Adolph A. Hoehling, *Vicksburg: 47 Days of Siege* (Mechanicsburg, PA: Stackpole Books, 1996), 2, 250.

86. The only Methodist Episcopal Church listed in Vicksburg stood at the corner of Cherry and Crawford Streets. Services began at 11:00 a.m. Born in Maine about 1813, the Rev. C. K. Marshall lived with his 48-year-old wife, Amanda, and three daughters and served as a Methodist preacher in Vicksburg. In 1860, Marshall owned $100,000 in real estate and a personal estate valued at $7,000. Born on December 25, 1838, James McMurray served as captain of Company G and assistant quartermaster of the 23rd Arkansas Infantry. After the war, he lived at Luna Landing and Lake Village and served

as the circuit clerk. He died on March 10, 1925. CSR, M376, Roll 16; *A General Directory for the City of Vicksburg,* 52; *Biographical and Historical Memoirs of Southern Arkansas,* 1062; *Eighth Census,* M653–592, 24.

87. The Vicksburg, Shreveport, and Texas Railroad operated a western terminus at DeSoto, Arkansas, opposite Vicksburg. This line made 6 stops over 74 miles and ended service at Monroe, Louisiana. By 1862, Federal troops occupied the eastern terminus at Shreveport. Swayze, *Rail-Road and Steam-Boat Guide,* 46.

88. Born in Georgia about 1826, William T. Brewer lived in Talladega Township in Jefferson County, Arkansas, with his 28-year-old wife, M. M. Brewer, a son, a daughter, and an overseer. He owned 35 slaves in 1860, as well as $14,900 in real estate and a personal estate valued at $40,000. Born in Georgia about 1817, Mrs. M. S. Whetstone lived on a farm in Ward 4 of Bastrop, Morehouse Parish, Louisiana, with five sons and four daughters. In 1860, she owned $10,000 in real estate and a personal estate valued at $48,000, as well as 44 slaves. *Eighth Census,* M653–44, 725; *Eighth Census, Slave Schedule* (Jefferson County, Arkansas), M653, Roll 53, 389; *Eighth Census,* M653–413, 336; *Eighth Census, Slave Schedule* (Morehouse Parish, Louisiana), M653–429, 132.

89. Mr. Woods could not be identified.

90. Born in Arkansas about 1819, Joseph W. Pennington lived in Pennington Township near the Bradley County town of Warren. Pennington lived with his 37-year-old wife, Lenora, five sons, and three daughters. In 1860, he owned $4,650 in real estate and a personal estate valued at $500. *Eighth Census,* M653–38, 530.

91. Born in Kentucky about 1800, Drew White lived on a Pine Bluff plantation in Jefferson County with his 55-year-old wife, Jane, two sons, and several apparent boarders. White established one of the earliest taverns in Pine Bluff. In 1860, he owned $60,000 in real estate and a personal estate valued at $30,000. Judge Campbell could not be identified. *Eighth Census,* M653–44, 794; Dallas T. Herndon, ed., *Centennial History of Arkansas* (Chicago: S. J. Clarke Publishing Company, 1922), 882.

92. James G. Downhour, "Claiborne Fox Jackson," in *Encyclopedia of the American Civil War: A Political, Social, and Military History,* ed. David S. Heidler and Jeanne T. Heidler (Santa Barbara: ABC-Clio), 2:1055–56.

93. While in command of the Trans-Mississippi Department, Thomas C. Hindman attempted to secure northwestern Arkansas. He attacked the isolated division of James G. Blunt with a cavalry column under John S. Marmaduke. Blunt, however, seized the offensive initiative and engaged Marmaduke at Cane Hill on November 28, 1862, in a fluid fight that forced the Confederate column steadily southward. Afterward, Blunt returned to Cane Hill and Marmaduke rejoined Hindman. Blunt reported 8 killed and 36 wounded, while the Confederates suffered 10 killed and approximately 70 wounded or missing. Although a tactical Confederate defeat, Blunt's force remained isolated from the nearest Union reinforcements. Hindman, therefore, moved northward toward Prairie Grove to attack Francis J. Herron's column as it attempted to reinforce Blunt. *OR,* 1:22 (Part 1), 138; William L. Shea, *Fields of Blood: The Prairie Grove Campaign* (Chapel Hill: University of North Carolina Press, 2009), 92–108; William L. Shea, "Battle of Cane Hill," in *Encyclopedia of the American Civil War,* ed. Heidler and Heidler, 1:353.

94. The Union gained a strategic victory at Prairie Grove on December 7, 1862. Hindman estimated Confederate casualties at Cane Hill and Prairie Grove as "about 350" killed, wounded, and missing. He estimated Federal losses as 1,000 killed and wounded, along with "about 300" prisoners, 20 wagons, and 4 stands of colors. The official Union figures included 263 captured or missing, as well as 175 killed and 813 wounded, for an aggregate of 1,251 casualties. Confederate losses at Prairie Grove amounted to 1,483 and consisted of 204 killed, 872 wounded, and 407 missing. Historian William L. Shea questions whether Confederate commanders, particularly Missourians, reported complete losses for Prairie Grove. Dr. John H. Carroll's mother could not be identified. *OR*, 1:22 (Part 1), 46, 138–46; Shea, *Fields of Blood*, 145–242, 261–62.

95. For several days after Prairie Grove, Hindman and Blunt engaged in a lively debate over claim of victory. Hindman's repeated claims, as well as attempts to downplay the overall failure of his northwestern Arkansas campaign, undoubtedly fueled early Confederate reports of Prairie Grove as a victory. Historian William L. Shea notes that many Southern soldiers considered the battle a victory until Hindman retreated. *OR*, 1:22 (Part 1), 69–82, 86, 138; Shea, *Fields of Blood*, 239–42, 254–55.

96. Born in South Carolina about 1826, L. H. Belser owned a farm in Marion Township in Drew County. He lived with his 28-year-old wife, Mary, three sons, and a daughter. He served as a state senator for Chicot, Ashley, and Drew Counties from 1860 to 1862 and served in the state's Confederate legislature in Washington, Arkansas, in 1864. Bayou Bartholomew extends through southeastern Arkansas and northern Louisiana. *Eighth Census*, M653–41, 112; *Biographical and Historical Memoirs of Southern Arkansas* (Chicago: Goodspeed Publishing Company, 1890), 1063; Dallas T. Herndon, *Centennial History of Arkansas* (Chicago: S. J. Clarke Publishing Company, 1922), 132.

97. Born about 1815 in Virginia, Johnson Chapman lived in Oden Township with his 35-year-old wife, Elizabeth, two sons, and three daughters and served as Chicot County clerk between 1838 and 1844. In 1860, he owned $45,000 in real estate and a personal estate valued at $40,000, as well as 63 slaves. Born in Maryland about 1814, Dr. Stephen Proctor lived in Old River Township with his 33-year-old wife, Mary. He owned $10,000 in real estate and a personal estate valued at $3,000. *Eighth Census*, M653–38, 922, 950; *Eighth Census, Slave Schedule* (Chicot County, Arkansas), M653, Roll 53, 97; *Biographical and Historical Memoirs of Southern Arkansas*, 1062.

98. Born in Virginia about 1804, John R. Llewellyn lived in Oden Township with his 46-year-old wife, Susan, three sons, and four daughters. Llewellyn owned 1,200 acres of plantation lands, including property opposite "Island Eighty-Two." In 1860, he reported $100,000 in real estate and a personal estate valued at $60,000, as well as 53 slaves. He lost most of his holdings after the war and died on July 1, 1878. The title "Colonel" appears to be honorary. *Eighth Census*, 1860, M653–38, 950; *Eighth Census, Slave Schedule* (Chicot County, Arkansas), M653, Roll 53, 97; *Biographical and Historical Memoirs of Southern Arkansas*, 1064, 1077.

99. Born in Kentucky about 1815, Mrs. Mildred P. Davies lived in Old River Township with her 62-year-old husband, Anthony H. Davies, and their eight children

along with five children of his deceased first wife. In 1860, Mr. Davies owned $124,200 in real estate and a personal estate of $154,000. A. H. Davies died of flux on September 10, 1862. The sister of prominent Chicot County planter Richard M. Gaines, Mrs. Davies lived on "Lake Hall" plantation and owned 139 slaves in 1860. Exempt from the general amnesty of May 29, 1865, due to personal wealth of more than $20,000, Mrs. Davies applied for a special presidential pardon. Endorsed by Gov. Isaac Murphy, she received a pardon on November 9, 1865. Born in Virginia about 1821, Mrs. Susan Read resided as a planter in Old River Township along with her three children, a sister-in-law, a private tutor, and two hired persons. In 1860, Mrs. Read owned $27,480 in real estate, a personal estate valued at $42,700, and 91 slaves. Exempt from the general amnesty due to personal worth of more than $20,000, she applied for a special presidential pardon. Endorsed by Murphy and U.S. district attorney Orville Jennings, she received a pardon on November 9, 1865. *Eighth Census,* M653–38, 922; *Eighth Census, Slave Schedule* (Chicot County, Arkansas), M653, Roll 53, 102–3; *Biographical and Historical Memoirs of Southern Arkansas,* 1063–64, 1074; Douthat, *Special Presidential Pardons,* 1:170, 173.

100. Born in Maine about 1815, the Rev. Otis Hackett and his 38-year-old wife, Abigail, lived in Old River Township. The Hackett family included four daughters and two sons. In 1860, Rev. Hackett held a personal estate valued at $1,000. He presided over one of five Protestant Episcopal congregations in Arkansas in the late 1850s. *Journal of the Proceedings of the Bishops, Clergy and Laity of the Protestant Episcopal Church* (Philadelphia: King and Baird, 1857), 334; *Eighth Census,* M653–38, 919.

101. Bayou Macon extends through southeastern Arkansas and northeastern Louisiana, between the Boeuf and Mississippi Rivers, and converges with the Tensas River. James Dunwoody Brownson DeBow, *DeBow's Review of the Western and Southern States* (New Orleans: J.D.B. DeBow, 1852), 411.

102. Born in Illinois about 1823, R. Stuart Diamond worked as an overseer in Louisiana Township and lived with his 21-year-old wife, Mary, and three daughters. In 1860, he reported a personal estate of $10,000, including 2 slaves. *Eighth Census,* M653–38, 949; *Eighth Census, Slave Schedule* (Chicot County, Arkansas), M653, Roll 53, 93.

103. The battle of Murfreesboro occurred while Reynolds was at home on furlough. The report by Harper differs only slightly in content from the report published in the *Official Records.* After moving to relieve St. John R. Liddell and twice driving Federal troops from their position, McNair removed himself from the field due to exhaustion caused by several days of poor health. Col. Robert W. Harper assumed command of the brigade for the rest of the engagement. Harper cited Maj. Lee M. Ramseur for gallantry as "acting Lieutenant Colonel." According to Robert H. Dacus, the 1st Arkansas Mounted Rifles remained at Loudon, Tennessee, from late October until "sometime in December" when they moved to Murfreesboro just prior to the battle. The Arkansas Brigade and Ector's Texas Brigade opened the battle "before sunrise" and charged across a field toward a Federal position in a cedar brake. These brigades captured a Union battery before sunrise. About one hour after sunrise, the Arkansas troops captured a second battery. *OR,* 1:20 (Part 1), 662, 949. Dacus, *Reminiscences,* 5.

104. For a full account of the battle of Stones River at Murfreesboro, Tennessee, see

Peter Cozzens, *No Better Place to Die: The Battle of Stones River* (Champaign: University of Illinois Press, 1991).

105. Clark D. Jenkins mustered in as a private in Company D of the 1st Arkansas Mounted Rifles on June 9, 1861. Awarded the Badge of Distinction for service at Murfreesboro, Jenkins also earned promotion to sergeant. Born December 6, 1831, in Chillicothe, Ohio, Joshua Woodrow Sill graduated from West Point in 1853 and taught geography, history, and ethics at the academy. He resigned in January 1861 but returned to command the 33rd Ohio Infantry. Promoted to brigadier general on July 16, 1862, he died at Murfreesboro on December 31, 1862, and received burial at Grandview Cemetery in Chillicothe. Fort Sill, Oklahoma, bears his name. Born at "Elmsley" Plantation near Woodville, Mississippi, on September 6, 1815, St. John Richardson Liddell entered West Point in 1833 but soon withdrew and owned a plantation in Catahoula Parish, Louisiana. Liddell served as an aide-de-camp on the staff of William J. Hardee and earned an appointment to brigadier general on July 17, 1862. After Chattanooga, he transferred to the Trans-Mississippi Department and surrendered at Fort Blakely, Alabama, on April 9, 1865. He returned to Catahoula Parish and died on February 14, 1870, during an altercation on a steamboat. He received burial on his plantation. *OR*, 1:20 (Part 1), 948–49; CSR, M376, Roll 12; U.S. War Department, *List of Staff Officers of the Confederate States Army, 1861–1865* (Washington, DC: Government Printing Office, 1891), 98; Warner, *Generals in Blue*, 448–49; Terry L. Jones, "St. John Liddell," in *Confederate General*, ed. Davis and Hoffman, 4:74–75.

106. McNair reported "a large number" of Union troops captured, as well as 14 pieces of artillery, caissons, ordnance stores, small arms, and equipage. He also reported the capture of August Willich. *OR*, 1:20 (Part 1), 944–46.

107. Major and acting lieutenant colonel Lee M. Ramseur commanded the 1st Arkansas Mounted Rifles at Murfreesboro after Harper assumed command of the brigade. Ramseur survived a severe wound on December 31, 1862. Dacus credited Cleburne's Division with saving the brigade from annihilation by filling a gap that opened to the right of the Arkansas Brigade when the division assigned there failed to advance. With the gap closed, the Confederates advanced against the Federal right and pushed the enemy back against their center. Bragg reported 4,000 Federals captured, with 31 pieces of artillery and 200 wagons and mules. *OR*, 1:20 (Part 1), 946, 949; Dacus, *Reminiscences*, 5.

108. The official casualty figures differ only slightly from Harper's aggregate of 96. The 1st Arkansas Mounted Rifles suffered 9 killed, 82 wounded, and 4 missing on December 31, 1862, for an aggregate of 95 casualties. McNair reported an aggregate of 427 killed, wounded, and missing for his brigade and cited the work of Dr. Gammage, along with "the regimental surgeons, with their assistants." Charles D. Cotton mustered in as a private with Company A of the 1st Arkansas Mounted Rifles on June 15, 1861, and earned promotion to sergeant and regimental color bearer in 1862. Wounded at Atlanta on July 27, 1864, he is not listed after August 31, 1864. *OR*, 1:20 (Part 1), 681, 944–49; CSR, M376, Roll 5.

109. Robert E. Foote served as an assistant adjutant general on the staff of Evander McNair. Foote earned promotion to major on November 1, 1862. At the battle of

Murfreesboro, McNair commanded the 3rd Brigade of John P. McCown's Division until ordered to retire due to ill health. Robert W. Harper commanded the brigade for the rest of the battle. McNair cited Foote for "valuable assistance." Harper submitted a regimental report, as well as the brigade report referenced by Reynolds. In his regimental report, Harper cited Foote for prompt and courageous service. Foote served as assistant adjutant general to Bushrod R. Johnson from November 4, 1864, until February 8, 1865. *OR*, 1:20 (Part 1), 946–49; CSR, M818, Roll 8; War Department, *List of Staff Officers*, 56.

THREE

1. For a discussion of the Vicksburg campaign and its strategic significance, see Michael B. Ballard, *Vicksburg: The Campaign That Opened the Mississippi* (Chapel Hill: University of North Carolina Press, 2004).

2. Thomas Lawrence Connelly, *Autumn of Glory: The Army of Tennessee, 1862–1865* (Baton Rouge: Louisiana State University Press, 1971), 4–5, 69–92; James Lee McDonough and Thomas Lawrence Connelly, *Five Tragic Hours: The Battle of Franklin* (Knoxville: University of Tennessee Press, 1983), 6–9.

3. J. G. McCown, who served in Ector's Brigade as a private in Company K of the 32nd Texas Cavalry, said that Walker expressed "a poor opinion" of the discipline in Ector's and McNair's Brigades during operations in Mississippi. Walker apologized for his comments after Chickamauga. McNair's Brigade transferred to the division of Samuel Gibbs French on June 22, 1864. According to Robert H. Dacus, "all hated General French." J. G. McCown, "About Ector's and McNair's Brigades," *Confederate Veteran* (March 1901): 113; Robert H. Dacus, *Reminiscences of "Company H," First Arkansas Mounted Rifles* (Dardanelle, AR: Post-Dispatch Printing, 1897), 30; Peter Cozzens, *This Terrible Sound: The Battle of Chickamauga* (Urbana: University of Illinois Press, 1992), 401–2.

4. Signed November 17, 1863, Reynolds's appointment as colonel ranked from September 20. "Appointments," Daniel Harris Reynolds Papers, Special Collections, University Libraries, Fayetteville, Box 1, Folder 7, Item 127 (hereafter cited as DHR Papers).

5. After Sherman's unsuccessful assault on Chickasaw Bayou, Adm. David D. Porter's Mississippi Squadron transported troops down the Mississippi River on January 2, 1863, where they joined John A. McClernand's forces at Milliken's Bend for operations against Fort Hindman at Arkansas Post. *OR*, 1:17 (Part 1), 700–710; Ballard, *Vicksburg*, 146–47.

6. Former U.S. district judge Ben Johnson owned "Tecumseh" plantation with his brother Richard Mentor Johnson, former vice president of the United States. In 1869, Reynolds and William B. Streett purchased "Tecumseh." Born in Louisiana about 1822, Franklin Dunn lived in Oden Township and worked as an overseer in 1860. Born in Virginia on December 21, 1821, Thomas A. Hunnicutt lived in Oden Township and worked as an overseer. In 1860, he owned $5,000 in real estate and a personal estate of $3,500. He enlisted as a corporal in Company F of the 12th Arkansas Cavalry (also

known as Wright's Arkansas Cavalry) on November 10, 1863, and served as sheriff between 1864 and 1868. After the war, he served as a Freedmen's Bureau agent but lost this position after seven months due to financial and sexual improprieties. He died at Lake Village on October 12, 1888. Bureau of the Census, *Eighth Census of the United States, 1860* (Washington, DC: National Archives and Records Administration, 1860), M653–38, 950, 953; U.S. War Department, Compiled Service Records of Confederate Soldiers Who Served in Organizations from the State of Arkansas, National Archives, Microcopy 376, Roll 12 (hereafter cited as CSR with microfilm and roll numbers); *Biographical and Historical Memoirs of Southern Arkansas* (Chicago: Goodspeed Publishing Company, 1890), 1062, 1065; Paul A. Cimbala and Randall M. Miller, eds., *The Freedmen's Bureau and Reconstruction: Reconsiderations* (New York: Fordham University Press, 1999), 100–101.

7. George W. Polk, brother of Episcopal bishop and Confederate lieutenant general Leonidas Polk, owned plantation property in Chicot County's Louisiana Township but did not reside in the county. In 1860, he reported 88 slaves. Macon Hills run alongside Bayou Macon in southeastern Arkansas. Born in Tennessee about 1796, Hiram Ralph lived as a planter in Bayou Mason Township with his 45-year-old wife, Ellen, five sons, and two daughters. In 1860, Ralph owned $6,500 in real estate and a personal estate of $21,500, as well as 39 slaves. Born in Louisiana about 1827, Caleb P. Bennett lived as a planter in Louisiana Township with his 28-year-old wife, Britton, and an overseer named William M. Simmons. In 1860, he owned $48,000 in real estate and a personal estate of $20,000, as well as 20 slaves. The titles "Colonel" and "Captain" appear to be honorary. *Eighth Census*, M653–38, 944, 947; Bureau of the Census, *Eighth Census of the United States, 1860, Agriculture Schedule and Slave Schedule* (Chicot County, Arkansas), M653–53, 88B, 91, 93B; James Dunwoody Brownson DeBow, *DeBow's Review of the Western and Southern States* (New Orleans: J.D.B. DeBow, 1852), 411; *Biographical and Historical Memoirs of Southern Arkansas*, 1065.

8. Aaron Goza owned Gossypia Plantation on Old River Lake in Ward 3 of Carroll Parrish, Louisiana. Born in Georgia about 1805, he lived with his 46-year old wife, Amanda, two sons, and three daughters. Goza owned 260 slaves in 1860 and reported $385,000 in real estate and a personal estate valued at $200,000. Union troops raided his plantation in 1863 due to its use as a refuge for Confederate soldiers. Govey Hood owned 62 slaves on his Black Bayou Place plantation near Lake Providence, Louisiana, as well 117 slaves on property in Louisiana and Kentucky, and fought a protracted legal battle over lands lost to wartime debts. *Eighth Census*, M653–409, 373; *Eighth Census, Slave Schedule* (Carroll Parish, Louisiana), M653, Rolls 427, 329, 336, 347; Federal Writers Project, *Louisiana: A Guide to the State* (New York: Hastings House 1945), 590; Robert Desty, ed., *The Federal Reporter: Cases Argued and Determined in the Circuit and District Courts of the United States, June–August 1882* (St. Paul, MN: West Publishing Company, 1882), 763–68; William Kauffman Scarborough, *Masters of the Big House: Elite Slaveholders of the Mid-Nineteenth-Century South* (Baton Rouge: Louisiana State University Press, 2003), 135.

9. Born in Virginia about 1800, Rice C. Ballard owned several plantations in the southern Mississippi Valley but lived in Louisville, Kentucky, with his 37-year-old wife,

Louisa, and three daughters. In 1860, he owned $30,000 in real estate and a personal estate of $35,000, as well as approximately 500 slaves across Mississippi, Louisiana, and Arkansas. Ballard kept 76 slaves on his Louisiana Township property in 1860. He died in 1860. His papers are held by the Wilson Library at the University of North Carolina at Chapel Hill. *Eighth Census,* M653–375, 728; *Eighth Census, Slave Schedule* (Chicot County, Arkansas), M653, Roll 53, 92; Scarborough, *Masters of the Big House,* 124–25.

10. Oak Grove Plantation stood three miles from Tallulah, Louisiana, near Milliken's Bend. The overseer named Bird could not be identified. Gary D. Joiner, Marilyn S. Joiner, and Clifton D. Cardin, eds., *No Pardons to Ask, nor Apologies to Make: The Journal of William Henry King, Gray's 28th Louisiana Infantry Regiment* (Knoxville: University of Tennessee Press, 2006), 57.

11. Born in Germany about 1815, William Trowbridge moved from Corning, New York, to Vicksburg, Mississippi, with his 35-year-old wife, Catharine, three sons, and two daughters. Trowbridge operated the "Mechanics Boarding-House" at the corner of Walnut and Grove Streets. In 1860, he owned $5,000 in real estate and a personal estate of $4,000. Trowbridge died in Vicksburg on July 25, 1860. *Eighth Census,* M653–592, 918; *General Directory for the City of Vicksburg: Containing the Name and Address of Every Professional and Business Man and Resident of the City* (Vicksburg: H. C. Clarke, Publisher, 1860), 71; Mary Smith Jackson, *Death Notices from Steuben County New York Newspapers, 1797–1884* (Westminster, MD: Heritage Books, 1998), 251.

12. British satirist George Colman the Younger wrote the comedy *Blue-Beard, or Female Curiosity* about a wife-murdering nobleman, based on the 1698 fairy tale by Charles Perrault. First performed at Drury Lane Theater in London in 1798, it remained popular throughout the nineteenth century. Phyllis Hartnoll, ed., *The Oxford Compendium to the Theatre* (Oxford: Oxford University Press, 1983), 167; Mark Hawkins-Dady, ed., *International Dictionary of Theatre* (Detroit: St. James Press, 1994), 2:212.

13. John Augustus Stone wrote *Metamora or The Last of the Wampanoag.* First performed at the Park Theatre in New York City in 1829, it tells the story of a Native American chief and his struggle against conquest by white settlers; it enjoyed tremendous popularity throughout the nineteenth century. British playwright Thomas Morton wrote *A Pretty Piece of Business,* a comedy about Americans in Paris. First performed at London's Royal Haymarket Theatre in 1853, it received favorable reviews. *Dramatic Register for 1853* (New York: T. Hailes Lacy, 1854), 56, 116; *Bentley's Monthly Review, Or, Literary Argus: November 1853 to April 1854* (London: Piper, Stephenson and Spence, 1854), 430; Gerald Bordman, ed., *The Oxford Companion to American Theatre* (New York: Oxford University Press, 1984), 474–75.

14. Designed by architect Samuel Holt and owned by Thompson Tyler and Company, the Exchange Hotel opened in November 1847 at the corner of Montgomery and Commerce Streets in Montgomery, Alabama. J. C. Swayze, *Hill and Swayze's Confederate States Rail-Road and Steam-Boat Guide, Containing the Time-Tables, Fares, Connections and Distances on all the Rail-Roads of the Confederate States; also, the Connecting Lines of Rail-Roads, Steam-Boats and Stages. And will be Accompanied by a Complete Guide to the Principal Hotels, with a Large Variety of Valuable Information*

(Griffin, GA: Hill and Swayze, 1862), 5; James Frederick Sulzby, *Historic Alabama Hotels and Resorts* (Tuscaloosa: University of Alabama Press, 1960), 125–26.

15. The Nashville and Chattanooga Railroad operated between Chattanooga and Tullahoma, Tennessee. At Wartrace, 2 stops after Tullahoma, a branch of the McMinnville and Manchester Railroad connected to Shelbyville, Tennessee. Swayze, *Rail-Road and Steam-Boat Guide,* 38, 47.

16. Born in Louisiana about 1833, Jefferson Stone lived in Batesville in Independence County and worked as a clerk. In 1860, he owned $6,700 in real estate and a personal estate of $10,000. He mustered in as captain of Company K of the 1st Arkansas Mounted Rifles on June 9, 1861, and served until killed at Chickamauga on September 20, 1863. *Eighth Census,* M653–43, 10; M376, Roll 22.

17. Born on June 3, 1861, at McConnellsville, Ohio, Otho French Strahl attended Ohio Wesleyan University with Reynolds. Strahl practiced law in Dyersburg, Tennessee. He served as a captain in the 4th Tennessee Infantry but commanded the regiment by January 1863. He earned promotion to brigadier general on July 28, 1863. Although primarily part of Cheatham's Corps, Strahl's Brigade served in Alexander P. Stewart's Division of John C. Breckinridge's Corps during the Chattanooga campaign and served in John C. Brown's Division of Cheatham's Corps during the 1864 invasion of Tennessee. Killed at Franklin and initially buried at St. John's Church in Ashwood, Tennessee, his remains now rest in Dyersburg's Old City Cemetery. Beth Beach (Registrar's Office, Ohio Wesleyan University) to Robert Patrick Bender, July 16, 2009, in possession of the editor; Charles M. Cummings, "Otho French Strahl: 'Choicest Spirit to Embrace the South,'" *Tennessee Historical Quarterly* 24 (1965): 341–55; Edwin C. Bearss, "Otho French Strahl," in *Confederate General,* ed. Davis and Hoffman, 6:14–17.

18. John A. McClernand and the Army of the Mississippi captured Arkansas Post (Fort Hindman) on January 11, 1863, which helped secure Federal communication between Vicksburg and Memphis while Grant continued operations against Vicksburg. *OR,* 1:24 (Part 1), 5; *OR,* 1:7, 700–709.

19. Reynolds cites the proper official regulations for captains and their obligations as officer-of-the-day. Confederate States of America War Department, *Regulations for the Army of the Confederate States 1863* (Richmond: J. W. Randolph, 1863), 68, 74.

20. Born in North Carolina about 1831, James A. Williamson lived in his father's household in Ozan Township in the Hempstead County town of Washington, Arkansas, and practiced law. He mustered in as captain of Company H of the 2nd Arkansas Mounted Rifles on August 4, 1861, and earned promotion to colonel. He lost a leg at Resaca, Georgia, on May 14, 1864. He settled in Columbus, Arkansas, represented Hempstead County, and prospered as a planter and attorney. He married Annie Pearsall Johnson in 1873. Walter C. Carrington joined the staff of Evander McNair as an aide-de-camp on November 19, 1862, and resigned on January 16, 1864. Born in Tennessee about 1834, S. H. Mulherrin moved to Carolina Township in Prairie County and became a merchant. In 1860, he owned $1,000 in real estate and a personal estate of $4,000. He joined McNair's staff in 1862 as a major and served as chief of subsistence. On June 19, 1864, he joined E. C. Walthall's staff but served as Reynolds's chief of sub-

sistence from November 4, 1864, until May 1865. U.S. War Department, Index to Compiled Service Records of Confederate Soldiers Who Served in Organizations Raised Directly by the Confederate Government and of Confederate General and Staff Officers and Non-Regimental Enlisted Men, National Archives, Microcopy 818, Roll 5 (hereafter cited as CSR with microfilm and roll numbers); M376, Roll 25; M818, Roll 17; *Eighth Census,* M653–42, 723; *Eighth Census,* M653–48, 944; Wesley Thurman Leeper, *Rebels Valiant: Second Arkansas Mounted Rifles, Dismounted* (Little Rock: Pioneer Press, 1964), 243, 321; Crute, *Confederate Staff Officers,* 163; U.S. War Department, *List of Staff Officers of the Confederate States Army, 1861–1865* (Washington, DC: Government Printing Office, 1891), 28, 119.

21. In accordance with the congressional act of October 13, 1862, the Confederate Adjutant and Inspector General's Office issued General Order No. 93 on November 22, 1862, which authorized "medals and badges of distinction" to recognize "courage and good conduct" on the battlefield. Awarded by majority vote, one non-commissioned officer or private in each company received the honor after each victory. Unable to obtain medals and badges, the Adjutant and Inspector General's Office established a "Roll of Honor" on October 3, 1863, with General Order No. 131. Pat Calahan mustered in as a private in Company A ("the Chicot Rangers") of the 1st Arkansas Mounted Rifles on June 15, 1862. He received parole at Jamestown, North Carolina, on April 30, 1865. Born in Tennessee about 1840, William T. Blakemore lived on his father's farm in Prairie County in White River Township in Des Arc. He mustered in as a private in Company B ("the Des Arc Rangers") on June 9, 1861. Born in Arkansas about 1840, James Pearson lived on his father's farm in Perry Township in Johnson County. He mustered in as a private in Company C ("the Johnson Rifles") on June 6, 1861. Hospitalized at Yazoo City, Mississippi, in June 1863 and at LaGrange, Georgia, in July 1864, he later served in Company B and received parole at Greensboro, North Carolina, on April 28, 1865. For Clark Jenkins, see note 105 in chapter 2. Born in Arkansas about 1838, Thomas J. Underwood lived on his mother's farm in Strawberry Township in Lawrence County. He mustered in as a private in Company E ("the Lawrence County Rifles") on June 9, 1861. William S. Colburn mustered in as first sergeant in Company G ("the Napoleon Cavalry") on May 12, 1861, and was wounded at Atlanta on July 28, 1864. Born in Tennessee about 1842, Thomas Thomson (sometimes spelled "Thompson" in records). lived on his mother's farm in Dardanelle Township in Yell County. He mustered in as a private in Company H ("the Yell County Rifles") on June 9, 1861, and earned promotion to corporal. Born in Georgia about 1836, Isaac L. Caston worked as a laborer and lived in his brother's household in the Conway County town of Lewisburg. He mustered in as a corporal in Company I ("the McCulloch Rangers") in June 1861 and was wounded and captured at Murfreesboro. George B. House mustered in as a private in Company K ("The Independence County Rifles") on June 9, 1861, and served until killed at Murfreesboro. CSR, M376, Roll 4; M376, Roll 3; M376, Roll 3; M376, Roll 18; M376, Roll 24; M376, Roll 5; M376, Roll 23; M376, Roll 4; M376, Roll 11; *OR,* 1:11 (Part 2), 992; *Eighth Census,* M653–48, 1000; *Eighth Census,* M653–44, 1075; *Eighth Census,* M653–45, 322; *Eighth Census,* M653–52, 1028; *Eighth Census,* M653–39, 447.

22. Born on February 3, 1807, in Farmville, Virginia, Joseph E. Johnston graduated from West Point in 1829. He earned a brevet during the Seminole War and two more in the Mexican War. He earned promotion to brigadier general on June 28, 1860, but resigned after the secession of Virginia. Commissioned as a brigadier general on May 14, 1861, he played a vital role at First Manassas. His appointment to full general dated from July 4, 1861. In late 1862, he commanded the Department of the West and frequently disagreed with Jefferson Davis. Relieved of command during the Atlanta campaign, he returned to command during the Carolina campaign and surrendered to William T. Sherman on April 26, 1865, at Bennett Station, North Carolina. He lived in Georgia and Virginia after the war, wrote a memoir, and served in congress. He died of pneumonia on March 21, 1891, and received burial in Green Mount Cemetery in Baltimore, Maryland. Richard M. McMurry, "Joseph Eggleston Johnston," in *Confederate General,* ed. Davis and Hoffman, 3:192–97; Gilbert E. Govan and James W. Livingood, *General Joseph E. Johnston, C.S.A.: A Different Valor* (New York: Konecky and Konecky, 1993), 11–15, 162–71.

23. Led by former Ohio representative Clement L. Vallandigham, the Democratic Party fueled antiwar debate based on concerns for constitutional liberties, military setbacks, and opposition to abolition as a war goal. By early 1863, such issues inspired discussion about a potential alliance between the Old Northwest and the South. In a related move, the lower houses of the Indiana and Illinois state legislatures passed resolutions in favor of armistice and a peace conference. Although unsuccessful, these movements bolstered Confederate hopes that the North could not sustain a unified war effort. McPherson, *Battle Cry of Freedom,* 591–97.

24. The 4th Arkansas Infantry regiment and 4th Arkansas Infantry Battalion served in Evander McNair's Brigade of John Porter McCown's Division in Edmund Kirby Smith's Department of East Tennessee. The 1st and 2nd Arkansas Mounted Rifles (Dismounted), 30th Arkansas Infantry, 31st Arkansas Infantry, and Capt. J. T. Humphreys's Arkansas Battery comprised the remainder of McNair's Brigade. *OR,* 1:20 (Part 2), 413.

25. Lodges serve as the basic unit of the Masonic Order. Individual lodges belong to a recognized (or "regular") Grand Lodge. "Military" or "Traveling Lodges" may organize under temporary "Traveling Warrants," which expire at the conclusion of the conflict, and members revert to their local lodges. The worshipful master, senior warden, and junior warden serve as the primary officers of a lodge. Other lodge officers include secretary, treasurer, senior deacon, junior deacon, marshal, chaplain, stewards, and a Tyler or doorkeeper. A member holds the rank of "Master Mason" after completion of the 33rd degree of the order, after completing the ranks of "Entered Apprentice" and "Fellow Craft." John B. Hardwick mustered in with Company B of the 1st Arkansas Mounted Rifles on June 6, 1861. He became captain after John S. Pearson received a slight wound at the battle of Oak Hills. Hardwick received parole at Greensboro, North Carolina, on April 28, 1865. CSR, M376, Roll 10; *Biographical and Historical Memoirs of Western Arkansas* (Chicago: Goodspeed Publishing Company, 1891), 15; Desmond Walls Allen, *Abstracts from Masonic Records, Grand Lodge of Arkansas, 1862–1869* (Conway, AR: Arkansas Research, 2003), 9, 127; Albert G. Mackey, *Encyclopedia of Freemasonry*

(Philadelphia: McClure Publishing Company, 1916), 321, 472–74, 492–93, 501, 826; William J. Whalen, *Handbook of Secret Organizations* (Milwaukee: Bruce Publishing Company, 1966), 51–55; Clement Anselm Evans, ed., *Confederate Military History: A Library of Confederate States History, Written by Distinguished Men of the South* (Atlanta: Confederate Publishing Company, 1899), 10:45, 49.

26. Complaints about medical care reflect shortages of personnel and supplies after Stones River. Glenna R. Schroeder-Lein, *Confederate Hospitals on the Move: Samuel H. Stout and the Army of Tennessee* (Columbia: University of South Carolina Press, 1996), 63–64.

27. Born in Rogersville, Tennessee, on October 2, 1821, Alexander Peter Stewart graduated from West Point in 1842 but resigned in 1845 to teach mathematics. He commanded the Heavy and Water Batteries at Belmont, Missouri, and earned promotion to brigadier general on November 8, 1861. He earned promotion to major general on June 2, 1863. Stewart succeeded Polk to corps command, with rank as lieutenant general to date from June 23, 1864. He received parole at Greensboro, North Carolina, in May 1865. He engaged in business interests, served as president of the University of Mississippi, and as commissioner of the Chickamauga-Chattanooga National Military Park. Stewart died in Biloxi, Mississippi, on August 30, 1908, and received burial in St. Louis in Bellefontaine Cemetery. William C. Davis, "Alexander Peter Stewart," in *Confederate General,* ed. Davis and Hoffman, 6:10–11.

28. Eli Hufstedler mustered in as captain of Company A in the 30th Arkansas Infantry (later renamed the 25th Arkansas Infantry) and earned promotion to lieutenant colonel after the resignation of Henry Remington. CSR, M376, Roll 12.

29. Because the Alabama and Mississippi Rivers Railroad did not operate east of Montgomery, a fleet of steamboats traveled a daily route on the Alabama River from Montgomery to Selma. The fleet included the *Southern Republic, St. Nicholas, Jeff Davis, Henry J. King, Senator, St. Charles, Claudis,* and *La Grande.* Swayze, *Rail-Road and Steam-Boat Guide,* 44–45.

30. The Alabama and Mississippi Rivers Railroad operated a route between Selma and Demopolis, with a stop at Uniontown. From Demopolis passengers traveled up the Tombigbee River to McDowell on the steamboat *Marengo.* Swayze, *Rail-Road and Steam-Boat Guide,* 44.

31. The Alabama and Mississippi Rivers Railroad operated between McDowell and Meridian, Mississippi. Swayze, *Rail-Road and Steam-Boat Guide,* 44.

32. On May 3 and 5, 1863, Beauregard ordered States Rights Gist to proceed to Jackson, Mississippi, in command of his and W.H.T. Walker's Brigades, to aid Pemberton at Vicksburg. Born in Union District, South Carolina, on September 3, 1831, States Rights Gist graduated from South Carolina College in 1852 and Harvard University Law School in 1854. Thereafter, he practiced law. He served as a volunteer aid to Barnard E. Bee and received a commission as a brigadier general on March 20, 1862. He served until killed at Franklin. Initially buried in Franklin, his remains now rest in Trinity Episcopal Churchyard in Columbia, South Carolina. W. T. Edwards served as assistant commissary as of November 1862. Charles C. Ferguson became sergeant major in 1862. *OR,* 1:14, 925; *OR,* 1:24 (Part 3), 833, 883–84; Walter Brian Cisco,

States Rights Gist: A South Carolina General of the Civil War (Gretna, LA: Pelican Publishing Company, 2008), 38–47, 132–53; Ezra J. Warner, *Generals in Gray: Lives of the Confederate Commanders* (Baton Rouge: Louisiana State University Press, 1959), 106–7.

33. The Southern (Mississippi) Railroad operated a route between Meridian and Jackson, Mississippi. Swayze, *Rail-Road and Steam-Boat Guide,* 50.

34. While in route to join Pemberton, Gist received instructions from Joseph E. Johnston to post his command 40 or 50 miles from Jackson, Mississippi, in order to join Johnston. Gist posted his troops at Forest Station, Mississippi, 44 miles from Jackson and 45 miles from Canton. Union troops under William T. Sherman destroyed considerable military and civilian property during their occupation of Jackson. *OR,* 1:24 (Part 3), 883–84, 886, 889, 897; Ballard, *Vicksburg,* 280–81.

35. When Johnston went to Jackson, Gist took command of "some 12,000 men" at Canton. *OR,* 1:24 (Part 3), 919–20.

36. Born in Tennessee about 1836, W. T. Edwards lived on a farm in Harrison Township in White County with his 17-year-old wife, M. E. Edwards, and infant son. In 1860, he owned $1,000 in real estate. Edwards served as a first lieutenant and adjutant in the 1st Arkansas Mounted Rifles, with rank from September 25, 1861. Promoted to captain on September 22, 1863, he served thereafter as an assistant commissary of subsistence. *Eighth Census,* M653-52, 870; M376, Roll 7; *Journal of the Congress of the Confederate States of America, 1861–1865* (Washington, DC: Government Printing Office, 1904), 1:840; *Journal of the Congress of the Confederate States of America, 1861–1865* (Washington, DC: Government Printing Office, 1904), 4:239.

37. Born on November 26, 1816, in Augusta, Georgia, William Henry Talbot Walker graduated from West Point in 1837. Commissioned as a brigadier general on May 25, 1861, he resigned on October 29, 1861, and served as a major general of Georgia State Troops. Reappointed a brigadier general on February 9, 1863, and promoted to major general on May 23, 1863, he commanded a division under Joseph E. Johnston during the Vicksburg campaign. During the winter of 1863–1864, he led opposition to Cleburne's proposal to enlist slaves as soldiers. Killed at Atlanta on July 22, 1864, he received burial in Walker Cemetery in Augusta. Russell K. Brown, *To the Manner Born: The Life of General William H. T. Walker* (Macon, GA: Mercer University Press, 2005), 1–19, 217–302; Steve Davis, "A Georgia Firebrand: Major General W.H.T. Walker, C.S.A.," *Georgia Historical Quarterly* 63 (Winter 1979): 447–60; Arthur W. Bergeron Jr., "William Henry Talbot Walker," in *Confederate General,* ed. Davis and Hoffman, 6:98–99.

38. S. H. Crump served as a captain and assistant inspector general on the staff of W.H.T. Walker. CSR, M818, Roll 6; War Department, *List of Staff Officers,* 38.

39. Born in Lawrence County, Alabama, on September 28, 1828, John Gregg migrated to Texas in 1852, where he served as a district judge and a member of the Texas secession convention. Elected to the Confederate Congress, he resigned to serve as colonel of the 7th Texas Infantry. Promoted to brigadier general on August 29, 1862, he survived a wound at Chickamauga and, thereafter, commanded the Texas Brigade in the Army of Northern Virginia. Killed near Richmond on October 7, 1864, he received burial at Odd Fellows Cemetery in Aberdeen, Mississippi. Born in Putnam County,

Georgia, on February 28, 1822, Matthew Duncan Ector graduated from Centre College in Danville, Kentucky, and served in the Georgia state legislature. He moved to Texas in 1850, practiced law, and served in the state house of representatives. He served as adjutant to James L. Hogg until appointed colonel of the 14th Texas Cavalry. Promoted to brigadier general on August 23, 1862, he lost a leg during the Atlanta campaign and served in the defense of Mobile. He returned to Texas and served on the state court of appeals. He died in Tyler, Texas, on October 29, 1879, and received burial in Greenwood Cemetery in Marshall. In May 1863, Walker's staff consisted of Capt. Robert H. Anderson (aide-de-camp and acting assistant adjutant general), Capt. S. H. Crump (assistant inspector general), Capt. Joseph B. Cumming (assistant adjutant general), Maj. Alfred L. Dearing (commissary of subsistence), Maj. T. R. Heard (quartermaster), Lt. Thomas H. Kenan (aide-de-camp), Lt. G. De Rossett Lamar (aide-de-camp), Lt. Lawson W. Magruder (ordnance officer), Maj. Nathaniel O. Tilton (quartermaster), and Captain Troup (assistant adjutant general). J. G. McCown, "About Ector's and McNair's Brigades," *Confederate Veteran* (March 1901): 113; Joseph H. Crute Jr., *Confederate Staff Officers, 1861–1865* (Powhatan, VA: Derwent Books, 1982), 113, 202; Warner, *Generals in Gray,* 80–81, 118–19.

40. Reynolds's negative assessment does not reflect Walker's overall reputation. Quick tempered and inclined toward political machinations to advance his ambitions for promotion, Walker nonetheless enjoyed a good reputation as a division commander. Although never promoted to corps command, he commanded the reserve corps at Chickamauga. Brown, *To the Manner Born,* 153, 283; Connelly, *Autumn of Glory,* 248, 319–21, 449; Bergeron, "William Henry Talbot Walker," in *Confederate General,* ed. Davis and Hoffman, 6:98–99.

41. G. De Rosset "Derry" Lamar served as a volunteer aide-de-camp to Walker from March 1863 until his appointment as a lieutenant on May 23, 1863. After a personal quarrel with Walker, Lamar resigned during the Atlanta campaign. He later served on the staff of his brother-in-law, Brig. Gen. Alfred Cummings. Walker faced considerable difficulties while organizing his new division, during the time of Reynolds's complaints. With no division staff in place at the time of his promotion, Walker made due with his existing brigade staff. The necessity of this move further required the use of several regimental officers to fill vacancies on various brigade staffs. The resulting shuffle of officers may have left Reynolds with a perception of inefficient administration. Russell K. Brown to Robert Patrick Bender, November 15–16, 2010, in possession of the editor; War Department, *List of Staff Officers,* 94; Brown, *To the Manner Born,* 140–41, 156–57, 212.

42. Rev. D. S. Snodgrass served as pastor for the Baptist Church located at the east corner of Walnut and Crawford Streets in Vicksburg. On December 21, 1861, he received an appointment as a Confederate chaplain. *A General Directory for the City of Vicksburg* (Vicksburg: H. C. Clarke, 1860), 52; *Journal of the Congress of the Confederate States of America, 1861–1865,* 1:608.

43. Born in Gloucester County, New Jersey, on November 22, 1818, Samuel Gibbs French graduated from West Point in 1843 and earned two brevets for gallantry in the Mexican War. He resigned in 1856 and married into a Mississippi plantation family. He

served initially as chief of ordnance for Mississippi, until appointed as a brigadier general on October 23, 1861. He received promotion to major general on August 31, 1862, and transferred to the Western Theater in May 1864. He surrendered in April 1865 at Mobile, Alabama. Afterward, he lived as a planter and retired to Florala, Florida, where he died on April 20, 1910. He received burial in St. John's Cemetery in Pensacola. Mrs. Bowles could not be identified. McCown, "About Ector's and McNair's Brigades," 113; Samuel G. French, *Two Wars: The Autobiography and Diary of Gen. Samuel G. French, CSA* (Huntington, WV: Blue Acorn Press, 1999); William C. Davis, "Samuel Gibbs French," in *Confederate General,* ed. Davis and Hoffman, 2:148–49.

44. The division's movements near Jackson and Big Black River Bridge remained a source of contention after the war. Robert H. Dacus critically declared, "We were marched and countermarched, it seemed as much for diversion for himself [French] and staff as for any other visible reason, until Vicksburg fell." "Mr. Home" may refer to T. J. Holmes. Born in North Carolina about 1806, T. J. Holmes owned a farm in Township 5 of Hinds County, near Jackson, Mississippi, with his 25-year-old daughter, H. M. Holmes. In 1860, he owned $24,000 in real estate, 55 slaves, and a personal estate valued at $55,000. *Eighth Census,* M653–582, 540; *Eighth Census, Slave Schedule* (Hinds County, Mississippi) M653, Roll 597, 206–206B; Dacus, *Reminiscences,* 6.

45. Birdsong's Ferry crossed the Big Black River northeast of Vicksburg. Grant closely guarded its approach to prevent reinforcement by Johnston. Edwards Depot is located 2 stops and 18 miles from Vicksburg along the Southern (Mississippi) Railroad. Swayze, *Rail-Road and Steam-Boat Guide,* 50; Ballard, *Vicksburg,* 404–5; Gordon A. Cotton and Jeff T. Giambrone, *Vicksburg and the War* (Gretna, LA: Pelican Publishing Company, 2004), 98.

46. Born in Tennessee about 1835, James T. Smith lived on his father's farm in Clear Creek Township in Sevier County and practiced medicine. In 1860, he owned a personal estate of $200. He mustered in as second lieutenant in Company G ("the Sevier Rifles") of the 2nd Arkansas Mounted Rifles on July 27, 1861. Elected lieutenant colonel on August 18, 1861, he served until killed at Atlanta on July 28, 1864. According to Dacus, French separated Reynolds's and Ector's Brigades due to their disdain for him, expressed through insubordinate singing and whistling as his staff rode through brigade lines. *Eighth Census,* M653–51, 121; M376, Roll 21; Dacus, *Reminiscences,* 29–30.

47. Born on February 3, 1824, in Marion, South Carolina, Nathan George "Shanks" Evans graduated from West Point in 1848 and served on the frontier. He played a crucial role at First Manassas and was promoted to brigadier general on October 21, 1861. During the Vicksburg campaign, he served under Joseph E. Johnston. After the war, he served as a high school principal in Midway, Alabama, where he died on November 23, 1868. He received burial in Cokesbury, South Carolina. Warner, *Generals in Gray,* 83–84.

48. For a description of the role played by the 1st Arkansas Mounted Rifles during the engagements around Jackson, Mississippi, in early July, see the official report of Col. Henry G. Bunn of the 4th Arkansas Infantry. *OR,* 1:24 (Part 2), 658–59.

49. The 1st Arkansas Mounted Rifles and the 4th Arkansas Infantry alternated at the center, between the 4th Louisiana Infantry on the right and the 2nd Arkansas Mounted Rifles on the left. For a description of the role played by the 1st Arkansas Mounted

Rifles in front of Jackson on July 11 and 12, 1863, see the report of Henry G. Bunn of the
4th Arkansas Infantry. Born in Lexington, Kentucky, on January 16, 1821, John C.
Breckinridge studied at Centre College, the College of New Jersey, and Transylvania
University. He served as major in the 3rd Kentucky Volunteers during the Mexican
War. Afterward, Breckinridge practiced law and won seats in the Kentucky legislature
and U.S. Congress. In 1856, he won election as vice president of the United States under
James Buchanan and ran unsuccessfully for president four years later. Although
Kentucky remained in the Union, Breckinridge joined the Confederacy. Appointed a
brigadier general on November 2, 1861, he earned promotion to major general on April
14, 1862, and served under Johnston during the Vicksburg campaign. He commanded
the Department of Southwest Virginia in 1864. Appointed as the secretary of war in
February 1865, he oversaw the demise of the Confederate government. He returned to
Kentucky after a brief exile, practiced law, engaged in business, and supported national
reconciliation. Breckinridge died on May 17, 1875, and received burial in Lexington
Cemetery. *OR,* 1:24 (Part 2), 658–59; William C. Davis, "John Cabell Breckinridge," in
Confederate General, ed. Davis and Hoffman, 1:126–27. For a full discussion of the life
and career of John C. Breckinridge, see William C. Davis, *Breckinridge: Statesman,
Soldier, Symbol* (Baton Rouge: Louisiana State University Press, 1992).

50. Born in Tennessee about 1838, James P. Eagle lived on his father's farm in the
Brownsville Township in Richwoods in Prairie County. In 1860, he worked as a deputy
sheriff and owned $3,500 in real estate and a personal estate of $800. Eagle mustered in
as second lieutenant of Company C in the 2nd Arkansas Mounted Rifles on August 20,
1861. He earned promotion to captain on May 8, 1862. Wounded and captured at
Murfreesboro, he received exchange on April 29, 1863. He earned promotion to major
on May 20, 1863, and survived a wound on July 19, 1864. After consolidation, Eagle
served as lieutenant colonel and received parole at Greensboro, North Carolina, on
April 28, 1865. For a description of the activities of French's Division and McNair's
Brigade between July 7 and 16, 1863, see Eagle's report. *OR,* 1:24 (Part 2), 657–58; *Eighth
Census,* M653–48, 912; M376, Roll 7.

51. During the siege of Jackson, Mississippi, Breckinridge's Division served as the
left flank of Johnston's line, positioned south of the city's downtown. The 1st Arkansas
Mounted Rifles served in French's Division, positioned to the immediate right of
Breckinridge, facing the Raymond, Robinson, and Clinton Roads and the western
approach of the Southern Railroad. The divisions of W.H.T. Walker and William W.
Loring lined up northwest of downtown, to protect the northern entrance of the rail-
road to New Orleans. Born in Wilmington, North Carolina, on December 4, 1818,
William Wing Loring grew up in Florida, studied law, served in the state legislature,
and received a direct commission into the U.S. Army in 1846. He lost an arm in the
Mexican War but served until May 13, 1861, when he resigned. Appointed a brigadier
general seven days later, he earned promotion to major general on February 15, 1862.
After a clash with Stonewall Jackson, Loring served with the Army of Tennessee.
Afterward, he served as a general in the army of the Khedive of Egypt until 1879. He
died in New York City on December 30, 1886, and received burial in Woodlawn
Cemetery in St. Augustine, Florida. Ballard, *Vicksburg,* 407–8; James W. Raab, *W. W.*

Loring: Florida's Forgotten General (Manhattan, KS: Sunflower University Press, 1996), 1–5, 8–9, 36, 40, 48–62, 100–122, 201–16, 235–42; Robert K. Krick, "William Wing Loring," in *Confederate General,* ed. Davis and Hoffman, 4:96–99.

52. No report by Reynolds exists for the period mentioned. The only known report of actions taken by the 1st Arkansas Mounted Rifles during this period is that of Col. Henry G. Bunn of the 4th Arkansas Infantry. *OR,* 1:24 (Part 2), 658–59.

53. Such conditions held no weight within the stipulations of the Confederate Conscription Act of 1862. Individuals and companies retained the right to apply for a transfer, but such requests fell within the discretionary needs of the department. *OR,* 4:1, 1099.

54. The Grand Lodge for Arkansas granted several dispensations in 1863 for the creation of traveling lodges within various Confederate regiments, including the "Harper Traveling Lodge." Masonic Grand Lodges organize on a territorial basis and serve as the supreme administrative body for the lodges within their area. Each Grand Lodge is presided by a grand master mason, senior and junior grand wardens, grand secretary, and grand treasurer. Elbert H. English served as grand master of Masons in Arkansas from 1859 until 1868, the longest tenure in the state's history. He also served many years as the chief justice of the Arkansas Supreme Court. *Proceedings of the MW Grand Lodge of Free and Accepted Masons of the State of Arkansas, Held in the Town of Washington* (Little Rock: J. D. Butler, Book and Job Printer, 1866), 5; Mackey, *Encyclopedia of Freemasonry,* 319–21.

55. Born in Kentucky about 1836, George S. Laswell lived in Lewisburg in Conway County and worked as a druggist. Laswell mustered in with Company I of the 1st Arkansas Mounted Rifles on June 6, 1861. Following Robert W. Harper's election to major, Laswell became captain. He later served as lieutenant colonel. *Eighth Census,* M653–39, 444; M376, Roll 14; *Biographical and Historical Memoirs of Western Arkansas,* 15.

56. Harpin Davis mustered in as a private in Company G of the 23rd Arkansas Infantry on March 27, 1862, and earned promotion to corporal and forage master on June 28, 1862. He served as a volunteer aide-de-camp on Reynolds's staff from April to August 1864 and is sometimes listed "Harper Davis." CSR, M376, Roll 6, and M818, Roll 7; Crute, *Confederate Staff Officers,* 163.

57. For a description of the practical and symbolic characteristics of Masonic furniture, see William D. Moore, *Masonic Temples: Freemasonry, Ritual Architecture, and Masculine Archetypes* (Knoxville: University of Tennessee Press, 2006).

58. Each Masonic Lodge displays a set of six jewels, three "moveable" and three "immovable." The moveable jewels consist of the "Rough Ashlar," the "Perfect Ashlar," and the "Trestle Board." These objects do not have a fixed place. The immovable jewels consist of the "Square," the "Level," and the "Plumb." The Square faces to the east, the Level to the west, and the Plumb to the south. The reference to stars appears to refer to the insignia of two stars worn by Confederate lieutenant colonels. Reynolds's rank as lieutenant colonel dated from May 1, 1862. "Appointments," DHR Papers, Box 1, Folder 7, Item 127; Mackey, *Encyclopedia of Freemasonry,* 382–83.

59. Born in Savannah, Georgia, on October 30, 1830, John Stevens Bowen graduated from West Point in 1853 and worked as an architect in St. Louis. He served as a captain

and chief of staff to Daniel M. Frost during the crisis over Camp Jackson. Appointed colonel of the 1st Missouri Infantry, Bowen earned promotion to brigadier general on March 14, 1862, and major general on May 25, 1863. He died from dysentery during the Vicksburg campaign on July 13, 1863, and received burial in Vicksburg's Confederate Cemetery. Crute, *Confederate Staff Officers*, 19–20; Phillip Thomas Tucker, *The Forgotten "Stonewall of the West": Major General John Stevens Bowen* (Macon, GA: Mercer University Press, 1997), 1–116, 293–324; Edwin C. Bearss, "John Stevens Bowen," in *Confederate General*, ed. Davis and Hoffman, 1:110–11.

60. The Mobile and Ohio Railroad made 24 stops on its 127-mile journey between Meridian and Okolona, Mississippi. Swayze, *Rail-Road and Steam-Boat Guide*, 48–49.

61. Rev. L. Eathe could not be identified.

62. In mid-August 1863, Grant conducted expeditions from Big Black River, Mississippi, and La Grange, Tennessee, against ordnance and commissary stores at Grenada, Mississippi, but no substantial reports exist for those operations. One such raid destroyed or captured $8,000,000 to $10,000,000 in contraband, including 60 locomotives, 450 rail cars, and miscellaneous supplies. James R. Chalmers commanded the Confederate cavalry that defended against such raids, but Union forces occupied Grenada on August 20, 1863. *OR*, 1:30 (Part 4), 497–500; Marion Morrison, *A History of the Ninth Regiment Illinois Volunteer Infantry, with the Regimental Roster* (Carbondale: Southern Illinois University Press, 1997), 91; J. N. Reece, *Report of the Adjutant General of the State of Illinois: Containing Reports for the Years 1861–66* (Springfield: Phillips Brothers, 1900), 1:461.

63. T he Union army captured the steamboat *Coquette* during operations against Mobile, Alabama. E. Kay Gibson, comp., *Dictionary of Transports and Combatant Vessels Steam and Sail Employed by the Union Army, 1861–1868* (Camden, ME: Ensign Press, 1995), 71.

64. Between 1863 and 1864, Confederate officers and civilians engaged in heated debate over proposals to enroll slaves in noncombat or combat roles. Neither of the letters in this exchange could be located on microfilm. Bruce Levine, *Confederate Emancipation: Southern Plans to Free and Arm Slaves during the Civil War* (New York: Oxford University Press, 2006), 17–19.

65. After the Gettysburg campaign, James Longstreet and the First Corps of the Army of Northern Virginia transferred to the Army of Tennessee and served in the Chickamauga campaign. James Longstreet, *From Manassas to Appomattox: Memoirs of the Civil War in America* (New York: Da Capo Press, 1992), 433–44.

66. Bushrod R. Johnson and David Coleman reported the movements of McNair's Brigade in this skirmish, prior to the battle of Chickamauga. *OR*, 1:30 (Part 2), 451–53, 499.

67. Born on April 1, 1823, in Hart County, Kentucky, Simon Bolivar Buckner graduated from West Point in 1844. He earned two brevet promotions during the Mexican War but resigned in 1855 to pursue business interests. Commissioned as a brigadier general to date from September 14, 1861, he served in Tennessee and Kentucky. Captured at Fort Donelson, he earned promotion to major general in August 1862, and commanded a corps at Chickamauga. Promoted to lieutenant general on September

20, 1864, he transferred to the Trans-Mississippi Department. He died on January 8, 1914, and received burial in the State Cemetery at Frankfort, Kentucky. Born in York District, South Carolina, on July 12, 1821, Daniel Harvey Hill graduated from West Point in 1842. He served in the Mexican War but resigned to pursue a teaching career. He served as colonel of the 1st North Carolina Infantry until promoted to brigadier general on July 10, 1861. Promoted to major general on March 26, 1862, and lieutenant general on July 11, 1863, he commanded a corps at Chickamauga. Conflicts with Bragg cost him approval of the promotion to lieutenant general, and he commanded a division as a major general at the end of the war. Afterward, he served as president of the University of Arkansas and Middle Georgia Military and Agricultural College. He died in Charlotte, North Carolina, on September 24, 1889, and received burial in the Davidson College Cemetery. William Page enlisted as a private in Company D on June 9, 1861, and served until taken prisoner at Chickamauga on September 19, 1863. R. J. Green mustered in as a lieutenant with Company F of the 1st Arkansas Mounted Rifles on June 15, 1861, and earned promotion to captain. Nehemiah Cravens mustered in as second lieutenant with Company C of the 1st Arkansas Mounted Rifles on June 6, 1861. He survived a wound at Chickamauga. Robert J. Prather mustered in as a private in Company D on June 9, 1861, before promotion to regimental adjutant. He survived a wound at Murfreesboro. The 1st Arkansas Mounted Rifles captured the regimental colors of the 8th Kansas Infantry at Chickamauga, but the reports contain no mention of a captured ambulance. *OR*, 1:30 (Part 2), 453–56, 499–500, 502; CSR, M818, Roll 4; U.S. War Department, Compiled Service Records of Confederate Soldiers Who Served in Organizations from the State of North Carolina, National Archives, Microcopy M230, Roll 18 (hereafter cited as CSR with microfilm and roll numbers); M376, Roll 19; M376, Roll 18; M376, Roll 9; M376, Roll 6; Hal Bridges, *Lee's Maverick General: Daniel Harvey Hill* (Lincoln: University of Nebraska Press, 1991), 195–224; Lawrence L. Hewitt, "Simon Bolivar Buckner," in *Confederate General,* ed. Davis and Hoffman, 1:138–43; Gary W. Gallagher, "Daniel Harvey Hill," in *Confederate General,* ed. Davis and Hoffman, 3:102–5. For a full discussion of the life and career of Simon Bolivar Buckner, see Arndt M. Stickles, *Simon Bolivar Buckner: Borderland Knight* (Chapel Hill: University of North Carolina Press, 1940).

68. Robert W. Harper received a mortal wound while in command of McNair's Brigade. Command then fell to David Coleman of the 39th North Carolina Infantry, who led a successful charge across Dyer Field against the guns of the 8th Indiana and 1st Michigan batteries. This performance prompted W.H.T. Walker to apology for derogatory remarks made in Mississippi. Coleman submitted the brigade's report. His casualty figures agree with those cited by Reynolds. The 1st Arkansas Mounted Rifles entered battle with 254 effectives and suffered the heaviest losses in the brigade, with an aggregate of 106. Bushrod R. Johnson, commanding the Provisional Division that included McNair's Brigade, cited Reynolds for "faithful toil and heroic conduct." Born in Giles County, Tennessee, on January 6, 1827, John Calvin Brown graduated from Jackson College in 1846, practiced law, supported the 1860 Bell-Everett ticket, and served as colonel of the 3rd Tennessee Infantry. Captured and exchanged at Fort Donelson, he earned promotion to brigadier general on August 30, 1862, survived a

wound at Perryville, and commanded a brigade at Chickamauga. He earned promotion to major general on August 4, 1864, and survived another wound at Franklin. He received parole at Greensboro, North Carolina, in May 1865. Afterward, he practiced law in Pulaski and won two terms as governor in 1870 and 1872. Defeated in 1875 for the U.S. Senate by former president Andrew Johnson, Brown served as president of various railroad companies. He died in Red Boiling Springs, Tennessee, on August 17, 1889, and received burial in Maplewood Cemetery in Pulaski. *OR*, 1:30 (Part 2), 360–66, 451–67, 471–79, 483, 499–506; Peter Cozzens, *This Terrible Sound: The Battle of Chickamauga* (Urbana: University of Illinois Press, 1992), 401–2; Edwin C. Bearss, "John Calvin Brown," in *Confederate General*, ed. Davis and Hoffman, 1:130–33.

69. After Chickamauga, McNair, Ector, and Orme's Brigades went to Mississippi. The 1st Arkansas Mounted Rifles established winter camp at Meridian, Mississippi. *OR*, 1:30 (Part 1), 216; Dacus, *Reminiscences*, 7–8.

70. The Mobile and Great Northern Railroad operated between Mobile and Pollard, with boat service across Mobile Bay. Swayze, *Rail-Road and Steam-Boat Guide*, 47.

71. Numerous vessels named *Natchez* worked the Mississippi River, but Reynolds's reference to *Natchez No. 2* may refer to a vessel owned by Capt. Thomas Leathers. Built in Cincinnati in 1849, *Natchez* operated the New Orleans to Vicksburg trade. Sold several times in the mid-1850s, *Natchez* served as a wharf boat in Mobile and foundered on March 10, 1866. Frederick Way Jr., comp., *Way's Packet Directory, 1848–1994: Passenger Steamboats of the Mississippi River System since the Advent of Photography in Mid-Continent America* (Athens: Ohio University Press, 1994), 337.

72. Born in Virginia about 1805, A. L. Burwell lived on a farm in Beat 4 Township in the town of Sageville in Lauderdale County, Mississippi, with his 45-year-old wife, Elizabeth, three sons, and three daughters. In 1860, he owned $16,600 in real estate and a personal estate valued at $2,100. *Eighth Census*, M653–585, 132.

73. The *Official Records* does not contain a report by Reynolds for Chickamauga.

74. Born in Arkansas about 1841, William A. Wilburn lived on his father's farm in White Rock Township in Franklin County. He mustered in as second lieutenant of Company E and assistant quartermaster with the 25th Arkansas Infantry on March 10, 1862. He served as a captain and assistant adjutant general on Reynolds's staff from July 16, 1864, until May 1865. "Sage Village Lodge No. 86" should be "Sageville Lodge #186." Located west of Meridian, Mississippi, Sageville formed a lodge in 1853, with Benjamin F. Gaddis as the first worshipful master. Lodge #186 moved to Meridian in 1866, returned to Sageville in 1873, and finally settled at Meridian in 1877. The lodge disbanded in 1879. *Eighth Census*, M653–41, 327; M376, Roll 25, and M818, Roll 26; Mickey McMahan (Grand Secretary of Masons for the state of Mississippi) to Robert Patrick Bender, March 31, 2009, in possession of the editor; *The Grand Lodge Proceedings of 1854* (Natchez, MS: Daily Courier Book and Job Office, 1854), 65, 357; Crute, *Confederate Staff Officers*, 163.

75. The Southern (Mississippi) Railroad operated out of Vicksburg, with a stop at Brandon, 14 miles east of Jackson and 59 miles from Vicksburg. Jefferson Davis arrived at the camps of the Army of Tennessee at Meridian, Mississippi, on October 17, 1863, where he sent and received several messages. Capt. Nat Jones could not be identified.

Swayze, *Rail-Road and Steam-Boat Guide,* 50; *OR,* 2:52 (Part 2), 545. For a full discussion of the life and career of Jefferson Davis, see William J. Cooper Jr., *Jefferson Davis: American* (New York: Alfred A. Knopf, 2000).

76. Born in Kentucky about 1839, Alexander W. Jones Jr. lived in Bay Township in Jackson County and worked as a bookkeeper in 1860. He mustered in as a sergeant with Company D of the 1st Arkansas Mounted Rifles on June 9, 1861, but received promotion to second lieutenant. Union troops captured Jones on November 22, 1864, on furlough in Woodruff County. *Eighth Census,* M653–44, 558; M376, Roll 13.

77. Born in Tennessee about 1833, Lafayette L. Noles lived in Cache Township in Monroe County with his 26-year-old wife, Nancy, and a daughter. In 1860, Noles worked as a brick mason and owned $500 in real estate and a personal estate of $200. He mustered in as major of the 25th Arkansas Infantry on March 10, 1862. *Eighth Census,* M653–46, 787; M376, Roll 17.

78. Born in Gallatin, Tennessee, on September 19, 1815, Charles Burton Mitchel graduated from the University of Nashville in 1833 and Jefferson Medical College of Philadelphia in 1836. He served in the Arkansas House of Representatives, practiced medicine, and lived with his 27-year-old wife, Margaret, one son, and two daughters in Washington, Arkansas. In 1860, he owned $20,000 in real estate and a personal estate of $20,000. He served briefly in the U.S. Senate. In November 1861, the state legislature elected Mitchel and Robert W. Johnson to the Confederate Senate, where Mitchel advocated the defensive and financial needs of the Trans-Mississippi. Mitchel died in Little Rock on September 20, 1864, and received burial at Presbyterian Cemetery in Washington, Arkansas. Augustus H. Garland succeeded Mitchel on November 8, 1864. On November 21, 1862, James Alexander Seddon became the fourth Confederate secretary of war. He served until February 5, 1865. *Eighth Census,* M653–42, 723; *OR,* 4:3, 1185, 1187, and 1189; Ezra J. Warner and W. Buck Yearns, eds., *Biographical Register of the Confederate Congress* (Baton Rouge: Louisiana State University Press, 1975), 176–77; Thomas William Herringshaw, *Herringshaw's National Library of American Biography* (Chicago: American Publishers Association, 1914), 196.

79. Robert H. Dacus shared Reynolds's low opinion of French and the "set of dudes" on his staff. Dacus, *Reminiscences,* 29–30.

80. Born in Buncombe County, North Carolina, on February 5, 1824, David Coleman graduated from the University of North Carolina and the U.S. Naval Academy. He left the U.S. Navy in 1850, practiced law, and represented Buncombe County in the state senate. Coleman commanded the Confederate steamer *Ellis.* On December 10, 1861, he became major of an infantry battalion later attached to the 39th North Carolina. Despite a reputation as a hard drinker, he earned promotion to lieutenant colonel on February 16, 1862, became colonel on May 19, 1862, and survived a wound at Murfreesboro. He received parole at Shreveport, Louisiana, on June 15, 1865, practiced law in Buncombe County, and served at the 1875 state constitutional convention. Devastated by defeat, Coleman frequently walked alone at night dressed in his Confederate uniform. Coleman died in Asheville, North Carolina, on March 5, 1883, and received burial in Riverside Cemetery. CSR, M230, Roll 8; Bruce S. Allardice, *Confederate Colonels: A Biographical Register* (Columbia: University of Missouri Press, 2008), 105–6.

81. Born in Kentucky about 1826, William H. Elstner worked as a machinist in Franklin Township in Sevier County with his 26-year-old wife, Ann, three sons, and a daughter. In 1860, he owned $10,000 in real estate and a personal estate of $1,000. Elstner served as a captain and quartermaster on the staff of Evander McNair. Promoted to major on March 31, 1864, he served as quartermaster on Reynolds's staff until May 1865. Despite Reynolds's reference to a transfer west of the Mississippi River, Elstner is not with any Trans-Mississippi command. *Eighth Census,* M653–51, 29; CSR, M376, Roll 7; M818, Roll 8; War Department, *List of Staff Officers,* 50.

82. Born on July 22, 1814, in Scott County, Kentucky, Robert Ward Johnson moved to Arkansas in 1821 after his father's appointment to the Arkansas Territorial Superior Court. He graduated from Yale Law School in 1836, married Sarah S. Smith, and fathered six children. Johnson served in the U.S. House of Representatives and U.S. Senate and advocated pro-slavery positions. The state legislature chose Johnson and Charles B. Mitchel to serve in the Confederate Senate, where Johnson supported the Davis administration. Financially ruined, he moved to Texas, but he returned to Arkansas and practiced law with Albert Pike. He died in Little Rock on July 26, 1879, and received burial in Mount Holly Cemetery. *OR,* 4:3, 1185, 1187, 1189; Warner and Yearns, *Biographical Register of the Confederate Congress,* 132–34; James M. Woods, "Robert Ward Johnson," in *Arkansas Biography: A Collection of Notable Lives,* ed. Nancy A. Williams and Jeannie M. Whayne, 152–53 (Fayetteville: University of Arkansas Press, 2000).

83. Born in Alabama about 1838, Jesse A. Ross practiced law in Washington, Arkansas. He mustered in as first lieutenant in Company C in the 4th Arkansas Infantry Battalion on October 11, 1861, and earned promotion to major on November 10, 1862. *Eighth Census,* M653–42, 689; M376, Roll 20.

84. Born in Monroe County, Kentucky, on February 6, 1828, Lewis Byrum Mitchell moved to Lonoke County, Arkansas, by way of Tennessee. He graduated from the University of Nashville in 1858 and practiced medicine in Austin, Arkansas. He enlisted as a private in Company I of the 25th Arkansas Infantry but received an appointment as assistant surgeon in the 4th Arkansas Infantry Battalion. Mitchell requested assignment as assistant surgeon for the 2nd Arkansas Mounted Rifles after the capture of Dr. W.A.C. Sayle. Dr. Gammage praised Mitchell's skill. Mitchell received parole at Greensboro, North Carolina, on April 28, 1865, returned to Arkansas, married Sarah J. St. Clair, and fathered six sons and three daughters. In 1888, he moved his medical and pharmaceutical practices to Brinkley, Arkansas. He died on November 7, 1906, and received burial in Brinkley at Oaklawn Cemetery. CSR, M376, Roll 16; *Biographical and Historical Memoirs of Eastern Arkansas* (Chicago: Goodspeed Publishing Company, 1890), 546–47; W. L. Gammage, *The Camp, the Bivouac, and the Battlefield: Being the History of the Fourth Arkansas Regiment* (Little Rock: Arkansas Southern Press, 1958), 130–31.

FOUR

1. Comments related to Reynolds's court-martial appear in his entry dated January 20–31, 1864. French barely mentions Reynolds in his autobiography.

Throughout the spring of 1864, debate over Cleburne's proposal fueled angry comments and alliances within the Army of Tennessee. U.S. War Department, Compiled Service Records of Confederate Soldiers Who Served in Organizations from the State of Arkansas, National Archives, Microcopy 376, Roll 19 (hereafter cited as CSR with microfilm and roll numbers); Samuel G. French, *Two Wars: An Autobiography of Gen. Samuel G. French* (Huntington, WV: Blue Acorn Press, 1999), 188; Thomas Lawrence Connelly, *Autumn of Glory: The Army of Tennessee, 1862–1865* (Baton Rouge: Louisiana State University Press, 1971), 235–78, 318–21.

2. Signed on March 12 and received on March 26, Reynolds's promotion to brigadier general ranked officially from March 5, 1864. "Appointments," Daniel Harris Reynolds Papers, University Libraries, Fayetteville, Box 1, Folder 7, Item 127 (hereafter cited as DHR Papers).

3. The transfer of Col. David Coleman's 39th North Carolina Infantry for Col. Isaac L. Dunlop's 9th Arkansas Infantry occurred on May 25, 1864, during operations near New Hope Church, Georgia. U.S. War Department, Compiled Service Records of Confederate Soldiers Who Served in Organizations from the State of North Carolina, National Archives, Microcopy M230, Roll 8 (hereafter cited as CSR with microfilm and roll numbers); M376, Roll 7; *Biographical and Historical Memoirs of Southern Arkansas* (Chicago: Goodspeed Publishing Company, 1890), 1084.

4. The Democratic Party's "Chicago Platform" fell short of accepting Southern independence but did offer immediate cessation of hostilities along with vague statements for a negotiated reunion of the states. Connelly, *Autumn of Glory,* 279–493; John C. Waugh, *Reelecting Lincoln: The Battle for the 1864 Presidency* (New York: Crown Publishers, 1997), 276–94.

5. The bodies placed on the back porch of Carnton Plantation included generals John Adams, Patrick Cleburne, Hiram Granbury, and Otho French Strahl. Derek Smith, *The Gallant Dead: Union and Confederate Generals Killed in the Civil War* (Mechanicsburg, PA: Stackpole Books, 2005), 313–27; Stanley F. Horn, *The Decisive Battle of Nashville* (Knoxville: University of Tennessee Press, 1968), v–xiii, 154–66.

6. Born on April 10, 1806, in Raleigh, North Carolina, Leonidas Polk graduated from West Point in 1827 but resigned to study theology. Thereafter, he served as an Episcopal minister and bishop. Appointed a major general on June 25, 1861, he earned promotion to lieutenant general on October 10, 1862, and commanded a corps until killed at Pine Mountain, Georgia, on June 14, 1864. U.S. War Department, Index to Compiled Service Records of Confederate Soldiers Who Served in Organizations Raised Directly by the Confederate Government and of Confederate General and Staff Officers and Non-Regimental Enlisted Men, National Archives, Microcopy 818, Roll 19 (hereafter cited as CSR with microfilm and roll numbers); Ezra J. Warner and W. Buck Yearns, eds., *Generals in Gray: Lives of the Confederate Commanders* (Baton Rouge: Louisiana State University Press, 1959), 242–43; Glenn Robins, *The Bishop of the Old South: The Ministry and Civil War Legacy of Leonidas Polk* (Macon, GA: Mercer University Press, 2006), 1–34, 151–93.

7. Born on June 11, 1832, in Tipton County, Tennessee, Augustus Hill Garland moved to Washington, Arkansas, in 1836. He graduated from St. Joseph's College in

1849 and taught in Sevier County, Arkansas. He married Sarah Virginia Sanders in 1853, practiced law, and supported John Bell in 1860. He served as a Unionist delegate for Pulaski County in the state secession convention but accepted secession after Lincoln called for state troops. Garland served in the Confederate House of Representatives until appointed to replace the late Sen. Charles B. Mitchel on November 8, 1864. He practiced law after the war. Exempt from the general amnesty of May 29, 1865, due to his tenure in the Confederate Congress, Garland applied for a special presidential pardon. Endorsed by Gov. Isaac Murphy, former Confederate acting-brigadier-general-turned-scalawag Edward W. Gantt, W. D. Fishback, Elisha Baxter, R. T. White, and U.S. district attorney Orville Jennings, Garland received a pardon on July 15, 1865. In 1865, he successfully argued for the right of former Confederates to practice before the U.S. Supreme Court. Elected governor in 1874, he helped ratify the state's new constitution. He served in the U.S. Senate between 1876 and 1885 and as U.S. attorney general under President Grover Cleveland. He suffered a stroke while arguing a case before the U.S. Supreme Court and died on January 26, 1899. He received burial in Little Rock's Mount Holly Cemetery. U.S. War Department, *The War of the Rebellion: A Compilation of the Official Records of the Union and Confederate Armies* (Washington, DC: Government Printing Office, 1900), series 4, 3:1185 (hereafter cited as *OR* or *Official Records*); James L. Douthat, comp., *Special Presidential Pardons of Confederate Soldiers: A Listing of Former Confederates Requesting Full Pardon from President Andrew Johnson* (Signal Mountain, TN: Mountain Press, 1999), 1:23; Ezra J. Warner and W. Buck Yearns, eds., *Biographical Register of the Confederate Congress* (Baton Rouge: Louisiana State University Press, 1975), 95–96; J. Wayne Jones, "Augustus Hill Garland," in *Arkansas Biography: A Collection of Notable Lives,* ed. Nancy A. Williams and Jeannie M. Whayne (Fayetteville: University of Arkansas Press, 2000), 118–19.

   8. Believing his men to be the target of intentional insult and abusive behavior, Reynolds refused to discipline them for sarcastic singing and whistling at the approach of French's staff officers. Reynolds's allusion to French's "disgraceful and disorganizing acts" appears unwarranted. Although unpopular, French proved competent. CSR, M376, Roll 19; Robert H. Dacus, *Reminiscences of Company "H," First Arkansas Mounted Rifles* (Dardanelle, AR: Private publication, 1897), 29–30; Jack A. Bunch, *Roster of the Courts-Martial in the Confederate States Armies* (Shippensburg, PA: White Mane Books, 2001), 288.

   9. The Southern (Mississippi) Railroad made 12 stops in 95 miles between Meridian and Jackson, Mississippi. Swayze, *Rail-Road and Steam-Boat Guide,* 50.

   10. Brandon, Mississippi, is 2 stops and 14 miles from Jackson on the Southern (Mississippi) Railroad. Swayze, *Rail-Road and Steam-Boat Guide,* 50.

   11. The Southern (Mississippi) Railroad made 4 stops in 30 miles between Newton Station and Meridian, Mississippi. The Mobile and Ohio Railroad connected to the Southern Railroad at Meridian, Mississippi, and made 27 stops on its 134-mile journey toward Mobile, Alabama. Swayze, *Rail-Road and Steam-Boat Guide,* 48–50.

   12. Enterprise, Mississippi, is located 2 stops and 14 miles from Meridian on the route of the Mobile and Ohio Railroad. Swayze, *Rail-Road and Steam-Boat Guide,* 48.

   13. One of three Confederate fortifications at Mobile Bay, Fort Powell guarded the

shallow southwestern approach through Grant's Pass. Forts Gaines and Morgan
guarded the main entrance. On February 16, 1864, Farragut bombarded Fort Powell to
divert attention from movements against Atlanta. Born in Knoxville, Tennessee, on July
5, 1801, David Glasgow Farragut received direct appointment as a midshipman in 1810.
He served in the War of 1812 and in Mexico and earned promotion to captain by 1855.
Farragut remained loyal and commanded the West Gulf Blockading Squadron by
December 1861. During the war, he captured New Orleans and Mobile Bay and played
vital roles at Vicksburg and Port Hudson. Farragut became the first officer to earn the
ranks of rear admiral, vice admiral, and admiral of the U.S. Navy. Farragut died in
Portsmouth, New Hampshire, on August 14, 1870. He received burial in Woodlawn
Cemetery in the Bronx, New York. James P. Duffy, *Lincoln's Admiral: The Civil War
Campaigns of David Farragut* (New York: John Wiley and Sons, 1997), 3–13, 16–37, 39–
45, 54–58, 101–14, 119, 125–48, 158–59, 169–93, 215, 222, 225–26, 236, 257–60; Charles R.
Haberlein Jr., "Damn the Torpedoes," in *The Civil War Times Illustrated Photographic
History of the Civil War: Vicksburg to Appomattox,* ed. William C. Davis and Bell Irvin
Wiley (New York: Black Dog Publishing, 1996), 2:962; Frances H. Kennedy, ed., *The
Civil War Battlefield Guide* (New York: Houghton Mifflin Harcourt, 1998), 574.

14. In addition to the surrender and occupation of Little Rock the previous
September, events in Chicot County may have inspired concerns among Reynolds and
his men for the safety of their homes and families. On February 14, 1864, 22 self-
described "half bushwhackers" of Capt. Tuck Thorp's 9th Missouri Cavalry wiped out
32 Union soldiers from the 1st Mississippi Infantry (African Descent) while they for-
aged on Benjamin Johnson's "Tecumseh" plantation near Grand Lake. According to
one account, Confederates pinned the Union corpses to the ground with their own
bayonets. No report exists for this incident, officially known as "the engagement at
Ross's Landing," but it is listed on the summary of events for operations in Louisiana
and the Trans-Mississippi states for January 1 through June 30, 1864. In addition, a skirmish occurred at Lake Village on February 10, 1864, for which no report exists. Such
events characterized life in Chicot County in the spring of 1864. *OR,* 1:34 (Part 1), 2–3,
1162; Weed Marshall, "A Fight to the Finish near Lake Village, Ark.," *Confederate
Veteran* 19 (April 1911): 169; Thomas A. DeBlack, "'A Model Man of Chicot County':
Lycurgus Johnson and Social Change," in *The Southern Elite and Social Change: Essays
in Honor of Willard B. Gatewood, Jr.,* ed. Randy Finley and Thomas A. DeBlack
(Fayetteville: University of Arkansas Press, 2002), 29.

15. Harris Flanagin served as Confederate governor of Arkansas from 1862 through
1864. Born on November 3, 1817, in Roadstown, New Jersey, Flanagin received his education in Quaker schools. By 1839, he practiced law in Arkadelphia, Arkansas, and spec-
ulated in land. Flanagin served as a delegate to the state secession convention and
reluctantly supported secession. He served as captain of Company E in the 2nd
Arkansas Mounted Rifles and succeeded James McIntosh after Elkhorn Tavern. In the
1862 gubernatorial election, he defeated Henry M. Rector. Flanagin supported the
defensive needs of Arkansas and twice raised state troops for this purpose. Following
the capture of Little Rock, Flanagin fled south and established a government-in-exile at
Washington, Arkansas. After the war, he returned to Arkadelphia, practiced law, and

served on the 1874 state constitutional committee. Exempt from the general amnesty of
May 29, 1865, due to his status as a Confederate governor, Flanagin applied for special
presidential pardon in June 1865. Endorsed by Gov. Isaac Murphy, W. M. Fishback, E.
W. Gantt, Elisha Baxter, and U.S. district judge Henry C. Caldwell, he received a pardon
on December 9, 1865. Flanagin died of congestive heart failure on October 23, 1874, and
received burial in Rose Hill Cemetery in Arkadelphia. National Archives and Records
Service, Case Files of Applications from Former Confederates for Presidential Pardons:
1865–1867 ("Amnesty Papers"), Record Group 94; Michael B. Dougan, "Harris
Flanagin," in *Arkansas Biography,* ed. Williams and Whayne, 104–5.

16. The Mobile and Great Northern Railroad made 6 stops on its 50-mile journey
between Tensas Station and Pollard, Alabama. Swayze, *Rail-Road and Steam-Boat
Guide,* 47.

17. Captain Slaughter could not be identified. Born in North Carolina about 1843,
Isaac N. Lane lived on his father's farm in Center Township in Polk County. He
enlisted on August 17, 1861, as a sergeant in Company K of the 4th Arkansas Infantry
regiment and earned promotion to second lieutenant and ordnance officer by
December 1862. Bureau of the Census, *Eighth Census of the United States, 1860*
(Washington, DC: National Archives and Records Administration, 1860),
M653–48, 608.

18. "Appointments," DHR Papers, Box 1, Folder 7, Item 127.

19. Issued on April 6, 1864, Special Orders No. 81 designated the defenses for Mobile
as "the District of the Gulf" within the Department of Alabama, Mississippi, and East
Louisiana, under command of Dabney H. Maury. In addition to the 1st and 2nd
Arkansas Mounted Rifles (Dismounted), 4th Arkansas, 25th Arkansas, and 39th North
Carolina Infantry regiments, Reynolds commanded a detachment of the 7th Alabama
Cavalry, 15th Confederate Cavalry, Tarrant's Alabama Battery, and Tobin's Tennessee
Battery. These units reported 1,942 aggregate troops in April 1864. *OR,* 1:32 (Part 3),
751–52, 860–61.

20. *OR,* 1:38 (Part 4), 659–60, 668; Dacus, *Reminiscences,* 8.

21. Reynolds's Brigade moved immediately from the train cars to the picket post at
Dug Gap, west of Dalton, Georgia. *OR,* 1:38 (Part 4), 674; Dacus, *Reminiscences,* 8.

22. Believing their position impregnable, the regiment did not expect an attack.
Confederate signal troops, however, discovered Hooker's movement across a field west
of Dug Gap. Johnston's report for operations from December 23, 1863, to July 17, 1864,
states that two regiments of Reynolds's Brigade and Warren Grigsby's Brigade of dismounted Kentucky cavalry held their position on May 8 against an assault by a division of Hooker's 20th Corps. Dacus described this action as "some of the hardest
fighting that we did during the war." Born in Arkansas about 1836, Thomas L. Preston
lived on his mother's Richland Township farm in Desha County. He mustered in as a
corporal in Company G on June 15, 1861. Wounded at Murfreesboro, he earned promotion to first lieutenant on June 10, 1863. *OR,* 1:38 (Part 3), 614; *OR,* 1:38 (Part 4), 679;
Eighth Census, M653–41, 69; Dacus, *Reminiscences,* 8–9; Albert Castel, *Decision in the
West: The Atlanta Campaign of 1864* (Lawrence: University of Kansas Press, 1992),
130–35; Lee Kennett, *Sherman: A Soldier's Life* (New York: HarperCollins, 2001), 237–56;

James Willis, *Arkansas Confederates in the Western Theater* (Dayton: Morningside House, 1998), 471–77.

23. Although Reynolds did not report specific casualty figures for this engagement, James Cantey reported an aggregate loss of 26 killed and 405 wounded for his brigade during engagements from Dalton to the Etowah River between May 7 and 20, 1864. Born in Camden, South Carolina, on December 30, 1818, Cantey graduated from South Carolina College and practiced law. He served with the Palmetto Regiment during the Mexican War, moved to Russell County, Alabama, and became a planter. He served as colonel of the 15th Alabama Infantry through the summer of 1862. After a transfer to the Western Theater, he earned promotion to brigadier general on January 8, 1863. During this skirmish on May 9, Cantey apparently hid in a bombproof shelter. He suffered frequent bouts of ill health but surrendered with the Army of Tennessee. He returned to his plantation and died there on June 30, 1874. He received burial in the Crowell Family Cemetery at Fort Mitchell, Alabama. *OR*, 1:38 (Part 3), 686; Jeffry D. Wert, "James Cantey," in *The Confederate General*, ed. William C. Davis and Julie Hoffman (Harrisburg, PA: National Historical Society, 1991), 1:160–61, 43.

24. Reynolds's reports for operations in northern Georgia do not include descriptions or casualty figures for this engagement. Johnston reported only "brisk skirmishing" on May 13, 1864. *OR*, 1:38 (Part 3), 615.

25. Augustus W. Belt enlisted as a private with Company E of the 1st Arkansas Rifles on October 30, 1861. His surname is sometimes listed "Bell." He served as a first sergeant and aide-de-camp on Reynolds's staff from March 31, 1864, until mortally wounded at Resaca, Georgia, on May 14, 1864. Born in Georgia about 1837, Henry Waldrop lived in Arkadelphia and worked as a store clerk. In 1860, he owned $800 in real estate. He served as a sergeant in Company E of the 2nd Arkansas Mounted Rifles until promoted to first lieutenant. In 1862, he became an assistant adjutant general on the staff of Evander McNair. He served as an assistant adjutant general on Reynolds's staff from March 31, 1864, until May 1865. *OR*, 1:38 (Part 3), 615; CSR, M376, Roll 2; M376, Roll 24, and M818, Roll 25; *Eighth Census*, M653–39, 74; War Department, *List of Staff Officers*, 173, 178; Joseph H. Crute Jr., *Confederate Staff Officers, 1861–1865* (Powhatan, VA: Derwent Books, 1982), 163.

26. Reynolds's reports for operations in northern Georgia do not include descriptions or casualty figures, but Johnston reported severe skirmishing on May 15, 1864. *OR*, 1:38 (Part 3), 615.

27. Reynolds's reports for operations in northern Georgia do not include descriptions or casualty figures for May 19. See Johnston's report. *OR*, 1:38 (Part 3), 615–16.

28. Johnston's report indicates he ordered this retreat primarily in response to the opinions of lieutenant generals Leonidas Polk and John Bell Hood, both of whom believed their positions at Cassville "untenable" due to Federal artillery. *OR*, 1:38 (Part 3), 616.

29. For a discussion of opinion in the Army of Tennessee about the leadership of Joseph E. Johnston, see Connelly, *Autumn of Glory*, 281–426.

30. Born in South Carolina about 1836, Isaac L. Dunlop lived in Pennington Township in Bradley County and worked as a bookkeeper. In 1860, he owned a per-

NOTES TO PAGES 127–28

sonal estate of $10,000. He mustered in as second lieutenant with Company D of the 9th Arkansas Infantry on July 25, 1861. Elected colonel on January 12, 1862, he served until killed on September 9, 1864. In accordance with Special Orders No. 126, issued May 5, 1864, the 39th North Carolina Infantry transferred to Ector's Brigade of French's Division. Born in Owingsville, Kentucky, on June 1, 1831, John Bell Hood graduated from West Point in 1853, served in California and Texas, and resigned on April 17, 1861. Appointed colonel of the 4th Texas Infantry, he earned promotion to brigadier general on March 3, 1862. Promoted to major general on October 10, 1862, he survived wounds at Gettysburg and Chickamauga and received promotion to lieutenant general on February 1, 1864, with rank from September 20, 1863. He commanded a corps under Joseph E. Johnston and succeeded Johnston as commander of the Army of Tennessee in July 1864, with promotion to full general on July 18, 1864. Relieved of command at his own request after Franklin and Nashville, he reverted to lieutenant general and received parole at Natchez, Mississippi, on May 31, 1865. He served as president of an insurance company in New Orleans and died of yellow fever on August 30, 1879. He received burial in New Orleans at Metairie Cemetery. *Eighth Census,* M653–38, 550; M376, Roll 7; *OR,* 1:38 (Part 4), 668; Richard McMurry, *John Bell Hood and the War for Southern Independence* (Lexington: University Press of Kentucky, 1982), 1–35, 93–115; Ezra J. Warner, *Generals in Gray: Lives of the Confederate Commanders* (Baton Rouge: Louisiana State University Press, 1959), 142–43.

31. Born in Augusta, Georgia, on September 10, 1836, Joseph Wheeler graduated from West Point in 1859. He resigned on April 22, 1861, and received an appointment as colonel of the 19th Alabama Infantry. On July 13, 1862, he became chief of cavalry under Braxton Bragg. Appointed as brigadier general on October 30, 1862, he earned promotion to major general on January 20, 1863, and commanded cavalry troops for most of the war. On May 20, 1864, Wheeler routed Federal cavalry commanded by Kenner Garrard at Cassville, Georgia, and captured 70 to 80 wagons, 182 prisoners, 300 horses, saddles, and mules, and stores. Captured in Georgia in May 1865 and confined at Fort Delaware until June 8, 1865, Wheeler settled in Alabama after the war. He served in the U.S. House of Representatives and as a major general of U.S. Volunteers during the Spanish-American War. Wheeler died in Brooklyn, New York, on September 10, 1900, and received burial in Arlington National Cemetery. *OR,* 1:38 (Part 3), 616–17, 946–48; Edward G. Longacre, *A Soldier to the Last: Joseph Wheeler in Blue and Gray* (Dulles, VA: Potomac Books, 2008), 2–3, 7, 9–14, 16–17, 61, 144–49, 151–53, 203–6, 208, 211–15, 220–24, 232–35; Edwin C. Bearss, "Joseph Wheeler," in *Confederate General,* ed. Davis and Hoffman, 6:124–29.

32. This skirmish lasted from May 25 to May 27, 1864. Johnston placed Polk's and Hardee's Corps between Hood's Corps at New Hope Church and the Atlanta Road, with Hardee's left flank covering the road. *OR,* 1:38 (Part 3), 616.

33. Born in Bledsoe's Lick, Tennessee, on October 7, 1826, William Brimage Bate served in Mexico, edited a newspaper, and studied law. He served as colonel of the 2nd Tennessee Infantry until promoted to brigadier general on October 3, 1862, and major general on February 23, 1864. He practiced law in Nashville and served as governor and U.S. senator. He died in Washington, D.C., on March 9, 1905, and received burial in

Nashville at Mount Olivet Cemetery. Lawrence L. Hewitt, "William Brimage Bate," in *Confederate General,* ed. Davis and Hoffman, 1:70–73.

34. Born on October 1, 1834, near Warrensburg, Missouri, Francis Marion Cockrell graduated from Chapel Hill College in 1853 and practiced law. He commanded the Missouri Brigade during the Vicksburg campaign and earned promotion to brigadier general on July 18, 1863. Wounded at Franklin, he surrendered at Mobile. He practiced law in Missouri and served in the U.S. Senate. He died in Washington, D.C., on December 15, 1915, and received burial in Sunset Hill Cemetery in Warrensburg. Anne Bailey, "Francis Marion Cockrell," in *Confederate General,* ed. Davis and Hoffman, 2:6–7.

35. Born in Nashville, Tennessee, on October 20, 1820, Benjamin Franklin Cheatham served in Mexico and owned a plantation. Commissioned as a brigadier general on July 9, 1861, he earned promotion to major general on March 10, 1862. He commanded a corps after Chickamauga. He was severely blamed by Hood for the failure to block the Union army at Spring Hill, and his troops suffered heavy losses at Franklin. He served under Johnston in the Carolinas and surrendered in April 1865. He served as superintendent of Tennessee state prisons and postmaster of Nashville. He died in Nashville on September 4, 1886, and received burial in Mount Olivet Cemetery. CSR, M818, Roll 5; Edwin C. Bearss, "Benjamin Franklin Cheatham," in *Confederate General,* ed. Davis and Hoffman, 1:174–81. For a full discussion of Frank Cheatham's Civil War career, see Christopher Losson, *Tennessee's Forgotten Warriors: Frank Cheatham and His Confederate Division* (Knoxville: University of Tennessee Press, 1989).

36. On June 14, 1864, generals Johnston, Hardee, and Polk rode to the top of Georgia's Pine Mountain to assess the Union position. The group came under Federal artillery fire, which instantly killed Polk. Initially buried in St. Paul's Church Cemetery in Augusta, he received final burial in Christ Church Episcopal Cathedral in New Orleans. Robins, *The Bishop of the Old South,* 192–93, 195; Warner, *Generals in Gray,* 242–43.

37. Although initially driven back, Reynolds reestablished his skirmish line within an hour. Reynolds reported losses of 1 officer and 4 men killed, as well as 9 men wounded. Maj. L. L. Noles of the 25th Arkansas Infantry received a mortal wound while in command of Reynolds's skirmish line. Born in Tennessee on August 8, 1820, Winfield Scott Featherston served as colonel of the 17th Mississippi Infantry but earned promotion to brigadier general on March 4, 1862. He commanded a brigade in Loring's Division of Polk's Corps during and after the Vicksburg campaign and received parole at Greensboro, North Carolina, in May 1865. He practiced law, opposed Reconstruction government, and served in the state legislature and constitutional convention. He died in Holly Springs, Mississippi, on May 28, 1891, and received burial in Hill Crest Cemetery. Born in Virginia on April 4, 1831, Edward Cary Walthall moved to Mississippi and received his education at St. Thomas Hall in Holly Springs. He served as first lieutenant in the 15th Mississippi Infantry until appointed colonel of the 29th Mississippi Infantry in 1862. He earned promotion to brigadier general on December 13, 1862. Promoted to major general during the Atlanta campaign, his rank dated from July 6, 1864. He received parole at Greensboro on May 1, 1865, and returned to Mississippi. He practiced law and served in the U.S. Senate, where he opposed federal

legislation to ensure political equality among African American voters. He died in
Washington, D.C., on April 21, 1898. He received burial in Holly Springs Cemetery. The
Department of Archives and History of the J. D. Williams Library at the University of
Mississippi holds his papers. U.S. War Department, Compiled Service Records of
Confederate Soldiers Who Served in Organizations from the State of Mississippi,
National Archives, Microcopy M232, Roll 42 (hereafter cited as CSR with microfilm
and roll numbers); M818, Roll 25; *OR*, 38 (Part 3), 922–24, 934–35; *OR*, 38 (Part 4), 748,
753, 755; *Biographical and Historical Memoirs of Mississippi* (Gretna, LA: Pelican
Publishing Company, 1999), 2:977–79; Warner, *Generals in Gray*, 86–87, 325–26.

38. Born on February 8, 1820, in Lancaster, Ohio, William Tecumseh Sherman graduated from West Point in 1840. He resigned after service in California during the
Mexican War, struggled at business in St. Louis, and served as president of a military
academy that became Louisiana State University. Appointed as colonel on May 14, 1861,
he earned promotion to brigadier general on August 7, 1861, and major general on May
1, 1862. By the summer of 1864, he commanded all Union troops in the Western
Theater. Kennett, *Sherman*, 237–56; Ezra J. Warner, *Generals in Blue: Lives of the Union
Commanders* (Baton Rouge: Louisiana State University Press, 1964), 441–44.

39. Robert H. Dacus described this exchange of artillery as "one of the greatest
artillery duels . . . witnessed on land during the whole of the war." Dacus,
Reminiscences, 11.

40. Born near Jamestown, Virginia, on July 4, 1825, William Andrew Quarles grew
up in Christian County, Kentucky, and studied law at the University of Virginia. He
moved to Tennessee and served as a circuit court judge and state supervisor of banks.
He served as colonel of the 42nd Tennessee Infantry. Captured and exchanged at Fort
Donelson, he earned promotion to brigadier general, to rank from August 25, 1863.
Wounded at Franklin, he received parole on May 25, 1865. He practiced law and served
in the Tennessee state legislature. He died in Kentucky on December 28, 1893, and
received burial in Flat Lick Baptist Cemetery in Christian County. Arthur W. Bergeron
Jr., "William Andrew Quarles," in *Confederate General*, ed. Davis and Hoffman,
5:66–67.

41. Reynolds's troops served as support for cavalry and destroyed the bridge when
the Confederates withdrew south of Peachtree Creek. *OR*, 38 (Part 3), 935.

42. During the Atlanta campaign, Oliver Otis Howard and John M. Palmer com-
manded the 4th and 14th corps in the Army of the Cumberland, respectively, while
Grenville M. Dodge commanded the 16th Corps in the Army of the Tennessee and
John M. Schofield commanded the 23rd Corps that constituted the Army of the Ohio.
On July 15, 1864, Sherman's forces crossed the Chattahoochee River and established a
line along Peachtree Creek. Wallace P. Reed, ed., *History of Atlanta, Georgia* (Syracuse:
D. Mason and Company, 1889), 172–73; Shelby Foote, *The Civil War: Red River to
Appomattox* (New York: Random House, 1958), 409; Warner, *Generals in Blue*, 127–28,
238–39, 358–59, 425–26.

43. *OR*, 1:38 (Part 3), 935.

44. Born on July 1, 1825, in Nashville, Tennessee, John Adams graduated from West
Point in 1846 and earned two brevets in the Mexican War. He resigned on May 31, 1861.

Initially commissioned as a Confederate captain, he earned promotion to colonel in May 1862 and brigadier general on December 29, 1862. He served under Joseph E. Johnston during the Vicksburg and Atlanta campaigns. Killed at Franklin, he received burial in Maplewood Cemetery in Pulaski, Tennessee. Born in Dinwiddie Courthouse, Virginia, on May 10, 1830, Alfred Jefferson Vaughan Jr. graduated from Virginia Military Institute in 1851 and served as a civil engineer in California. By 1856, he owned a plantation in Marshall County, Mississippi. He served as colonel of the 13th Tennessee Infantry, earned promotion to brigadier general on November 18, 1863, and lost a leg during the Atlanta campaign. He settled in Memphis and served as the clerk of the Shelby County Court. He died in Indianapolis, Indiana, on October 1, 1899, and received burial in Memphis in Elmwood Cemetery. Reynolds's reference to the time at which Gist relieved the majority of his brigade is incomplete, referring only to the half hour. In his official report, Reynolds stated that Gist relieved his brigade at 1:00 p.m. John Adams suggests in his report that Reynolds did not act in concert with the supporting force on Adams's left flank (the 15th Mississippi Infantry and two companies of the 6th Mississippi Infantry under Col. Michael Farrell). According to Reynolds, the gap occurred because Farrell did not advance as directed, which forced Reynolds to adjust his line as indicated in his diary and report. Reynolds believed they could have held that portion of the line and captured more prisoners, had the 15th Mississippi been positioned more efficiently. Reynolds's report lists the same casualty figures as his diary. He estimated that the Union troops engaged with his command suffered an aggregate of 500 killed, wounded, and captured. John A. Kirkpatrick enlisted on August 4, 1861, as a corporal in Company H of the 2nd Arkansas Mounted Rifles but earned promotion to third lieutenant on May 8, 1862. Reynolds reported Eagle and Kirkpatrick as "severely wounded." Born on March 2, 1828, Jefferson Columbus Davis earned a direct commission in the U.S. Army after service in Mexico. Appointed colonel of the 22nd Indiana Infantry in August 1861, he earned promotion to brigadier general in December and commanded a division against Atlanta. Wiley M. Dyer mustered in as first lieutenant in Company B of the 1st Arkansas Mounted Rifles on June 9, 1861. On July 19, 1864, he became an assistant inspector general on Reynolds's staff. Captured while attempting to position the 15th Mississippi Infantry for the second time, he spent the rest of the war at Johnson's Island. The 9th Arkansas Infantry captured two flags in this engagement. CSR, M818, Roll 1; M376, Roll 13; *OR*, 1:38 (Part 3), 891–94, 924–25, 935–37; Crute, *Confederate Staff Officers*, 163; Warner, *Generals in Gray*, 2, 316–17; Warner, *Generals in Blue*, 115–16.

45. William C. Preston served as the division's chief of artillery until killed on July 20, 1864, while placing Selden's Battery. Reynolds reported 540 effectives, with losses of 6 killed, 52 wounded, and 9 missing. A rumor of Johnston's return to command circulated prior to the charge. Dacus suspected an intentional deception to inspire a better effort. *OR*, 1:38 (Part 3), 925–26, 938, 969; Dacus, *Reminiscences*, 13–14.

46. Officially named "the Western and Atlantic Railroad," many referred to this route as "the Atlanta and Chattanooga." The Western and Atlantic made 24 stops in 138 miles between Atlanta and Chattanooga. *OR*, 1:38 (Part 3), 925–26, 700; Swayze, *Rail-Road & Steam-Boat Guide*, 41; David Evans, *Sherman's Horsemen: Union Cavalry*

Operations in the Atlanta Campaign (Bloomington: Indiana University Press, 1999), 1.

47. Youngblood's Georgia Battalion of Government Mechanics (also called Youngblood's Battalion of Georgia Infantry), commanded by Maj. E. H. Youngblood, served temporarily with Walthall's Division as part of Reynolds's Brigade. *OR*, 1:38 (Part 3), 926; U.S. War Department, Compiled Service Records of Confederate Soldiers Who Served in Organizations from the State of Georgia, National Archives, Microcopy M266, Roll 577 (hereafter cited as CSR with microfilm and roll numbers); Claud Estes, comp., *List of Field Officers, Regiments and Battalions in the Confederate States Army, 1861–1865* (Macon, GA: J. W. Burke Company, 1912), 23.

48. Mr. Trawick and Mr. Wages could not be identified. On May 18, 1864, during the Red River campaign, Andrew Jackson Smith engaged John A. Wharton in a sharp fight at Yellow Bayou, Louisiana, near the Atchafalaya River south of Chicot County. In July, Smith led the 16th and 17th Corps on an expedition from La Grange, Tennessee, to Tupelo, Mississippi. He occupied Tupelo on July 13, inflicted severe casualties, and repulsed an attack by Nathan Bedford Forrest on July 14. Ruffin, James Hunt, Wiley, and John Jones could not be identified. David S. Heidler and Jeanne T. Heidler, "Andrew Jackson Smith," in *Encyclopedia of the American Civil War: A Political, Social, and Military History*, ed. David S. Heidler and Jeanne T. Heidler (Santa Barbara: ABC-Clio, 2000), 4:1806–7; David S. Heidler and Jeanne T. Heidler, "Yellow Bayou (Bayou de Glaize), Louisiana," in *Encyclopedia of the American Civil War*, ed. Heidler and Heidler, 4:2161.

49. Born in Madison County, Kentucky, on May 19, 1808, Samuel Jameson Gholson lived in Alabama and Mississippi, practiced law, and served as a U.S. district circuit judge, Mississippi state legislator, and U.S. congressman. He commanded cavalry troops in Chalmers's Division of Forrest's Corps throughout Mississippi, eastern Louisiana, and Alabama. He earned promotion to brigadier general on May 6, 1864, and lost a leg in December 1864 at Egypt, Mississippi. He served in the state legislature until removed by the Reconstruction Act of 1867. He died in Aberdeen, Mississippi, on October 16, 1883, and received burial in the Odd Fellows Cemetery. Col. John McGuirk commanded Gholson's Brigade during its temporarily service with Reynolds's Brigade. Reynolds reported 400 effectives, with an aggregate loss of 167 killed and wounded. Reynolds reported Gholson's Brigade at 450 effectives, with an aggregate loss of 144 killed, wounded, and missing. He reported Youngblood's Battalion at 150 effectives, with a loss of 9 wounded. Reynolds's command lost 320 casualties, including several officers. In addition to Smith, Hufstedler, Bunn, and Galloway, Reynolds's aide-de-camp (Lt. James H. Hart) received a severe wound in the left arm. Bunn received wounds to the right arm and both thighs. *OR*, 1:38 (Part 3), 926–28, 939–40; Ted R. Worley, ed., *They Never Came Back: The War Memoirs of Captain John W. Lavender, C.S.A.* (Pine Bluff, AR: Perdue Company, 1956), 98; Arthur W. Bergeron Jr., "Samuel Jameson Gholson," in *Confederate General*, ed. Davis and Hoffman, 2:182–83.

50. Georgia State Troops occupied part of the position formerly held by Walthall's Division. According to Dacus, Reynolds rode "Robert" (also known as "Old Bob") since the regiment crossed the Mississippi River in the spring of 1862. *OR*, 1:38 (Part 3), 928; Dacus, *Reminiscences*, 24.

51. Reynolds probably refers to the second battle of Kernstown, Virginia, fought on July 24, 1864. This victory led to Confederate raids against Martinsburg, West Virginia, the Baltimore and Ohio Railroad, and Chambersburg, Pennsylvania, and renewed questions about the North's hopes for a general victory in the war. Scott C. Patchan, *Shenandoah Summer: The 1864 Valley Campaign* (Lincoln: University of Nebraska Press, 2007), 2.

52. Born in Clarke County, Virginia, in April 1816, Alexander Welch Reynolds graduated from West Point in 1838. Appointed a captain in March 1861, he became colonel of the 50th Virginia Infantry on July 10, 1861, and earned promotion to brigadier general on September 14, 1863. During the Atlanta campaign, he commanded a brigade in Carter L. Stevenson's Division of William J. Hardee's Corps and survived a wound at New Hope Church. He served in northern Alabama and middle Tennessee at the end of the war. In 1869, he joined the army of the Khedive of Egypt and died on May 26, 1876, in Alexandria, Egypt. He was reportedly buried in Alexandria, but a marker rests in the Cemetery of St. James the Lesser in Philadelphia. Arthur W. Bergeron Jr., "Alexander Welch Reynolds," in *Confederate General,* ed. Davis and Hoffman, 5:82–83.

53. On August 18, 1864, Walthall received orders to withdraw his command from the trenches and take a reserve position near the main headquarters. *OR,* 1:38 (Part 3), 928.

54. Located on the west side of the Chattahoochee River, West Point, Georgia, served as the junction for the Atlanta and West Point Railroad and the Montgomery and West Point Railroad. Lt. Col. Aaron S. Godwin's 48th Tennessee Infantry, of William A. Quarles's Brigade, served under Reynolds at Lovejoy's Station. Located on the line between Campbell and Fayette Counties, the village of Fairburn, Georgia, hosted a stop on the Atlanta and West Point Railroad 19 miles from Atlanta. The Macon and Western Railroad operated between Macon and Atlanta with stops at Lovejoy's Station, Jonesboro, and East Point, Georgia. Born in Paris, Tennessee, on October 1, 1835, William Hicks "Red" Jackson graduated from West Point in 1856 and served with a regiment of mounted rifles until he resigned in May 1861. Jackson survived a wound at Belmont and earned promotion to colonel of the 1st Tennessee Cavalry. He earned promotion to brigadier general on December 29, 1862, and commanded the cavalry corps during the Atlanta campaign. Thereafter, he commanded two cavalry divisions under Forrest. In 1868, he married into the Harding family of Nashville. He died at "Belle Meade" horse farm on March 30, 1903, and received burial at Mount Olivet Cemetery in Nashville. Located in Fayette County, the village of East Point is 6 miles and 1 stop from Atlanta. Jonesboro is 22 miles and 4 stops from Atlanta. Lovejoy's Station is located 29 miles and 5 stops from Atlanta. Born on November 22, 1835, at the Choctaw Agency of the Indian Territory, Frank Crawford Armstrong received a direct commission into the U.S. Army in 1855. Elected colonel of the 3rd Louisiana Infantry after Elkhorn Tavern, he earned promotion to brigadier general on January 20, 1863, and commanded cavalry for the rest of the war. He died at Bar Harbor, Maine, on September 8, 1909, and received burial in Rock Creek Cemetery in Georgetown, District of Columbia. Sherman temporarily raised the siege of Atlanta and deployed the main body of his army against Confederate communications. Hood reported that Jackson and Reynolds "routed" the Federals at Lovejoy's Station. *OR,* 1:38

(Part 1), 79–80; *OR*, 1:38 (Part 3), 928–29; *OR*, 1:38 (Part 5), 981–82; "Gen. William H. Jackson," *Confederate Veteran* 2 (June 1894): 176–77; Swayze, *Rail-Road and Steam-Boat Guide*, 7, 42–43; Warner, *Generals in Gray*, 12–13, 152–53; Samuel J. Martin, *Kill-Cavalry: The Life of Union General Hugh Judson Kilpatrick* (Mechanicsburg, PA: Stackpole Books, 2000), 185–88.

55. After Lovejoy Station, Kilpatrick withdrew to the north and east and reached Decatur on August 22, 1864. Born in Charleston, South Carolina, on November 3, 1834, Samuel Wragg Ferguson graduated from West Point in 1857. He resigned in March 1861, joined the staff of P.G.T. Beauregard, and saw extensive cavalry service during the Vicksburg campaign. He earned promotion to brigadier general on July 23, 1863. He lived in Greenville, Mississippi, practiced law, and served on the Mississippi River Commission. He died on February 3, 1917, and received burial at Greenwood Cemetery in Jackson, Mississippi. Born in Bentonsport, Iowa, on September 27, 1838, Lawrence Sullivan Ross grew up in Texas. He graduated from Alabama's Wesleyan University in 1859 and served as a captain in the Texas Rangers. He enlisted as a private but received a commission as colonel of the 6th Texas Cavalry on May 14, 1862. He earned promotion to brigadier general on December 21, 1863. Ross engaged Kilpatrick at Jonesboro on August 18, 1864, prior to the fight at Lovejoy's Station. He returned to Texas and served as McLennan County sheriff and in the constitutional convention. He served two terms as governor and, thereafter, as president of the Agricultural and Mechanical College of Texas. He died at College Station on January 3, 1898, and received burial in Oakwood Cemetery in Waco. Born on January 14, 1836, near Deckertown, New Jersey, Hugh Judson Kilpatrick graduated from West Point in the May class of 1861. He advanced from captain with the 5th New York Infantry to colonel of the 2nd New York Cavalry by December 1862. Kilpatrick received promotion to brigadier general on June 14, 1863, and served with the Army of the Potomac until April 1864. He commanded Sherman's cavalry during the Atlanta and Carolina campaigns and received brevet promotions to major general of regulars and volunteers in March and June 1865. He served as minister to Chile during the Johnson and Arthur administrations and died in Santiago on December 4, 1881. Initially buried in Peru, he received final burial at West Point in 1882. *OR*, 1:38 (Part 1), 79–80; Judith Ann Benner, *Sul Ross: Soldier, Statesman, Educator* (College Station: Texas A&M University Press, 2005), 3–6, 16–21, 33–35, 73–77, 81–87, 103–11, 130–97, 198–233; Martin, *Kill-Cavalry*, 11–12, 15–21, 28, 57, 89, 173, 185–88, 208, 225, 234–36, 238, 260–63; Warner, *Generals in Gray*, 87, 263–64. Warner, *Generals in Blue*, 266–67.

56. The *Official Records* contain no telegrams between Reynolds and Hood for the fight at Lovejoy's Station.

57. S amuel R. Watkins, "The Fighting Forty-Eighth Tennessee Regiment," in *The Southern Bivouac* (Louisville: B. F. Avery and Sons, 1884), 2:246–51; David Evans, *Sherman's Horsemen: Union Cavalry Operations in the Atlanta Campaign* (Bloomington: Indiana University Press, 1999), 416.

58. Camp revivals and religious activities increased in the Confederate army throughout 1864. Steven Woodworth, *While God Is Marching On: The Religious World of Civil War Soldiers* (Lawrence: University of Kansas Press, 2001), 234–44.

59. See Edward Cary Walthall's report for operations by his division from July 18, 1864, through the end of the Atlanta campaign. *OR,* 1:38 (Part 3), 929.

60. Born on October 29, 1824, Joseph Horace Lewis graduated from Centre College and practiced law. He served as colonel of the 6th Kentucky (Confederate) Infantry and commanded the Orphan Brigade upon promotion to brigadier general, with rank to date from September 30, 1863. Ordered to assist in the defense of the West Point Railroad, Lewis moved his command to Jonesboro by rail on August 28, 1864. (In his report, Reynolds praised both Wilburn and Waldrop as "very efficient.") A part of Jefferson Davis's final escort, Lewis received parole at Washington, Georgia, on May 9, 1865. He practiced law in Glasgow and served in the Kentucky state legislature and the U.S. Congress and as chief justice on Kentucky Court of Appeals. After retirement, he lived on a farm in Scott County. He died on July 6, 1904, and received burial in the Glasgow Municipal Cemetery. *OR,* 1:38 (Part 3), 929, 937; *OR,* 1:38 (Part 5), 998; William C. Davis, "Joseph Horace Lewis," in *Confederate General,* ed. Davis and Hoffman, 4:70–71.

61. Born in Tennessee about 1831, John C. Bratton lived in Pennington Township in Bradley County with his 29-year-old wife, Harriet, two sons, and two daughters and worked as a grocery keeper. In 1860, he owned $4,800 in real estate and a personal estate of $3,000. Bratton mustered in as first lieutenant in Company D of the 9th Arkansas Infantry on July 25, 1861. Promoted to captain, major, and lieutenant colonel, he later commanded the regiment and survived a wound at Franklin. Born in Charleston, South Carolina, on September 22, 1833, Stephen Dill Lee graduated from West Point in 1854. He resigned on February 20, 1861, and served as an aide to P.G.T. Beauregard. He earned promotion to brigadier general on November 20, 1862, and served under Pemberton at Vicksburg. Promoted to major general on August 3, 1863, he commanded cavalry in the Department of Mississippi, Alabama, West Tennessee, and East Louisiana until advanced to lieutenant general on June 23, 1864. He commanded a corps until the end of the war. He farmed in Mississippi, served in the state senate, held the presidency of Mississippi State University, and became commander-in-chief of the United Confederate Veterans. Lee died at Vicksburg on May 28, 1908, and received burial in Friendship Cemetery. *Eighth Census,* M653–38, 547; M376, Roll 3; Herman Hattaway, *General Stephen D. Lee* (Jackson: University Press of Mississippi, 1988), 3–61, 99–111, 126–67; Herman Hattaway, "Stephen Dill Lee," in *Confederate General,* ed. Davis and Hoffman, 4:58–63.

62. Born about 1833 in Baltimore, Maryland, Robert Charles Tyler served in William Walker's first Nicaragua filibuster and later settled in Memphis. He enlisted in the 15th Tennessee Infantry on April 18, 1861, but won election as colonel by 1862. He survived a wound at Shiloh and commanded William B. Bate's former brigade at Missionary Ridge, where he lost a leg. He did not rejoin this brigade, but it continued under the name "Tyler's Brigade." Tyler received promotion to brigadier general on February 23, 1864, and commanded Fort Tyler at West Point, Georgia. He died on April 16, 1865, during a cavalry attack by James H. Wilson. Tyler received burial in the Fort Tyler Cemetery. M. B. McMicken served as a lieutenant colonel and assistant chief quartermaster under Bragg with rank from July 17, 1862. He became chief quartermaster on

Bragg's staff on June 10, 1863, and chief quartermaster of the Army of Tennessee that November. He also served as chief quartermaster of the Department of South Carolina, Georgia, and Florida and on Joseph E. Johnston's staff. CSR, M818, Roll 24; M818, Roll 16; *OR*, 1:38 (Part 5), 1007–8; War Department, *List of Staff Officers*, 111; Stuart W. Sanders, "One Last Gallant Defense," *Military History Quarterly* (Spring 2006): 44–51; Smith, *Gallant Dead*, 346–48; William C. Davis, "Robert Charles Tyler," in *Confederate General*, ed. Davis and Hoffman, 6:66–67.

63. On the evening of September 1, 1864, Walthall's Division established camp about 6 miles outside of Atlanta in the direction of McDonough, Georgia. Special Orders No. 207, issued on September 1, 1864, ordered all noncommissioned Arkansas officers and privates captured at Vicksburg or Port Hudson, and separated from their Trans-Mississippi commands and present in Mississippi and Alabama, to report to Reynolds's Brigade once officially declared exchanged. *OR*, 1:38 (Part 3), 929; *OR*, 1:39 (Part 2), 811.

64. Walthall's Division turned toward Lovejoy's Station and took position on the right of Hardee's line, in support of Cleburne's Division, in the evening. Previously known as Goode's Texas Battery, Capt. James P. Douglas's Texas Battery served in Alfred R. Courtney's Artillery Battalion as part of Stephen D. Lee's Corps. *OR*, 1:38 (Part 3), 674, 929; Joseph H. Crute Jr., *Units of the Confederate States Army* (Midlothian, VA: Derwent Books, 1987), 343–44.

65. Born on May 30, 1832, in Hillsboro, North Carolina, George Doherty Johnston grew up in Alabama, graduated from Howard College, earned a law degree from Cumberland University, and practiced in Marion. He served as second lieutenant with Company G of the 4th Alabama Infantry but became major of the 25th Alabama Infantry in January 1862 and colonel by September 1863. Promoted to brigadier general on July 26, 1864, he survived a severe leg wound two days later at Ezra Church. He worked in education, civil service, and Alabama state politics. He died in Tuscaloosa, Alabama, on December 8, 1910, and received burial in Greenwood Cemetery. Terry L. Jones, "George Doherty Johnston," in *Confederate General*, ed. Davis and Hoffman, 3:190–91.

66. For a discussion of the Democratic Party's "Chicago Platform" and Confederate hopes during the presidential election of 1864, see John C. Waugh, *Reelecting Lincoln: The Battle for the 1864 Presidency* (New York: Crown Publishers, 1997), 149–51, 276–94; Phyllis F. Field, "Election of 1864," in *Encyclopedia of the American Civil War*, ed. Heidler and Heidler, 2:640–42.

67. William M. Lea mustered in as regimental chaplain for the 1st Arkansas Mounted Rifles on June 9, 1861, and served until paroled at Greensboro, North Carolina, on April 28, 1865. CSR, M376, Roll 14.

68. Between June 1861 and March 1865, Jefferson Davis proclaimed nine days of fasting to promote unity. Ted Ownby, "Fast Days," in *Encyclopedia of the Confederacy*, ed. Richard N. Current (New York: Simon and Schuster, 1993), 2:568.

69. Born in Boonville, Missouri, on January 1, 1838, William Hugh Young grew up in Texas. He attended Washington College, McKenzie College, and the University of Virginia. He served as captain of Company C in the 9th Texas Infantry but earned promotion to colonel after Shiloh. During the Atlanta campaign, the 9th Texas served in

Ector's Brigade. After Ector received a serious leg wound, Young succeeded to brigade command, with promotion to brigadier general on August 15, 1864. Severely wounded and captured at Allatoona, Young remained at Johnson's Island until July 24, 1865. He practiced law and sold real estate in San Antonio. He died on November 28, 1901, and received burial in the San Antonio Confederate Cemetery. Lawrence L. Hewitt, "William Hugh Young," in *Confederate General,* ed. Davis and Hoffman, 6:172–73.

70. Jefferson Davis arrived at John Bell Hood's headquarters camp on September 25, 1864, in the company of two aides. They departed for Montgomery, Alabama, on September 27. *OR,* 1:39 (Part 1), 805.

71. Davis reviewed the army on September 26, 1864. The muted affair lacked enthusiasm. Robert H. Dacus stated that many soldiers, dissatisfied with the removal of Joseph E. Johnston, planned to shout his name while they passed before Davis and Hood. Under threat of court-martial, the soldiers instead stood silent, heads down, and refused to cheer. *OR,* 1:39 (Part 1), 805; Dacus, *Reminiscences,* 12.

72. Reynolds reported the capture of 1 Federal officer and 83 enlisted men in the skirmish at Moon Station, Georgia. He reported 6 men killed, including Sgt. Maj. John Tim Walton, who originally served in Company H of the 9th Arkansas Infantry. *OR,* 1:39 (Part 1), 812, 825; CSR, M376, Roll 24.

73. Reynolds burned the stockade at Moon's Station, Georgia. *OR,* 1:39 (Part 1), 812, 825.

74. Born in Saint Bernard Parish, Louisiana, on May 28, 1818, Pierre Gustave Toutant Beauregard graduated from West Point in 1838. He served on the staff of Winfield Scott during the Mexican War and earned two brevet promotions. Suspicions about his loyalties cut short his tenure as superintendent of West Point, and he resigned in February 1861. Commissioned as a brigadier general on March 1, 1861, he commanded the bombardment against Fort Sumter. He earned promotion to full general on July 21, 1861. He served mainly in the Western Theater but returned to Virginia during the 1864 campaigns around Richmond and Petersburg. On October 17, 1864, he commanded the Military Division of the West, including the Department of Tennessee and Georgia and the Department of Alabama, Mississippi, and East Louisiana. He surrendered in April 1865. He lived in New Orleans, engaged in railroad business, and managed the Louisiana Lottery. He died in New Orleans on February 20, 1893, and received burial in Metairie Cemetery. *OR,* 1:39 (Part 1), 801–2; T. Harry Williams, *P.G.T. Beauregard: Napoleon in Gray* (Baton Rouge: Louisiana State University Press, 1955), 1–80, 133–49, 166–84, 212–35, 319–29; Gary W. Gallagher, "Pierre Gustave Toutant Beauregard," in *Confederate General,* ed. Davis and Hoffman, 1:84–93; David S. Heidler and Jeanne T. Heidler "Departments, Military, C.S.A.," in *Encyclopedia of the American Civil War,* ed. Heidler and Heidler, 2:583–86.

75. See the report of Edward Cary Walthall for operations of his division from July 18, 1864, to January 14, 1865. *OR,* 1:39 (Part 1), 825.

76. *OR,* 1:39 (Part 1), 825–26.

77. Col. Lewis Johnson of the 44th United States Colored Troops surrendered a garrison at Dalton, Georgia, on October 13, 1864, after a short skirmish with Hood. Johnson reported the surrender of 751 troops, including 600 soldiers and 26 officers

from the 44th USCT, 50 soldiers and 2 officers from Company F of the 57th Illinois Infantry, 50 soldiers and 3 officers from Company B of the 7th Kentucky Cavalry, and 20 soldiers from one section of the 20th Ohio Artillery. Johnson also surrendered 650 muskets, one 12-pound Napoleon cannon, one damaged 3-inch Rodman gun, and less than 150 rounds of artillery ammunition. Despite Johnson's personal protest, Hood returned several black soldiers to supposed owners at Villanow, Georgia, and forced others to destroy a 2-mile section of railroad track. Johnson reported the murder of six black soldiers. Confederates shot one black soldier who refused to assist in the destruction of the railroad and killed five others deemed too sick to march to Tunnel Hill. Paroled on October 15, 1864, Johnson requested reprisal, but none occurred. Hood briefly mentioned the capture of Dalton in his autobiography (and over-estimated the number of captured Union troops at 1,000) but remained silent on the issue of prisoner abuse. The 15th Pennsylvania Cavalry liberated approximately 20 of the black soldiers on January 1, 1865, in Itawamba County, Mississippi, during operations through Alabama and Mississippi. The Western and Atlantic (State) Railroad operated one stop on the 9 miles between Tilton and Dalton as part of its 138-mile route between Atlanta and Chattanooga. *OR*, 1:39 (Part 1), 717–24, 802, 812, 825; *OR*, 1:45 (Part 2), 540–42; Richard N. Current, ed., *Advance and Retreat: Personal Experiences in the United States and Confederate States Armies by J. B. Hood* (Bloomington: Indiana University Press, 1959), 262; Swayze, *Rail-Road and Steam-Boat Guide*, 41.

78. Robert H. Dacus did not share Reynolds's assessment of Hood. Dacus acknowledged Hood's courage but expressed "no confidence" in his abilities as an army commander (especially in comparison to Joseph E. Johnston). Dacus, *Reminiscences*, 13.

79. Abraham Fryer mustered in as a private in Company I of the 1st Arkansas Mounted Rifles at Camp Yancey on July 18, 1862. During the reorganization at Corinth, Mississippi, Fryer earned election as lieutenant. Promoted to captain after George S. Laswell's promotion to lieutenant colonel, Fryer served until killed in action on October 27, 1864. CSR, M376, Roll 8; *Biographical and Historical Memoirs of Western Arkansas* (Chicago: Goodspeed Publishing Company, 1891), 15.

80. Stephen D. Lee ordered two brigades of Johnson's Division across the Tennessee River 2½ miles above South Florence, Alabama, while Gibson's Brigade of Clayton's Division crossed at South Florence. *OR*, 1:39 (Part 1), 811, 826.

81. Major Moore could not be identified.

82. On November 8, 1864, Augustus H. Garland succeeded the late Charles Mitchel in the Confederate Senate. Felix I. Batson filled Garland's vacant seat in the Confederate House of Representatives. *OR*, 4: 3, 1190; Warner and Yearns, *Biographical Register of the Confederate Congress*, 18–19, 95–96.

83. Beauregard conducted an informal review of Stewart's Corps on November 12, 1864. Hood expressed disapproval over the propriety of this review, in relation to the proximity of the Union army. Despite Hood's complaints, Beauregard reported his intent to review Cheatham's and Lee's corps as well. *OR*, 1:39 (Part 3), 913–14.

84. Born in Bedford County, Tennessee, on July 13, 1821, Nathan Bedford Forrest recruited and equipped a mounted battalion and served as lieutenant colonel. Promoted to colonel of the 3rd Tennessee Cavalry in the spring of 1862, he commanded

a brigade by June and earned promotion to brigadier general on July 21, 1862. After repeated quarrels with Braxton Bragg, Forrest received an independent command in northern Mississippi and western Tennessee, with promotion to major general on December 4, 1863. He commanded the cavalry during Hood's 1864 Tennessee campaign and earned promotion to lieutenant general on February 28, 1865. He surrendered in April at Selma, Alabama, and became a planter and railroad president. He died in Memphis on October 29, 1877, and received burial in Elmwood Cemetery. Edwin C. Bearss, "Nathan Bedford Forrest," in *Confederate General,* ed. Davis and Hoffman, 2:138–45; Brian Steel Wills, *A Battle from the Start: The Life of Nathan Bedford Forrest* (New York: HarperCollins, 1992), 4–56, 120–47, 274–93.

85. Walthall's Division held the center of the corps position, with Quarles's Brigade on the right, Reynolds's Brigade on the left, and Cantey's Brigade (under Charles M. Shelley) in reserve. They advanced around 4 p.m., but a brier thicket blocked Reynolds's Brigade. The movement to skirt this obstacle forced Reynolds from his position. Subsequently, Cantey's (Shelley's) Brigade held the left, with Reynolds in reserve. Francis M. Cockrell's Missouri Brigade (of French's Division) consisted of the consolidated "1st and 4th Missouri," the "2nd and 6th Missouri," and the "3rd and 5th Missouri" Infantry regiments, as well as the 1st Missouri Cavalry and 3rd Missouri Cavalry Battalion. The Missourians suffered 98 killed, 129 wounded, and 92 missing, for an aggregate loss of 319. Their casualties included 5 officers of regimental or higher rank, including Cockrell. The only members of Strahl's staff listed killed at Franklin are Capt. James W. Johnston, former regimental adjutant of the 4th Tennessee Infantry and acting assistant adjutant general since August 5, 1863, and Lt. John T. Marsh, assistant inspector general. The 6 Confederate generals killed at Franklin were John Adams, John C. Carter, Patrick Cleburne, States Rights Gist, Hiram Granbury, and Otho French Strahl. Five other Confederate general officers sustained wounds at Franklin: A. M. Manigault, T. M. Scott, F. M. Cockrell, W. A. Quarles, and John C. Brown. In addition, the Federals captured G. W. Gordon. According to Robert H. Dacus, Reynolds's horse sustained a wound and Walthall lost two horses. Hood underestimated Confederate casualties at 4,500 and exaggerated Union losses as "equal or near our own." Confederate losses totaled 6,261 in killed, wounded, and missing, while Union losses amounted to only 189 killed, along with 1,033 wounded and 1,194 missing or captured, for an aggregate of 2,416. *OR,* 1:45 (Part 1), 343, 654, 684–86, 716, 720–21; CSR, M818, Roll 1; U.S. War Department, Compiled Service Records of Confederate Soldiers Who Served in Organizations from the State of Tennessee, National Archives, Microcopy M231, Roll 8 (hereafter cited as CSR with microfilm and roll numbers); M818, Roll 5; M376, Roll 5; M818, Roll 5; M818, Roll 9; U.S. War Department, Compiled Service Records of Confederate Soldiers Who Served in Organizations from the State of Texas, National Archives, Microcopy M227, Roll 14 (hereafter cited as CSR with microfilm and roll numbers); M818, Roll 10; M231, Roll 42; M818, Roll 23; M231, Roll 23; Dacus, *Reminiscences,* 17–18; Crute, *Confederate Staff Officers,* 186–87; James Lee McDonough and Thomas Lawrence Connelly, *Five Tragic Hours: The Battle of Franklin* (Knoxville: University of Tennessee Press, 1983), 129, 147–49, 160–66; Jack D. Welsh, *Medical Histories of Confederate Generals* (Kent, OH: Kent State University Press, 1999), 259.

86. Walthall reported Quarles as "severely wounded" at Franklin. Shattered by a cannonball, his left leg required amputation. Federals captured Quarles on December 18, 1864, as he recuperated in a nearby house. Reynolds's Brigade suffered an aggregate of 102 casualties at Franklin: 20 killed and 82 wounded. These losses included 5 officers killed and 15 wounded. After the war, Reynolds claimed a slight wound at Franklin, but he remained on duty and did not officially report the injury. *OR,* 45 (Part 1), 721, 726; *Biographical and Historical Memoirs of Southern Arkansas* (Chicago: Goodspeed Publishing Company, 1890), 1085; Welsh, *Medical Histories,* 178, 259.

87. William Dudley Gale and Katherine (Polk) Gale, son-in-law and daughter of Leonidas Polk, lived in a home near Nashville. From February 6, 1863, until August 12, 1864, Gale served on the staff of Polk and Alexander P. Stewart. Montgomery's house stood on Montgomery Hill, a fortified position on the Confederate left flank that Hood eventually abandoned. Crute, *Staff Officers,* 154, 185; U.S. War Department, *List of Staff Officers of the Confederate States Army, 1861–1865* (Washington, DC: Government Printing Office, 1891), 58; Jerry Keenan, *Wilson's Cavalry Corps: Union Campaigns in the Western Theatre, October 1864 through Spring 1865* (Jefferson, NC: McFarland and Company, 1998), 96, 98–99.

88. Reynolds's Brigade withdrew from Walthall's line and reinforced Ector's Brigade. They checked the enemy but could not secure a line of retreat along Franklin Pike. Felix Compton purchased this property in 1858; it was built in 1844 on an original 1811 structure. By 1860, he owned 750 acres and 37 slaves. Located across the road from Confederate Redoubt 5, the Compton home served as a hospital for both sides at different times during the battle of Nashville. Virginia Bradford owned a farm near Nashville, where she lived with three sons and three daughters. Located along Stewart's line of retreat, the Bradford home witnessed a dramatic moment. Bradford's oldest daughter, Mary, ran into the midst of heavy fire to encourage the Confederates, to no avail. Impressed with her heroism, Hood mentioned her in his memoir. Born in Sullivan County, Tennessee, on December 28, 1833, Charles Miller Shelley moved to Talladega, Alabama. He served as a captain in the 5th Alabama Infantry. By January 1862, he earned promotion to colonel of the 30th Alabama Infantry, which he commanded until captured at Vicksburg. He received promotion to brigadier general on September 17, 1864. He later served in Congress and promoted Alabama industry. He died in Birmingham on January 20, 1907, and received burial in Talladega at Oak Hill Cemetery. Born in Peru on November 8, 1817, Claudius Wistar Sears graduated from West Point in 1841 and resigned after the Seminole War. He served with the 17th Mississippi Infantry until appointed colonel of the 46th Mississippi Infantry. Captured and exchanged at Vicksburg, he earned promotion to brigadier general on March 1, 1864, and lost a leg at Nashville on December 15, 1864. Captured during the Confederate retreat, he remained a prisoner until June 23, 1865. Afterward, he taught mathematics and civil engineering at the University of Mississippi. He died in Oxford, Mississippi, on February 15, 1891, and received burial in Saint Peter's Cemetery. Born in Georgia about 1836, Green B. W. Mercer worked on a farm in Sulphur Fork Township in Lafayette County. In 1860, he owned a personal estate of $2,000. He mustered in as a private in Company D of the 4th Arkansas Infantry on August 17, 1861, at Mt. Vernon,

Missouri. He earned promotion to second lieutenant and survived wounds at Murfreesboro and Nashville. Felix P. Koonce enlisted as a sergeant on August 17, 1861, and earned promotion to adjutant and captain in Company A when the 4th Arkansas Infantry reorganized on May 8, 1862. Born in Tennessee about 1828, Gilbert W. Ralston practiced medicine in Dudley Lake Township in Jefferson County. Listed "G. W. Rolston" in the 1860 census, he owned a personal estate of $250. Ralston mustered into Company H of the 9th Arkansas Infantry as a private on July 27, 1861, but earned promotion to second lieutenant on September 20, 1861, and captain on December 18, 1862. Captured at Vicksburg, he received parole on July 8, 1863. He survived a wound at Nashville on December 16, 1864, but lost a leg and remained a prisoner until March 18, 1865. Born in Alabama about 1838, Jesse A. Ross lived in the Hempstead County town of Washington and practiced law. He mustered in as first lieutenant in Company C of the 4th Arkansas Infantry Battalion on October 12, 1861, and earned promotion to adjutant on November 10, 1862. Captured at Nashville, he remained a prisoner until June 4, 1865. Born in Tennessee about 1833, John W. Lavender lived in the Montgomery County town of Mount Ida with his 19-year-old wife, Elizabeth, and worked as a mechanic. In 1860, he owned $150 in real estate and a personal estate of $250. He mustered in as a lieutenant in Company F of the 4th Arkansas Infantry regiment on August 17, 1861. Promoted to captain on June 30, 1862, he served until captured on December 15, 1864, and remained a prisoner until June 16, 1865. He published a memoir after the war. *OR*, 1:45 (Part 1), 710–11; U.S. War Department, Compiled Service Records of Confederate Soldiers Who Served in Organizations from the State of Alabama, National Archives, Microcopy M374, Roll 40 (hereafter cited as CSR with microfilm and roll numbers); M818, Roll 21; M376, Roll 16; M376, Roll 13; M376, Roll 19; M376, Roll 20; M376, Roll 14; *Eighth Census*, M653–42, 689; *Eighth Census*, M653–44, 763; *Eighth Census*, M653–46, 874; *Eighth Census*, M653–45, 51; *Eighth Census*, M653–1246, 198; W. L. Gammage, *The Camp, the Bivouac, and the Battlefield: Being a History of the Fourth Arkansas Regiment, from Its First Organization down to the Present Date* (Little Rock: Arkansas Southern Press, 1958), 33–34; Ted R. Worley, ed., *They Never Came Back: The War Memoirs of Captain John W. Lavender, C.S.A.* (Pine Bluff, AR: Perdue Company, 1956), 119–29; Richard N. Current, ed., *Advance and Retreat: Personal Experiences in the United States and Confederate States Armies by J. B. Hood* (Bloomington: Indiana University Press, 1959), 304; Winston Groom, *Shrouds of Glory: From Atlanta to Nashville: The Last Great Campaign of the Civil War* (New York: Atlantic Monthly Press, 1995), 249; Warner, *Generals in Gray*, 271–72, 274–75; James A. Hoobler, *A Guide to Historic Nashville Tennessee* (Charleston: History Press, 2008), 7, 9–10, 123.

89. John W. Lavender stated after the war that, as captain of the picket line on December 15, he detected this flanking movement and reported it to brigade but heard no response. The pickets attempted to hold but fell back to the regiment's original position behind a stone fence. Walthall detached Reynolds's Brigade to meet a threat to the left from Union troops across the Hillsborough Pike in the woods near Compton's house. The division's other brigades extended to fill the gap created by this shift. With his left flank connected to Cantey's Brigade, Reynolds formed diagonally across the

woods and refused his left flank. As the Federal troops extended to the left, Reynolds lengthened his front. Walthall received troops to reinforce Reynolds, but they remained insufficient to prevent retreat. Walthall singled out Reynolds for praise in his report. Terry H. Cahal served as a second lieutenant in Company K of the 45th Tennessee Infantry. On July 9, 1864, he joined the staff of Alexander P. Stewart as an assistant inspector general with rank of major. *OR*, 1:45 (Part 1), 722–23; CSR, M818, Roll 5, and M231, Roll 7; Worley, *They Never Came Back*, 111–17, 119–39; Crute, *Confederate Staff Officers*, 184–85.

90. Dr. Bryan of Columbia, Tennessee, could not be identified.

91. "Misses B. and W." cannot be identified.

92. On December 20, 1864, Hood placed five additional brigades in Walthall's Division and directed him to report to Nathan Bedford Forrest as part of the army's rear guard. On December 22, 1864, a Union force crossed the Duck River by pontoon near Columbia, Tennessee. In response, Forrest ordered Walthall to move up the Pulaski Pike and take a defensive position 2½ miles from Lynnville, Tennessee, where they continued to support the movements of Forrest's Cavalry. At the onset, David Coleman commanded Ector's Brigade. Due to reduced numbers, Walthall consolidated the brigades, with Reynolds in command of his and Ector's Brigades. W. S. Featherston commanded his and Quarles's Brigades. Col. J. B. Palmer commanded his and Smith's Brigades. Col. Hume R. Feild commanded Maney's and Strahl's Brigades. Born in Franklin, Tennessee, on August 24, 1826, George Earl Maney graduated from the University of Nashville in 1845 and served in the Mexican War. He practiced law in Franklin and served in the Tennessee state legislature. Maney served as colonel of the 1st Tennessee Infantry until promoted to brigadier general on April 16, 1862. After Maney sustained a serious wound at Chattanooga, John C. Carter commanded the brigade until killed at Franklin. Maney surrendered with the Army of Tennessee and returned to his law practice and railroad business interests. He served in the state legislature as a Republican and received appointments as U.S. minister to Colombia and Bolivia. He died in Washington, D.C., on February 9, 1901, and received burial in Nashville at Mount Olivet Cemetery. Born in Rutherford County, Tennessee, on November 1, 1825, Joseph Benjamin Palmer graduated from Union University, practiced law, and served in the Tennessee state legislature. He served as colonel of the 18th Tennessee Infantry until promoted to brigadier general on November 15, 1864. He received parole at Greensboro, North Carolina, on May 1, 1865, and returned to his law practice. He died at Murfreesboro on November 4, 1890, and received burial in Evergreen Cemetery. Born in Maury County, Tennessee, on July 1, 1831, James Argyle Smith graduated from West Point in 1853 and served on the frontier. He resigned on May 9, 1861, and served on the staff of Leonidas Polk. After Shiloh, he served as colonel of the 5th Confederate Infantry until promoted to brigadier general on September 20, 1863. After Franklin, he commanded Cleburne's Division. Smith received parole at Greensboro, North Carolina, on May 1, 1865. He lived on a Mississippi farm after the war and served as state superintendent of public education. He died in Jackson, Mississippi, on December 6, 1901, and received burial in Greenwood Cemetery. Walthall praised the endurance of his men, in spite of severe weather, privations, and

a general sense of depression since Franklin and Nashville. Walthall did not report casualties. *OR,* 1:45 (Part 1), 22, 726–28, 758, 772; Seth Warner, "George Earl Maney: Soldier, Railroader, and Diplomat," *Tennessee Historical Quarterly* 65, no. 2 (Summer 2006): 130–47; Lawrence L. Hewitt, "George Earl Maney," in *Confederate General,* ed. Davis and Hoffman, 4:150–51; Edwin C. Bearss, "Joseph Benjamin Palmer," in *Confederate General,* ed. Davis and Hoffman, 4:208–9, Edwin C. Bearss, "James Argyle Smith," in *Confederate General,* ed. Davis and Hoffman, 5:176–77.

93. Hume R. Feild served as a captain of Company H in the 1st Tennessee Infantry until promoted to colonel. Feild commanded Maney's and Strahl's Brigades after Franklin. Sam Watkins expressed considerable respect for Feild's leadership and courage. CSR, M231, Roll 14; Sam R. Watkins, *"Co. Aytch": A Side Show of the Big Show* (Wilmington, NC: Broadfoot Publishing Company, 1994), 52–53, 55, 73–74.

94. Nathan Bedford Forrest misidentified this portion of Walthall's command as Ector's and Granbury's Brigades. Lawrence S. Ross identified them as Reynolds's and Ector's Brigades. Walthall identified them as Reynolds's and Feild's Brigades. *OR,* 1:45 (Part 1), 726, 758, 772.

FIVE

1. Many soldiers in the Army of Tennessee revered Joseph E. Johnston and welcomed his return to command because he did not recklessly waste their lives. Robert H. Dacus, *Reminiscences of Company "H," First Arkansas Mounted Rifles* (Dardanelle, AR: Private publication, 1897), 12–13; Craig L. Symonds, *Joseph E. Johnston: A Civil War Biography* (New York: W. W. Norton, 1992), 357; James Lee McDonough and Thomas Lawrence Connelly, *Five Tragic Hours: The Battle of Franklin* (Knoxville: University of Tennessee Press, 1983), 4–6.

2. For a detailed analysis of the final campaign in the Western Theater and the surrender of the Army of Tennessee, see Mark L. Bradley, *This Astounding Close: The Road to Bennett Place* (Chapel Hill: University of North Carolina Press, 2006).

3. Reynolds included his parole document in his diary entry for May 2, 1865. Reynolds to Andrew Johnson, August 21, 1865, Daniel Harris Reynolds Papers, University Libraries, Fayetteville, Box 1, Folder 5, Item 108 (hereafter cited as DHR Papers).

4. William E. Estes served as major of the 32nd Texas Cavalry (Dismounted). U.S. War Department, Compiled Service Records of Confederate Soldiers Who Served in Organizations from the State of Texas, National Archives, Microcopy 227, Roll 11 (hereafter cited as CSR with microfilm and roll numbers).

5. Cullin Redwine Earp mustered in as first lieutenant in Company D of the 10th Texas Cavalry (Dismounted) but earned promotion to colonel. French commended Earp for his leadership during the battle of Allatoona, Georgia, on October 5, 1864. U.S. War Department, *War of the Rebellion: Official Records of the Union and Confederate Armies* (Washington, DC: Government Printing Office, 1880–1901) (hereafter cited as *OR* or *Official Records*), 1:39 (Part 1), 819; CSR, M227, Roll 11.

6. The Mobile and Ohio Railroad stopped at Verona, Mississippi, 4 miles from Tupelo and 54 miles from Corinth. J. C. Swayze, *Hill and Swayze's Confederate States*

Rail-Road & Steam-Boat Guide, Containing the Time-Tables, Fares, Connections and Distances on all the Rail-Roads of the Confederate States; also, the Connecting Lines of Rail-Roads, Steam-Boats and Stages. And will be Accompanied by a Complete Guide to the Principal Hotels, with a Large Variety of Valuable Information (Griffin, GA: Hill and Swayze, 1862), 49.

7. No such order is found in the *Official Records*.

8. "Ewing's Place" may refer to the property of D. Ewing. Born in South Carolina about 1790, Ewing owned a farm in the Eastern Division of Monroe County, Mississippi, near Aberdeen Post Office. In 1860, he owned $720 in real estate and a personal estate of $790. The Mobile and Ohio Railroad stopped at Prairie Station, Mississippi, 4 stops and 29 miles from Verona. Swayze, *Rail-Road and Steam-Boat Guide,* 49; U.S. Bureau of the Census, *Eighth Census of the United States, 1860* (Washington, DC: National Archives and Records Administration, 1860), M653–587, 356.

9. Recruited from Blount, Shelby, Talladega, Barbour, Russell, Montgomery, Bibb, and Conecuh Counties, the 29th Alabama Infantry formed in February 1862 at Pensacola, Florida. Stationed between Pollard and Pensacola for more than a year, the regiment moved to Mobile and stayed until spring of 1864. Transferred to the Army of Tennessee, as part of Cantey and Shelley's Brigade, the 29th Alabama saw action from Resaca to Nashville, as well as in Kinston and Bentonville. James M. Shell mustered in as a private in Company D of the 1st Arkansas Mounted Rifles on June 9, 1861, and later served with Company A. U.S. War Department, Compiled Service Records of Confederate Soldiers Who Served in Organizations from the State of Arkansas, National Archives, Microcopy 376, Roll 21 (hereafter cited as CSR with microfilm and roll numbers); Joseph H. Crute Jr., *Units of the Confederate States Army* (Midlothian, VA: Derwent Books, 1987), 22.

10. The Mobile and Ohio Railroad made 18 stops along the 93-mile journey between West Point and Marion Station, Mississippi. Meridian is 1 stop and 5 miles beyond Marion Station. Mobile, Alabama, is 27 stops and 134 miles from Meridian on the Mobile and Ohio route. Swayze, *Rail-Road and Steam-Boat Guide,* 48–49.

11. Written in 1832 by Alexandre Dumas, *La Tour de Nesle* depicts the Tower of Nesle as a scene of orgies and regicide. The role of Capt. Jehan Buridan, who triumphs over a vampire-witch, made the play popular throughout the nineteenth century. The actor named "Hamilton" may refer to Claude Hamilton. Born in New York in 1831, Claude Hamilton debuted in 1851 in the role of Blunt in *Richard III* at the American Theatre in Cincinnati. Throughout his career, he performed both leading and character roles. Martin Banham, ed., *The Cambridge Guide to Theatre* (New York: Cambridge University Press, 1995), 314; T. Allston Brown, *History of the American Stage: Containing Biographical Sketches of Nearly Every Member of the Profession That Has Appeared on the American Stage, from 1733 to 1870* (New York: Benjamin Blom, 1969), 158.

12. According to Robert H. Dacus, many officers and men shared Reynolds's contempt for French. Reynolds refers to his men as "Jakes," but other sources show their nickname as "Joshes." According to J. G. McCown of the 32nd Texas Cavalry, Ector's men bore the nickname of "Chubs" and McNair's/Reynolds's Brigade carried the

nickname "Joshies." Gammage cites the May 1862 formation of McCown's "Division of Joshes and Chubs" in Corinth as the origin of the nickname. Dacus, *Reminiscences*, 30; J. G. McCown, "About Ector's and McNair's Brigades," *Confederate Veteran* (March 1901): 113; W. L. Gammage, *The Camp, the Bivouac, and the Battlefield: Being a History of the 4th Arkansas Regiment* (Little Rock: AR Southern Press, 1958), 76–79.

13. Born in Kentucky about 1835, James H. Hart lived in Railroad Township but reported no occupation in 1860. He mustered in on June 9, 1861, as first sergeant in Company D of the 1st Arkansas Mounted Rifles. From July 19, 1864, until May 1865 he served as second lieutenant and aide-de-camp on Reynolds's staff. Hart sustained a severe wound in the left arm at Atlanta on July 28, 1864. The Montgomery and West Point Railroad made 19 stops on its 95-mile journey between Montgomery, Alabama, and Columbus, Georgia. *OR*, 1, 38 (Part 3), 926–28, 939–40; CSR, M376, Roll 10; U.S. War Department, Index to Compiled Service Records of Confederate Soldiers Who Served in Organizations Raised Directly by the Confederate Government and of Confederate General and Staff Officers and Non-Regimental Enlisted Men, National Archives, Microcopy 818, Roll 11 (hereafter cited as CSR with microfilm and roll numbers); *Eighth Census*, M653–38, 957; Swayze, *Rail-Road and Steam-Boat Guide*, 43; Crute, *Confederate Staff Officers*, 163.

14. The Central (Georgia) Railroad operated out of Savannah and made 4 stops in 17 miles between Milledgeville and Macon. Swayze, *Rail-Road and Steam-Boat Guide*, 56–57.

15. The Georgia Railroad stopped at Camak, Georgia, 6 stops and 47 miles from Augusta en route to Atlanta. Swayze, *Rail-Road and Steam-Boat Guide*, 8.

16. The South Carolina Railroad operated between Charleston, South Carolina, and Augusta, Georgia, with a stop at Graniteville, South Carolina. Swayze, *Rail-Road and Steam-Boat Guide*, 10–11.

17. This movement occurred due to a store of cotton at Augusta, then under threat by Sherman and Kilpatrick. Cheatham held a position at Bath Mills, South Carolina. Wheeler conducted reconnaissance throughout Aiken County but began a movement toward Orangeburg, South Carolina, on February 12, 1865. *OR*, 1:53, 410–11.

18. Norris's Store lay approximately 15 miles southwest of Columbia. David Williamson, *The Third Mississippi Battalion Infantry and the 45th Mississippi Regiment: A Civil War History* (Jefferson, NC: McFarland, 2003), 304.

19. Previously known as Lee's Ferry, McNary's Ferry crossed the Saluda River northwest of Columbia. Williamson, *The Third Mississippi Battalion*, 304.

20. Born in North Carolina on July 4, 1829, Daniel Chevilette Govan grew up in Mississippi. Educated at the University of South Carolina, he went to California during the Gold Rush. In 1860, Govan lived on a Richland Township farm in Phillips County with his 25-year-old wife, Mary, two sons, and two daughters. He owned $12,000 in real estate and a personal estate of $22,000. He served as lieutenant colonel of the 2nd Arkansas Infantry. Promoted to brigadier general on February 29, 1863, he commanded a brigade in Cleburne's Division. He lived in Arkansas until 1894, when President Grover Cleveland appointed him an Indian agent in Washington State. He died in Memphis on March 12, 1911, and received burial in Hillcrest Cemetery in Holly Springs,

Mississippi. *Eighth Census,* M653–47, 354; M376, Roll 9, and M818, Roll 10; Daniel E. Sutherland, "No Better Officer in the Confederacy: The Wartime Career of Daniel C. Govan," *Arkansas Historical Quarterly* 54, no. 3 (Autumn 1995): 269–303; Ezra J. Warner, *Generals in Gray: Lives of the Confederate Commanders* (Baton Rouge: Louisiana State University Press, 1959), 112–13.

21. Jones's Ferry forded the Enoree River between Laurens and Union Counties, South Carolina. Federal Writers' Project, *South Carolina Slave Narratives: A Folk History of Slavery in South Carolina from Interviews with Former Slaves* (Bedford, MA: Applewood Books, 2006), 89.

22. Pomaria, South Carolina, is located 5 stops and 31 miles from Columbia, on the Greenville and Columbia Railroad. Swayze, *Rail-Road and Steam-Boat Guide,* 12.

23. The Charlotte and South Carolina Railroad operated between Columbia and Statesville, North Carolina. Charlotte is located 7 stops and 43 miles from Chester, South Carolina, along this route. Swayze, *Rail-Road and Steam-Boat Guide,* 14.

24. The North Carolina Railroad made a stop at Salisbury, 43 miles and 6 stops from Charlotte on the route between Charlotte and Goldsboro. Swayze, *Rail-Road and Steam-Boat Guide,* 15.

25. A. G. Moore mustered in with Company D of the 1st Arkansas Mounted Rifles on June 9, 1861. He succeeded Lee M. Ramseur as captain after Ramseur's promotion to lieutenant colonel. Thomasville is located 3 stops and 28 miles from Salisbury on the North Carolina Railroad route between Charlotte and Goldsboro. CSR, M376, Roll 17; Swayze, *Rail-Road and Steam-Boat Guide,* 15.

26. Raleigh is located 15 stops and 96 miles from Thomasville on the North Carolina Railroad. Swayze, *Rail-Road and Steam-Boat Guide,* 15.

27. Goldsboro is located 4 stops and 48 miles from Raleigh on the North Carolina Railroad. Daniel H. Hill reported on the engagements near Kinston at Southwest Creek and Monroe's Crossroads on March 7–10, 1865. *OR,* 1:47 (Part 1), 1086–89.

28. For a discussion of Joseph E. Johnston's return to command of the Army of Tennessee, see Thomas Lawrence Connelly, *Autumn of Glory: The Army of Tennessee, 1862–1865* (Baton Rouge: Louisiana State University Press, 1971), 517–25; Nathanial Cheairs Hughes Jr., *Bentonville: The Final Battle between Sherman and Johnston* (Chapel Hill: University of North Carolina, 2006), 38.

29. According to Robert H. Dacus, the Alabama Brigade of Walthall's Division refused to occupy its assigned position at Bentonville due to lack of protection from an open field in their front. Reynolds agreed to switch places. While engaged in this move-ment, in the company of D. H. Hill and other generals, Reynolds and his horse, "Robert," sustained serious wounds from artillery fire up the Goldsboro Road. Surgeons amputated Reynolds's left leg above the knee. Brigade command fell to Henry G. Bunn of the 4th Arkansas Infantry, although Walthall initially rallied the brigade. Bunn received orders to position the brigade in an open field to the right of Robert F. Hoke's Division, in support of one or two batteries of artillery. Ordered to advance at 2:45 p.m., the brigade moved obliquely to its right, charged the enemy, drove them, and pursued for several hundred yards. The line then halted to reform and, at about 4 p.m., advanced through a swamp. At about 5 p.m., Reynolds's (Bunn's)

and Quarles's (under George D. Johnston) Brigades formed as the left flank of the line and received an attack in an unprotected position but held their ground. Bunn sustained a slight wound and left the field at twilight. He described this attack as "more obstinate" than any other part of the battle. Bunn reported 7 killed, 33 wounded, and 1 missing, for an aggregate of 41 casualties out of "about 150" effectives. Dr. John T. Darby served as staff surgeon under G. W. Smith from June until September 1862, when he joined the staff of John Bell Hood. On July 7, 1864, he joined the staff of Alexander P. Stewart and later served as medical director for the Army of Tennessee. Vol King mustered in as first lieutenant in Company E of the 1st Arkansas Mounted Rifles on August 17, 1861, and served until paroled at Greensboro, North Carolina. *OR,* 1:47 (Part 1), 1101–5; CSR, M818, Roll 7; M376, Roll 13; Dacus, *Reminiscences,* 24; War Department, *List of Staff Officers,* 41; Jack D. Welsh, *Medical Histories of Confederate Generals* (Kent, OH: Kent State University Press, 1999), 184; Hughes, *Bentonville,* 54.

30. Smithfield is located 2 stops and 27 miles from Raleigh along the North Carolina Railroad. Dr. F. J. Haywood practiced medicine in Smithfield. In 1848, he performed the first surgical procedure in the state with the use of chloroform. Swayze, *Rail-Road and Steam-Boat Guide,* 15; Guion Griffis Johnson, *Ante-Bellum North Carolina: A Social History* (Chapel Hill: University of North Carolina Press, 1937), 745.

31. Dr. Robert A. Price served as regimental surgeon for the 9th Arkansas Infantry. Born in Alabama about 1836, F. W. Ragland practiced law and lived with his brother E. B. Ragland in Vaugine Township in Jefferson County. F. W. Ragland joined Company H of the 9th Arkansas Infantry as a private but earned promotion to first lieutenant and aide-de-camp under Reynolds from July 17, 1863, to July 19, 1864. Promoted to captain, Ragland served as Reynolds's assistant inspector general from July 19, 1864, until May 1865. Henry G. Bunn cited Ragland for gallantry at Bentonville. *Eighth Census,* M653– 44, 808; M376, Roll 19; M376, Roll 19, and M818, Roll 20; *OR,* 1:47 (Part 1), 1105; U.S. War Department, *List of Staff Officers of the Confederate States Army, 1861—1865* (Washington, DC: Government Printing Office, 1891), 134.

32. On April 9, 1865, Joseph E. Johnston reorganized his army. Consolidated into a single regiment, Reynolds's Brigade served the final weeks of the war as the "1st Mounted Rifles (Consolidated) (Dismounted)" in Featherston's Brigade of Loring's Division and Stewart's Corps. George W. Wells mustered in as second lieutenant in Company E of the 1st Arkansas Mounted Rifles on July 9, 1861, and sustained a wound during the Atlanta campaign on July 20, 1864. Promoted to lieutenant colonel, he commanded the consolidated regiment. Morrisville is located 2 stops and 13 miles from Raleigh on the North Carolina Railroad. *OR,* 1:47 (Part 1), 1063; *OR,* 1:47 (Part 3), 773; CSR, M376, Roll 24; Swayze, *Rail-Road and Steam-Boat Guide,* 15.

33. Hillsboro is 3 stops and 26 miles from Raleigh on the North Carolina Railroad. The line continues another 7 stops and 42 miles to Greensboro. Swayze, *Rail-Road and Steam-Boat Guide,* 15.

34. Haw River Station is 2 stops and 16 miles from Hillsboro on the North Carolina Railroad. The Company Shops Station is 2 stops and 4 miles from Haw River. Greensboro is 3 stops and 22 miles from the village of Company Shops. Forerunner to the city of Burlington, Company Shops served as a maintenance facility for the North

Carolina Railroad. McLean's Station is located 8 miles from Greensboro. Thomas Hole could not be identified. Swayze, *Rail-Road and Steam-Boat Guide,* 15; Don Bolden, *Remembering Alamance County: Tales of Railroads, Textiles, and Baseball* (Charleston, SC: History Press, 2006), 9–13.

35. James E. Sloan served as assistant quartermaster for the state of North Carolina. After Bentonville, he offered use of his Goldsboro home until Reynolds could travel. Born in North Carolina about 1832, Russ Evans lived in Des Arc Township in White River in Prairie County with his 22-year-old wife, Nannie. In 1860, Evans worked as a mechanic and owned $31,000 in real estate and a personal estate valued at $11,000. He enlisted in Company C of the 25th Arkansas Infantry but transferred to the 1st Arkansas Mounted Rifles on March 13, 1862, and served in companies B ("the Des Arc Rangers") and A ("the Chicot Rangers"). James E. Sloan to D. H. Reynolds, March 27, 1865, Box 1, Folder 5, Item 103, DHR Papers; CSR, M818, Roll 22; M376, Roll 7; War Department, *List of Staff Officers,* 151; *Eighth Census,* M653–48, 986; Bradley, *This Astounding Close,* 153.

36. As Sherman and Johnston discussed terms of surrender, many Confederates expressed anxiety over postwar rights. To dispel such concerns, the surrender agreement signed on April 18, 1865, referred to retention of individual political and property rights. William T. Sherman, *Memoirs of General William T. Sherman* (New York: Da Capo Press, 1984), 352–57; Noah Andre Trudeau, *Out of the Storm: The End of the Civil War, April–June 1865* (Boston: Little, Brown and Company, 1994), 233–34.

37. Born in Franklin County, Tennessee, on February 16, 1822, James Patton Anderson commanded the 1st Mississippi Battalion during the Mexican War. He served as colonel of the 1st Florida Infantry until promoted to brigadier general on February 10, 1862. He earned promotion to major general on February 17, 1864. Anderson commanded the District of Florida until recalled to the Army of Tennessee during the Atlanta campaign and sustained a severe wound at Jonesboro. He owned an agricultural newspaper in Memphis and served as tax collector for Shelby County, Tennessee. He died in Memphis on September 20, 1872, and received burial in Elmwood Cemetery. *Eighth Census,* M653–51, 29; M818, Roll 1; Larry Rayburn, "'Wherever the Fight Is Thickest': General James Patton Anderson of Florida," *Florida Historical Quarterly* 60, no. 3 (January 1982): 313–36; Lawrence L. Hewitt, "James Patton Anderson," in *Confederate General,* ed. Davis and Hoffman, 1:22–25.

38. Abraham Lincoln's death on April 15, 1865, changed the political climate and led to congressional rejection of the initial peace terms. Trudeau, *Out of the Storm,* 237–44.

39. For a description of the second round of negotiations between Johnston and Sherman, see Trudeau, *Out of the Storm,* 237–44.

40. Col. Martin H. Cofer commanded the 6th Kentucky Mounted (Confederate) Infantry. Joseph E. Johnston appointed him provost marshal general for the Army of Tennessee on March 31, 1865. *OR,* 1:47 (Part 3), 729; U.S. War Department, Compiled Service Records of Confederate Soldiers Who Served in Organizations from the State of Kentucky, National Archives, Microcopy M377, Roll 3 (hereafter cited as CSR with microfilm and roll numbers).

41. William Hartsuff of Port Huron, Michigan, mustered in as captain of Company E in the 10th Michigan Infantry on October 1, 1861. He earned promotion to lieutenant

colonel and assistant inspector general for the 23rd Army Corps on May 13, 1863. He received the brevet rank of brigadier general and mustered out on July 10, 1865. CSR, M545, Roll 18; *History of St. Clair County, Michigan* (Chicago: A. T. Andreas and Company, 1883), 365.

42. A branch road of the North Carolina Railroad connected Greensboro, North Carolina, to Danville, Virginia. Swayze, *Rail-Road and Steam-Boat Guide,* 15.

43. Danville served as the southwestern terminus of the Richmond (Lynchburg) and Danville Railroad, which connected Richmond to Petersburg as one of the last supply lines to the Army of Northern Virginia. Located on the north side of the James River at Fourteenth Street, the Richmond and Danville Railroad intersected with the Southside Railroad about 40 miles west of Petersburg. Swayze, *Rail-Road and Steam-Boat Guide,* 15, 28–29; Noah Andre Trudeau, *The Last Citadel: Petersburg, Virginia, June 1864– April 1865* (Boston: Little, Brown and Company, 1991), 88; Nelson Lankford, *Richmond Burning: The Last Days of the Confederate Capital* (New York: Viking, 2002), 85.

44. Manchester, Virginia, is the first stop on the Richmond and Danville Railroad on the route out of town over the railroad bridge. The Powhatan House operated at the corner of Broad and Capitol Streets in Richmond. The city purchased the hotel in 1911 and razed the property. Swayze, *Rail-Road and Steam-Boat Guide,* 28; Louis Manarin, *Richmond on the James* (Charleston: Arcadia Publishing, 2001), 60.

45. Charlottesville, Virginia, is located 16 stops and 97 miles from Richmond on the route of the Virginia Central Railroad. The town's proximity to railroads and the University of Virginia made it an ideal location for military hospitals. "Miss Nancy" could not be identified. Swayze, *Rail-Road and Steam-Boat Guide,* 30; Ervin L. Jordan Jr., *Charlottesville and the University of Virginia in the Civil War* (Lynchburg, VA: H. E. Howard, 1988), 47, 62.

46. On February 9, 1865, Virginia became the twelfth state to abolish slavery through ratification of the Thirteenth Amendment. On May 29, 1865, President Andrew Johnson issued a proclamation to define general amnesty for former Confederates and fourteen classes of exemption. The third class of exemption, status as a commissioned Confederate officer above the rank of colonel, applied to Reynolds and required an application for special presidential pardon. Paul H. Bergeron, ed., *The Papers of Andrew Johnson* (Knoxville: University Press of Tennessee, 1989), 8:128–31; Mason I. Lowance, ed., *A House Divided: The Antebellum Slavery Debates in America, 1776–1865* (Princeton, NJ: Princeton University Press, 2003), 31.

47. Thomas Jefferson designed "Jefferson Hall," on the West Range on the University of Virginia campus. It served as a Confederate hospital. Jordan, *Charlottesville and the University of Virginia,* 47, 62; John Shelton Patton, *Jefferson, Cabell, and the University of Virginia* (New York: Neale Publishing Company, 1906), 234.

48. Situated on the peninsula between the James and York Rivers, Fortress Monroe guarded the approach to Hampton Roads through Chesapeake Bay. In May 1865, one of the fort's casements served as a prison cell for Jefferson Davis. Reynolds's reference to the steamboat "*M. Martion*" probably refers to the *M. Martin,* which served under charter between October 29, 1864, and May 2, 1865. Owned by the Baltimore Steam Packet Company, the *Louisiana* worked the Rappahannock River trade. E. Kay Gibson,

comp., *Dictionary of Transports and Combatant Vessels Steam and Sail Employed by the Union Army, 1861–1868* (Camden, ME: Ensign Press, 1995), 207; Alexander Crosby Brown, *Steam Packets on the Chesapeake* (Cambridge, MD: Cornell Maritime Press, 1961), 38–42, 47, 49, 53, 59–60, 67, 162; James L. Nelson, *Reign of Iron: The Story of the First Battling Ironclads, the Monitor and the Merrimack* (New York: William Morrow, 2004), 35, 145, 298.

49. The Fountain House was located near the Baltimore and Ohio Railroad station in Baltimore. The Continental Hotel opened in Philadelphia on February 16, 1860, at the corner of Ninth and Chestnut Streets and catered to an elite clientele. Moses Foster Sweetser, ed., *The Middle States: A Handbook for Travellers* (Boston: James R. Osgood and Company, 1881), 394; Rudolph J. Walther, *Happenings in Ye Olde Philadelphia, 1680–1900* (Philadelphia: Walther Printing House, 1925), 184.

50. President Andrew Johnson proclaimed a day of national fasting, humiliation, and prayer on June 1, 1865, to mourn the death of Abraham Lincoln. Merrill D. Peterson, *Lincoln in American Memory* (New York: Oxford University Press, 1995), 23.

51. The reference to "Dr. Palmer" in Baltimore may refer to Dr. Henry Palmer. Born in New Hartford, New York, on July 30, 1827, Palmer graduated from Albany Medical College and established a practice in Janesville, Wisconsin. He married Edna A. Hoyt in November 1851 and fathered six children. Palmer served as regimental surgeon of the 7th Wisconsin Infantry and brigade surgeon for the Iron Brigade from 1861 to July 1862, when he became surgeon-in-charge at the U.S. Army Hospital in York, Pennsylvania. He received orders in the fall of 1864 to serve as medical inspector for the 8th Corps, with headquarters in Baltimore. He remained in Baltimore until June 9, 1865, when he received appointment as medical inspector to oversee closure of the prison hospital at Camp Douglas in Chicago. He mustered out on October 7, 1865. On March 13, 1866, he received a brevet promotion to lieutenant colonel for meritorious services, with rank to date from March 13, 1865. He returned to Janesville and practiced medicine. He died on June 14, 1895, and received burial in Oak Hill Cemetery. CSR, M559, Roll 23; *Portrait and Biographical Album of Rock County, Wisconsin* (Chicago: Acme Publishing Company, 1889), 364–66; *Dictionary of Wisconsin Biography* (Madison: State Historical Society of Wisconsin, 1960), 278–79; Malcolm Palmer Mouat, *Dr. Henry Palmer, "The Fighting Surgeon," 1827–1895* (Detroit: Harlo Press, 1977), 63–79, 201–6.

52. Designed in 1854 by either Griffith Thomas or John B. Snook, the one-thou-sand-room St. Nicholas Hotel stood along the 500 block of Broadway near West 155th Street. The hotel survived a November 1864 fire started by Confederate agents as part of a plot to burn the city and spread panic in the North. Gerard R. Wolfe, *New York, 15 Walking Tours: An Architectural Guide to the Metropolis* (New York: McGraw-Hill, 2003), 208–9.

53. The New York and Erie Railroad made regularly scheduled stops between New York City and Dunkirk, New York. New York and Erie Railroad, *Rates and Fares and Distances Between All the Stations on the New York and Erie Railroad: Hancock to Dunkirk* (New York: Printed at the Office of the Company, 1854), 2–3.

54. Maj. Smith could not be identified. Burghampton is located in Washington County, New York.

55. Located at the corner of Sixth and Washington Streets, the stylish Lindell Hotel served as headquarters for the provost marshal general in the Department of the Missouri. In 1864, it served as headquarters for the Executive Committee of the Mississippi Valley Sanitary Fair. Such varied wartime uses may account for its "poorly kept" appearance at this time. The Lindell burned in 1867. Frank L. Klement, *Dark Lanterns: Secret Political Societies, Conspiracies, and Treason Trials in the Civil War* (Baton Rouge: Louisiana State University Press, 1989), 76; Robert Patrick Bender, "'This Noble and Philanthropic Enterprise': The Mississippi Valley Sanitary Fair and the Meaning of Civil War Philanthropy," *Missouri Historical Review* (January 2001): 130; Robert W. Jackson, *Rails across the Mississippi: A History of the St. Louis Bridge* (Urbana: University of Illinois Press, 2001), 118.

56. Built in 1860 in Jeffersonville, Indiana, and owned by the St. Louis and Memphis Packing Company, the *Belle Memphis* worked the Mississippi River between St. Louis, Memphis, and New Orleans. The vessel served as U. S. Grant's headquarters at Belmont and as a troop transport into Fort Henry. Commonly referred to as the *Memphis,* the vessel spent much of March and early April 1864 stranded on a sandbar near Tiptonville, Tennessee. *Belle Memphis* sank on January 12, 1866, while anchored in ice at St. Louis. Frederick Way Jr., comp., *Way's Packet Directory, 1848–1994: Passenger Steamboats of the Mississippi River System since the Advent of Photography in Mid-Continent America* (Athens: Ohio University Press, 1994), 319; Charles Dana Gibson and E. Kay Gibson, eds., *Dictionary of Transports and Combatant Vessels, Steam and Sail, Employed by the Union Army, 1861–1868* (Camden, ME: Ensign Press, 1995), 326.

57. For a discussion of the immediate postwar sentiments about social and political rights for newly freed blacks, see Carl H. Moneyhon, *The Impact of the Civil War and Reconstruction on Arkansas: Persistence in the Midst of Ruin* (Fayetteville: University of Arkansas Press, 2002), 207–10.

58. Designed by James Dakin for entrepreneur Robertson Topp, the Gayoso House opened in the mid-1840s along the Memphis riverfront. David Cockrell owned the Gayoso House during the war, when it served variously as headquarters for Leonidas Polk and William T. Sherman. After the capture of Memphis, the Gayoso served as a Union hospital under the supervision of Mary Ann Bickerdyke. With a capacity for 900 patients, it earned a reputation as the best medical facility in the city. The original structure burned on July 4, 1899. *Tennessee State Gazetteer and Business Directory for 1860–61* (Nashville: John L. Mitchell, 1860), 150; Mary Ashton Rice Livermore, *My Story of the War: A Woman's Narrative* (Hartford: A. D. Worthington and Company, 1890), 289–90; Charles Bracelen Flood, *Grant and Sherman: The Friendship that Won the Civil War* (New York: Farrar Straus & Giroux, 2005), 142; David Bowman, "The Gayoso House," in *Metropolis of the American Nile: Memphis and Shelby County,* ed. John E. Harkins (Woodland Hills, CA: Windsor Publications, 1982), 63–64, 72.

59. Reynolds's reference to a steamboat named *Bostonia* probably refers to the *Bostona.* Built in Cincinnati in 1854 and owned by the Cincinnati, Maysville, and Portsmouth Packet Company, *Bostona* worked the Ohio River trade and the off-season trade between Cincinnati and St. Louis. Late in the war, *Bostona* operated between

Memphis and Vicksburg. Sold by the U.S. marshals due to debt, authorities sent the vessel to St. Louis and dismantled it. Way, *Way's Packet Directory*, 59.

60. Established in the 1830s, "Sunnyside" became one of the most prosperous plantations in Chicot County. In 1860, Elisha Worthington owned "Sunny Side," along with "Red Leaf," "Meanie," and "Eminence" plantations. Worthington owned $201,900 in real estate and a personal estate valued at $27,500. Born in Virginia about 1790, Claiborn W. Saunders lived with his 63-year old wife, Eliza, in the Oden Township. In 1860, he owned $50,000 in real estate and a personal estate valued at $52,500, as well as 90 slaves. Exempt from the general amnesty of May 29, 1865, for violation of the wartime amnesty issued on December 8, 1863, Saunders applied for special presidential pardon. Endorsed by Gov. Isaac Murphy, he received a pardon on October 9, 1865. *Eighth Census*, M653–38, 926, 950; *Eighth Census, Slave Schedule* (Chicot County, Arkansas), M653–53, 104; *Eighth Census, Slave Schedule* (Knox County, Kentucky), M653–404, 99; James L. Douthat, ed., *Special Presidential Pardons for Confederate Soldiers: A Listing of Former Confederate Soldiers Requesting Full Pardon from President Andrew Johnson* (Signal Mountain, TN: Mountain Press, 1999), 1:173; Willard B. Gatewood, "Sunnyside: The Evolution of an Arkansas Plantation, 1840–1945," in *Shadows over Sunnyside*, ed. Jeannie M. Whayne (Fayetteville: University of Arkansas Press, 1999), 3–24.

61. Born in Pennsylvania about 1830, Samuel N. Caughey lived in Louisiana Township with his 20-year-old wife, Rebecca, and two sons. Caughey served as Chicot County clerk from 1856 to 1858. In 1860, he owned $50,000 in real estate as well as a personal estate valued at $50,000 and 40 slaves. Nathan Bass owned 100 slaves on his property in Old River Township. Born in Ireland about 1831, James F. Robinson lived in Old River Township with his 22-year-old wife, Mary, and one son. In 1860, he practiced law and owned $70,000 in real estate, as well as a personal estate valued at $45,000 and 38 slaves. *Eighth Census*, M653–38, 920, 947, 949; *Eighth Census, Slave Schedule* (Chicot County, Arkansas), M653, Roll 53, 91, 102B–103; *Biographical and Historical Memoirs of Southern Arkansas* (Chicago: Goodspeed Publishing Company, 1890), 1062.

62. Born in Virginia about 1821, John Hunnicutt lived in Old River Township and worked as the hotelkeeper at the Buckhorn Hotel with his 24-year-old wife, Susan, three sons, and one daughter. Hunnicutt reported no assets in 1860. *Eighth Census*, M653–38, 921.

BIBLIOGRAPHY

PRIMARY SOURCES: MANUSCRIPTS

Daniel Harris Reynolds Papers. Special Collections, University of Arkansas Libraries, Fayetteville.

Richard and Connie Cox Collection. Lake Village, AR. Used by permission.

PRIMARY SOURCES: NEWSPAPERS AND JOURNALS

Arkansas Democrat (Little Rock, AR)

Arkansas Gazette (Little Rock, AR)

Atlanta Journal and Constitution (Atlanta, GA)

Chicot Press (Lake Village, AR)

Confederate Veteran

Confederate War Journal

Daily Constitutionalist (Augusta, GA)

PRIMARY SOURCES: PUBLIC DOCUMENTS

National Archives and Records Service. Case Files of Applications from Former Confederates for Presidential Pardons: 1865–1867 ("Amnesty Papers").

U.S. Bureau of the Census. *Population Schedules [Free] of the Fourth Census of the United States, 1820.* Washington, DC: National Archives and Records Administration, 1820.

———. *Population Schedules [Free] of the Sixth Census of the United States, 1840.* Washington, DC: National Archives and Records Administration, 1840.

———. *Population Schedules [Free] of the Eighth Census of the United States, 1860.* Washington, DC: National Archives and Records Administration, 1860.

———. *Population Schedules [Slave] of the Eighth Census of the United States, 1860.* Washington, DC: National Archives and Records Administration, 1860.

———. *Population Schedules of the Ninth Census of the United States, 1870.* Washington, DC: National Archives and Records Administration, 1870.

———. *Population Schedules of the Thirteenth Census of the United States, 1910.* Washington, DC: National Archives and Records Administration, 1910.

U.S. War Department. Compiled Services Records of Confederate General and Staff Officers and Non-Regimental Enlisted Men. National Archives. Microcopy 313.

———. Compiled Service Records of Confederate Soldiers Who Served in Organizations from the State of Alabama. National Archives. Microcopy M374.

———. Compiled Service Records of Confederate Soldiers Who Served in Organizations from the State of Arkansas. National Archives. Microcopy 317.

———. Compiled Service Records of Confederate Soldiers Who Served in

Organizations from the State of Arkansas. National Archives. Microcopy 376 and M383.

———. Compiled Service Records of Confederate Soldiers Who Served in Organizations from the State of Georgia. National Archives. Microcopy M266.

———. Compiled Service Records of Confederate Soldiers Who Served in Organizations from the State of Kentucky. National Archives. Microcopy M377 and M386.

———. Compiled Service Records of Confederate Soldiers Who Served in Organizations from the State of Louisiana. National Archives. Microcopy M378.

———. Compiled Service Records of Confederate Soldiers Who Served in Organizations from the State of Mississippi. National Archives. Microcopy M232.

———. Compiled Service Records of Confederate Soldiers Who Served in Organizations from the State of Missouri. National Archives. Microcopy M380.

———. Compiled Service Records of Confederate Soldiers Who Served in Organizations from the State of North Carolina. National Archives. Microcopy M230.

———. Compiled Service Records of Confederate Soldiers Who Served in Organizations from the State of Tennessee. National Archives. Microcopy M231.

———. Compiled Service Records of Confederate Soldiers Who Served in Organizations from the State of Texas. National Archives. Microcopy M227.

———. Index to Compiled Service Records of Confederate Soldiers Who Served in Organizations Raised Directly by the Confederate Government and of Confederate General and Staff Officers and Non-Regimental Enlisted Men. National Archives. Microcopy 818.

———. *List of Staff Officers of the Confederate States Army, 1861–1865.* Washington, DC: Government Printing Office, 1891.

———. *War of the Rebellion: Official Records of the Union and Confederate Armies* (Washington, DC: Government Printing Office, 1880–1901). (Cited in the notes as *OR* or *Official Records.*)

PRIMARY SOURCES: ARTICLES, BOOKS, AND PAMPHLETS

A General Directory for the City of Vicksburg. Vicksburg: H. C. Clarke, 1860.

Bentley's Monthly Review, Or, Literary Argus: November 1853 to April 1854. London: Piper, Stephenson and Spence, 1854.

Bible Record of Francis Madison McGehee. Transcription in possession of Carolyn Golowka, used by permission. Available online at http://files.usgwarchives.org/ar/cleveland/bible/m2000001.txt.

Biographical and Historical Memoirs of Eastern Arkansas. Chicago: Goodspeed Publishing Company, 1890.

Biographical and Historical Memoirs of Mississippi. Gretna, LA: Pelican Publishing Company, 1999.

Biographical and Historical Memoirs of Pulaski, Jefferson, Lonoke, Faulkner, Grant, Saline, Perry, Garland, and Hot Spring Counties, Arkansas. Chicago: Goodspeed Publishing Company, 1889.

Biographical and Historical Memoirs of Southern Arkansas. Chicago: Goodspeed
    Publishing Company, 1890.
Biographical and Historical Memoirs of Western Arkansas. Chicago: Goodspeed
    Publishing Company, 1891.
Dramatic Register for 1853. New York: T. Hailes Lacy, 1854.
"Gen. William H. Jackson," *Confederate Veteran* 2 (June 1894): 176–77.
A General Directory for the City of Vicksburg. Vicksburg: H. C. Clarke, 1860.
The Grand Lodge Proceedings of 1854. Natchez, MS: Daily Courier Book and Job Office,
    1854.
Historical Reminiscences and Biographical Memoirs of Conway County, Arkansas. Little
    Rock: Arkansas Historical Publishing Company, 1890.
*History of Benton, Washington, Carroll, Madison, Crawford, Franklin and Sebastian
    Counties, Arkansas.* Chicago: Goodspeed Publishing Company, 1889.
History of St. Clair County, Michigan. Chicago: A. T. Andreas and Company, 1883.
Journal of the Congress of the Confederate States of America, 1861–1865. Washington, DC:
    Government Printing Office, 1904.
*Journal of the Proceedings of the Bishops, Clergy and Laity of the Protestant Episcopal
    Church.* Philadelphia: King and Baird, 1857.
Portrait and Biographical Album of Rock County, Wisconsin. Chicago: Acme Publishing
    Company, 1889.
*Proceedings of the MW Grand Lodge of Free and Accepted Masons of the State of Arkansas,
    Held in the Town of Washington.* Little Rock: J. D. Butler, Book and Job Printer, 1866.
The Southern Business Directory and General Commercial Advertiser. Charleston: Steam
    Power Press of Walker and James, 1854.
Tennessee State Gazetteer and Business Directory for 1860–61. Nashville: John L. Mitchell,
    1860.

PRIMARY SOURCES: MEMOIRS AND PUBLISHED RECORDS

Allen, Desmond Walls. *Abstracts from Masonic Records, Grand Lodge of Arkansas, 1862–
    1869.* Conway, AR: Arkansas Research, 2003.
————. *First Arkansas Confederate Mounted Rifles.* Conway, AR: Arkansas Research,
    1988.
Bergeron, Paul H., ed. *The Papers of Andrew Johnson.* Knoxville: University Press of
    Tennessee, 1989.
Brown, Allston. *History of the American Stage: Containing Biographical Sketches of
    Nearly Every Member of the Profession That Has Appeared on the American Stage,
    from 1733 to 1870.* 1870. Reprint, New York: Benjamin Blom, 1969.
Bunn, Henry G. "Gen. Evander McNair." *Confederate Veteran* 11 (1903): 265–66.
Campbell, Robert Allen. *Campbell's Gazetteer of Missouri.* St. Louis: R. A. Campbell,
    Publisher, 1875.
Confederate States of America War Department. *Regulations for the Army of the
    Confederate States 1863.* Richmond: J. W. Randolph, 1863.
Crute, Joseph H., Jr., ed. *Confederate Staff Officers, 1861–1865.* Powhatan, VA: Derwent
    Books, 1982.

Dacus, Robert H. *Reminiscences of Company "H," First Arkansas Mounted Rifles.* Dardanelle, AR: Post-Dispatch Printing, 1897.

Davis, Robert S., Jr., ed. *Requiem for a Lost City: Sallie Clayton's Memoir of Civil War Atlanta.* Macon, GA: Mercer University Press, 1999.

DeBow, James Dunwoody Brownson. *DeBow's Review of the Western and Southern States.* New Orleans: J.D.B. DeBow, 1852.

Douthat, James L., comp. *Special Presidential Pardons of Confederate Soldiers.* Signal Mountain, TN: Mountain Press, 1999.

Federal Writers Project. *South Carolina Slave Narratives: A Folk History of Slavery in South Carolina from Interviews with Former Slaves.* Bedford, MA: Applewood Books, 2006.

Forman, Jacob Gilbert. *The Western Sanitary Commission: A Sketch of Its Origins, History, Labors for the Sick and Wounded of the Western Armies, and Aid Given to Freedmen and Union Refugees, with Incidents of Hospital Life.* St. Louis: R. P. Studley and Company, 1864.

French, Samuel G. *Two Wars: The Autobiography and Diary of Gen. Samuel G. French, CSA.* Huntington, WV: Blue Acorn Press, 1999.

Gammage, Washington Lafayette. *The Camp, the Bivouac, and the Battle Field: Being a History of the Fourth Arkansas Regiment, from Its First Organization Down to the Present Date.* Little Rock: Arkansas Southern Press, 1958.

Gould, Emerson W. *Fifty Years on the Mississippi; or, Gould's History of River Navigation: Containing a History of the Introduction of Steam as a Propelling Power on Ocean, Lakes and Rivers.* St. Louis: Nixon-Jones Printing Company, 1889.

Jewett, Clayton E., ed. *Rise and Fall of the Confederacy: The Memoir of Senator Williamson S. Oldham, CSA.* Columbia: University of Missouri Press, 2006.

Leeper, Wesley Thurman. *Rebels Valiant: Second Arkansas Mounted Rifles, Dismounted.* Little Rock: Pioneer Press, 1964.

Livermore, Mary Ashton Rice. *My Story of the War: A Woman's Narrative.* Hartford, CT: A. D. Worthington and Company, 1890.

Longstreet, James. *From Manassas to Appomattox: Memoirs of the Civil War in America.* New York: Da Capo Press, 1992.

Marshall, Weed. "A Fight to the Finish near Lake Village, Ark." *Confederate Veteran* 19 (April 1911): 169.

McCorkle, John. *Three Years with Quantrill: A True Story Told by His Scout.* New York: Buffalo-Head Press, 1966.

Monks, William. *A History of Southern Missouri and Northern Arkansas: Being an Account of the Early Settlements, the Civil War, the Ku-Klux, and Times of Peace.* West Plains, MO: West Plains Journal Company, 1907.

Morrison, Marion. *A History of the Ninth Regiment Illinois Volunteer Infantry, with the Regimental Roster.* Carbondale: University of Southern Illinois Press, 1997.

New York and Erie Railroad. *Rates and Fares and Distances Between All the Stations on the New York and Erie Railroad: Hancock to Dunkirk.* New York: Printed at the Office of the Company, 1854.

Parker, Nathan Howe. *The Missouri Handbook: Embracing a Full Description of the State of Missouri.* St. Louis: P. M. Pinckard, 1865.

Reece, J. N. *Report of the Adjutant General of the State of Illinois: Containing Reports for the Years 1861–66.* Springfield, MO: Phillips Brothers, 1900.

Scott, Kim Allen, ed. *Loyalty on the Frontier or Sketches of Union Men of the South West with Incidents and Adventures in Rebellion on the Border.* Fayetteville: University of Arkansas Press, 2003.

Sherman, William T. *Memoirs of General William T. Sherman.* New York: Da Capo Press, 1984.

Swayze, J. C. *Hill and Swayze's Confederate States Rail-Road & Steam-Boat Guide, Containing the Time-Tables, Fares, Connections and Distances on all the Rail-Roads of the Confederate States; also, the Connecting Lines of Rail-Roads, Steam-Boats and Stages. And will be Accompanied by a Complete Guide to the Principal Hotels, with a Large Variety of Valuable Information.* Griffin, GA: Hill and Swayze, 1862.

Tunnard, W. H. *A Southern Record: The History of the Third Regiment Louisiana Infantry.* Fayetteville: University of Arkansas Press, 1997.

Urwin, Gregory J. W., and Cathy Kunzinger Urwin, eds. *History of the 33d Iowa Infantry Volunteer Regiment 1863–66.* Fayetteville: University of Arkansas Press, 1999.

Watkins, Samuel R. "The Fighting Forty-Eighth Tennessee Regiment." In *The Southern Bivouac*, 2:246–51. Louisville: B. F. Avery and Sons, 1884.

Way, Frederick, Jr., comp. *Way's Packet Directory, 1848–1994: Passenger Steamboats of the Mississippi River System since the Advent of Photography in Mid-Continent America.* Athens: Ohio University Press, 1994.

Woodruff, W. E. *With the Light Guns in '61–'65: Reminiscences of Eleven Arkansas, Missouri and Texas Light Batteries, in the Civil War.* Little Rock: Central Printing Company, 1903.

SECONDARY SOURCES: ARTICLES AND CHAPTERS

Arey, Frank. "'The Place Is Well Fortified . . .': Massard Prairie and the Confederate Attack on Fort Smith." *Journal of the Fort Smith Historical Society* 27 (April 2003): 3–9.

Bender, Robert Patrick. "Daniel Harris Reynolds." In *Arkansas Biography: A Collection of Notable Lives*, edited by Nancy A. Williams and Jeannie M. Whayne, 239–40. Fayetteville: University of Arkansas Press, 2000.

———. "'This Noble and Philanthropic Enterprise': The Mississippi Valley Sanitary Fair and the Meaning of Civil War Philanthropy." *Missouri Historical Review* (January 2001): 117–39.

Bird, Allen W., II. "U.M. Rose." In *Arkansas Biography: A Collection of Notable Lives*, edited by Nancy A. Williams and Jeannie M. Whayne, 250–51. Fayetteville: University of Arkansas Press, 2000.

———. "U.M. Rose: Arkansas Attorney." *Arkansas Historical Quarterly* 64 (Summer 2005): 171–205.

Cummings, Charles M. "Otho French Strahl: 'Choicest Spirit to Embrace the South.'" *Tennessee Historical Quarterly* 24 (1965): 341–55.

Davis, Steve. "A Georgia Firebrand: Major General W.H.T. Walker, C.S.A." *Georgia Historical Quarterly* 63 (Winter 1979): 447–60.

DeBlack, Thomas A. "'A Model Man of Chicot County': Lycurgus Johnson and Social Change." In *The Southern Elite and Social Change: Essays in Honor of Willard B. Gatewood, Jr.,* edited by Randy Finley and Thomas A. DeBlack, 16–33. Fayetteville: University of Arkansas Press, 2002.

Dorris, J. T., "Pardoning the Leaders of the Confederacy." *Mississippi Valley Historical Review* 15, no. 1 (June 1928): 3–21.

Dougan, Michael B. "Harris Flanagin." In *Arkansas Biography: A Collection of Notable Lives,* edited by Nancy A. Williams and Jeannie M. Whayne, 104–5. Fayetteville: University of Arkansas Press, 2000.

Elkins, F. Clark. "Thomas James Churchill, 1881–1883." In *Governors of Arkansas: Essays in Political Biography,* edited by Timothy Paul Donovan, William B. Gatewood Jr., and Jeannie M. Whayne, 72–76. Fayetteville: University of Arkansas Press, 1995.

"Ferries." Vertical File, Research Division, Oklahoma Historical Society, Oklahoma City, OK.

Gatewood, Willard B. "The Arkansas Delta: The Deepest of the Deep South." In *The Arkansas Delta: Land of Paradox,* edited by Willard B. Gatewood and Jeannie M. Whayne, 3–29. Fayetteville: University of Arkansas Press, 1996.

———. "Sunnyside: The Evolution of an Arkansas Plantation, 1840–1945." In *Shadows over Sunnyside,* edited by Jeannie M. Whayne, 3–24. Fayetteville: University of Arkansas Press, 1999.

Haberlein, Charles R., Jr. "Damn the Torpedoes." In *The Civil War Times Illustrated Photographic History of the Civil War: Vicksburg to Appomattox,* edited by William C. Davis and Bell Irvin Wiley, 2:962. New York: Black Dog Publishing, 1996.

Holley, Donald. "The Plantation Heritage: Agriculture in the Arkansas Delta." In *The Arkansas Delta: Land of Paradox,* edited by Jeannie Whayne and Willard B. Gatewood, 238–77. Fayetteville: University of Arkansas Press, 1996.

Hughes, Susan Lyons. "Camp Dick Robinson." In *The Kentucky Encyclopedia,* edited by John E. Kleber, 157–58. Lexington: University Press of Kentucky, 1992.

Ingham, Howard M. "Captain Valentine Merriwether M'Gehee." *Publications of the Arkansas Historical Association* (edited by John Hugh Reynolds) 4 (1917): 140–51.

Jones, J. Wayne. "Augustus Hill Garland." In *Arkansas Biography: A Collection of Notable Lives,* edited by Nancy A. Williams and Jeannie M. Whayne, 118–19. Fayetteville: University of Arkansas Press, 2000.

McCown, J. G. "About Ector's and McNair's Brigades." *Confederate Veteran* (March 1901): 113.

Melton, Emory. "Civil War Days in Barry County." *White River Historical Quarterly* 5, no. 1 (Fall 1973): 8–11.

Pierce, Aaron B. "St. John's College." *Pulaski County Historical Review* 36 (Summer 1988): 39–44.

Piston, William Garrett. "'Springfield Is a Vast Hospital': The Dead and Wounded at the Battle of Wilson's Creek." *Missouri Historical Review* 93, no. 4 (July 1999): 345–66.

Rayburn, Larry. "'Wherever the Fight Is Thickest': General James Patton Anderson of Florida." *Florida Historical Quarterly* 60, no. 3 (January 1982): 313–36.

Roberts, Bobby L. "General T. C. Hindman and the Trans-Mississippi District."
    Arkansas Historical Quarterly 32 (Winter 1973): 297–311.
Rose, F. P. "Hugh Anderson Dinsmore." *Arkansas Historical Quarterly* 11 (Spring 1952):
    69–78.
Scroggs, Jack B. "Arkansas in the Secession Crisis." *Arkansas Historical Quarterly* 12,
    no. 3 (Autumn 1953): 179–224.
Smith, John David. "James F. Robinson." In *Kentucky's Governors,* edited by Lowell H.
    Harrison, 89–92. Lexington: University Press of Kentucky, 2004.
Smith, Ted J. "Mastering Farm and Family: David Walker as Slaveholder." *Arkansas
    Historical Quarterly* 58, no. 1 (Spring 1999): 61–79.
Stuart W. Sanders. "One Last Gallant Defense." *Military History Quarterly* 18 (Spring
    2006): 44–51.
Sutherland, Daniel E. "No Better Officer in the Confederacy: The Wartime Career
    of Daniel C. Govan." *Arkansas Historical Quarterly* 54, no. 3 (Autumn 1995):
    269–303.
Utley, Joseph S. "Graves of Eminent Men." In *Publications of the Arkansas Historical
    Association,* edited by John Hugh McReynolds, 2:265. Little Rock: Democrat
    Printing and Lithographing Company, 1908.
Warner, Seth. "George Earl Maney: Soldier, Railroader, and Diplomat." *Tennessee
    Historical Quarterly* 65, no. 2 (Summer 2006): 130–47.
Whayne, Jeannie M. "Henry Massie Rector." In *Arkansas Biography: A Collection of
    Notable Lives,* edited by Nancy A. Williams and Jeannie M. Whayne, 234–35.
    Fayetteville: University of Arkansas Press, 2000.
Woods, James M. "Ambrose Hundley Sevier." In *Arkansas Biography: A Collection of
    Notable Lives,* edited by Nancy A. Williams and Jeannie M. Whayne, 259–60.
    Fayetteville: University of Arkansas Press, 2000.
———. "Robert Ward Johnson." In *Arkansas Biography: A Collection of Notable Lives,*
    edited by Nancy A. Williams and Jeannie M. Whayne, 152–53. Fayetteville:
    University of Arkansas Press, 2000.
Woodward, Earl F. "The Brooks and Baxter War in Arkansas, 1872–1874." *Arkansas
    Historical Quarterly* 30 (Winter 1971): 315–36.

SECONDARY SOURCES: BOOKS AND ENCYCLOPEDIAS

Abel, Annie Heloise. *The American Indian as Participant in the Civil War.* Cleveland:
    Arthur H. Clark Company, 1919.
Allardice, Bruce S. *Confederate Colonels: A Biographical Register.* Columbia: University
    of Missouri Press, 2008.
———. *More Generals in Gray.* Baton Rouge: Louisiana State University Press, 1995.
The American Heritage Dictionary. New York: Dell Publishing Company, 1985.
Ballard, Michael B. *Vicksburg: The Campaign that Opened the Mississippi.* Chapel Hill:
    University of North Carolina Press, 2004.
Banham, Martin, ed. *The Cambridge Guide to Theatre.* New York: Cambridge
    University Press, 1995.

Benner, Judith Ann. *Sul Ross: Soldier, Statesman, Educator.* College Station: Texas A&M University Press, 2005.

Bolden, Don. *Remembering Alamance County: Tales of Railroads, Textiles, and Baseball* Charleston, SC: History Press, 2006.

Bordman, Gerald, ed. *The Oxford Companion to American Theatre.* New York: Oxford University Press, 1984.

Bradley, Mark L. *This Astounding Close: The Road to Bennett Place.* Chapel Hill: University of North Carolina Press, 2006.

Brannon, Sheila Farrell, ed. *A Tribute to Chicot County.* Dermott, AR: Brannon, 2000.

Bridges, Hal. *Lee's Maverick General: Daniel Harvey Hill.* 1961. Reprint, Lincoln: University of Nebraska Press, 1991.

Brown, Alexander Crosby. *Steam Packets on the Chesapeake.* Cambridge, MD: Cornell Maritime Press, 1961.

Brown, Russell K. *To the Manner Born: The Life of General William H. T. Walker.* Macon, GA: Mercer University Press, 2005.

Brown, Walter Lee. *A Life of Albert Pike.* Fayetteville: University of Arkansas Press, 1997.

Carter, Arthur B. *The Tarnished Cavalier: Major General Earl Van Dorn, C.S.A.* Knoxville: University of Tennessee Press, 1999.

Castel, Albert. *Decision in the West: The Atlanta Campaign of 1864.* Lawrence: University of Kansas Press, 1992.

———. *General Sterling Price and the Civil War in the West.* Baton Rouge: Louisiana State University Press, 1993.

Cimbala, Paul A., and Randall M. Miller, eds. *The Freedmen's Bureau and Reconstruction: Reconsiderations.* New York: Fordham University Press, 1999.

Cisco, Walter Brian. *States Rights Gist: A South Carolina General of the Civil War.* Gretna, LA: Pelican Publishing Company, 2008.

Confer, Clarissa W. *The Cherokee Nation.* Norman: University of Oklahoma Press, 1997.

Connelly, Thomas Lawrence. *Autumn of Glory: The Army of Tennessee, 1862–1865.* Baton Rouge: Louisiana State University Press, 1971.

Cooling, Benjamin Franklin. *Forts Henry and Donelson: The Key to the Confederate Heartland.* Knoxville: University of Tennessee Press, 1987.

Cooper, William J., Jr. *Jefferson Davis: American.* New York: Alfred A. Knopf, 2000.

Cotton, Gordon A., and Jeff T. Giambrone. *Vicksburg and the War.* Gretna, LA: Pelican Publishing Company, 2004.

Cozzens, Peter. *No Better Place to Die: The Battle of Stones River.* Champaign: University of Illinois Press, 1991.

———. *This Terrible Sound: The Battle of Chickamauga.* Urbana: University of Illinois Press, 1992.

Crute, Joseph H., Jr. *Units of the Confederate States Army.* Midlothian, VA: Derwent Books, 1987.

Cunningham, Frank. *General Stand Watie's Confederate Indians.* Norman: University of Oklahoma Press, 1998.

Current, Richard N., ed. *Advance and Retreat: Personal Experiences in the United States and Confederate States Armies by J. B. Hood.* Bloomington: Indiana University Press, 1959.

———. *Encyclopedia of the Confederacy.* New York: Simon and Schuster, 1993.

Cutrer, Thomas W. *Ben McCulloch and the Frontier Military Tradition.* Chapel Hill: University of North Carolina Press, 1993.

Davis, William C. *Breckinridge: Statesman, Soldier, Symbol.* Baton Rouge: Louisiana State University Press, 1992.

Davis, William C., and Julie Hoffman, eds. *The Confederate General.* Harrisburg, PA: National Historical Society, 1991.

Dedmondt, Glenn. *The Flags of Civil War Arkansas.* Gretna, LA: Pelican Publishing Company, 2006.

Desty, Robert, ed. *The Federal Reporter: Cases Argued and Determined in the Circuit and District Courts of the United States, June–August 1882.* St. Paul, MN: West Publishing Company, 1882.

———. *Supreme Court Reporter: Cases Argued and Determined in the United States Supreme Court. Vol. 14, October Term 1893.* St. Paul: West Publishing Company, 1894.

Detzer, David. *Allegiance: Fort Sumter, Charleston, and the Beginning of the Civil War.* New York: Harcourt, 2001.

Dictionary of Wisconsin Biography. Madison: State Historical Society of Wisconsin, 1960.

Eno, Clara B. *History of Crawford County, Arkansas.* Van Buren, AR: Press-Argus, 1951.

Estes, Claud, comp. *List of Field Officers, Regiments and Battalions in the Confederate States Army, 1861–1865.* Macon, GA: J. W. Burke Company, 1912.

Evans, David. *Sherman's Horsemen: Union Cavalry Operations in the Atlanta Campaign.* Bloomington: Indiana University Press, 1999.

Federal Writers Project. *Louisiana: A Guide to the State.* New York: Hastings House, 1945.

Fellman, Michael. *Inside War: The Guerrilla Conflict in Missouri during the American Civil War.* New York: Oxford University Press, 1990.

Fletcher, John Gould. *Arkansas.* Chapel Hill: Univeristy of North Carolina Press, 1947.

Flood, Charles Bracelen. *Grant and Sherman: The Friendship that Won the Civil War.* New York: Farrar, Straus & Giroux, 2005.

Foote, Shelby. *The Civil War: Red River to Appomattox.* New York: Random House, 1958.

Garrison, Webb. *The Encyclopedia of Civil War Usage: An Illustrated Compendium of the Everyday Language of Soldiers and Civilians.* Nashville: Cumberland House, 2001.

Gibson, Charles Dana, and E. Kay Gibson, comp. *Dictionary of Transports and Combatant Vessels Steam and Sail Employed by the Union Army, 1861–1868.* Camden, ME: Ensign Press, 1995.

Govan, Gilbert E., and James W. Livingood. *General Joseph E. Johnston, C.S.A.: A Different Valor.* 1956. Reprint, New York: Konecky and Konecky, 1993.

Groom, Winston. *Shrouds of Glory: From Atlanta to Nashville: The Last Great Campaign of the Civil War.* New York: Atlantic Monthly Press, 1995.

Harkins, John E. *Metropolis of the American Nile: Memphis and Shelby County.* Woodland Hills, CA: Windsor Publications, 1982.

Hartnoll, Phyllis, ed. *The Oxford Compendium to the Theatre.* Oxford: Oxford University Press, 1983.

Hattaway, Herman. *General Stephen D. Lee.* Jackson: University Press of Mississippi, 1988.

Hauptman, Laurence M. *Between Two Fires: American Indians in the Civil War.* New York: Free Press, 1995.

Hawkins-Dady, Mark, ed. *International Dictionary of Theatre.* Detroit: St. James Press, 1994.

Heidler, David S., and Jeanne T. Heidler, eds. *Encyclopedia of the American Civil War: A Political, Social, and Military History.* Santa Barbara: ABC-Clio, 2000.

Herndon, Dallas T. *Centennial History of Arkansas.* Chicago: S. J. Clarke Publishing Company, 1922.

Herringshaw, Thomas William. *Herringshaw's National Library of American Biography.* Chicago: American Publishers Association, 1914.

Hess, Earl J. *Banners to the Breeze: The Kentucky Campaign, Corinth, and Stones River.* Lincoln: University of Nebraska Press, 2000.

Hirsch, E. D., Joseph F. Kett, and James S. Trefil. *The New Dictionary of Cultural Literacy.* New York: Houghton Mifflin Harcourt, 2002.

Hoehling, Adolph A. *Vicksburg: 47 Days of Siege.* Mechanicsburg, PA: Stackpole Books, 1996.

Hoobler, James A. *A Guide to Historic Nashville, Tennessee.* Charleston: History Press, 2008.

Horn, Stanley F. *The Decisive Battle of Nashville.* Knoxville: University of Tennessee Press, 1968.

Hughes, Nathanial Cheairs, Jr. *Bentonville: The Final Battle between Sherman and Johnston.* Chapel Hill: University of North Carolina, 2006.

———. *General William J. Hardee: Old Reliable.* Baton Rouge: Louisiana State University Press, 1992.

Jackson, Mary Smith. *Death Notices from Steuben County New York Newspapers, 1797–1884.* Westminster, MD: Heritage Books, 1998.

Jackson, Robert W. *Rails across the Mississippi: A History of the St. Louis Bridge.* Urbana: University of Illinois Press, 2001.

Johnson, E. Polk. *A History of Kentucky and Kentuckians: The Leaders and Representative Men in Commerce, Industry and Modern Activities.* Chicago: Lewis Publishing Company, 1912.

Johnson, Guion Griffis. *Ante-Bellum North Carolina: A Social History.* Chapel Hill: University of North Carolina Press, 1937.

Joiner, Gary D., Marilyn S. Joiner, and Clifton D. Cardin, eds. *No Pardons to Ask, nor Apologies to Make: The Journal of William Henry King, Gray's 28th Louisiana Infantry Regiment.* Knoxville: University of Tennessee Press, 2006.

Jordan, Ervin L., Jr. *Charlottesville and the University of Virginia in the Civil War.* Lynchburg, VA: H. E. Howard, 1988.

Keenan, Jerry. *Wilson's Cavalry Corps: Union Campaigns in the Western Theatre, October 1864 through Spring 1865.* Jefferson, NC: McFarland and Company, 1998.

Kennedy, Frances H., ed. *The Civil War Battlefield Guide.* New York: Houghton Mifflin Harcourt, 1998.

Kennett, Lee. *Sherman: A Soldier's Life.* New York: HarperCollins, 2001.

Klement, Frank L. *Dark Lanterns: Secret Political Societies, Conspiracies, and Treason Trials in the Civil War.* Baton Rouge: Louisiana State University Press, 1989.

Lankford, Nelson. *Richmond Burning: The Last Days of the Confederate Capital.* New York: Viking, 2002.

Leeper, Wesley Thurman. *Rebels Valiant: Second Arkansas Mounted Rifles, Dismounted.* Little Rock, AR: Pioneer Press, 1964.

Levine, Bruce. *Confederate Emancipation: Southern Plans to Free and Arm Slaves during the Civil War.* New York: Oxford University Press, 2006.

Longacre, Edward G. *A Soldier to the Last: Maj. Gen. Joseph Wheeler in Blue and Gray.* Dulles, VA: Potomac Books, 2008.

Losson, Christopher. *Tennessee's Forgotten Warriors: Frank Cheatham and His Confederate Division.* Knoxville: University of Tennessee Press, 1989.

Lowance, Mason I., ed. *A House Divided: The Antebellum Slavery Debates in America, 1776–1865.* Princeton, NJ: Princeton University Press, 2003.

Mackey, Albert G. *Encyclopedia of Freemasonry.* Philadelphia: McClure Publishing Company, 1916.

Manarin, Louis. *Richmond on the James.* Charleston: Arcadia Publishing, 2001.

Martin, Samuel J. *Kill-Cavalry: The Life of Union General Hugh Judson Kilpatrick.* Mechanicsburg, PA: Stackpole Books, 2000.

McDonough, James Lee, and Thomas Lawrence Connelly. *Five Tragic Hours: The Battle of Franklin.* Knoxville: University of Tennessee Press, 1983.

McMurry, Richard. *John Bell Hood and the War for Southern Independence.* Lexington: University Press of Kentucky, 1982.

McPherson, James M. *Battle Cry of Freedom: The Civil War Era.* New York: Oxford University Press, 1988.

McReynolds, John Hugh. *Makers of Arkansas History.* New York: Silver, Burdett and Company, 1905.

McWhiney, Grady, and Judith Lee Hallock. *Braxton Bragg and Confederate Defeat.* Vol. 2. Tuscaloosa: University of Alabama Press, 1991.

Miller, Gregory K. *The Civil War and Campbell County, Tennessee.* Jacksboro, TN: Action Printing, 1992.

Moneyhon, Carl H. *The Impact of the Civil War and Reconstruction on Arkansas: Persistence in the Midst of Ruin.* Fayetteville: University of Arkansas Press, 2002.

Moore, Albert Burton. *Conscription and Conflict in the Confederacy.* Columbia: University of South Carolina Press, 1996.

Moore, William D. *Masonic Temples: Freemasonry, Ritual Architecture, and Masculine Archetypes.* Knoxville: University of Tennessee Press, 2006.

Mouat, Malcolm Palmer. *Dr. Henry Palmer, "The Fighting Surgeon," 1827–1895.* Detroit: Harlo Press, 1977.

Neal, Diane, and Thomas W. Kremm. *Lion of the South: General Thomas C. Hindman.* Macon, GA: Mercer University Press, 1997.

Neely, Mark E. *Southern Rights: Political Prisoners and the Myth of Confederate Constitutionalism.* Charlottesville: University of Virginia Press, 1999.

Nelson, James L. *Reign of Iron: The Story of the First Battling Ironclads, the Monitor and the Merrimack*. New York: William Morrow, 2004.

Parks, Joseph Howard. *General Edmund Kirby Smith, C.S.A.* Baton Rouge: Louisiana State University Press, 1954.

Patchan, Scott C. *Shenandoah Summer: The 1864 Valley Campaign*. Lincoln: University of Nebraska Press, 2007.

Patton, John Shelton. *Jefferson, Cabell, and the University of Virginia*. New York: Neale Publishing Company, 1906.

Peterson, Merrill D. *Lincoln in American Memory*. New York: Oxford University Press, 1995.

Phillips, Christopher. *Missouri's Confederate: Claiborne Fox Jackson and the Creation of Southern Identity in the Border West*. Columbia: University of Missouri Press, 2000.

Piston, William Garrett, and Richard Hatcher III. *Wilson's Creek: The Second Battle of the Civil War and the Men Who Fought It*. Chapel Hill: University of North Carolina Press, 2000.

Potter, David M., and Don E. Fehrenbacher. *The Impending Crisis: 1848–1861*. New York: HarperCollins, 1976.

Raab, James W. *W. W. Loring: Florida's Forgotten General*. Manhattan, KS: Sunflower University Press, 1996.

Ragsdale, William Oates. *They Sought a Land: A Settlement in the Arkansas River Valley, 1840–1870*. Fayetteville: University of Arkansas Press, 1997.

Ramage, James A. *Rebel Raider: The Life of General John Hunt Morgan*. Lexington: University Press of Kentucky, 1986.

Reed, Wallace P., ed. *History of Atlanta, Georgia*. Syracuse: D. Mason and Company, 1889.

Roberts, Bobby, and Carl Moneyhon, eds. *Portraits of Conflict: A Photographic History of Arkansas*. Fayetteville: University of Arkansas Press, 1987.

Robins, Glenn. *The Bishop of the Old South: The Ministry and Civil War Legacy of Leonidas Polk*. Macon, GA: Mercer University Press, 2006.

Rosen, Hannah. *Terror in the Heart of Freedom: Citizenship, Sexual Violence, and the Meaning of Race in the Post-Emancipation South*. Chapel Hill: University of North Carolina Press, 2008.

Scarborough, William Kauffman. *Masters of the Big House: Elite Slaveholders of the Mid-Nineteenth-Century South*. Baton Rouge: Louisiana State University Press, 2003.

Schroeder-Lein, Glenna R. *Confederate Hospitals on the Move: Samuel H. Stout and the Army of Tennessee*. Columbia: University of South Carolina Press, 1996.

Shannon, B. Clay. *Still Casting Shadows: A Shared Mosaic of U.S. History*. Lincoln, NE: iUniverse, 2006.

Shea, William L. *Fields of Blood: The Prairie Grove Campaign*. Chapel Hill: University of North Carolina Press, 2009.

Shea, William L., and Earl J. Hess. *Pea Ridge: Civil War Campaign in the West*. Chapel Hill: University of North Carolina Press, 1992.

Shirk, George H. *Oklahoma Place Names*. Norman: University of Oklahoma Press, 1987.

Silverstone, Paul H. *Civil War Navies, 1855–1883*. New York: Routledge, 2006.

Smith, Derek. *The Gallant Dead: Union and Confederate Generals Killed in the Civil War*. Mechanicsburg, PA: Stackpole Books, 2005.

Smith, Kenneth L. *Buffalo River Handbook*. Fayetteville: University of Arkansas Press, 2006.

Starr, Emmet. *History of the Cherokee Indians and Their Legends and Folk Lore*. Oklahoma City: Warden Company, 1921.

Stickles, Arndt M. *Simon Bolivar Buckner: Borderland Knight*. Chapel Hill: University of North Carolina Press, 1940.

Stiles, T. J. *Jesse James: Last Rebel of the Civil War*. New York: Alfred A. Knopf, 2002.

Sulzby, James Frederick. *Historic Alabama Hotels and Resorts*. Tuscaloosa: University of Alabama Press, 1960.

Sweetser, Moses Foster, ed. *The Middle States: A Handbook for Travellers*. Boston: James R. Osgood and Company, 1881.

Symonds, Craig L. *Joseph E. Johnston: A Civil War Biography*. New York: W. W. Norton, 1992.

———. *Stonewall of the West: Patrick Cleburne and the Civil War*. Lawrence: University of Kansas, 1997.

Taylor, Orville W. *Negro Slavery in Arkansas*. Durham: Duke University Press, 1958.

Trudeau, Noah Andre. *The Last Citadel: Petersburg, Virginia, June 1864–April 1865*. Boston: Little, Brown and Company, 1991.

———. *Out of the Storm: The End of the Civil War, April–June 1865*. Boston: Little, Brown and Company, 1994.

Tucker, Phillip Thomas. *The Forgotten "Stonewall of the West": Major General John Stevens Bowen*. Macon, GA: Mercer University Press, 1997.

Violette, Eugene Morrow. *A History of Missouri*. New York: D. C. Heath and Company, 1918.

Walther, Eric H. *William Lowndes Yancey and the Coming of the Civil War*. Chapel Hill: University of North Carolina Press, 2006.

Walther, Rudolph J. *Happenings in Ye Olde Philadelphia, 1680–1900*. Philadelphia: Walther Printing House, 1925.

Warner, Ezra J., and W. Buck Yearns, eds. *Biographical Register of the Confederate Congress*. Baton Rouge: Louisiana State University Press, 1975.

———. *Generals in Blue: Lives of the Union Commanders*. Baton Rouge: Louisiana State University Press, 1964.

———. *Generals in Gray: Lives of the Confederate Commanders*. Baton Rouge: Louisiana State University Press, 1959.

Watkins, Sam R. *"Co. Aytch": A Side Show of the Big Show*. Wilmington, NC: Broadfoot Publishing Company, 1994.

Waugh, John C. *Reelecting Lincoln: The Battle for the 1864 Presidency*. New York: Crown Publishers, 1997.

Welsh, Jack D. *Medical Histories of Confederate Generals*. Kent, OH: Kent State University Press, 1999.

Whalen, William J. *Handbook of Secret Organizations*. Milwaukee: Bruce Publishing Company, 1966.

Williams, Edward F., and Ted Williams. *Early Memphis and Its River Rivals.* Memphis: Historical Hiking Trails, 1968.

Williams, T. Harry. *P.G.T. Beauregard: Napoleon in Gray.* Baton Rouge: Louisiana State University Press, 1955.

Williamson, David. *The Third Mississippi Battalion Infantry and the 45th Mississippi Regiment: A Civil War History.* Jefferson, NC: McFarland, 2003.

Willis, James. *Arkansas Confederates in the Western Theater.* Dayton: Morningside Press, 1998.

Wills, Brian Steel. *A Battle from the Start: The Life of Nathan Bedford Forrest.* New York: HarperCollins, 1992.

Wolfe, Gerard R. *New York, 15 Walking Tours: An Architectural Guide to the Metropolis.* New York: McGraw-Hill, 2003.

Woodworth, Steven. *While God Is Marching On: The Religious World of Civil War Soldiers.* Lawrence: University of Kansas Press, 2001.

Worley, Ted R., ed. *They Never Came Back: The War Memoirs of Captain John W. Lavender, C.S.A.* Pine Bluff, AR: Perdue Company, 1956.

Youatt, William, and Walter Watson. *The Horse: With a Treatise on Draught.* London: Longmans, Green, 1880.

SECONDARY SOURCES: CORRESPONDENCE WITH THE EDITOR

Beth Beach, Registrar's Office, Ohio Wesleyan University, to Robert Patrick Bender, July 16, 2009, in possession of the editor.

Russell K. Brown to Robert Patrick Bender, November 15–16, 2010, in possession of the editor.

Mickey McMahan, Grand Secretary of Masons for the state of Mississippi, to Robert Patrick Bender, March 31, 2009, in possession of the editor.